WORLD PREHISTORY
Studies in Memory of Grahame Clark

Alexander Csáky

Grahame Clark

PROCEEDINGS OF THE BRITISH ACADEMY · 99

WORLD PREHISTORY

Studies in Memory of Grahame Clark

Edited by

JOHN COLES, ROBERT BEWLEY & PAUL MELLARS

Published for THE BRITISH ACADEMY
by OXFORD UNIVERSITY PRESS

Oxford University Press, Great Clarendon Street, Oxford OX2 6DP

Oxford New York
Athens Auckland Bangkok Bogota Bombay
Buenos Aires Calcutta Cape Town Dar es Salaam
Delhi Florence Hong Kong Istanbul Karachi
Kuala Lumpur Madras Madrid Melbourne
Mexico City Nairobi Paris Singapore
Taipei Tokyo Toronto Warsaw

and associated companies in
Berlin Ibadan

Published in the United States by
Oxford University Press Inc., New York

British Library Cataloguing in Publication Data
Data available

ISBN 0-19-726196-5

Typeset by Wyvern 21, Bristol
Printed in Great Britain
on acid-free paper
at the Alden Press
Oxford

Contents

List of Plates

A photograph of participants at the 'Grahame Clark and World Prehistory' conference, held at the British Academy on 22 November 1997, appears on page xiv.

Notes on Contributors

J. DESMOND CLARK
Department of Anthropology, University of California, Berkeley, California 94720, USA
Professor Clark is Professor Emeritus of Anthropology at the University of California, Berkeley. He was formerly Director of the Rhodes-Livingstone Museum in Livingstone, Northern Rhodesia (Zambia) and Secretary of the National Monuments Commission from 1938 to 1961. He has conducted archaeological research in Africa, India, and China, mostly in Palaeolithic archaeology. He is the author of more than 300 books and papers in scientific journals.

JEAN CLOTTES
11, rue du Fourcat, 09000 Foix, France
Jean Clottes is Scientific Advisor for prehistoric art to the French Ministry of Culture and Chairman of the International Committee for Rock Art (ICOMOS). His research is mostly related to prehistoric rock art and especially its preservation and recording, dating problems, the study of its archaeological context, and problems of epistemology and the search for meaning. He is currently in charge of the study of the Chauvet Cave. His publications include *La Grotte Cosquer. Peintures et gravures de la caverne engloutie* (1994), with Jean Courtin; *Les Cavernes de Niaux. Art préhistorique en Ariège* (1995); and *Les Chamanes de la Préhistoire. Transe et magie dans les grottes ornées* (1996), with David Lewis-Williams.

MARK COLLARD
Department of Anthropology, University College London, London, UK
Mark Collard is a Wellcome Trust Bioarchaeology Postdoctoral Fellow in the Department of Anthropology at UCL and before that held an NERC Research Studentship in the Hominid Palaeontology Research Group at The University of Liverpool. His doctoral and postdoctoral research has been directed at improving our understanding of human phylogeny.

BRIAN FAGAN
Department of Anthropology, University of California, Santa Barbara, California 93106, USA
Brian Fagan is Professor of Anthropology at the University of California, Santa Barbara and a graduate of Pembroke College, Cambridge. He spent his early career in Zambia and East Africa working on Iron Age archaeology and early African history. He is now a generalist and the author of many books on archaeology for the wider audience, including *The Rape of the Nile* (1975), *The Adventure of Archaeology* (1985), *Time Detectives* (1995), *Clash of Cultures* (second edition, 1997), *People of the Earth* (ninth edition 1998), and *From Black Land to Fifth Sun* (1998).

CHARLES HIGHAM
Department of Anthropology, University of Otago, Dunedin, New Zealand
Charles Higham is Professor of Anthropology at the University of Otago, New Zealand. He has directed excavations in Thailand since 1969, including Ban Na Di, Khok Phanom Di, Nong Nor, and Ban Lum Khao. His current project involves the excavation of the Iron Age settlement of Noen U-Loke. His publications include *The Archaeology of Mainland Southeast Asia* (1989), *The Bronze Age of Southeast Asia*

(1996), *Khok Phanom Di: Adaptation to the World's Richest Habitat* (1994), with R. Thosarat, and *Prehistoric Thailand, from First Settlement to Sukhothai* (1998), with R. Thosarat.

IAN HODDER
Department of Archaeology, University of Cambridge, Downing Street, Cambridge CB2 3DZ, UK
Ian Hodder is Professor of Archaeology at the University of Cambridge and Director of the Çatalhöyük Research Project. His main interests are in archaeological theory and European prehistory and he excavated mainly in Britain before undertaking fieldwork in Turkey. His main publications include *Symbols in Action* (1982), *Reading the Past* (1986 and 1991), *The Domestication of Europe* (1990), *Theory and Practice in Archaeology* (1992), and about to appear *The Archaeological Process* (1998).

RHYS JONES
Department of Archaeology and Natural History, Research School of Pacific and Asian Studies, The Australian National University, Canberra, ACT 0200, Australia
Rhys Jones holds a personal Chair in Archaeology at the Australian National University. He began his independent field research in Tasmania in 1963, completing his PhD in 1971 on the excavation of the coastal midden sequence at Rocky Cape. He has carried out exploratory excavations on early sites in many parts of the Australian continent, in particular at Lake Mungo, western NSW, on the Franklin River in south-west Tasmania and in Kakadu and the Kimberley in the tropical north. In 1972, together with Betty Meehan, he made a detailed ethno-archaeological study of the hunting and gathering ecology of the Gidjingarli Aboriginal people of the north coast of Arnhem Land, a study which has led to a lifetime's involvement in Aboriginal issues.

LARS LARSSON
Institute of Archaeology, Lund University, Sandgatan 1, S-223 50 Lund, Sweden
Lars Larsson is Professor of Archaeology at Lund University, southern Sweden. He has directed excavations mainly in the southernmost part of Sweden and in recent years in Portugal and Zimbabwe. His research has concentrated on the Mesolithic and Neolithic with a special interest in the relation between coastal and inland settlement. His range of publications includes *Ageröd I:B–I:D. A Study of Early Atlantic Settlement in Scania* (1978), *The Skateholm Project. Late Mesolithic Settlement at a South Swedish Lagoon* (1988), *Settlement and Environment during the Middle Neolithic and Late Neolithic* (1992), with others, and *The Colonization of South Sweden During the Deglaciation* (1996).

LEENDERT LOUWE KOOIJMANS
Faculty of Archaeology, Leiden University, NL 2300 RA Leiden, Netherlands
Leendert Louwe Kooijmans graduated in Physical Geography at the University of Utrecht and in Prehistory at Leiden. He worked as Curator of the Department of Prehistory at the National Museum of Antiquities from 1966 onward and was appointed to the Chair of Prehistory at Leiden University in 1982. His main work and interests are in the Neolithic and in wetland archaeology of the Lower Rhine Basin. His main publications include *The Rhine/Meuse Delta* (1974) and *Verleden Land* (1982). He is supervising a handbook on Dutch prehistory, to appear in 1999.

JOHN MULVANEY
128 Schlich Street, Yarralumla, ACT 2600, Australia
Emeritus Professor D.J. Mulvaney AO, CME, is a History graduate from the University of Melbourne and a graduate in Archaeology from Cambridge. Following extensive archaeological fieldwork in Australia, in 1971 he became Foundation Professor in Prehistory in the Faculty of Arts, Australian National University, and was an Australian Heritage Commissioner from 1976 to 1982. His publications include

The Prehistory of Australia (1969, 1975), *Encounters in Place, Outsiders and Aboriginal Australians 1606–1985* (1989), and *Cricket Walkabout. The Aborigines in England 1868* (1967, 1988).

JOHN PARKINGTON
Department of Archaeology, University of Cape Town, Rondebosch, Cape 7700, South Africa
John Parkington is Professor of Archaeology at the University of Cape Town. He began teaching there in 1966 and has focused on the prehistory of the Cape, excavating various caves and rock shelters and recording rock paintings. His main research interests are in coastal archaeology, hunter gatherers, and rock art. He has written many chapters and journal articles and is currently editing a volume on the results of excavations at Elands Bay Cave.

PETER ROWLEY-CONWY
Department of Archaeology, University of Durham, Science Site, South Road, Durham DH1 3LE, UK
Peter Rowley-Conwy is a Reader in Environmental Archaeology at the University of Durham, where he has worked since 1990. His main specialization is zooarchaeology; he has examined the Mesolithic and early agricultural assemblages from Denmark, Sweden, Britain, Portugal, and Italy as well as the Russian Far East, and has worked on the Tell Abu Hureyra project. He is currently writing a book on the Mesolithic assemblages and is also working on pig domestication. He also works on plant remains, and is studying the desiccated material from Qasr Ibrim in southern Egypt. His publications include *Star Carr Revisited. A Re-analysis of the Large Mammals* (co-authored with Tony Legge).

BERNARD WOOD
Department of Anthropology, The George Washington University, 2110 G Street, NW, Washington, DC 20052, USA
Bernard Wood is the Henry R. Luce Professor of Human Origins at George Washington University and an Adjunct Senior Scientist in the Smithsonian Institution, at the National Museum for Natural History. Until 1997, he was Head of the Department of Human Anatomy and Cell Biology, and Dean of Medicine, at The University of Liverpool. His main research interests are the reconstruction of human evolutionary history, particularly the phylogenetic and functional analysis of early hominids. His publications include: *Hominid Cranial Remains from Koobi Fora* (1991) and the *Origin and Evolution of the Genus* Homo (1992).

The 'Grahame Clark and World Prehistory' symposium
was co-sponsored by
THE PREHISTORIC SOCIETY

This publication of the proceedings
has been generously assisted by a grant from
THE PREHISTORIC SOCIETY

Preface

Among the many contributions of Grahame Clark to archaeology, his commitment to the theme of world prehistory is perhaps the one for which he will be most remembered. The successive editions of *World Prehistory: an Outline*, progressively revised, updated, and expanded, have been translated into numerous languages. Many of Grahame's students made major contributions to the study of world prehistory. His legendary map on the wall of his study, marking the far-flung points on the globe to which Cambridge-trained prehistorians had been despatched, was not a figment of the imagination (as some of us had assumed) but a physical reality, regularly updated as each new recruit was sent off to Canberra, Dunedin, Cape Town, or Santa Barbara.

The decision to organize a symposium in memory of Grahame Clark's contributions to world prehistory jointly by the Prehistoric Society and the British Academy seemed appropriate on many counts. The initial creation of the Prehistoric Society in 1935 was largely a product of Grahame's own vision, and he served as either President of the Society or the editor of its *Proceedings* for 35 years. His commitment to the British Academy was equally strong. He served as Chairman of the Archaeology section of the Academy from 1974 to 1978, and was the driving force behind the creation of the British Academy Major Research Project on the Early History of Agriculture in 1966. The establishment of the Grahame Clark Medal for Prehistory of the British Academy and the annual 'Europa' Lecture series of the Prehistoric Society were both a product of Grahame's personal generosity—the latter arising from his own award of the highly prestigious Erasmus Prize of the Netherlands Erasmus Foundation in 1990.

The symposium was held in the Academy's rooms in Cornwall Terrace, attended by a capacity audience, and was chaired by Paul Mellars, Clive Gamble, Bryony Coles, and Tim Champion. The choice of topics and speakers for the conference was intended to reflect as wide a span of current issues and developments in world prehistory as could reasonably be achieved within the confines of a single day meeting—especially those areas in which Grahame himself had a special interest. As the papers in the present volume reveal, the topics ranged from the origins of our own genus in Africa around two million years ago, to the issues of the Later Stone Age and emergence of civilization in northern Europe, Anatolia, and south-east Asia. Over two-thirds of the papers were given by either former students or colleagues of Grahame—several of whom had travelled from areas as far afield as Australia, New Zealand, South Africa, and California to be present at the meeting. It was especially fitting to be able to include contributions from Desmond Clark and John Mulvaney, who gave the opening and closing addresses to the meeting respectively, and paid tribute to Grahame's own special contributions to the world prehistory theme.

As the academic organizers of the event we are particularly indebted to the President of the Prehistoric Society, Professor Tim Champion, and the Secretary of the British Academy, Peter Brown, for their personal support in the planning of the conference, and above all to Rosemary Lambeth for her tireless efforts in all the administrative arrangements for the meeting. We are equally indebted to James Rivington, Janet English, and Sheila Chatten for their help in the editing and publication of the present volume. Financial support for the meeting was provided jointly by the British Academy and the Prehistoric Society.

Finally, it was a special pleasure to be able to welcome Lady (Mollie) Clark and Philip Clark to the meeting, and to the ensuing conference dinner for the speakers. Their presence added a special personal touch to an event devoted to a man who, perhaps more than any other, established the study of human prehistory on a truly world-wide scale.

John Coles
Robert Bewley
Paul Mellars
July 1998

Note. The memoir of Grahame Clark published in the *Proceedings of the British Academy* for 1996 (Vol. 94) is reproduced as an Appendix to the present volume.

Speakers, Chairmen, Lady Clark and son Philip on the occasion of the joint British Academy and Prehistoric Society meeting in honour of Professor Sir Grahame Clark, 22 November 1997. *From left to right:* T. Champion, P. Mellars, P. Rowley-Conwy, J. Coles, J. Clottes, R. Jones, L. Larsson, I. Hodder, Lady Clark, L. Louwe Kooijmans, B. Wood, J.D. Clark, B. Coles, P. Clark, J. Mulvaney, C. Higham, C. Gamble and J. Parkington. (Photo by Bob Bewley)

Grahame Clark and World Prehistory: A Personal Perspective

J. DESMOND CLARK

GRAHAME CLARK WAS SO SUCCESSFUL in providing us with the first masterly and comprehensive synthesis of humankind's biological and cultural evolution because of his great ability to assimilate, order, and understand the nature and direction of the processes that underlie the progress from foraging to civilization. This was indeed a formidable task that few could have been capable of in the years immediately after the Second World War. To understand how this work came about it is necessary to follow Grahame's developing ideology and conception of what archaeological data can tell us about behaviour, economics, and society. Clark's *World Prehistory* stands apart with that other great comprehensive masterpiece H.G. Wells' *The Outline of History* published in 1920. Today this volume makes singular, salutary reading. Fundamentalism was rife, there was no time frame before history other than guesswork, the focus was directed to evolution in Europe with an excursion to south-west Asia and China. Eoliths and Piltdown were in the limelight, the Neandertals were put on the back burner and only the French and northern Spanish caves with their cultural sequence and art provided some solid data for documenting the earlier progressive stages in the evolution of the human lineage. As Wells begins his *Outline of History*, 'The origin of man and his relationship to other animals has been the subject of great controversies during the past one hundred years' (Wells 1920, 62). How very true this still is today, and as Wells goes on to say, 'The task of the historian is to deal, not with what is seemly, but with what is truth'. And still today we might ask with 'jesting Pilate' what *is* 'truth', and some of us also are not prepared to wait for the answer.

This was the milieu in which Grahame grew up and it was most likely that he was influenced by Wells' comprehensive outlook on understanding the causes and effects of change in human societies. He also read Darwin's *On the Origin of Species* (1859) and *The Descent of Man* (1871), Huxley's *Evidence as to Man's Place in Nature* (1863), and Charles Lyell's *The Antiquity of Man* (1873). Indeed, I am the honoured possessor of his copy of *Origin of Species* that he used as an undergraduate. It must have been works such

Proceedings of the British Academy, **99**, 1–10

as these and the earlier anthropological publications that made a deep impression on Grahame's ideas and turned his interests away from taxonomy, then the normal way of looking at archaeological finds, and focusing them towards understanding what his collections of flints and potsherds might mean in terms of the behavioural traits they might represent about the individuals and groups who made them, especially when examined in the light of the climatic and environmental changes that the glacial/interglacial framework provided. It is likely, also, that he was influenced by Gordon Childe's *The Dawn of European Civilization* (1925), with its 'diffusionist hypothesis'. This was the general way in which change was explained at that time in both the Palaeolithic sequence in the French caves, pioneered by Lartet and Christy (1865–75), and in later cultural contexts. Grahame, however, was looking beyond migration as the explanation for cultural change, and on several occasions in those early years he expressed his belief that such changes could also have come about as a result of the spread of ideas and new technology.

Grahame must have been equally conversant with the precision and advanced methods of excavation that General Pitt-Rivers had introduced to British archaeology in the last 20 years of the nineteenth century, in particular at his estate of Cranborne Chase in Wiltshire. With such a backdrop, Grahame set about developing his own ideas about how technology *in its context* could be used to show something of the behaviour and lifeways of the prehistoric groups that had made and used these artefacts.

Grahame's interest in and excitement with prehistory was all-abiding and his research went ahead with speed and foresight and efficiency within the limited facilities at his disposal. His first piece of research at Cambridge was predominantly taxonomic using typology and patterns of geographical distribution to explain differences and variability in time and region. *The Mesolithic Age in Britain* (Clark 1932) conformed to the ideas and format of the day in which, however, he showed his early appreciation of the value of distribution maps used in environmental contexts. This doctoral dissertation gave him a foot- perhaps one should say a toe-hold at Cambridge, putting him in a position so that he could develop his methodology to document the changes that had taken place since the end of the Last Glacial in terms of climate and environment and the human behavioural changes within a chronological framework. In this he was inspired by the post-glacial varve chronology developed by Baron de Geer in Sweden based on the varve history in receding glacial lakes over the past 12,000 years (de Geer 1910).

The new research Grahame initiated was based on interdisciplinary team coordination in which various natural scientists brought their expertise and support to identify the contextual habitats, so enabling the archaeologist to begin to understand the economic base of the prehistoric population whose archaeological residues were associated in time and space. So was formed the Fenland Research Committee, the history of which has been well documented recently by Pamela Smith (1997). This was the beginning of a new focus and dimension in prehistoric archaeology in Britain. It also was the beginning of the input from the natural sciences working in close collaboration with archaeologists that, over the years, has become all important and continues today to expand methodology and provide new meaning to behavioural models in prehistory. The initiative and organization for maintaining the impetus of the 'new archaeology', as it has rightly been called by Smith, came from Grahame and his close association with the Godwins and the small group of like-minded young archaeologists he had recruited to the Committee: C.W. Phillips, Stuart Piggott, Christopher Hawkes, 'Oggs' Crawford, and others, some of whom I had the privilege of listening to over tea with Grahame in his office or house. Plantation and Peacock's Farms excavations demonstrated for the first time the nature of the post-glacial/early Holocene changes in environment and those in technical and organizational adaptations in the human societies with which these climatic changes were associated. Stratigraphic methods and archaeological excavation were rigorous and meticulous. Everything was collected and the full range of technology, as shown by the artefact assemblages, was analysed, illustrated, and proportionally examined. The results and analyses that followed also made possible a comparative study of the record from Scandinavia due to Grahame's knowledge of the sites, artefacts, and literature there. The relative chronology that these Fenland excavations established was the best available before radiometric dating methods were developed, by which also it stands confirmed today.

The success of the Fenland Research Committee led to Grahame's giving a course on Mesolithic European Prehistory in 1934 that started his long association with the Cambridge Faculty. The course was so successful in attracting new students to the Department of Archaeology and Anthropology that he was appointed as an Assistant Lecturer in the Faculty in 1935. This, and his continued close association with the Fenland Research Committee, now enabled him and his associates on the Committee to vote on a change in the name and objectives of the Prehistoric Society of East Anglia, and to rename it The Prehistoric Society. The Society's *Proceedings* were the major influence in broadening horizons and introducing new perspectives to British prehistory. Under Grahame, as the Honorary Editor, the *Proceedings* became international and interdisciplinary in their contents. This was, indeed, the beginning of the new archaeology, but it took the discipline more generally some 15 to 20 more years to rethink and reorganize, no doubt in no small part due to the intervention of the Second World War.

My own association with Grahame began in the summer of 1935 and at the end of the year that followed I took Part One of the Archaeology and Anthropology Tripos. *The Mesolithic Settlement of Northern Europe* (Clark 1936) was a revelation for a would-be prehistorian after having previously read History for two years. This book and, of course, his lectures introduced *people*, their socio-economic organization and material culture, all within a relative chronological time frame, and post-glacial environmental changes based on sound excavated data. The book was a superb piece of scholarship that made a deep impression on me and the other some half-dozen students taking Part One that year. It dictated for me the pattern of my African research from 1938 onwards. Two other books at that time were equally important for my African work: Louis Leakey's *Adam's Ancestors* (1934), and his Munro Lectures *Stone Age Africa* (1936). Louis and Grahame were near contemporaries at Cambridge but they mostly went their respective ways, the one in the

Holocene and the other in the Pleistocene. Both, however, insisted on the recovery of the 'hard data'—the archaeological residues in their contexts, and the interdisciplinary input from science as the essential basis on which to attempt to identify any behavioural traits of the prehistoric population that had made and used them. The success of reconstructing prehistoric lifeways depends on the amount of reliable data on which the scenario is based, and, to this end, they both stressed the need for precision in excavation and recording and, also, the importance of a sound knowledge of lithic technology based on experiment.

Grahame was well versed in lithics, and he took his undergraduate students to study the Brandon flint-knappers during excursions to archaeological sites in East Anglia. This inevitably led to experimentation on my part.

It was nine years between 1937, when I went down, and 1946 before I met up again with Grahame, though by means of his books that filtered through to central Africa, I was able to keep up to some extent with the expansion of his ideology. Back in Cambridge in that cruel winter of 1946 and most of 1947 I wrote my thesis for the Ph.D.; Miles Burkitt was my Supervisor and Dorothy Garrod the Disney Professor. On this and subsequent long vacations from Northern Rhodesia every two-and-a-half to three years, we would rent a cottage in a village outside Cambridge to catch up with the changing ideas and methodology that were being developed during the times that we were back in Africa. Those vacations in Cambridge were enormously stimulating, exciting, and enjoyable; and it was possible to renew old friendships and make new ones with the excellent new archaeology faculty that Grahame was developing there. In particular, it was a great joy to be again with Charles McBurney and discuss his research in North Africa and mine in south-central Africa. We had been contemporaries taking the Tripos together in 1936–7 and we were both, during the quieter times of military service, able to continue our interest in prehistory, and the sites that we discovered and the artefacts that we were able to collect provided much important new evidence. The appointment of Charles McBurney to the Faculty is an indication of Grahame Clark's acumen in appointing the right person and Charles' influence on those specializing in the Palaeolithic was outstanding. He went on to excavate the great cave of Haua Fteah in Cyrenaica, Libya, which is the most complete sequence of upper Pleistocene and Holocene cultural assemblages yet known from any single site in north Africa. As my war service took me also north to the Horn of Africa, we had much in common to discuss; and, as it now turns out, both our areas are crucial for understanding the origins and spread of modern humans.

One book that perhaps sets out best the way Grahame's ideas of prehistoric archaeology and where its focus should be in the immediately pre-war years is his *Archaeology and Society* (Clark 1939). It shows the move away from the study of material antiquities to their behavioural implications; the changed focus from *things* to *people*. It was written for both the prehistorian and the interested layperson and it was aimed at making prehistory a popular science which it had never been before. The book shows the methodology of discovery, preservation, and excavation, and goes on to explain how the surviving residues, though always circumstantial, can be used to construct a temporal sequence for the economies and social behaviour of those who once camped or settled there. The scientific method is clearly demonstrated here: the recovery of the data, the formation of premises, and by testing and the elimination of alternatives the adoption of the most probable model for the behavioural implications. Grahame's belief in the need for an influential public is stated here. 'If we are ever to recover the story of a common past, it can only be through the pressure of an informed public opinion' (Clark op. cit., viii). The last chapter of the book, entitled 'Archaeology and Society', shows the extent of Grahame's reading and archaeological knowledge at this time. Though the emphasis is still on Europe it is, indeed, now global in its approach and coverage though, as the maps show, there are many blank regions. His ideology of a world prehistory was clearly about to take off. In his own words, 'To see big things whole they must be seen from a distance, and that is what archaeology enables one to do. The history of mankind, when any phase of it is studied at close quarters, appears to be a maze of inconsequences; it is only when viewed from the perspective of prehistory that the broad sweeps become easily appreicated and the history of men gives place to the history of man' (Clark op. cit., 212).

It was not until 1946 that prehistoric research became possible once more. *From Savagery to Civilization* (Clark 1946) pays attention to the Palaeolithic including the Chinese and Torralba finds, and emphasizes the need to examine the effects of climate change, but adds little that is new. From the war years Grahame gained experience with and recognized the significance of using aerial photography for archaeology.

The 1950s and 1960s were times of intense activity for prehistorians, and, in particular, the evidence now coming from Africa showed that the continent was not the backwater that prehistorians had thought it to be. The fossil hominid remains it was yielding and the excavation of land surfaces with assemblages of artefacts and faunal remains in near primary contexts made possible, not only a better understanding of the immensity of the timescale of hominid evolution, both biological and cultural, but also showed the ways in which climate was a major factor in bringing about change and variability in the Pleistocene. The Australopithecines became respectable due in large part to Sir Wilfred LeGros Clark's study and interpretation of Raymond Dart's and Robert Broom's discoveries in the South African limestone caves. Louis and Mary Leakey's work at Olorgesailie and Olduvai Gorge revitalized methodology for the investigation of Pleistocene sites throughout the world. Chronologies became more precise and reliable in terms of years before the present by the radiocarbon method (1950) and potassium–argon (K/Ar) dating (1960) in conjunction with the palaeomagnetic reversal chronology. Studies of what primates might tell us about how ancestral hominids might have behaved, especially the pioneer studies of Sherwood Washburn and Irven DeVore on the social organization and diet of *Papio*, and, in particular, the studies of the African and Asian great apes were rich sources of behavioural information. Though, as far as I know, Grahame never set foot in Africa, he was fully conversant with the progress of these new discoveries and the new methodology adopted from science the better to understand these beginning grades in the human lineage. In this, his close association and friendship with Kenneth Oakley at the

British Museum must have been important for Oakley had visited many of these sites and studied the fossils and artefacts.

Grahame's own research in the 1950s was primarily concerned with Europe, and perhaps the most important of his books for the impact it had on prehistorians throughout the world at this time was *Prehistoric Europe: The Economic Basis* (Clark 1952). This is a major erudite piece of scholarship that showed as never before on this scale the way archaeological data can be used to reveal the economy of foraging and farming communities, the strategies, diet and nutrition, settlement patterning, and social organization. 'This book', he says, 'is concerned with the ways in which early man, in competition with other forms of life, maintained himself on European soil since the end of the Pleistocene Ice Age, and with how he managed not merely to survive, but to raise his standards from those of savages to those of peasants ready to support the full weight of civilization' (Clark op. cit., vii). The volume is full of verified archaeological data, and exhaustive knowledge of material culture and art used to amplify and clarify the buried cultural residues. It firmly established Grahame's international reputation wherever prehistorians were at work. This reputation was confirmed even more by the site report on his excavations at the early Mesolithic site of Star Carr in Yorkshire (Clark 1954). This was one of the finest site reports that had ever been written for the meticulous methods of excavation, preservation, and recording, for the detailed documentation of the ecological context, and the interdisciplinary collaboration of botanists and palaeontologists which, with the skilful use of evidence for seasonal availability of animals and plants provided the means for reconstructing the way of life, the technology, and group identity of the human inhabitants. For its clarity, completeness, and great deductive interpretation, this book was a landmark publication.

In the 1950s and 1960s, the 'new archaeology' began to get underway, especially in the Americas, stimulated by, on the one hand, the Wenner-Gren Conference of anthropologists and archaeologists that gave us *Anthropology Today* (Kroeber 1953), and, on the other, Gordon Willey's and Philip Phillips' *Method and Theory in American Archaeology* (1958). This was an impressive synthesis of North American archaeology, and for clarifying developmental interpretation within a new evolutionary framework. Grahame must have read and been impressed by these works as he was a Visiting Lecturer at Harvard in 1957, and he and Gordon Willey became close friends. This 'new archaeology' has been explicitly described and documented by David Clarke's *Models in Archaeology* (1972).

With his established institutional base at Cambridge, Grahame was able to travel and thereby extend his knowledge of other preliterate societies in continents beyond Europe and western Asia. He visited New Zealand in 1964, and the same year he was also in Australia. These visits gave him the opportunity that he needed to visit sites, study technology, and have discussions with local archaeologists, ethnographers, linguists, and demographers. In particular, he now had a much better opportunity of understanding aborigines in their own habitat, enriching his ideas on the course of cultural evolution and the ability and ingenuity of so-called simple foragers, and the time depth of their lifeways.

The excavations at Devon Downs and Fromm's Landing particularly impressed him by the skill with which they were undertaken, and the long close association of Australian and Cambridge archaeology dates from this time.

The Stone Age Hunters (Clark 1967) reflects his impression that Australian aborigine culture and technology, as well as those of other foragers, can enrich the models for much older prehistoric societies. Voyages of discovery from the late fifteenth century onwards produced a voluminous literature about the peoples encountered in various different parts of the world, and this was later used, not only to demonstrate the progress of humanity into the civilized western world, but also to suggest that other social and economic systems were living survivals of these earlier stages of evolution. As a result of these too literal attempts to identify various extant foragers with different stages in prehistoric cultural evolution, such as can be seen in Sollas' *Ancient Hunters* (1924), archaeologists became disenchanted with using ethnography to help reconstruct past socio-economic behaviour. Now, however, new studies by anthropologists and archaeologists in Australia, Africa, and the New World, particularly in the Amazonian forests as well as in the Pacific, reflect a more critical examination of ethnographic sources from which certain generalizations on lifeways can be identified and may be equally applicable to the prehistoric record. The book shows that Grahame was quick to appreciate this especially if continuity within the region can be established. His first global synthesis, *World Prehistory: An Outline* (Clark 1961), was worldwide in its outlook so far as this was possible at the time. The volume is still essentially processual in its treatment, and the emphasis is still on Europe though this is understandable because of the inadequate nature of the data coming from other parts of the world, with the exception of the early civilizations of Asia, Egypt, and the New World. A new edition, *World Prehistory: A New Outline* appeared in 1969. This new volume takes full advantage of his journeys outside Europe, and includes the long biological and cultural evolutionary evidence coming from the new African discoveries that enables him, also, to set out his views on the evolution of lithic technology as a succession of 'Modes', numbered from 1 to 6. Modes represented a technological progress, the first appearance of each being temporally, loosely defined, and each Mode being typologically more advanced than that which went before. The degree of temporal and spatial overlap, Grahame considered, showed that it was ideas within a cultural tradition that were the main cause of change, not migration of a population. At the same time, regional variability could be explained in response to adaptations as to how best to exploit the resources of a new habitat. Grahame further expanded on his definition of Modes in his Hitchcock Professor Lectures at the University of California, Berkeley, also in 1969. Here he associated with Sherwood Washburn, Glynn Isaac, and myself and we had long discussions on human origins and how to reconstruct the behaviour of the earliest toolmakers in the Lower Palaeolithic. The concept of technical Modes is still useful, bearing in mind Grahame's caveat that no close relationship with hominid grades is recognized. These three lectures were published in *Aspects of Prehistory* (1970), and he also included distribution maps of the earlier Modes which he was able to use in later editions. When this second edition of *World Prehistory* appeared in 1969 it was offered as, I quote, 'virtually a new book'.

> This is even truer of the 1977 edition *World Prehistory in New Perspective.* It is substantially longer and is much more fully illustrated. It has benefited from another decade of research and it has been written in a world in which some of the trends noted in the last edition have become more pronounced. It is now even more apparent that we should view the archaeology, that is the material embodiment of the culture of each territory, as something worthy of study on its own merits.
>
> The notion of a single and implicitly western stereotype no longer survives in any conscious sense. Interest is focussed on adaptive capacity and inventiveness of men and every pattern of culture is assumed to have its own validity. Diffusion and migration can hardly be ignored, but can no longer be accepted as explanations of change. Where they can be proved to have operated, they are seen not as replacing so much as enriching the endowments of societies whose main characteristic has been their capacity to survive. [...] It is essential to appreciate that the value of any attempt to describe, let alone to account for, what happened in prehistory must depend for its success on the quality of the data themselves and on the insight brought to bear on them.
>
> (Clark 1977, xv–xx)

And again, concerning chronology, 'The enterprise of world prehistory is founded on the availability of a system of world-wide validity'. The depth of the coverage shows the immensity of Grahame's ability to absorb, digest, and comprehend the huge volume of data now available from primate societies, behavioural studies of foragers and farmers, fossil hominid morphology, climatic and environmental changes in the Quaternary, and the reliability of the chronology. The breadth of this volume is immense: from the Palaeolithic through Neolithic farming to urbanization, the population of the Pacific, occupation of the Arctic, of Tierra del Fuego and Tasmania, through prehistory, proto-history to historic archaeology. It is very, very impressive: the volume is a turning point in changing prehistorians from focusing on a national past to thinking internationally and realizing that modern humans are not only unique in the speed with which they spread to colonize the world in some 40 thousand years or so, but in the close genetic relationships and the range of shared behaviour to be seen in the different ethnic populations in the world today. Now that genetics has entered the field, this can be seen even more clearly. This was, I think, the essential message Grahame intended to convey in his 1977 *World Prehistory*. We have a common ancestry which we need to be aware of, to know what is the nature of this inheritance, and, where necessary, how to control it since we share with the animals and other organisms of our planet the need to conserve, not to continue to destroy, our common environmental resources. At one time, perhaps in the Lower Palaeolithic, sources were seemingly limitless, but now, due to the density of humanity today and with the technological advances of this century, and particularly of the last 30 years, we now have the ability to destroy not only most other sources of life on this planet but ourselves as well. The knowledge of our biological and cultural past, its lessons as well as those of more recent history if we but understand and learn from them, can help to stimulate global collaboration for controlling our destiny.

Grahame's success is reflected in his ability as Disney Professor (1952–74) to 'pick a winner' and thereby, through the Faculty he recruited, to produce an erudite, innovative, and progressive group of archaeological colleagues in the Cambridge School. Its success is to be seen also in the number of brilliant students it produced working globally today. Grahame was always accessible to us in my day and after. He has, however, been described as reserved and certainly his personality could not be described as 'macho'. He did not seek the limelight as other more flamboyant prehistorians did and do. He devoted himself to his research and thereby became one of, indeed I believe, the most, influential prehistorian of this century. This was due in very large part to the support he always received from his wife, herself an archaeologist, and his family. Grahame acknowledged this in his books, but it needs stressing that the ability to produce innovative work depends upon the circumstances in which to think and write. I can vouch for this in my own case. In 1977 Grahame says, 'In closing, [his Preface] I wish to acknowledge the immense debt I owe to my wife for enduring and assisting the writing of this book'.

The continued success of interdisciplinary teaching and research at Cambridge, in very large part the result of Grahame's groundwork, can be seen in his 1989 volume *Prehistory at Cambridge and Beyond.* Gordon Willey sums it up well in his review of the book in the *Journal of Field Archaeology* (1991): 'This successful bringing together of prehistorians, anthropologists, Classical and Middle Eastern archeologists, historians, linguists, and people from the natural sciences has been the Cambridge achievement, and I believe that this is the reason why Cambridge, in the scope of the 20th Century, has led the way in making the world conscious of the importance of prehistory'. Cambridge archaeology and the global importance of *World Prehistory* are Grahame's legacy to us all.

References

CHILDE, V.G. 1925. *The Dawn of European Civilization.* London: Paul, Trench, Trubner & Co.
CLARK, J.G.D. 1932. *The Mesolithic Age in Britain.* Cambridge: Cambridge University Press.
CLARK, J.G.D. 1936. *The Mesolithic Settlement of Northern Europe.* Cambridge: Cambridge University Press.
CLARK, J.G.D. 1939. *Archaeology and Society.* London: Methuen.
CLARK, J.G.D. 1946. *From Savagery to Civilization.* London: Cobbett Press.
CLARK, J.G.D. 1952. *Prehistoric Europe: The Economic Basis.* Cambridge: Cambridge University Press.
CLARK, J.G.D. 1954. *Excavations at Star Carr.* Cambridge: Cambridge University Press.
CLARK, J.G.D. 1961. *World Prehistory: An Outline.* Cambridge: Cambridge University Press.
CLARK, J.G.D. 1967. *The Stone Age Hunters.* London: Thames and Hudson.
CLARK, J.G.D. 1969. *World Prehistory: A New Outline.* Cambridge: Cambridge University Press.
CLARK, J.G.D. 1970. *Aspects of Prehistory.* Berkeley, California: California University Press.
CLARK, J.G.D. 1977. *World Prehistory in New Perspective.* Cambridge: Cambridge University Press.
CLARK, J.G.D. 1989. *Prehistory at Cambridge and Beyond.* Cambridge: Cambridge University Press.
CLARKE, D.L. (ed.) 1972. *Models in Archaeology.* London: Methuen.
DARWIN, C. 1859. *On the Origin of Species.* London: John Murray.
DARWIN, C. 1871. *The Descent of Man and Selection in Relation to Sex.* London: John Murray.

DE GEER, G. 1910. A geochronology of the last 12,000 years. Stockholm, International Geological Congress. fasc. 1, 241–57.

HUXLEY, T.H. 1863. *Evidence as to Man's Place in Nature*. London: William and Margate.

KROEBER, A.L. (ed.) 1953. *Anthropology Today*. Chicago: Chicago University Press.

LEAKEY, L.S.B. 1934. *Adam's Ancestors*. London: Methuen.

LEAKEY, L.S.B. 1936. *Stone Age Africa*. Oxford: Oxford University Press.

LYELL, C. 1873. *The Antiquity of Man*. London: John Murray.

SMITH, P.J. 1997. Grahame Clark's new archaeology: the Fenland Research Committee and Cambridge prehistory in the 1930s. *Antiquity* 71, 11–30.

SOLLAS, W.J. 1924. *Ancient Hunters and their Modern Representatives.* London: MacMillan.

WELLS, H.G. 1920. *The Outline of History*. London: Cassells.

WILLEY, G.R. 1991. Review of *Prehistory at Cambridge and Beyond* by Grahame Clark. *Journal of Field Archaeology* 18, 222–4.

WILLEY, G.R. & PHILLIPS, P. 1958. *Method and Theory in American Archaeology.* Chicago: Chicago University Press.

‘Is *Homo* Defined by Culture?’

BERNARD WOOD & MARK COLLARD

The changing face of *Homo*

THE GENUS *HOMO* was established by Carolus Linnaeus as part of the 1758 edition of his monumental review, the *Systema Naturae*. As construed by Linnaeus, the genus *Homo* subsumed two species. One, *Homo sylvestris*, was ‘nocturnal’ and was only known from Java. We now realize that *H. sylvestris* was based on the orang-utan, which has since been referred to its own genus, *Pongo* Lacépède, 1799. It was to the ‘diurnal’ species that Linnaeus attached the name *Homo sapiens*. Two of the six groups he included within *H. sapiens*, namely the ‘wild’ and the ‘monstrous’ components are of historical rather than biological interest, but the remaining ones are geographical variants drawn from the four continents, Africa, America, Asia, and Europe, known to Linnaeus.

The first fossil evidence to be included within the genus *Homo* were the remains recovered from the Feldhofer cave in the Neander Valley in Germany, which were referred to *Homo neanderthalensis* King, 1864. Thereafter, the interpretation of the genus remained unaltered until the inclusion of *Homo heidelbergensis* Schoetensack, 1908. This added a specimen with a rather more primitive mandible than had been the case for *H. neanderthalensis*, but otherwise the inclusion of this material made little difference to the perception of *Homo*. Thereafter, *Homo rhodesiensis* Woodward, 1921 and *Homo soloensis* Oppenoorth, 1932 were added to the genus, and in 1940 Weidenreich proposed that *Pithecanthropus erectus* Dubois, 1892 and *Sinanthropus pekinensis* Black, 1927 be incorporated into *Homo* as *Homo erectus*. Robinson (1961) proposed a similar solution for *Telanthropus capensis* Broom and Robinson, 1949, and subsequently Le Gros Clark (1964) suggested that *Atlanthropus mauritanicus* Arambourg, 1954 and *Meganthropus palaeojavanicus* von Koenigswald, 1950 should also be included in the hypodigm of *H. erectus*.

By the time these modifications had been made the genus *Homo* had assumed a rather different character, and it had come to subsume substantially more variation than it had done in 1940 (Le Gros Clark 1964). Even so, the lower limit of cranial capacity was still 900 cc, and the posture and gait of its member species were both ‘fully erect’. In the lit-

Proceedings of the British Academy, **99**, 11–23

erature there are many references to the use of a 'cerebral rubicon' as a criterion for membership of the genus *Homo*. Many of these discussions quote Sir Arthur Keith (1948), but his decision about the location of the rubicon was not based on the fossil record, but on the differences between the living apes and modern humans. He selected 750 cc as the rubicon because it is midway between 650 cc, the 'highest gorilla' endocranial volume, and 855 cc, the 'lowest aborigine' volume (ibid., 206). Using this, he judges the 'fossil skulls of Java' to be 'human' and the smaller-brained *Paranthropus* crania to be 'anthropoid' (ibid., 206).

Many of these criteria changed with the addition, in 1964, of *Homo habilis* (Leakey *et al.* 1964). In their 'revised diagnosis of the genus *Homo*', the range of cranial capacity had to be lowered to 600 cc in order to accommodate *H. habilis.* They also refer to an 'erect posture and bipedal gait' as well as to the possession of a 'fully opposable' thumb and a 'precision grip' as criteria for inclusion within *Homo*. These statements were all made on the basis that they were consistent with the way the function of *H. habilis* was being interpreted at the time. However, since 1964 views about the posture, gait, and dexterity of *H. habilis* have changed, and new fossil evidence has been found. For example, contemporary interpretations suggest that *H. habilis* is not an obligate biped (Wood 1996a) and the case for it having a modern human-like 'precision grip' is a good deal weaker than it was in 1964 (Marzke 1996; 1997). The result of these reassessments is that the inclusion of *H. habilis* within the genus *Homo* leaves the latter with little in the way of functional coherence.

It has also been suggested that the material that had been accumulating either within *H. habilis*, or in the category known as 'early *Homo*', was more variable than was consistent with a 'single species' interpretation (reviewed in Wood 1991). Subsequently, it was suggested that the 'early *Homo*' fossils were a conflation of two species, *Homo habilis sensu stricto* and *Homo rudolfensis* (Wood 1992), and several investigations published since then have supported this interpretation (Kramer *et al.* 1995; Grine *et al.* 1996). The resorting of this material into two taxa yields rather different interpretations of the resulting species. One of them, *H. habilis sensu stricto*, has a relatively later *Homo*-like, but small-brained, cranium, combined with a primitive-looking postcranium (Johanson *et al.* 1987; Hartwig-Schrerer & Martin 1991). The other, *H. rudolfensis*, has an absolutely-larger brain, but it is combined with a face that is unlike that of later *Homo*. There are no postcranial remains reliably associated with the latter taxon.

The origins of culture

Almost all attempts to list the features that distinguish modern humans from the living apes make reference to the complexity of modern human culture. We live with evidence of this complexity all around us, but we do not have to go far back into human prehistory before the evidence is confined to those aspects of prehuman activity that involve durable materials. Wooden tools survive for a surprisingly long time in the archaeological record (Thieme 1997), and although bone tools are rare in the Lower Pleistocene, there are grounds for concluding that the modification of bone may date back to at least 1.5 Myr (Brain *et al.* 1988). Nevertheless, most of the early evidence for human culture comprises artefacts made from stone.

The first sound absolute dating evidence for stone tool manufacture in the Lower Pleistocene came when Evernden and Curtis applied the then novel method of K/Ar dating to volcanic detritus from Olduvai Gorge, Tanzania (Leakey *et al.* 1961; Evernden & Curtis 1965). These dates confirmed the antiquity of the relatively crudely-fashioned stone artefacts, previously referred to the Oldowan Industry (Leakey 1951), that had been, and were continuing to be, recovered from Bed I at Olduvai (Leakey 1966). The Olduvai evidence retained the distinction of being the 'oldest stone tools' until the discovery of Oldowan-like artefacts at what was then called East Rudolf, in Northern Kenya (M.D. Leakey 1970; R.E.F. Leakey 1970). They were found at the KBS locality within a horizon which was apparently securely-dated to 2.4 Myr (ibid.). However, when the dating evidence was re-examined (Drake *et al.* 1980; Gleadow 1980; McDougall *et al.* 1980) it was apparent that the case for such an old age could not be substantiated, and the date for the artefacts was subsequently revised to *c.*1.9 Myr (see Brown (1994) for an excellent review of the 'KBS' dating controversy). Meanwhile, simple artefacts, mainly quartz flakes, had been found in Member F of the Shungura Formation in southern Ethiopia (Howell *et al.* 1987), and these were reliably-dated to 2.3 Myr (Feibel *et al.* 1989). Other artefact assemblages have been reported from Member E in the same formation, and these would have pushed the onset of stone artefact manufacture back to close to 2.5 Myr, but in one locality the evidence is limited to surface finds (Howell *et al.* 1987), and in the other the outcrop from which the artefacts had been excavated could not be linked securely enough to the reference stratigraphy (ibid.). Subsequent discoveries elsewhere in the Turkana Basin have confirmed the presence of artefacts at *c.*2.3–2.4 Myr (Kibunjia *et al.* 1992; Kibunjia 1994). Even more recently discoveries made at Gona, a site on the north side of the lower reaches of the Awash River, have pushed the date for stone artefact manufacture back to between 2.5 and 2.6 Myr (Semaw *et al.* 1997).

Homo and stone tools

The link between stone tool manufacture and the genus *Homo* is a long-standing one. This was made particularly explicit by Kenneth Oakley in the title of his book *Man the Toolmaker* (Oakley 1949). Indeed, in the first edition Oakley proposed that 'the problem of the antiquity of man resolves itself into the question of the geological age of the earliest known artefacts' (ibid., 3). The link between *Homo* and artefact manufacture was broken temporarily in 1959 when *Zinjanthropus boisei*, then the only hominid known from

Bed I at Olduvai Gorge (Leakey 1959), was described 'as the oldest yet discovered maker of stone tools' (ibid., 493). However, when evidence of a 'more advanced tool maker' was found (Leakey *et al.* 1964, 9), the authors adjusted the definition of the genus *Homo* (ibid., 7 and see above) to accommodate the new fossils, and thus re-established the link between stone tool manufacture and the genus *Homo*.

Some idea of the strength of that link can be gauged from the statement made by Grahame Clark in the third edition of *World Prehistory* in which he wrote that if future research produced evidence of 'a yet more advanced hominid in Bed I', then 'there would be no problem from a paleontological point of view in downgrading *H. habilis* to a variety of *A. africanus*' (Clark 1977, 22). It is clear from this statement that Clark was one of many commentators who were prepared, at least in matters related to taxonomy, to let inferences about behaviour take precedence over morphological evidence.

The passage of time since Clark's statement was written has seen very little weakening of the link between *Homo* and culture. Tobias (1991) concedes that the ability to make stone artefacts may have been seen first in a 'derived *A. africanus*' ancestor of *Homo habilis sensu lato* as 'facultative' culture, but only credits the latter with 'cultural behaviour [which] must have become *obligate*' (ibid., 832). The proposal that the Chemeron temporal bone (KNM-BC1) may belong to *Homo* apparently 'made more tenable the idea that our genus is also or exclusively responsible for the origins of lithic culture' (Hill *et al.* 1992, 720), and when Kimbel and his colleagues reported the discovery at Hadar of Oldowan tools and a hominin maxilla apparently reliably-dated to 2.33±0.07 Myr, the authors referred to the discovery as representing 'the oldest association of hominid remains with stone tools, and possibly the earliest well-dated occurrence of the genus *Homo*' (Kimbel *et al.* 1996). It is clear from the emphasis of Kimbel *et al.*'s paper, and from the interest that it stimulated (Wood 1997), that the discovery of stone artefacts along with the remains of a maxilla attributed to an early hominin other than *Homo* would have evoked substantially less interest.

Tobias has long championed the link between *Homo* and the ability to communicate through spoken language (see Tobias (1991) for a review). He bases this primarily on evidence from endocranial casts and writes that 'in the endocranial casts of *H. habilis*, for the first time in the early hominid fossil record, there are prominences corresponding to both a well-developed speech area of Broca and a secondary speech area of Wernicke. These are two of the most important neural bases for language ability in the human brain' (ibid., 836). He links linguistic ability with cultural facility and claims that *H. habilis sensu lato* 'was the first culture-bound and language-dependent primate' (ibid., 840). However, despite recent claims to the contrary (Wilkins & Wakefield 1995), there is compelling evidence that function cannot always be reliably inferred from the gross appearance of the brain (Galaburda & Pandya 1982; Falk 1986; Donald 1995; Lieberman 1995; Whitcombe 1995; Gannon *et al.* 1998). We suggest that while it is attractive to link culture and language with 'the emergence of the genus *Homo* and the arrival of *Homo habilis*' and the attainment of a 'new level of organization' (Tobias 1991, 844), we caution that there is little hard evidence to support such a scenario.

How many candidates for the pioneer 'tool-maker'?

As long as human evolution was considered to be made up of a series of time-successive species, assembled in a ladder-like lineage running from an ape-like ancestor at the base of the ladder, to modern humans at the top, the identification of a tool-maker was not difficult. Indeed the possession of culture was at the heart of the 'single-species' hypothesis which was espoused by Bartholomew, Birdsell, Brace and others (eg Bartholomew & Birdsell 1953; Brace 1967) and which maintained that the principle of 'competitive exclusion' would ensure that no more than one species at a time could exploit the 'culture niche'. No matter how sound, or unsound, the principle of 'competitive exclusion' (Gause 1934), with the discovery of *Homo habilis* and *Zinjanthropus boisei* (now more usually referred to as *Paranthropus boisei*) in the hominin fossil record from Bed I at Olduvai (Leakey *et al.* 1964), and the recovery at Koobi Fora, in northern Kenya, of the remains of early African *Homo erectus/Homo ergaster* and *Paranthropus boisei* from the same strata (Leakey & Walker 1976), the 'single-species' interpretation of the early phases of the hominin fossil record became untenable.

The hominin fossil record is now generally recognized as being more speciose than it was even 20 years ago (Wood 1996b), and there were several occasions during human evolutionary history when as many as three sympatric hominin species were extant (Figure 1). For example, at the time of what we presently understand to be the earliest evidence of stone artefacts, *c.*2.5 Myr, there are at least two, and possibly four—if we include the suggestion that *H. habilis* may be as old as, if not older than, 2.3 Myr (Tobias 1989; Kimbel *et al.* 1996; Suwa *et al.* 1996), and the possibility of temporal overlap between *Paranthropus aethiopicus* and *Paranthropus boisei* (Suwa *et al.* 1996)—hominins in the East African fossil record. However, in the light of the thumbnail sketches given above, are either *H. rudolfensis* or *H. habilis sensu stricto* so 'advanced' that we can automatically assume that one or the other, or perhaps both of them, manufactured the stone artefacts known from this time? Are they functionally comparable to *H. ergaster*, or early African *H. erectus*? If not, can we be confident that they should be included in the genus *Homo*?

Is *Homo* a good genus?

Ernst Mayr (1950) provides a good guide to what a genus is. He suggested that 'a genus consists of one species, or a group of species of common ancestry, which differ in a pronounced manner from other groups of species and are separated from them by a decided morphological gap' (ibid., 110). He goes on to state that the genus 'has a very distinct biological meaning. Species that are united in a given genus occupy an ecological situation which is different from that occupied by the species of another genus, or, to use the terminology of Sewall Wright, *they occupy a different adaptive plateau*' (our italics) (ibid.).

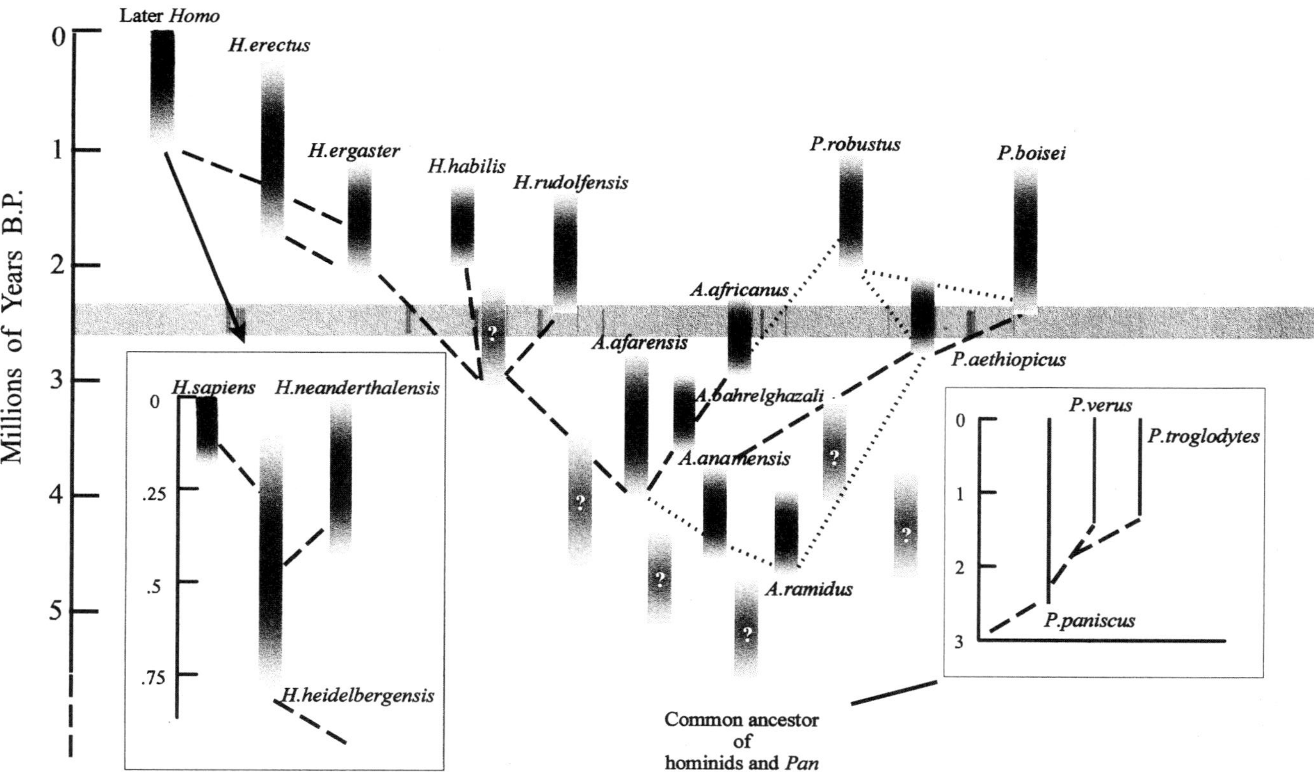

Figure 1. Approximate time ranges of hominin species groups. The columns with a question mark represent species groups that are likely to exist, but which are, for the moment, not recognized in the hominin fossil record. The horizontal grey band corresponds to the time of appearance of the earliest recognizable stone tools.

Thus, a genus has to be a group of species of 'common ancestry' that is adaptively homogeneous.

Evidence about the first of these criteria can be examined using the method of phylogenetic analysis, also known as cladistics. If all the species presently allocated to *Homo* form a well-supported 'monophyletic group', or clade, then that would satisfy one of the two necessary conditions for a genus. The second condition, that of adaptive homogeneity, can, in fossil taxa, only be investigated by looking at the distribution of morphological features which have functional and adaptive implications. How well does the genus *Homo*, as presently defined, satisfy these two criteria?

Monophyly

Although cladistic methods have been applied to the early hominin fossil record for more than two decades, since Eldredge and Tattersall's pioneering analysis was published in 1975, relatively few studies have considered the more recently recovered material attributed to 'early *Homo*', and fewer still have broken this evidence down into two taxonomic groups for the purpose of phylogenetic analysis. Of these, only Strait *et al.* (1997) conclude that the species presently included in *Homo* form a monophyletic group. The study by Lieberman *et al.* (1996) came to the conclusion that while there was evidence for linking *H. habilis sensu stricto* with later *Homo* taxa in a monophyletic group, with respect to *H. rudolfensis* there was as much evidence linking it with the *Paranthropus* clade as with that of *Homo*.

These results all relate to cladistic analyses that include only craniodental evidence. While it would be unwise to speculate about the results of studies that are not yet undertaken, it is worth bearing in mind that if the scope of the analysis was widened to include postcranial characters, then given even the little we know about the postcranial skeleton of *H. habilis sensu stricto* (Johanson *et al.* 1987), it is unlikely that this taxon would be part of a *Homo* clade, since its postcranial skeleton is at least as primitive as that of *A. afarensis* (Hartwig-Schrerer & Martin 1991).

Adaptive homogeneity

In an analysis which is reported elsewhere (Collard & Wood in press) we have examined information about early hominin taxa which reflect their body shape, locomotor behaviour, and the size of their neocortex, and we have analysed data which provide information about diet. We reasoned that one way of assessing how many adaptive strategies are represented in hominin evolution is to look for major differences in the way in which the component species go about maintaining homeostasis, acquiring food, and producing offspring. We also reasoned that a species' mode of locomotion, dietary choices, brain size, and the shape and size of its body would be significant factors in determining how it achieved homeostasis, an adequate food intake, and reproductive success.

While the importance of locomotion and diet is obvious, the significance of brain size and, especially, body shape and size requires some explanation. Brain size appears to determine the principal social interactions that are involved in reproduction (Dunbar 1992; 1995; Aiello & Dunbar 1993). Body shape is closely linked to temperature regulation, water balance, and habitat (Wheeler 1991; 1992; Ruff 1991; 1993; 1994; Ruff & Walker 1993). Ruff (1993) notes that in closed, forested environments with limited direct sunlight and little air movement a tall, linear physique loses its advantages. Moreover, humid environments decrease the usefulness of a relatively large surface area for evaporative cooling by sweating.

We assessed information and morphometric evidence for seven African early hominin species: *Australopithecus afarensis*, *Australopithecus africanus*, *Paranthropus robustus*, *Paranthropus boisei*, *Homo habilis*, *Homo rudolfensis*, and *Homo ergaster*. Other early hominin species, including *Ardipithecus ramidus* (White *et al.* 1994; 1995), *Australopithecus anamensis* (Leakey *et al.* 1995), and *Paranthropus aethiopicus* (Walker *et al.* 1986), were not considered, since at the time of the study their published fossil records were, and still are, too sparse. As functional inferences about fossil taxa can be made only by analogy with extant species, we also considered evidence for *H. sapiens* and *Pan troglodytes*.

Information about, and relevant data for the interpretation of, early hominin species is frustratingly sketchy. What is known, however, suggests that these species can be divided into two broad adaptive categories (see Figure 1). One of these is characterized by a combination of facultative bipedalism and an ability to move effectively in trees; a diet which was considerably more mechanically demanding than those of *H. sapiens* and *P. troglodytes*; a low to moderate encephalization quotient; and a body shape which in terms of thermoregulation was best suited to a relatively wooded environment. The other adaptive strategy is characterized by a form of locomotion which is much more similar to that practised by modern humans, ie obligatory bipedalism with a limited ability to climb within trees; a diet which had similar mechanical properties to those of *H. sapiens* and *P. troglodytes*; a moderate encephalization quotient; and a physique which would have been adaptive on the open savannah. With varying degrees of certainty, *A. afarensis*, *A. africanus*, *P. boisei*, *P. robustus*, *H. habilis*, and *H. rudolfensis* can all be assigned to the first group, whereas among the early hominin taxa, only *H. ergaster* can be assigned to the second. Among the first group there is substantial morphological variation, and there are several clades subsumed within it. It is possible that additions to the fossil record, together with appropriate analyses, may show that it consists of species which sample more than one adaptive strategy.

In sum, the data we reviewed suggest that *A. afarensis*, *A. africanus*, *P. robustus*, *P. boisei*, *H. habilis*, and *H. rudolfensis* were, to use Andrews' (1995) phrase, 'bipedal apes'. They spent much of their time moving about in trees, were equipped with a brain that was little bigger in relative terms than that of *P. troglodytes*, had an omnivorous diet which included a greater proportion of difficult-to-process items, such as seeds, than that of *P. troglodytes*, and would have found it easier to live in relatively wooded habitats than in the open. The data also suggest that *H. ergaster* should be recognized as having a different adaptive strategy from that of *A. afarensis*, *A. africanus*, *P. robustus*, *P. boisei*, *H. habilis*, and *H. rudolfensis*. While still relatively unencephalized, *H. ergaster* appears to have been a fully committed biped, whose adaptations allowed it, if necessary, to venture into the open savannah. It also had a diet that was no more mechanically demanding than those of *H. sapiens* and *P. troglodytes*.

Conclusions and implications

For a variety of reasons it is no longer tenable to regard the possession of culture and membership of the genus *Homo* as synonymous. There are several grounds for abandoning this simplistic association. Firstly, stone tools are a poor proxy for 'culture'. They just happen to be durable, and if they are to be surrogates for 'culture', then 'culture' has to be redefined and qualified to reflect this. Secondly, what we can infer about the functional capabilities of two of the taxa presently included in *Homo*, namely *H. habilis sensu stricto* and *H. rudolfensis*, suggests that there are few grounds for regarding them as so 'advanced', that they are the only possible candidates for the manufacture of the stone artefacts. The fossil record of the postcranial skeleton of the early hominin upper limb is generally poor, but there are sufficient hand bones preserved to fuel a lively debate about whether it would have been possible for hominins other than those in *Homo* to make tools (Susman 1988; 1994; 1998; Marzke 1997), and research aimed at trying to understand the role of the hand and forearm muscles in stone tool manufacture (eg Marzke 1997; Hamrick *et al.* 1998) promises to generate testable criteria against which such judgements can be made. However, even if it could be demonstrated that *H. habilis sensu stricto* and *H. rudolfensis* could make tools, it is clear that their inclusion in *Homo* strains the latter's credibility as a genus. Their inclusion probably violates the requirement for monophyly, and almost certainly weakens the claim that all the members of the genus *Homo* occupy the same location in the 'adaptive landscape'. We suggest that species should only be included in the genus *Homo* if they share the reduced teeth and jaws, the derived body shape and the morphological manifestations of a commitment to terrestrial bipedalism that are apparently first seen in the hominin fossil record in early *African H. erectus/H. ergaster.*

Acknowledgement

We are grateful to Arthur Cain for his encouragement and for his translations of Linnaeus. The research incorporated in this review was supported by The Leverhulme Trust and The Henry Luce Foundation (B.W.) and by The Natural Environment Research Council Research Studentship and The Wellcome Trust (M.C.).

References

AIELLO, L.C. & DUNBAR, R.I.M. 1993. Neocortex size, group size and the evolution of language. *Current Anthropology* 34, 184–93.

ANDREWS, P. 1995. Ecological apes and ancestors. *Nature* 376, 555–6.

BARTHOLOMEW, G.A. & BIRDSELL, J.B. 1953. Ecology and the protohominids. *American Anthropologist* 55, 481–98.

BRACE, C.L. 1967. *The Stages of Human Evolution*. Englewood Cliffs: Prentice Hall.

BRAIN, C.K., CHURCHER, C.S., CLARK, J.D., GRINE, F.E., SHIPMAN, P., SUSMAN, R.L., TURNER, A. & WATSON, V. 1988. *South African Journal of Science* 84, 828–35.

BROWN, F.H. 1994. Development of Pliocene and Pleistocene chronology of the Turkana basin, East Africa, and its relation to other sites. In R.S. Corruccini and R.L. Ciochon (eds), *Integrative Paths to the Past: Paleoanthropological advances in honor of F. Clark Howell*, 285–312. New Jersey: Prentice Hall.

CLARK, G. 1977. *World Prehistory in New Perspective* (3rd edn). Cambridge: Cambridge University Press.

COLLARD, M.C. & WOOD, B.A. in press. Grades among the early African hominids. In T. Bromage and F. Schrenk (eds), *African Biogeography, Climate Change and Human Evolution*. Oxford: Oxford University Press.

DONALD, M. 1995. Neurolinguistic models and fossil reconstructions. *Behavioral and Brain Sciences* 18(1), 188–9.

DRAKE, R.E., CURTIS, G.H., CERLING, T.E., CERLING, B.W., & HAMPEL, J.H. 1980. KBS Tuff dating and geochronology of tuffaceous sediments in the Koobi Fora and Shungura Formations, East Africa. *Nature* 283, 368–72.

DUNBAR, R.I.M. 1992. Neocortex size as a constraint on group size in primates. *Journal of Human Evolution* 22, 287–96.

DUNBAR, R.I.M. 1995. Neocortex size and group size in primates: a test of the hypothesis. *Journal of Human Evolution* 28, 287–96.

ELDREDGE, N. & TATTERSALL, I. 1975. Evolutionary models, phylogenetic reconstruction, and another look at hominid phylogeny. In F.S. Szalay (ed.), *Approaches to Primate Paleobiology*, 218–42. Contrib. Primat. No. 5. Karger: Basel.

EVERNDEN, J.F. & CURTIS, G.H. 1965. Potassium-argon dating of late Cenozoic rocks in East Africa and Italy. *Current Anthropology* 6, 343–64.

FALK, D. 1986. Endocranial casts and their significance for primate brain evolution. *Comparative Primate Biology* 1, 477–90.

FEIBEL, C.S., BROWN, F.H. & MCDOUGALL, I. 1989. Stratigraphic context of fossil hominids from the Omo Group deposits, northern Turkana basin, Kenya and Ethiopia. *American Journal of Physical Anthropology* 78, 595–622.

GALABURDA, A.M. & PANDYA, D.N. 1982. Role of architectonics and connections in the study of primate brain evolution. In E. Armstrong and D. Falk (eds), *Primate Brain Evolution: Methods and Concepts*, 203–16. New York: Plenum.

GANNON, P.J., HOLLOWAY, R.L., BROADFIELD, D.C. & BRAUN, A.R. 1998. Asymmetry of chimpanzee planum temporale: humanlike pattern of Wernicke's brain language area homolog. *Science* 279, 220–2.

GAUSE, G.F. 1934. *The Struggle for Existence*. Baltimore: Williams and Wilkins.

GLEADOW, A.J.W. 1980. Fission track age of the KBS Tuff and associated hominid remains in northern Kenya. *Nature* 284, 225–30.

GRINE, F.E., JUNGERS, W.L. & SCHULTZ, J. 1996. Phenetic affinities among early *Homo* crania from East and South Africa. *Journal of Human Evolution* 30, 189–225.

HAMRICK, M.W., CHURCHILL, S.E., SCHMITT, D. & HYLANDER, W.L. 1998. EMG of the human flexor pollicis longus muscle: implications for the evolution of hominid tool use. *Journal of Human Evolution* 34, 123–36.

HARTWIG-SCHRERER, S. & MARTIN, R.D. 1991. Was 'Lucy' more human than her 'child'? Observations on early hominid postrcranial skeletons. *Journal of Human Evolution* 21, 439–49.

HILL, A., WARD, S., DEINO, A., GARNISS, C. & DRAKE, R. 1992. Earliest *Homo*. *Nature* 355, 719–21.

HOWELL, F.C., HAESAERTS, P. & DE HEINZELIN, J. 1987. Depositional environments, archaeological occurrences and hominids from Members E and F of Shungura Formation (Omo Basin, Ethiopia). *Journal of Human Evolution* 16, 643–64.

JOHANSON, D.C., MASAO, F.T., ECK, G.G., WHITE, T.D., WALTER, R.C., KIMBEL, W.H., ASFAW, B., MANEGA, P., NDESSOKIA, P. & SUWA, G. 1987. New partial skeleton of *Homo habilis* from Olduvai Gorge, Tanzania. *Nature* 327, 205–9.

KEITH, A. 1948. *A New Theory of Human Evolution*. London: Watts & Co. Limited.

KIBUNJIA, M. 1994. Pliocene archaeological occurrences in the Lake Turkana basin. *Journal of Human Evolution* 27, 159–71.

KIBUNJIA, M., ROCHE, H., BROWN, F.H. & LEAKEY, R.E. 1992. Pliocene and Pleistocene archaeological sites west of Lake Turkana, Kenya. *Journal of Human Evolution* 23, 432–8.

KIMBEL, W.H., WALTER, R.C., JOHANSON, D.C, REED, K.E., ARONSON, J.L., ASSEFA, Z., MAREAN, C.W., ECK, G.G., BOBE, R., HOVERS, E., RAK, Y., VONDRA, C., YEMANE, T., YORK, D., CHEN, Y., EVENSEN, N.M. & SMITH, P.E. 1996. Late Pliocene *Homo* and Oldowan tools from the Hadar formation (Kada Hadar Member), Ethiopia. *Journal of Human Evolution* 31, 549–61.

KRAMER, A., DONNELLY, S.M., KIDDER, J.H., OUSLEY, S.D. & OLAH, S.M. 1995. Craniometric variation in large-bodied hominoids: Testing the single-species hypothesis for *Homo habilis*. *Journal of Human Evolution* 29, 443–62.

LEAKEY, L.S.B. 1951. *Olduvai Gorge*. Cambridge: Cambridge University Press.

LEAKEY, L.S.B. 1959. A new fossil skull from Olduvai. *Nature* 184, 491–3.

LEAKEY, L.S.B., EVERNDEN, J.F. & CURTIS, G.H. 1961. Age of Bed I, Olduvai Gorge, Tanganyika. *Nature* 191, 478–9.

LEAKEY, L.S.B, TOBIAS, P.V. & NAPIER, J.R. 1964. A new species of the genus *Homo* from Olduvai Gorge. *Nature* 202, 7–9.

LEAKEY, M.D. 1966. A review of the Oldowan culture from Olduvai Gorge, Tanzania. *Nature* 210, 462–6.

LEAKEY, M.D. 1970. Early artefacts from the Koobi Fora area. *Nature* 226, 228–30.

LEAKEY, M., FEIBEL, C.S., MCDOUGALL, I. & WALKER, A. 1995. New four million-year-old species from Kanapoi and Allia Bay, Kenya. *Nature* 376, 565–71.

LEAKEY, R.E.F. 1970. Fauna and artefacts from a new Plio-Pleistocene locality near Lake Rudolf in Kenya. *Nature* 226, 223–4.

LEAKEY, R.E.F & WALKER, A.C. 1976. *Australopithecus*, *Homo erectus*, and the single species hypothesis. *Nature* 261, 572–4.

LE GROS CLARK, W.E. 1964. *The Fossil Evidence for Human Evolution*. Chicago & London: University of Chicago Press.

LIEBERMAN, D.E., WOOD, B.A. & PILBEAM, D.R. 1996. Homoplasy and early *Homo*: An analysis of the evolutionary relationships of *H. habilis sensu stricto* and *H. rudolfensis*. *Journal of Human Evolution* 30, 97–120.

LIEBERMAN, P. 1995. Manual versus speech motor control and the evolution of language. *Behavioral and Brain Sciences* 18(1), 197–8.

LINNAEUS, C. 1758. Systema Naturae. Editio Decima, Reformata. Holmiae, Impensis Direct, Laurentii Salvii. (Facsimile reprint, 1956: London, British Museum (Natural History)).

MARZKE, M.W. 1996. Evolution of the hand and bipedality. In A. Lock and C.R. Peters (eds), *Human Symbolic Evolution*, 126–54. Oxford: Clarendon Press.

MARZKE, M.W. 1997. Precision grips, hand morphology, and tools. *American Journal of Physical Anthropology* 102, 91–110.

MAYR, E. 1950. Taxonomic categories in fossil hominids. Cold Spring Harbor Symposia on Quantitative Biology. Vol. XV, *Origin and Evolution of Man*, 109–18. Cold Spring Harbor, New York: The Biological Laboratory.

MCDOUGALL, I., MAIER, R., SUTHERLAND-HAWKES, P. & GLEADOW, A.J.W. 1980. K-Ar age estimate for the KBS Tuff, East Turkana, Kenya. *Nature* 284, 230–4.

OAKLEY, K.P. 1949. *Man the Tool-maker*. London: Trustees of the British Museum.

ROBINSON, J.T. 1961. The Australopithecines and their bearing on the origin of man and of stone tool-making. *South African Journal of Science* 57, 3–13.

RUFF, C.B. 1991. Climate and body shape in hominid evolution. *Journal of Human Evolution* 21, 81–105.

RUFF, C.B. 1993. Climatic adaptation and hominid evolution: the thermoregulatory imperative. *Evolutionary Anthropology* 2, 53–60.

RUFF, C.B. 1994. Morphological adaptation to climate in modern and fossil hominids. *Yearbook of Physical Anthropology* 37, 65–107.

RUFF, C.B. & WALKER, A. 1993. Body size and body shape. In A. Walker and R.E. Leakey (eds), *The Nariokotome Homo erectus Skeleton*, 234–65. Berlin: Springer Verlag.

SEMAW, S., RENNE, P., HARRIS, J.W.K, FEIBEL, C.S., BERNOR, R.L., FESSEHA, N. & MOWBRAY, K. 1997. 2.5-million-year-old stone tools from Gona, Ethiopia. *Nature* 385, 333–6.

STRAIT, D.S., GRINE, F.E. & MONIZ, M.A. 1997. A reappraisal of early hominid phylogeny. *Journal of Human Evolution* 32, 17–82.

SUSMAN, R.L. 1988. Hand of *Paranthropus robustus* from Member 1, Swartkrans: Fossil evidence for tool behavior. *Science* 240, 781–4.

SUSMAN, R.L. 1994. Fossil evidence for early hominid tool use. *Science* 265, 1570–3.

SUSMAN, R.L. 1998. Hand function and tool behaviour in early hominids. *Journal of Human Evolution* 35, 23–46.

SUWA, G., WHITE, T.D. & HOWELL, F.C. 1996. Mandibular postcanine dentition from the Shungura Formation, Ethiopia: crown morphology, taxonomic allocations, and Plio-Pleistocene hominid evolution. *American Journal of Physical Anthropology* 101, 247–82.

THIEME, H. 1997. Lower Paleolithic hunting spears from Germany. *Nature* 85, 807–10.

TOBIAS, P.V. 1989. The status of *Homo habilis* in 1987 and some outstanding problems. *Proceedings Second International Congress of Hominid Paleontology* 141–9.

TOBIAS, P.V. 1991. *Olduvai Gorge Volume 4: The skulls, endocasts and teeth of* Homo habilis, 1–921. Cambridge: Cambridge University Press.

WALKER, A.C., LEAKEY, R.E.F., HARRIS, J.M. & BROWN, F.H. 1986. 2.5 Myr *Australopithecus boisei* from west of Lake Turkana, Kenya. *Nature* 322, 517–22.

WHEELER, P. 1991. The influence of bipedalism on the energy and water budgets of early hominids. *Journal of Human Evolution* 21, 117–36.

WHEELER, P. 1992. The thermoregulatory advantages of large body size for hominid foraging in savannah environments. *Journal of Human Evolution* 23, 351–62.

WHITCOMBE, E. 1995. Palaeoneurology of language: Grounds for skepticism. *Behavioral and Brain Sciences* 18(1), 204–5.

WHITE, T.D., SUWA, G. & ASFAW, B. 1994. *Australopithecus ramidus*, a new species of early hominid from Aramis, Ethiopia. *Nature* 371, 306–12.

WHITE, T.D, SUWA, G. & ASFAW, B. 1995. *Australopithecus ramidus*, a new species of early hominid from Aramis, Ethiopia—a corrigendum. *Nature* 375, 88.
WILKINS, W.K. & WAKEFIELD, J. 1995. Brain evolution and neurolinguistic preconditions. *Behavioral and Brain Sciences* 18(1), 161–226.
WOOD, B.A. 1991. *Koobi Fora Research Project IV: Hominid Cranial Remains from Koobi Fora*. Oxford: Clarendon Press.
WOOD, B.A. 1992. Origin and evolution of the genus *Homo*. *Nature* 355, 783–90.
WOOD, B.A. 1996a. Origin and evolution of the genus *Homo*. *Contemporary Issues in Human Evolution* 21, 105–14.
WOOD, B.A. 1996b. Human evolution. *BioEssays* 18(12), 945–54.
WOOD, B.A. 1997. The oldest whodunnit in the world. *Nature* 385, 292–3.

Western Cape Landscapes

JOHN PARKINGTON

ARCHAEOLOGY IS THE INTEGRATION of the geological, the ecological, the social, and the symbolic. Archaeology is also, in Kent Flannery's famous words—'the most fun you can have with your trousers on'. For me these definitions are connected in that it is the freedom to use archaeology as an integration of many disciplines that makes it so much fun—with or without trousers. Grahame Clark once described archaeology as 'incessant if absorbing toil', and it is my impression that what absorbed him was the scope the subject offered for intellectual inquiry. When I arrived in South Africa in 1966 there were very few professional archaeologists. This meant that I was under no pressure to look for a specialized niche, but had the good fortune to be able to investigate all aspects of the landscape of the western Cape. Here I try to build some connections between the physical landscape, the ecological framework and former human settlement systems.

Geological contexts

The Atlantic coast of the western Cape is characterized as a series of half-heart shaped or long spiral bays of various lengths (Figure 1). The sizes and depths of these bays are determined by the interval between rocky spurs at sea level and the extent to which these reach west into the Atlantic. The sandy bays are massive suppliers of very shelly sand that is transported onshore by strong, southerly, summer winds to form very large dune plumes easily visible on satellite and air photographs. These plumes are characteristically not used for wheat production as are the more nutrient-rich shale soils further inland and are repetitively and cyclically vegetated and deflated. Sand supply is episodic and probably related to regressions of sea level which expose and make available the offshore sand blanket. Soil development alternates with depositional episodes.

Earlier dunefields are cemented and often transformed by soil development to form a fossil landscape ideal for bone preservation because of the high calcium carbonate content. These calcretes have been known as the Langebaan Limestone and were thought to

Proceedings of the British Academy, **99**, 25–35

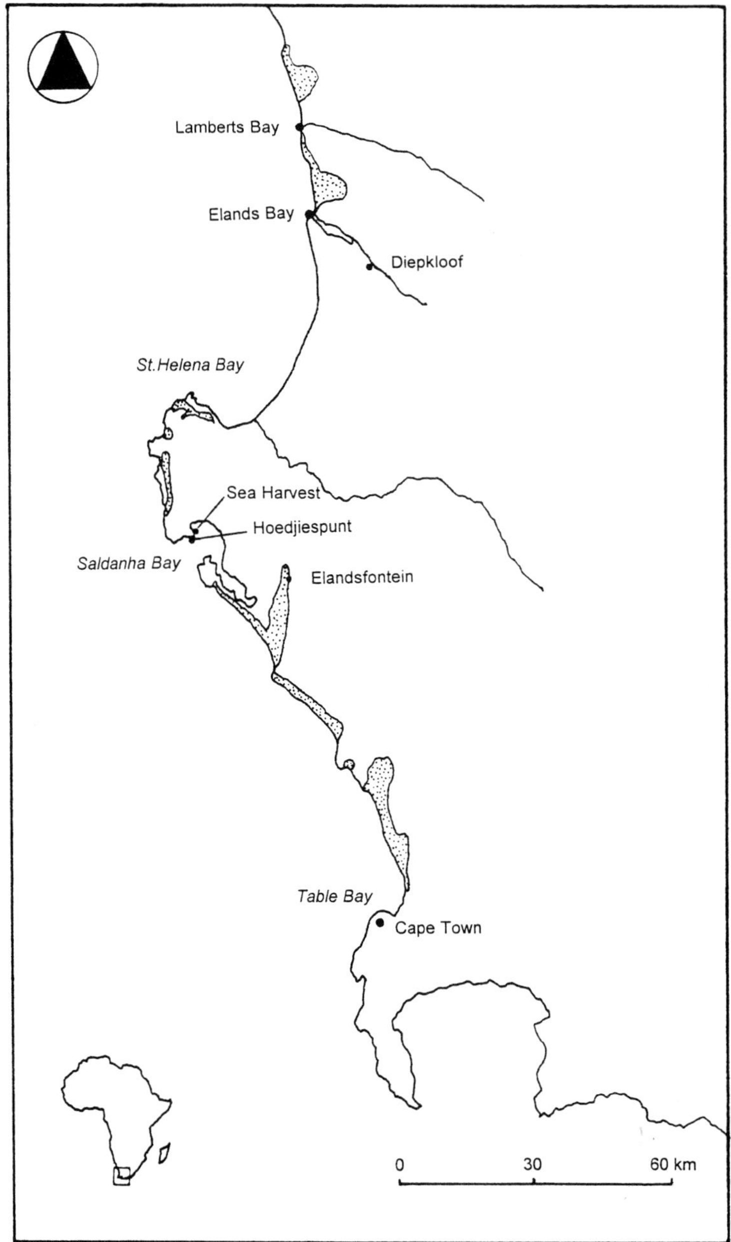

Figure 1. Map of the western Cape with dune plumes and sites mentioned in the text.

date from the Last Interglacial period. It is becoming increasingly clear, however, that the calcified dunes are often much older and that Early and Middle Pleistocene ages are likely for some of them. Perhaps the best known series of localities are those on the farm Elandsfontein from which the cranial roof known as Hopefield of Saldanha 'Man' was found in the early 1950s. These sites are in part palaeontological, but include Early, Middle, and Later Stone Age artefacts and probably span much of the last 0.5 million years. Dating is a major problem because deflation is common and there are no extensive marker horizons such as characterize the volcanic deposits in East African lake basins. Uranium series, electron spin resonance, and luminescence methods, along with rather embryonic biostratigraphic indicators from terrestrial and marine organisms are used for dating, but so far resolution is poor.

There are hyena, owl, and human derived faunal accumulations in these calcretes, almost all of them forming small pockets tucked away in cavities under calcrete shelves or eroding out in deflation hollows. The hyenas, probably mostly the brown hyena, are useful accumulators, vacuuming bones off the contemporary landscape and returning them helpfully to lairs in the lime-rich sands. Less helpfully they then systematically chew the rather spongy human bones and devour many of them. The durable hominid fragments that remain at Sea Harvest, for example, are invaluable because they can be excavated, dated, and properly contextualized. At the Hoedjiespunt site at Saldanha Bay we have four teeth, four or five small fragments of cranium, and two postcranial bones of one or two individuals from a hyena lair. The terrestrial character of the faunal remains and some preliminary uranium series dates on ostrich eggshell fragments may imply an age of 130,000 to 180,000 years for the hominids. It is sobering to think that—Klasies River Mouth aside—almost all the key human fossil specimens of Pleistocene southern Africa are without proper context. Kabwe was blasted out of a hillside by miners, Elandsfontein was found on a deflated surface and Florisbad was unearthed during the enlargement of a spring eye.

The human occupation sites in this calcrete landscape are even more remarkable in that they include many, probably hundreds of Middle Stone Age (MSA) shell middens with bone, ostrich eggshell, ochre, stone tools, and abundant marine shells, birds, and seals. Beyond the range of ^{14}C dating, these sites must date from a time of high sea level, most likely a part of oxygen isotope stage 5. Stratified above the hyena lair at Hoedjiespunt, for example, we have a series of MSA shell midden horizons with a quartz stone tool assemblage and abundant, sometimes bevelled and striated, ochre.

Although the ostrich eggshell fragments found so far at these coastal sites do not appear to come from water flasks, there are decorated fragments of ostrich eggshell not far away at the cave Diepkloof in the northern Sandveld (Figure 2). These are engraved fragments clearly associated with MSA stone tools, a reasonable faunal assemblage, and well-preserved charcoal. One fragment of decorated ostrich eggshell has been dated by AMS radiocarbon to more than 40,000 years and the sediment that contains the eggshell has a new luminescence date of about 63,000 years. This is as early as almost any claimed decorated object anywhere in the world. The contrast between the bone tools, abundant ochre, and

Figure 2. Two of 13 pieces of decorated ostrich eggshell from the late Middle Stone Age (Howiesons Poort) levels of Diepkloof.

decorated objects of the southern African MSA and their relative absence in the technologically similar Middle Palaeolithic assemblages of Europe and the Near East is an issue of growing interest.

But for me the excitement lies in the large number of undoubted shell middens along this coast, allowing us to contrast Holocene and Last Interglacial utilization of more or less the same set of resources. The idea of 'modern human behaviour' seems poorly defined but we have in the Cape a chance to look at large exposures of both MSA and LSA (Late Stone Age) domestic campsites and to assess changes over about 100,000 years. Already it is clear that MSA people left far more ochre, far more ostrich eggshell, ate a more restricted range of marine resources and ate, on average, larger limpets than their LSA descendants. Richard Klein's suggestion that there were fewer people in the MSA and that they used the landscape in a different way from later LSA people may well be correct and is certainly testable. It may also be that MSA integration of shellfish gathering into subsistence arrangements was less sophisticated than in later times.

Why, I'm wondering, do we have so many of these relatively early shellfish-gathering sites when they are so rare elsewhere on earth? It may be that we are simply lucky enough to have access to well-preserved repositories, which elsewhere are inundated by sea-level transgression or deeply buried under coastal sands. Alternatively, it may be that the origins of systematic shellfish gathering lie in this currently seasonal, mediterranean-type landscape at the southern tip of Africa. If this is so, we might begin to speculate about the antiquity of settlement systems that integrate spatially discrete and temporally complementary resources. Is the juxtaposition of an extremely rich near shore marine ecosystem with a seasonal and arguably unrewarding terrestrial ecosystem the significant factor? What do we know of other juxtapositions at this time elsewhere—in the Mediterranean, in Australia, in south-east Asia—or elsewhere in Africa?

Ecological contexts

The vegetation communities of the western Cape belong to the Fynbos Biome or the Cape Floral Kingdom, the smallest of the world's six plant kingdoms, arguably the most diverse and apparently the most threatened. Although characterized by botanists as heathlands and shrublands featuring many proteaceae, ericaceae, and restioniaceae, for hunter gatherers the key character is the abundance of geophytes, especially the many edible corms of the iridaceae family. There are no oil-based nuts or fruit-bearing trees such as are found in African savannas and the carbohydrate-rich corms are the best returns for gathering effort, requiring only a digging stick and carrying bag technology. The fynbos landscape is not very productive, has a low animal-carrying capacity and apparently was not conducive to the encouragement of formal domestication. The rainfall regime is strongly seasonal and results in a rhythmic pattern of corm development and edibility that may well have influenced hunter-gatherer movements and settlement.

Although there are many species of bulbous, tuberous, and corm-bearing plants, early traveller descriptions of the exploitation of plant foods by indigenous people refer regularly to 'uintjiestyd' or 'onion time', the period of the year when corms are fully developed but before the plant itself begins to make use of the stored carbohydrate. Indigenous gatherer hunters and gatherer herders knew the patterns of growth, edibility, and palatability of the local iridaceae and reckoned time by the availability cycle. Because most, but not all, of the western Cape geophytes flower in the spring and early summer, the growing months of the winter rainy season are lean periods for gatherers of corms. It is tempting to speculate that here is a seasonally restricted resource that needs to be integrated into a spatially coherent settlement strategy—arguably including coastal resources where available. Inter-tidal shellfish are as predictable and more spatially constrained than plant foods, and may have filled the gap left by the dearth of corms in winter.

As a sixties Cambridge graduate, these possibilities did not pass me by. Recently my reconstructions of seasonal mobility have been challenged by the isotope archaeometrists who have seen coastal populations as living permanently along the shores of the western Cape. Over the years it has become clear that there is no easy or direct relationship between a stable carbon isotope reading and the length of coastal residence. Pre-colonial organisms, including people, occupied an isotopically more enriched biosphere, collagen readings reflect only protein intake, not total diet, and coastal signatures, being derived from high protein shellfish diets, are exaggerated by rapid turnover in human skeletons. I know that some earlier reconstructions of seasonal rounds need modification, but I have no doubt that during parts of the Holocene, coastal visits were brief and seasonally scheduled. We need now to begin to study the seasonality of MSA coastal visits.

What is interesting in the context of subsistence patterns based on the exploitation of shellfish and underground corms is the complete absence of these staples or people gathering them from the painted repertoire of the hunter gatherers of the western Cape landscape. Not only that, but the landscape itself—topography, rivers, vegetation—

is not reflected in the paintings. Clearly the paintings are *in* but not *about* the physical landscape.

Social and symbolic contexts

The western Cape is a painted landscape with an estimated 10,000 painted rock shelters and caves scattered through the sandstone and quartzite hills and mountains. Although the age of the paintings is not yet well known it is likely that the paintings we can still see were made in the last 5000 years, although the tradition certainly extends back at least 10,000 years and is rooted in regular use of ochre in the MSA. Some broad stratigraphic patterns can be seen. Most clear is the superimposition of many handprints and some other finger-drawn images on fine line depictions of humans and animals, and the complete absence of the reverse. We take this to imply two periods during which dramatically different assemblages of images were made. I'd like to report our current views on the meaning of the fine line images.

These paintings are dominated by human images which outnumber animals by about 2 to 1. Humans are frequently depicted in lines, usually of either males or females, which are arguably representations of dances (Figure 3). Males are identified by prominent depictions of the penis, and women by breasts but more characteristically by well-defined, perhaps exaggerated, rounded buttocks (Figure 4). Many humans are too residual to be assigned as males or females, and there is some disagreement as to whether these were originally unambiguously one or the other. We think so. Although cloaked figures are technically impossible to classify by physiology, the regular association of bows, arrows, quivers, and hunting bags with cloaks has persuaded us they are male. The important points are that people are frequently painted naked, that men far outnumber women, that men almost always have bows, but that they very rarely are painted using them against animals, though not infrequently against one another. In the western Cape women are rarely depicted with the digging stick.

The fine line animals are very clearly not intended as a checklist of local fauna nor as a reflection of what was eaten. In fact the selection of animals to paint, and indeed the selection of images generally, point unambiguously toward the symbolic marking of the landscape with highly *socially* charged paintings. There are many paintings of small antelope, few of which are easily identified to species, and smaller but still substantial numbers of eland and elephant, some rhino, hartebeest, and sheep. Carnivores and small mammals such as dassies, porcupines, mongoose, hares, mole rats, and non-mammals such as tortoise and shellfish are either extremely rare or never painted. The frameworks for viewing this extra-ordinary selection are the archaeological, ethnographic, and historic documents which help us classify the local fauna in terms of economic, social, and symbolic values. Archaeologically, for example, shellfish, tortoises, dassies, small antelope, and plant foods provide the bulk of dietary intake, whereas eland bones are quite rare. Of

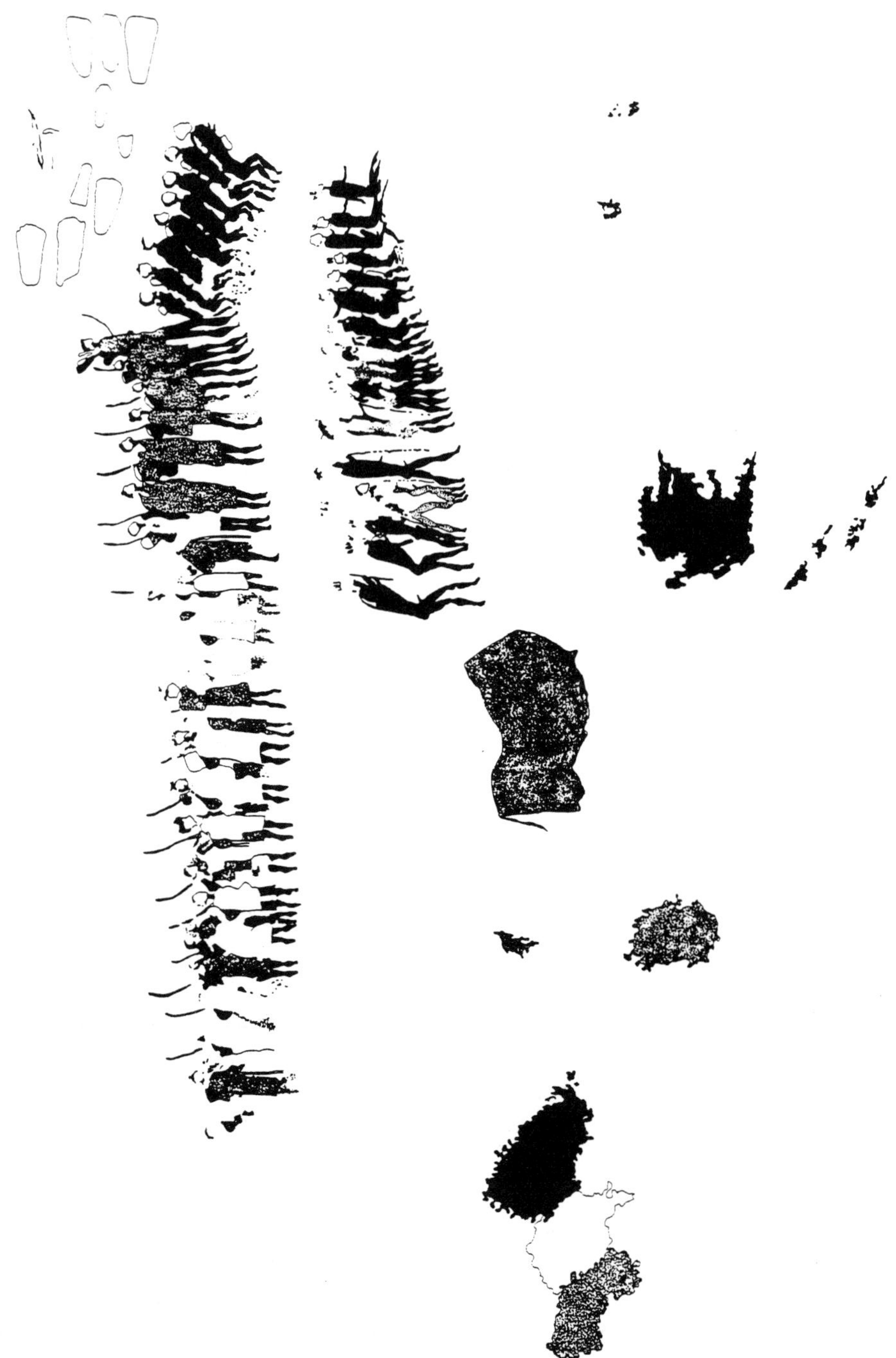

Figure 3. Lines of male figures from the farm Sevilla in the western Cape, probably an initiation event.

Figure 4. A line of female figures with one opposed male figure with bow from the farm Bushmanskloof in the western Cape.

the regular diet items only small antelope are painted. Ethnographically, by contrast, eland, along with gemsbok and kudu, the last two not found in the local fynbos, are very prominent in myth and folklore and form a group of animals hunted only by men with the bow and poisoned arrow.

One way to approach the selectivity of images and to try to suggest meanings for the paintings is to build a matrix which orders plants and animals of the landscape along economic, social, and symbolic dimensions and to compare the cell counts with the painted frequencies. Thus, carnivores are not hunted, large game are eagerly sought but rarely caught, small mammals are routinely killed, and corms and shellfish consumed almost daily. The larger the animal the greater the potential to share and develop social networks and the greater the amount of excitement caused by its capture. Women collect shellfish, may kill or collect small mammals and tortoises, but leave the killing of eland and other large game to men, who use bows and poisoned arrows. Risk, social value, and package size are somewhat related to one another and to gender roles.

In the Bleek and Lloyd archive (see for example Lloyd 1911), an extensive nineteenth-century collection of hunter-gatherer lore, mantis, porcupine, dassie, blue crane, mongoose, and tortoise exist as 'people of the early race', a time when the distinction between people and animals was not yet drawn. These animals are rarely or never depicted. Eland, however, were created at, and in fact create, the transformation to the present order when the distinctions *are* recognized and when the relationship between hunter and prey was established. The critical episode is the killing, by his children or grandchildren, of the mantis' favourite animal, an eland he had made and was keeping secretly near an isolated pool, rubbing it down with honey and referring to it as a person. When he discovers the killing, mantis complains that his permission was not sought and declares that from now on eland are meat and men are hunters. It is a moment of role definition and an event relived in all initiation ceremonies for hunters thereafter.

In Kalahari ethnographies a girl's first menstruation is marked by isolation and a ceremony attended by the adult women, but from which young adult men are excluded. This Eland Bull Dance, as it sometimes is called, is characterized by suggestive dancing by the women who frisk their waistbands like tails at an older man who represents the eland bull. The women are playing the role of eland cows and are welcoming the new maiden into the herd. The girl is now available as prey and as a mate for the young initiated men.

Eland thus occupy a very distinct economic, social, and symbolic position among southern African hunter-gatherer societies. As a large game species the eland offers an abundance of meat to be shared. It is exclusively the prey of men with the poisoned arrow, it is the kill that turns a boy into a man, it is the metaphor used to describe the transformation of a girl into a woman, and it is the animal of which the mantis/kaggen, a kind of trickster/creator/master of the game, was most fond. It was never a person 'of the early race', but appears in the Drakensberg, in the Karoo, and in Namibia at different times as an animal of particular, almost sexual, significance to the hunter (Figure 5).

Image choice in the paintings looks very interesting viewed along these dimensions. The absence of the collected component of diet and the rarity of the characters and themes of 'primal time' surely means that the paintings do not emphasize the economic role of women and do not illustrate the myths and legends of hunter-gatherer cosmology. Rather, a theme of the paintings is the social landscape, the approved relations between men and women. This line of argument might imply distinct meanings for the three kinds of animals regularly painted: small antelope, large herbivores, and very large beasts such as rhino and elephant. Here I tackle only the large herbivores represented in the western Cape by frequent depictions of eland.

The concept of n!ao in the Kalahari is a belief system that links the larger game—eland, kudu, gemsbok—with men's hunting abilities, women's childbearing and the weather. Significantly it is not as plant gatherers that women are opposed to men, but as sexual partners and childbearers. Significantly, also, the emphasis in paintings of women is not on the food quest but the erotic buttocks. Associated with n!ao is an extended verbal metaphor in which relations between adult men and women are spoken of in hunting terms—men pursue and eat women, as they hunt and eat large game. Women like meat,

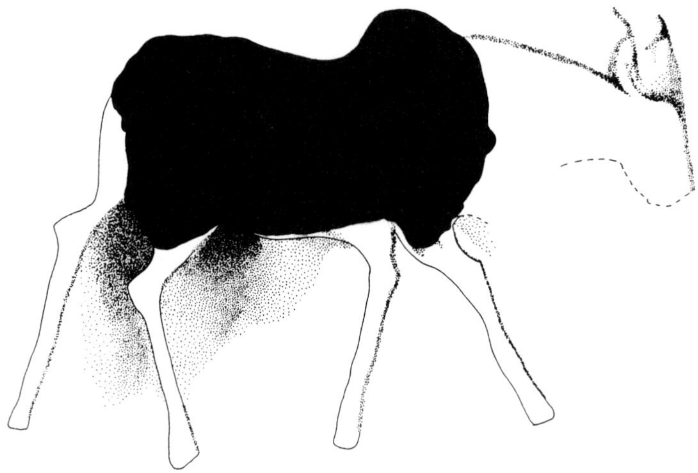

Figure 5. A bichrome eland from the farm Keurbos in the western Cape.

but women are also like meat as Megan Biesele (1993) has noted. Men become husbands and hunters at the same initiation ceremony. The assumption of the hunter–prey relationship refers back to the original eland death when a person became meat, when roles were established, when order was promulgated. Another Bleek and Lloyd story, about The Anteater's Laws, explains the transformation from primal to modern times as a kind of second creation, in the same way that an initiation event recreates the young man or woman under a new set of rules.

These metaphors seem to explain the prevalence of eland as painted subjects and their regular association with men and women painted to emphasize their sexual potential, and especially the processional dances that signal the achievement of sexual potential. My view is that many of the paintings in the western Cape and elsewhere in southern Africa, capture the tensions of the changing relationships between boys and girls, men and women, older men, and older women. Elephant, rhino, and small antelope fall into different cells of our multi-dimensional matrix and require other explanations.

In conclusion

Whatever else it is, the western Cape landscape is a wonderful palimpsest of traces from the past—a vessel that houses not only archaeological but also palaeontological, geological, botanical, zoological, architectural, and historical traces of what has been. We are currently developing a concept of the Landscape as combined museum framework and school curriculum in which we hope to return traces back to the landscape from which they came and to display them in context. The call in South African schools education is to dismantle disciplinary boundaries, to localize the content of the syllabus, to re-connect people to a pre-colonial past from which they have been severed and to focus on outcomes—numeracy, literacy, a conservation ethic. Archaeology is ideally placed to play an increasingly important role by integrating the museum case with the classroom and the present with the past. This may require incessant toil, but will be a truly absorbing task.

References

BERGER, L. & PARKINGTON, J. 1995. Brief communication: a new Pleistocene hominid-bearing locality at Hoedjiespunt, South Africa. *American Journal of Physical Anthropology* 98(4), 601–9.

BIESELE, M. 1993. *Women Like Meat*. Bloomington: Indiana University Press.

DOWSON, T. & LEWIS-WILLIAMS, D. (eds), 1994. *Contested Images: Diversity in Southern African Rock Art Research*. Johannesburg: Witwatersrand University Press.

GRINE, F.E. & KLEIN, R.G. 1993. Late Pleistocene human remains from Sea Harvest site, Saldanha Bay, South Africa. *South African Journal of Science* 89, 145–52.

KLEIN, R.G. & CRUZ-URIBE, K. 1991. The Bovids from Elandsfontein, South Africa and their implications for the age, palaeoenvironment, and the origins of the site. *The African Archaeological Review* 9, 21–79.

LLOYD, L.C. 1911. *Specimens of Bushmen Folklore*. London: George Allen.

PARKINGTON, J. 1996. What is an eland? N!ao and the politics of age and sex in the paintings of the Western Cape. In P. Skotnes (ed.), *Miscast*. Cape Town: University of Cape Town Press.

PARKINGTON, J. & MANHIRE, A. 1997. Processions and groups: human figures, ritual occasions and social categories in the rock paintings of the Western Cape, South Africa. In M.W. Conkey, O. Soffer, D. Stratmann and N.G. Jablonski (eds), *Beyond Art: Pleistocene Image and Symbol*. Memoirs of the California Academy of Sciences. No. 23. San Francisco.

RIGHTMIRE, G.P. & DEACON, H.J. 1991. Comparative studies of Late Pleistocene human remains from Klasies River Mouth, South Africa. *Journal of Human Evolution* 20, 131–56.

VOLMAN, T.P. 1978. Early archaeological evidence for shellfish collecting. *Science* 201, 911–13.

Dating the Human Colonization of Australia: Radiocarbon and Luminescence Revolutions

RHYS JONES

> If at Cambridge, prehistory sprang from anthropology and classics, it drew also consistently on the natural sciences for many of its methods and procedures. This was particularly true of dating.
>
> (Clark 1989, 79)

THE QUESTION OF THE ORIGINS and antiquity of Australian Aboriginal people goes back to the very beginning of the science of biogeography. Alfred Russel Wallace, in his paper 'On the varieties of man in the Malaya Archipelago' read to the Ethnological Society of London in 1865, rejoiced that one of the implications of the evolutionary theory was that now one had 'the permission . . . to place the origin of man at an indefinitely remote epoch . . . and we can speculate more freely on the parentage of tribes and races' (Wallace 1865, 209–10). Wallace's original 'Line' was an ethnological one (Moore 1997). He described how moving from Ternate to the neighbouring eastern island of Halmahera (Gilolo) 'Here then I had discovered the exact boundary line between the Malay and Papuan races . . . I was very much pleased at this determination, as it gave me a clue to one of the most difficult problems in Ethnology, and enabled me in many other places to separate the two races, and to unravel their intermixtures' (Wallace 1869, 243). He postulated that the Malays had a continental origin with affinities with other Asian peoples, whereas 'the races of Papuan type, including all to the east of the former, as far as the Fiji Islands, are derived not from any existing continent, but from lands which now exist or have recently existed in the Pacific Ocean' (Wallace op. cit., 15). Thomas Huxley took up Wallace's idea of a partly sunken continent on the Australian-Pacific rim, when he tried to explain what he considered to be close physical resemblances between the peoples of New Britain, New Caledonia, and Tasmania as having been due to cohabitation on a once contiguous land mass, most of which

Proceedings of the British Academy, **99**, 37–65

had since sunk, leaving these peoples as isolated relics of extremely ancient populations. This he felt was as good evidence of the high antiquity of man, as the direct testimony of the hand axes 'in the gravels of Hoxne and Amiens' (Wallace op. cit., 97).

Grahame Clark (1979, 2) considered that part of the reason for the rapid development of archaeology during the latter part of the nineteenth century came from 'the objective support it appeared to give to the idea of progress', that dominant paradigm of the Victorian era. Australian Aborigines were increasingly seen as having been a surviving relic from one of the earliest stages in this historical process, isolated in a remote and hostile land. This was expressed explicitly by W.A. Horn, the leader of a multidisciplinary scientific expedition to central Australia in 1894,

> The central Australian aborigine is the living representative of a stone age, who still fashions his spear-heads and knives from flint or sandstone . . . His origin and history are lost in the gloomy mists of the past.
>
> (Horn 1896, ix)

It was this expedition, by bringing together for the first time the Melbourne University biologist Baldwin Spencer and the telegraph postmaster at Alice Springs, Frank Gillen, that was to transform our knowledge of the social life of the Arunta Aborigines with their classic *Native Tribes of Central Australia* in 1899. Here, within the very heart of the desert, were people with minimal material possessions who lived through hunting and gathering for their food, yet who in their kinship relations, their religion, myth, and ceremonial life exhibited a degree of sophistication and complexity that astounded late Victorian scholars, steeped as they were in an assumption of an unilineal association of material and cultural wealth. Yet even Spencer and Gillen considered that through their studies, they were exploring earlier fossilized stages in human development (Mulvaney 1996). The work also profoundly influenced later thinkers such as Freud and Durkheim in their investigations as to the putative origins of human social and psychological phenomena. If, as Wallace put it, the Australian Aborigines were 'the remnant of an ancient and peculiar race' (Wallace 1888, 105), it is strange that this did not stimulate a major programme of archaeological research on the continent to investigate this antiquity. With a few exceptions this did not happen (Horton 1991). There was primarily an intellectual reason that the very archetype itself inhibited enquiry. The past would always resemble the present and peoples of a continuous stone age thus had no history (Jones 1984, 59).

Dubois' publication in 1893, of the *Pithecanthropus erectus* hominid remains from the banks of the Solo River in east Java, raised the expectation that the origins of man might lie in the tropics of south-east Asia. This kindled scientific interest in a long neglected carbonate-encrusted fossil skull with archaic morphological features, which had been discovered by accident in about 1884 at Talgai, on the Darling Downs of south-east Queensland. In 1914, the eminent geologist Edgeworth David presented evidence derived from both stratigraphic and morphological considerations, which indicated a Pleistocene age 'far older than any Aboriginal skulls that have ever been obtained in Australasia, and it proves that in Australia man attained to geological antiquity' (David & Wilson 1915, 531). Unfortunately, the formal anatomical description of the skull made comparisons with the Piltdown jaw, which naturally were not confirmed by subsequent work and so the significance of the Talgai skull became excessively diminished, only being re-established by the anatomist N.W.G. Macintosh (1967; 1969) in the 1960s when radiometric analyses suggested an age of at least 14,000 years.

Despite the efforts of Edgeworth David (1924) to provide further stratigraphic evidence for Pleistocene association of stone tools and middens, such evidence was flimsy or could not be replicated and disillusion set in (Meston 1937). The weight of opinion led by an influential group of stone artefact collectors and typologists based largely in Victoria moved away from a high antiquity for Aborigines in Australia towards a short chronology, to be measured perhaps only in terms of a few thousand years (Mulvaney 1961, 60; Golson 1993, 275; Griffiths 1996). One can make the somewhat ironic observation that it was during this time, the mid-1920s, that Gordon Childe left his native land for Europe to devote himself 'to identify the "primitive culture" of the Indo-Europeans and to locate their *Urheimat*' (Childe 1957 in Green 1981, 167).

In 1929, H.M. Hale and Norman Tindale published their account of an excavation at the limestone rock shelter of Devon Downs on the lower Murray River, where they proposed a sequence of typologically defined 'cultures' which spannned the Holocene. Tindale (1957) later proposed an earlier culture called the Kartan, which he argued was of late Pleistocene age because the distinctive pebble core tools and large scrapers had been found on Kangaroo Island off the coast of South Australia, as well as on the adjacent mainland, which implied that they had been made and left there by people prior to the post-glacial sea level rise. Nevertheless, persuasive though this argument was, it remained the case that up to the late 1950s the prehistory of Australia was confined to a narrow chronological constraint. Glyn Daniel in his *Hundred Years of Archaeology*, mentioned Australia only once, and then as part of a single sentence combining its prehistory within the 'Hoabinhian of south-east Asia, Australia and Japan' (Daniel 1950, 286). Gordon Childe, returning to Australia in 1957, wrote to O.G.S. Crawford in what may have been a somewhat satirical vein that

> Australian archaeology has possibilities though I could not possibly get interested. There are varieties of stone implement types—all horribly boring unless you're a flint fan—some stratified sites, rock drawings and paintings of uncertain age.
>
> (6 August 1957)

Grahame Clark, in the first edition of his *World Prehistory* (1961), devoted an entire chapter to 'Australasia and the Pacific'. His conclusion was that although a great deal of stone artefacts had been collected, 'the scientific pursuit of prehistory is still in its infancy over large areas of the vast Australian territories'; and concerning chronology, his defining phrase was that 'there is no convincing evidence for the immigration of man into Australia before Neothermal times' (Clark 1961, 243). What was to change this came not from archaeologists but from physicists.

Radiocarbon dating

The unstable isotope carbon 14 was first proposed as a theoretical possibility in 1934, during cloud chamber experiments on the fast neutron disintegration of nitrogen. It remained a curiosity until 1946, when Willard Libby, at the Institute for Nuclear Studies at the University of Chicago, theorized that the same process should be happening in nature through the collision of cosmic ray neutrons on nitrogen atoms in the outer atmosphere, and that this isotope as a constituent of carbon dioxide would enter the biosphere through photosynthesis. To test the critical assumption that the cosmic ray flux had remained relatively constant within the recent past, archaeological samples of known age, mostly from the Middle East were tested, the results showing a close fit with the measured C14 ages. Libby and his co-author, the chemist Jim Arnold, published their results in the 23 December 1949 issue of *Science*, in what Grahame Clark called the 'three-page article that was to shake the world' (1989, 84). It seems symbolically appropriate for what is probably the single most influential contribution to prehistoric archaeology in the twentieth century, that it should appear exactly at its mid-point.

Archaeologists now had a universal method to erect absolute chronologies for their sites, without recourse to comparative typologies and the various assumptions of diffusionist theories. Yet Childe also foreshadowed the danger of a loss of disciplinary autonomy and presciently observed in his 'Valediction' written in Australia in October 1957, a few weeks before his death, that 'archaeologists will abandon responsibility for chronology or themselves become nuclear physicists. In any case every prehistorian must master enough mathematics, physics and chemistry to appreciate the limitation of the information the latter can provide' (Green 1981, 167). This issue is the central theme of my paper.

Very quickly radiocarbon dating was applied to a series of key archaeological and palaeo-environmental problems, the bulk of them initially in North America and western Europe. Although there were some surprises, such as extending the antiquity of the earliest British Neolithic back almost a millennium, the impression that one now has from a more distant perspective is that, in general, radiocarbon tended either to confirm the existing chronologies or only change them to a limited extent. It is a credit to the rigour and autonomy of the traditional methods of archaeology that so much of the essential chronological edifice survived the radiocarbon examination.

In Australia and its neighbouring regions of New Guinea and the western Pacific, however, radiocarbon was utterly to transform the field, and probably nowhere else did this new technique have so much immediate impact. Australian archaeologists were quick to see the potential of the method. E.D. Gill sent samples from a midden near Warnambool on the south-west coast of Victoria to be dated by Libby and this result was published in the first corrected list of dates in 1951, alongside ones from the Danish site of Aamosen and Star Carr (Johnson 1951; Clark 1980, 26). In the mid-1950s, Athol Rafter set up the first radiocarbon laboratory in the south Pacific in Lower Hutt, New Zealand, and a series of dating programmes on Australian human fossil sites were initiated. Nevetherless, in his watershed synthesis 'The Stone Age of Australia', published in the *Proceedings of the Prehistoric Society* in 1961, which marked a critical hinge-point in the practice of Australian prehistory, John Mulvaney concluded that there was no firm carbon-dated evidence for any sites in Australia older than Holocene times, the oldest acceptable date being Tindale's date of 8700 BP for stone artefacts in a coastal sand dune at Cape Martin, South Australia. With access to the new technology, Clark (1980, 25–6) felt that 'Australian archaeologists were presented with a challenge almost as urgent as that with which Darwin and Huxley had once confronted the British and French pioneers of prehistory'.

Breakthrough into the Pleistocene

The first dates beyond the 'Pleistocene barrier' were obtained by Mulvaney himelf at Kenniff Cave in the highlands of south-east Queensland in 1962, when an age of 12,900 BP was obtained from a depth of seven feet, extended to 16,000 years BP a year later from lower down the section, and with further artefacts beneath. Within the next decade, this initiated a radical phase of field discovery, much of it carried out by recent graduates of Cambridge archaeology and by their students within newly established teaching and research posts in a few key Australian universities, notably at the Australian National University, which established its influential radiocarbon laboratory in 1965, at Sydney, and at the University of New England, Armidale. Institutional support was given by the Australian Institute of Aboriginal Studies, established by the Commonwealth Government in 1962, and which funded many critical discoveries and was prepared to back independent field projects by junior researchers. The dominant paradigm of this work was derived from an economic prehistory approach, rooted within the traditions and methods of integrated Quaternary research (Mulvaney 1993; Jones 1993, 106–8) and strongly influenced by the teaching and research of Clark (1989, 79–97), Charles McBurney, and Eric Higgs. Most projects involved the cooperation in the field of both archaeologists and Quaternary specialists such as geomorphologists and palynologists, which was reflected in the joint authorship of many of the key papers. The experience of working with indigenous people in northern Australia and New Guinea, together with a growing awareness of the vast ethnographic literature of the region, led to a powerful anthropological dimension (Meehan 1982; Golson 1986). Influences from the USA were strong: in particular the writings on cultural ecology by Julian Steward, work on shell middens by California archaeologists such as Heizer, and the analytical approaches of W.W. Taylor (1948) and Willey and Phillips in their *Method and Theory in American Archaeology* (1958). In many ways these trends echoed a similar integration within New Zealand archaeology, which had developed slightly earlier than in Australia, and much important work done in New Guinea was jointly carried out by Australian and New Zealand based researchers.

By 1967, dates of slightly over 20,000 years had been obtained from a variety of Australian sites, ranging from evidence of underground flint mining at the huge karst

Koonalda Cave on the Nullarbor Plain, or the sandstone shelter site of Burrill Lake on the coast of New South Wales, to several rock shelters in the Kakadu area of the Northern Territory. These latter sites, Malangangerr and Nawamoyn, caused a controversy, since in their basal levels dated to between 20,000 and 23,000 years ago, they contained small, well-made edge-ground hatchet heads made from volcanic or metamorphic rock with lateral hafting grooves on their sides presumably for hafting (C. White 1967; Schrire 1982). Edge-ground axe heads were also found in late Pleistocene contexts in caves in the highlands of New Guinea at Kafiavana and at Nombe (Golson 1971, 127; Mountain 1983, 94). Possibly analagous tools called 'waisted blades', usually made from volcanic rocks, consisting of large, flat, lenticular split-cobbles or flaked core rough-outs, with a pair of opposed notches on their sides or stemmed, and with their edges sharpened by grinding, were also found in Papua New Guinea. At the open Kosipe site they were dated to 26,000 years ago (White *et al.* 1970) and in limestone cave deposits in the highlands were found within terminal Pleistocene stratigraphic contexts, later dated back to about 30,000 years ago (Bulmer 1964; Mountain 1983). Within a remarkable series of tectonically uplifted coral terraces on the Huon Peninsula of north-eastern Papua New Guinea, these tools together with flakes and steep-edged cores were found *in situ* from the walls of a gully cutting the back-lagoon behind the uplifted reef terrace IIIa. This reef was itself dated by uranium series methods to between 45 and 53 ka, and a volcanic tephra covering this gully deposit was dated by thermo-luminescence (TL) to more than 40 ka, giving a minimum age for these artefacts (Groube *et al.* 1986).

Golson compared these northern Australian and New Guinean tools with similar ones from late Pleistocene contexts in south-east Asia and Japan and concluded that hafted ground axe/adzes were an integral part of the Pleistocene stone technology of this region, whose importance and antiquity had been long been masked by typological expectations carrying the 'burden of Europe' (Golson 1971, 129). This had led several scholars including Grahame Clark himself (White 1977) to present a somewhat Hobbesian verdict for the region that it was 'one of the most unenterprising parts of the Late Pleistocene world' (1968, 220).

New Guinea horticulture

Groube (1989) has ingeniously suggested that one of the functions for these waisted blades was as hafted axe/adzes to ring-bark trees so as to open up the rain forest canopy, thus allowing light to penetrate to the forest floor, where in the disturbed forest edge many potential food plants are found, such as yams and other vines and the mountain *Pandanus* with its high energy edible nuts. There is direct pollen and geomorphic evidence for landscape modification in the form of firing the higher margins of the forest as far back as about 30,000 years ago (Hope 1982; Haberle *et al.* 1990; Mountain 1991). The early Holocene saw the establishment of water drainage systems in intermontain swamps such as at Kuk in the Wahgi Valley from some 9000 years ago leading to a horticultural system there probably based on taro (Golson 1972, 17–18; 1989). With the land bridge between New Guinea and Australia being finally severed about 8000 years ago, the prehistories of the two land masses continued to diverge due both to physical separation and to the two subsistence trajectories; on the one hand the continuation of hunting and gathering on the savanna to the south with its long dry season and generally nutrient-poor soils of the continental plate, and on the other hand an intensification of horticulture which occurred in the younger upthrust mountain ranges with more continuous seasonal rainfall and volcanically enriched soil (Jones & Bowler 1980, 19–23).

Some implications from Mungo

The discoveries in 1969 at Lake Mungo, a fossil, now dry lake in the arid zone of southwestern New South Wales, were important in that a variety of archaeogical evidence could be closely integrated with palaeo-environmental reconstructions of a time period beyond the Last Glacial Maximum, when climatic conditions were much wetter than today (Bowler *et al.* 1970; Jones & Bowler 1980, 10). The cremated and smashed cranium of the Mungo I female dated to between 26,000 and 30,000 years old, indicated a modern sapient and gracile morphology. The Mungo III hominid, found within an older part of the dune more than 32 ka old, was an extended burial of a male in a grave which had been covered with red ochre, and it also exhibited modern morphological features (Bowler & Thorne 1976). There was evidence for a mixed foraging economy with gathering of freshwater unionid mussels and fishing from the lake edge, hunting small marsupial game, and collecting emu eggs from the desert scrub behind. Later research indicated a unionid shell midden in a nearby lake edge lunette dune dated to 35 ka (Bowler 1976, 59), and stone artefacts were excavated close to the base of the Mungo stratigraphic unit, with an assay on an extremely small carbon sample giving a value almost indistinguishable from background, and which was reported at the time as being *c.*40 ka old (Shawcross & Kaye 1980, 123).

At Mungo, flaked stone tools consisted of dome-shaped 'horsehoof' cores or core tools, and scrapers often made from thick flakes with steeply retouched edges, or with noses and deep notches possibly for use as spokeshaves. Their function was probably in the manufacture of wooden tools such as spears, digging sticks, and bowls, which were the primary implements for food production. Typologically, these were similar to assemblages from other late Pleistocene sites such as Kenniff Cave, Capertee in New South Wales, Ingaladdi in the Northern Territory, Mushroom Rock in Cape York, Kafiavana and Nombe in New Guinea, and within the entire Holocene sequence on the island of Tasmania, as many commentators had already noted—including Mulvaney and Joyce in their original Kenniff report (1965) and Grahame Clark in his review of the Australian stone tool sequence (1968, 20–2). In our description of the Mungo material, Harry Allen and I proposed the term 'Australian core tool and scraper tradition' for these industries, following the definition of 'tradition' by Willey and Phillips (1958, 37). Mindful of Childe's strictures that the culturally diagnostic usefulness of a type is proportional to its improbability (1956, 35–7), it might be argued that within this generalized suite of flake scraper types, there is not enough distinctiveness to imply some cultural reality behind it. Yet these kinds of tools are consistently found in Australian Pleistocene and early Holocene sites and so, if they are considered as constituting a distinctive 'technological mode' following Clark (1977) and Foley and Lahr (1997), then there is still predictive utility to the term. A regional exception to this general uniformity occurred in the mountainous region of south-west Tasmania during the Last Glacial Maximum, when the stone industries of people who concentrated their foraging on the hunting of wallabies were dominated by tiny thumbnail-shaped scrapers. This system came to an abrupt end during the early deglaciation at 13 ka when the region became revegetated by dense rainforest (Jones 1984, 52–7; 1989; 1995, 768–71; Allen 1989, 151; McNiven 1994).

Within the few well excavated and dated late Pleistocene sites in south-east Asia, the stone assemblages also bear a similarity to the Australian ones (Jones 1989, 750–4; Bowdler 1993, 65), as was noted as far back as 1970 by Fox in his account of the material from Tabun cave in Palawon Island, the Philippines (Fox 1970). Anderson's analysis of flaked stone tools from the pre-Hoabhinian layers at the limestone cave of Lang Rongrien in south Thailand dated to between 27 ka and greater than 38 ka (1990), and Glover's excavation at Leang Burung 2 on Sulawesi, between 20 ka and 32 ka (1981), have industries consisting of steep-edged and notched scrapers on flakes reminiscent of the Australian material. As Anderson (1990, 67) put it, 'Contrary to expectations built up from nearly a century of archaeological research and speculation, they suggest that flake tool industries and not pebble tool industries characterized the late Paleolithic in the region'. Hoabinhian industries only appeared in south-east Asia during terminal Pleistocene and Holocene times possibly extending down to as recently as 3 ka (Bellwood 1997, 158).

In Australia, typologically distinctive small stone tools such as unifacial and bifacial points, backed microliths, and flake adze pieces only appear within the mid Holocene, in most places at about 5000 years ago. These were probably the armatures of gum-hafted tools which would have included not only spears, but also tools for wood working. The linguist, Nicholas Evans, and I have argued that these technological changes were associated with the rapid spread of the Pama-Nyungan language family over most of the continent at that time, with an origin near south-eastern Arnhem Land (Evans & Jones 1997). These may have reflected a transformational reorganization of Aboriginal ritual and modes of trading relationships at that time, but we believe that they were also rooted within core Aboriginal belief systems which had a much greater antiquity. When considering the evidence from Mungo, while being conscious of the danger of repeating the nineteenth century archetype of an unchanging people, I felt that with the exception of seed grinding, no aspect of the economic nor funerary behaviour of the people there was inconsistent with the ethnographic record. (Jones 1975, 28) The direct evidence from the archaeological record seemed to indicate some trajectory of deep historical continuity.

The oldest radiocarbon dates

In a period of research extending just over a decade, from 1962 to about 1975, the radiocarbon chronology for the human occupation of Australia was pushed back from 10,000 to about 37,000 years ago, with successively older results being announced on a regular basis (Mulvaney 1964; 1975; Jones 1973; 1979; Flood 1995). Then a plateau seemed to have been reached with no older dates, but ones of this same order of antiquity began to be obtained from many disparate parts of the continent. A recent systematic review of the data by Smith and Sharp in 1993, indicated that there were some 170 sites with basal occupation dated to more than 10,000 years ago. These sites were distributed across the entire continent including all the major ecological zones, from the highlands of New Guinea at the equator, to the mountains of south-west Tasmania, a span of 42 degrees of latitude, and on an east-to-west traverse from the humid Pacific coast and the tropical savannas through the core of the desert to the isolated temperate region of the extreme south-west of Western Australia. Recently Aru Island, situated on the very north-west edge of the Sahul shelf, and famously associated with A.R. Wallace's travels, has been shown to have occupation extending back to at least 26,000 years (Veth *et al.* in press), completing the documentation of Pleistocene occupation of all of the former parts of the eustatically exposed continental shelf. Of particular interest was the discovery of Pleistocene sites extending back to between 30 and 35 ka on the truly oceanic islands to the east of the New Guinea shelf, on New Britain, New Ireland, and the northern Solomons, indicating that the capacity to make sea crossings in these tropical waters was not confined to the acts that led to the initial colonization of the continent itself (Allen *et al.* 1989; Pavlides & Gosden 1994). The oldest radiocarbon dates within all of of these different regions of the continent ranged back to between about 33 and 37 ka years ago. At present the oldest carbon dates from a secure stratigraphic context in Australia come from Carpenter's Gap, a large open shelter in the side of a Devonian age coral reef called Napier Range which forms a vertical limestone wall, fringing the southern margin of the King Leopold Range on the southern edge of the Kimberley in north-western Australia. Here, two AMS dates of 39,220±870 (AMS NZA 3803) and 39,7000±1000 (AMS NZA 3802), stratigraphically associated with stone artefacts, were obtained by Susan O'Connor (1995) from the base of one of her units. Underneath this was another unit of fine powdery silt without carbon but which also contained stone tools.

The radiocarbon barrier

In a broad-ranging review written in 1989, Jim Allen took this array of radiocarbon dates at their face value, and argued that they represented the real dates which documented the rapid colonization of the continent, which he believed to have been made by about 35,000 years ago, suggesting the first landfall at no older than 40,000 years, a view which he has entrenched in later papers (Allen 1994; Allen & Holdoway 1995; O'Connell & Allen 1998). He was followed by J. Hope (1993) in her assessment of the Willandra lakes situation, and by Bowdler (1989; 1993, 65), who concluded for both the Australian and south-east Asian material that 'there is no evidence that Homo sapiens was present in southeast Asia before 40,000 BP'.

I took a different view: that dates of this order of magnitude were so close to the theoretical limits of the radiocarbon method that maybe the 'plateau' was really an illusion (Jones 1982, 30; 1989, 762). At this order of antiquity, because we are so close to the asymptote of the decay curve, were one to take a 'radiocarbon dead' sample and add only 1 per cent of modern carbon, then the apparent age of the mixed sample would be counted as being about 37,000 years old (Aitken 1990). The question revolves less about the capabilities of the counting technology, which theoretically can extend back to *c*.50 ka or even more, but rather about the fundamental assumption that a prehistoric dating sample has remained closed to all exchanges of carbon from the time of its formation to the time of its measurement (Chappell *et al.* 1996). On Australian materials, while most contamination by mobile organic compounds can be removed by the standard pretreatments, experimentation has shown that further more intensive cleaning can produce a series of different ages on the same sample, indicating the extraordinary persistence of low level contamination (Gillespie *et al.* 1991; Magee *et al.* 1995). Thus the limits of AMS radiocarbon technology at present lie with the capacity to prepare utterly pure elemental carbon targets (Bird & Grocke 1997).

Deep pollen cores such as at Pulbeena Swamp in north-west Tasmania (Colhoun *et al.* 1982) and Lake George in southern New South Wales (Singh & Geissler 1985) follow a coherent relationship with depth up until about 35 ka and then values at this same order of magnitude are maintained below this, even though the real age of the deposits may extend back to quarter of a million years or more. At the critically important Williams Point site, a high bluff of lacustrine and dune deposits fronting the southern edge of Lake Eyre, the base of the sequence is correlated with the Last Interglacial, at oxygen isotope stage 5e some 125 ka ago. The top of the sequence is dated by several methods to 40–50 ka. A combination of amino acid racemization (AAR) on eggshell, thermo-luminescence (TL), optically stimulated luminescence (OSL), and thorium/uranium dating methods on these deposits, showed a steady increase with depth throughout this sequence. In contrast all of the C14 results were less than 45 ka, even though at least five of these had been assayed by AMS, with a state-of-the-art rigorous programme of oxidative pretreatment in an attempt to remove contaminants (Magee *et al.* 1995; Chappell *et al.* 1996).

There were several archaeological sites in Australia-New Guinea where artefacts occurred in stratigraphic situations below the lowest carbon (Jones 1979, 451–3; 1989, 762–4; Bowler 1976, 62–4). Of particular relevance to my own experience was the section at the Nauwalabila rock shelter in Deaf Adder Gorge, Kakadu in the Northern Territory which I had excavated in 1981 (Jones & Johnson 1985). Here was a sequence which had radiocarbon dating back to *c*.25 ka at a depth of 1.7 m; and beneath this there were numerous stone artefacts down to the base of the sand sheet and also within a underlying compacted rubble, to a maximim depth of 3 m. There were independent geomorphological indicators of great age for these basal deposits, including a deep orange colour for the sands, and the fact that the lowest silcrete artefacts showed weathering rinds when split (Jones & Johnson op. cit., 178–83).

Luminescence dating of sands

A solution for this impasse was offered by innovative applications of luminescence techniques to the dating of Quaternary sediments (Wintle & Huntley 1979; Wintle *et al.* 1984). Thermo-luminescence, a phenomenon originally described to the Royal Society of London by Robert Boyle in 1663, consists of the thermally stimulated emission of light from a semiconductor, following the previous absorption of energy from ionizing radiation. In the case of quartz crystals, buried as sand, electrons become steadily displaced into metastable traps within defects in the crystal lattices due to alpha, beta, and gamma rays which are derived from the decay of the primordial radionuclides which occur in the surrounding deposits; together with cosmic rays, if the depth of deposit is shallow. When such a grain is heated or exposed to sunlight, these electrons are evicted from their traps and in a process known as radiative recombination, photons are emitted. The exposed sand is said to have been 'bleached' and the luminescence clock set to zero. One of the critical assumptions of the method is that there remains no 'residual signal' when the grains are later reburied and the process recommenced, otherwise falsely older dates will be obtained. To measure the age of the deposit, the 'palaeodose' which is the total radiation dose which the sand grains had acquired since burial, is divided by the annual dose rate delivered to it from the surrounding soil; the latter being measured in the field with a gamma spectrometer and in the laboratory from soil samples. To measure the palaeodose, TL intensity is plotted against temperature in what is called a 'glow curve', which contains important information about electron traps mainly associated with the 325°C and the 375°C peaks. The latter is bleached slowly and only by ultraviolet wave lengths and is mainly responsible for the residual TL signal discussed above. Red desert sands are covered with a thin film of clay containing iron oxide which tends to shield them from solar radiation and thus they can sometimes carry a residual signal before reburial (Smith *et al.* 1997).

The more sophisticated, optically stimulated luminescence method developed in the late 1980s (Huntley *et al.* 1985) uses light to evict the traps and the OSL signal has been shown to correspond to the 325°C peak, which is extremely light sensitive; being emptied by a brief exposure of less than a minute to direct sunlight (Spooner 1994; Roberts & Jones 1994). There are also internal checks to see whether or not the sample had been fully bleached prior to burial. In TL this is called the 'plateau test' where a palaeodose plateau which extends from 270°C to 450°C indicates that the sample was well bleached in antiquity (Roberts & Jones 1994, 7), and there is an analagous 'shine down' test with OSL (Huntley *et al.* 1985). There are other assumptions concerning possible leaching of some of the daughter radionucleides in the deposit, so that detailed measurements of the decay isotopes have to be made and compared with the predicted values (Roberts & Jones 1994, 7–8). Luminescence methods in typical Australian conditions can be used to date an age range of a few hundred years back to about 200,000 years and thus provide the critical new tool to explore the time period beyond the radiocarbon barrier.

TL was first used to date Australian Quaternary deposits by Readhead (1982) on sands at the Mungo site. In the late 1980s Richard Roberts was engaged in a research programme using TL to date sand aprons situated at the base of cliffs in the Kakadu area of Western Arnhem Land. Within his auger columns, from which he obtained a series of consistent TL dates extending back in time to about 120,000 years, he was not able to obtain charcoal samples below a few centimetres from the ground for corroborative C14 dating, because carbon in this environment is rapidly recycled by biogenic agents. However, within the deposits of archaeological sites of the region, because so much firewood had been concentrated there by Aborigines in the past, there was enough charcoal to buffer some of these decomposing processes, so that although density of charcoal decayed rapidly with depth, there was still enough surviving to give dates that extended back to about 25,000 years ago (Jones & Johnson 1985). In 1988, a project was planned to pair TL dates against the known C14 chronology within these archaeological sequences, and if they matched, then to use TL to attempt to date the lowest artefact-bearing deposits beyond the limits of charcoal.

Malakunanja

Malakunanja II, first investigated by Kamminga and Allen (1973), is sheltered under the high sloping cliff of a quartzite outlier, detached a few kilometres from the main Arnhem Land escarpment. A sand apron with a low angled slope has accumulated at its foot, and excavations in 1988–9 revealed a total depth of 4.6 m of sand capped by a small shell midden. Within every excavation unit of the upper 2.6 m of deposit, there were numerous flaked stone artefacts, in total numbering several thousand. Yet within the entire bottom 2.0 m of the deposit there were none. The break was sharp, extending over only a single spit of 5 cm depth. A TL sample just below the surface gave a value of only 200 years, indicating that the assumption of total bleaching in the sand sample had been attained. At a depth of 1.5 m, a TL date of 15 ka was stratigraphically bracketed between two calibrated C14 dates of 15 ka and 18 ka; and at 2.0 m depth, a TL date of 24 ka corresponded reasonably well with a calibrated C14 value of between 20 and 22 ka (Roberts *et al.* 1990a, 153; Roberts & Jones 1994, 14). Beneath these, where charcoal was no longer preserved, there were three further TL dates associated with artefacts; the zone of first occupation of this site being bracketed between 53 ka and 60 ka ago. Underneath this within the culturally sterile deposits, were four further TL dates extending from 65 ka back to 107 ka at the base. The error estimate for each individual TL date was large, being some 15 per cent of the mean; but all the dates were in the correct chronological order as compared to their stratigraphic positions (Roberts *et al.* 1990a; Roberts & Jones 1994). A linear least-squares regression with the assumption of a uniform rate of accumulation of the sand deposit, showed that all samples lay within one random uncertainty of the 95 per cent confidence limit for this best fit curve. A conservative interpretation would indicate that the zone of first human occupation at this site would be around 50,000 years old (Roberts *et al.* 1990b, 127–8), with a possible extension back to *c.*60 ka.

We put forward two propositions: not only that humans were present in Australia at this time, but also that the Malakunanja II sequence indicated that there was nobody here before *c.*60 ka, since we regarded the total absence of any artefacts at this site over the previous 50,000 years as being highly significant (Roberts *et al.* op. cit., 128). This was because of the strategic location of the site at the first line of high terrain facing the then eustatically exposed Arafura Plain. With its gullies and gorges containing deepwater pools and rain forest pockets, this landscape constitutes one of the most biodiverse and stable landscapes on the entire Australian continent, which once found would never be relinquished.

Adding as they did, potentially a 50 per cent increase to the antiquity of humans on the Australian continent, these results were subject to fierce criticism (Bowdler 1990; Frankel 1990), only some of which was scientifically informed. Hiscock (1990) made the reasonable suggestion that although the TL dating of the sands themselves might be correct, the first artefacts might have been pushed or trodden into lower and much older stratigraphic contexts by the human activities of living on a sandy camp surface. We tried to answer this by pointing out that the luminescence method dates the time since the last exposure of sand to sunlight. Thus in a scuff zone which is normal in an occupation site, any sand kicked up by people's domestic activities would instantly be zeroed of its TL signal. In this taphonomic context, the method is paradoxically a more reliable indicator of the last time that the deposit finally bedded down than is the dating of charcoal, which can move up or down a stratigraphic column due to disturbance, while its C14 value is unaffected (Roberts *et al.* 1990b).

Nauwalabila

In order to try and replicate these results, in 1992 we returned to the Nauwalabila site, 60 km south, which previously we could not sample due to access restrictions following the burial nearby of two senior Badmardi men who had worked with me on the original excavation (Jones & Johnson 1985, 167). By this time, the OSL methodology was available at Martin Aitken's Oxford laboratory and five OSL samples were dated from this site. One from just below the surface gave a value of 300 years, indicating that the conditions of total bleaching had been achieved. At a depth of 1.1 m, an OSL date of 13.5 ka, consistent both with a TL date of 14.6 ka and a set of three radiocarbon samples dated to between 11 ka and 13 ka indicated a close chronological fit between the two methods. At 1.7 m, the lowest level where charcoal survived, there was a calibrated C14 date of *c.*27 ka, which was reasonably consistent with a TL date of 28 ka and an OSL one of 30 ka. Below that, where no charcoal existed at the base of the sand column at a depth of 2.4 m, there was an OSL date of 53 ka. Underneath this sand was a tightly packed rubble which also contained some 300 stone artefacts, and beneath the rubble was a small sand lens. An OSL sample from this at a depth of 3.0 m gave a date of 60 ka, and another OSL sample from an auger at the same general depth on the sand sheet outside the rock shelter gave a value of 58 ka. The lowest occupation at this site therefore was bracketed between dates of 53 and 60 ka, and here, there was no possibility of artefacts being worked down to lower levels due to any conceivable taphonomic process (Roberts *et al.* 1994b; Roberts & Jones 1994).

Comparison of OSL and carbon 14 methods: Allen's Cave and Ngarrabullgan

Work at other sites around the continent to try and replicate these results is proceeding, and a major effort has been put into trying to compare OSL with reliable C14 chronologies, especially those based on adequate pretreatment to produce pure elemental carbon. At the karst Allen's Cave on the Nullarbor Plain, a single well-defined hearth at the top of the basal red unit had three C14 dates (two being liquid scintillation and one AMS determination) with calibrated mean ages between 10.0 and 10.5 ka. An OSL sample from unburnt deposit immediately beneath this feature gave a value of 10.1±0.6 ka, indicating close correspondence of the two methods (Roberts *et al.* 1996, 14).

A detailed study has been made at Ngarrabullgan Cave, situated at the top of the Mount Mulligan sandstone plateau massif in north Queensland. Here, the shelter situated at the very highest point of the watershed has a depositional regime where the only accumulation of sand has come from the roof itself, with no other component washed in. As a consequence, there was an intensely compressed and highly coherent stratigraphy at this site. From within a single well-defined stratigraphic unit towards its base, a series consisting of 20 separate pieces of charcoal were dated individually using AMS, and their means showed a Gaussian distribution with a weighted mean age of 32,540±110 years BP. From this same level, an OSL date of 34,700±2,000 was obtained, which at 2 ka greater than the C14 mean, was the same difference that Bard *et al.* (1993) also obtained when they compared C14 and Ur/Th ages from Barbados coral at this 30–40 ka age period (David *et al.* 1997, 187). Where the appropriate methods are used, and where the various assumptions of the methods are met, there is a close correlation of C14 and OSL dating methods.

The rubble problem

A potentially serious problem concerning the application of luminescence dating at certain kinds of sandstone sites, was indicated during investigations at the Mushroom Rock shelter in Cape York, northern Queensland. As its name implies, this is a small undercut outlier off a main plateau of coarse-grained sandstone of Cretaceous age, and it overlooks a low angled sloping sand sheet. This site had originally been excavated by Richard Wright in 1962–3, when he found numerous stone artefacts within all excavation units in this sand down to a depth of 4.5 m, where they abruptly stopped. A further 1.3 m of sand in the excavation contained no artefacts (Wright 1964; Clark 1989, 117). In 1991, this site was re-excavated by Mike Morwood; and with a series of TL dates done by D. Price, extending back to 29 ka at a depth of 3.8 m, suggested, on an age-depth correlation, that the age for initial occupation at the site might have been prior to some 40 ka (Morwood *et al.* 1995, 137). Because this situation was analagous to that at Malakunanja II, Roberts and I joined Morwood in a further excavation at Mushroom Rock in 1994, where we excavated down to a total depth of 6 m making it one of the deepest archaeological sites in Australia. An OSL sample near the lowest artefacts gave unexpectedly old apparent age. Further research indicated that this was due to the inclusion in the sample of sand grains which had been derived from friable *in situ* weathered bedrock or *saprolite*. Never having been exposed to sunlight, these carried a saturated signal, and gave a falsely old age. Since it was difficult to distinguish these by microscopic methods this presented a formidable problem to the luminescence dating method at this type of site.

A similar problem was identified at the Puritjarra rock shelter in central Australia some 350 km west of Alice Springs (Smith *et al.* 1997). Here the TL and OSL dates done by John Prescott, with exemplary precautions as to possible errors, were persistently a small amount older than the C14 dates, except in the deepest part of the site, where both seemed to converge on a basal date of some 35 ka. These discrepancies were possibly explained by incorporation of *in situ* disintegration of old material from the bedrock.

The solution to this problem lay in miniaturization, which was analagous to the trend of research in radiocarbon. In luminescence dating, normally a value is obtained from an array of some 2000 grains of sand. However, if, say, 20 separate equal samples or 'aliquots' of a hundred or less sand grains are individually dated, then there is a reasonable statistical chance that in many of these the unbleached saprolite grains will be missing, and thus the contaminated samples easily identified. The ultimate is to be able to obtain luminescence dates from individual grains of sand, and this was technically achieved at the ANU in late 1995 (Murray & Roberts 1997).

The Jinmium controversy

In 1996, Fullagar, Price, and Head published TL dating results from a small sandstone rock shelter of Jinmium, situated a short distance from the north Australian coast at the border between the Northern Territory and Western Australia. They claimed that this site indicated stone tools stratified between TL dates of 116 ka and 176 ka; ochre between 75 ka and 116 ka; and a piece of rock with two pecked depressions buried between levels dated to 58 ka and 75 ka (Fullarger *et al.* 1996, 764–5, 771). On the shelter wall, there is a large panel of such features called 'cupules', believed by some to be the oldest expression of art in Australia. These results gained widespread international coverage (Bahn 1996; Holden 1996; Dayton & Woodford 1996; Gore 1997, 107–8), and John Noble Wilford in the science pages of the *New York Times*, headlined his extensive piece as 'In Australia, signs of artists who predate *Homo sapiens*' (1996).

Because of our scepticism as to the validity of these dates, Richard Fullagar invited Roberts and me to reinvestigate the chronology of the site, which we did in the field in July 1995, when samples were collected for OSL dating. Our doubts concerned the fact that the apparent compressed rate of deposition within the shelter, where there was much friable rubble, was only a tenth of that within the general sand sheet outside. The one published dose response curve for sample W 1752 with a TL age of 50 ka (Fullagar *et al.* 1996, 767), does not pass the plateau test, indicating that the sample had been incompletely reset on deposition (Spooner 1998). Geomorphologically, there were no marked stratigraphic breaks, despite dating indications of great time differences over a narrow depth of deposit, and it showed none of the pedogenic staining which is characteristic of Pleistocene deposits, both in the vicinity of the site itself and elsewhere in tropical Australia.

The new samples have been subjected to an intensive multi-method dating regime, involving OSL dating of single grains, and, in a parallel study, AMS dates from specially prepared elemental carbon samples designed to eliminate any organic carbon contamination. These results indicate that all of the deposit within the shelter is less than 10 ka years old, and that the levels in which the engraved rock was buried are also less than 4 ka (Roberts *et al.* 1998a). The single-grain OSL results agreed closely with the AMS dates within the error margins of both systems. The erroneous old ages at this site had been due to two factors: firstly that the TL signal had been incompletely reset at the time of sediment deposition, and secondly there had been contamination by unbleached grains derived from weathered bedrock.

Whereas the Jinmium example shows that luminescence dating of some sandstone rock shelters must be proceeded with due care, on the other hand, appropriate high-precision techniques have now been developed which can isolate the problems identified. A further programme of research has been initiated at both Malakunanja and Nauwalabila using single-grain OSL techniques to test the integrity of the previous results. At Malakunanja, where the initial work had involved TL dating, internal evidence such as confirmation of the behaviour of samples to the plateau test, and comparison with radiocarbon dates in the upper levels, had given confidence that the sediments at this site had been adequately bleached at the time of their deposition. A new set of OSL dates carried out at this site confirm the previous results (Roberts *et al.* 1998b). The oldest stone artefacts in the site had been bracketed between samples KTL 164 which gave a conventional TL date of 45±9 ka, and sample KTL 162 associated stratigraphically with the lowest artefacts with a TL date of 61±13 ka. Optical dates have since been measured for these samples. Multi-grained *c*.800 grains) OSL dates gave values of 46±4 ka for KTL 164, and 61±8 ka for KTL 162. Finally, individual sand grains were assayed from both samples; the results from the highest precision grains being 43±5 ka from KTL 164 and 56±8 ka from KTL 162. These multi-method results are within statistical accord of each other and despite the somewhat carping comments of O'Connell and Allen (1998, 135) on our previous work, confirm our claim that people were present in this region of north tropical Australia by about 50–60 ka.

Crossing Wallacea

With the presence of *erectus* populations in Java on the Sunda shelf back to about a million years ago (de Vos 1994), there has always been the issue of whether or not these people had the capacity to cross any of the water barriers to or even through Wallacea. Some elements of the large Asian mammalian fauna such as elephants and the related extinct Stegodontidae managed some of these crossings. On Luzon in the Philippines, with one water crossing, there were two species of stegodon, one extinct elephant, and an extinct rhino; on Sulawesi, also with a single crossing, there were two stegodons, one elephant, and some suids. Finally on both Flores and Timor, with several narrow water crossings along the Lesser Sunda Chain, there were a pigmy *S. sompoensis* and a large *S. trigonocephalus* (Hooijer 1972; Sondaar *et al.* 1994). In the early 1970s, claims were made for stone artefacts being associated with Middle Pleistocene fauna at the Cagayan Valley in northern Luzon, but these have not as yet been confirmed by further work.

A much better case is the one recently being reinvestigated on Flores. At Mata Menge in the west central part of the island, in the shadow of a large volcano, Maringer and Verhoeven (1970) reported finding stone artefacts in association with stegodon fossils in a water-lain tuffaceous sandstone. New excavations by Sondaar *et al.* (1994) found further stone tools of basalt flakes and fractured pebbles in the same Ola Bula Formation, stratigraphically associated with the large *S. trigonocephalus* located in the sequence immediately above the Bruhnes-Matuyama magnetic reversal, indicating an age for these artefacts of *c.*700 ka. Further analysis of stone artefacts within this formation was carried out by M. Morwood *et al.* (1997), and dating work is proceeding with a paper reporting fission track dates for this deposit dated to *c.*800 ka which was consistent with previous age estimates (Morwood *et al.* 1998). There is no doubt as to the authenticity of the stone artefacts, nor the general order of age for the stegodon fossils. It remains to be seen whether or not the ongoing geomorphological and taphonomic research can confirm the genuine association of tools and fossils in this tectonically dynamic region. If it does, then it will set an important claim for the capacity of *erectus* humans to cross limited stretches of tropical sea in Middle Pleistocene times.

Occupying the continent

My view is that it was only modern *Homo sapiens* who made the final journey to the Sahul shore, and that this was done at the order of 60 ka ago. This corresponds to the end of the isotope stage 4 (Linsley 1996, 236), and the palaeoenvironmental record from Lake Eyre indicates that this was close to the end of a far wetter period, when lake-full phases held as much as a hundred times the present flood events, implying a long-term average rainfall some four to five times greater than the present value (Magee *et al.* 1995). During the next 10 ka, there was a deterioration in the rainfall regime, leading eventually to slow desiccation of the Centre which reached its maximum at the Last Glacial Maximum. As Mulvaney (1961, 62) pointed out, there is a natural road into the heart of the Australian continent, south from the Gulf of Carpentaria, where there is only an imperceptible watershed on a wide plain separating the northerly rivers from those that flow south-west through western Queensland to feed Lake Eyre, whose basin encompasses a seventh of the area of the entire continent; or via the Paroo into the headwaters of the Darling-Murray basin. During rare but huge flood events fed by tropical monsoons, even in today's climate, rivers such as the Diamantina within the appropriately named Channel Country, form a network of braided streams and floodsheets of slowly moving water hundreds of kilometres wide, with an explosion of fish and aquatic bird life. During a wetter period, this would have been even more dramatic, allowing the probing colonization of core areas of the eastern half of Australia to be effected in a very short time, even within the timescale of a few generations and certainly to be measured as an instantaneous event given the errors of our dating methods (Webb & Rindos 1997).

There remains the question of the potential impact of the human arrival on the process of megafaunal extinction, when about a third of the marsupial species of Australia and New Guinea became extinct; almost all of these genera being much larger than existing forms. A similar process was also seen with some birds and reptiles. The central problem in investigating this issue has been that the extinction events may have occurred during a time period beyond the range of C14 dating, so that it has been impossible to erect a firm chronology for these events. The best record that we have so far, using new dating methods of any extinction event, is that concerning the giant flightless *Genyornis*, a bird about twice the weight of an emu. In the Lake Eyre sequence, both *Genyornis* and emu eggshells have been dated by amino acid racemization, and whereas emus continue through all of the vicissitudes of climatic change, including the deeply arid phase of the Last Glacial Maximum, *Genyornis* suddenly collapses about 45–50 ka, at about the time of human arrival (Miller *et al.* 1997; J. Magee pers. comm.).

In the swamp site of Cuddie Springs in western New South Wales, in a low energy riverine environment, hundreds of stone tools have been found in close stratigraphic association with bones of *Genyornis* and the marsupial Diprotodon (Furby *et al.* 1993; Pain 1997). This deposit has been dated by both C14 and OSL to about 34 ka ago, and fascinating though this site is, it remains to be entirely proven that there has been no slumping of older bone beds within this periodically saturated context. ESR dates on the teeth of the extinct fauna should be a critical test. I remain convinced that the megafauna which had existed and radiated over a period of more than five million years and survived at least 20 ice age events during the Pleistocene was somehow fatally affected by the arrival of the new human superpredator, either through direct hunting, or more likely through landscape modification by imposing a new firing regime (Jones 1975; Diamond 1997, 43–4).

Among the first modern humans out of Africa?

Genetic evidence over the past 15 years has accumulated a powerful case for a recent single origin for modern humans dated back to about 150 ka in sub-Saharan Africa (Klein 1995; Foley & Lahr 1997, 4). In the spread out of Africa, there were several genetic bottlenecks, notably in north-east Africa (Tishkoff *et al.* 1996), and the human spread out of this region may date to only some 80 ka ago. The Australian archaeological data are critical to this debate, since they provide some of the best chronometric evidence for the spread of modern humans out of an African bottleneck. Recently reported results from M. Stoneking presented to the Human Evolution Meeting, October 1997 at the Cold Spring Harbor Laboratory, suggested from a study of DNA sequences recognized by the restriction enzyme *Alu,* that the major split between African and non-African populations occurred about 140 ka ago. In addition, population samples from Sahul, both New Guineans and Australian Aborigines, are as close to the presumed ancestral state of the human Alu family as are samples from African populations, suggesting that 'a migration to Southeast Asia must have been one of the first "out of Africa" excursions of modern humans' (Wood 1997, 120). The route along the Parallel of the tropical savanna, from west to east was the obvious new terrain to people adapted to closely similar conditions in east Africa. The savannas of northern Australia only required short sea crossings to get into them.

There exist some fossil skulls in Australia which exhibit remarkable archaic characteristics. This is perhaps most exemplified by the Willandra Lakes (WLH) 50 skull, which has a vase shape to the top of the cranium, prominent post-orbital constriction and a broad flat occipital shape inviting anatomical comparison of some of these features with those of the Ngandong hominids (Frayer *et al.* 1994, 427–8). Whether or not these characteristics in the Australian fossil material indicate some direct genetic input from late Solo populations in Indonesia, as Weidenreich originally suggested, and as has been argued consistently by Thorne as a central element of his 'Multi-regional hypothesis' (Thorne & Wolpoff 1992; Frayer *et al.* 1994; Wolpoff *et al.* 1984), or whether they represent the retention within the isolated Australian region of generalized archaic characteristics of the first modern humans (Stringer & Brauer 1994), is an issue of contemporary debate (see Klein 1995, 179–83; Foley & Lahr 1997, 4). New dating programmes now underway on some of the Mungo hominid sites (Oyston 1996; Grün & Thorne pers. comm.), may help to clarify some of these issues, at least to place the various fossils into a firm chronological framework.

Dating rock art

Rock shelters, whose stone tool assemblages may carry little specific cultural information, often have walls and ceilings covered with fragmentary superimpositions of different styles of paintings, containing potentially the greatest information as to how the people conceptualized their world view. The problem has been to date these and thus to fix them into a historical context. Detailed superimposition studies over the past three decades in northern Australia, notably in Cape York, Kakadu, and the Kimberley have resulted in broadly accepted comparative sequences of the major styles (Chaloupka 1985; 1993; Chippindale & Taçon 1993; Cole *et al.* 1995; Walsh 1994) The question now is to be able to pin critical points within these floating sequences into an absolute timeframe. The solution also lies in the miniaturization of the dating techniques. AMS has been used to date beeswax forming parts of pictures back to 4 ka (Nelson *et al.* 1995). These oldest dates from a large rock shelter near Kakadu came from a representation of a turtle, conforming stylistically to Chaloupka's most recent 'Estuarine' phase, estimated on other grounds to extend back to some five thousand years (Chaloupka 1985). One of these dated figures overlays at least five further sets of weathered paintings. Chaloupka's oldest phase in his Kakadu sequence is argued to extend back to the late Pleiostocene and includes depictions of extinct animals such as *Thylacine*.

In Cape York mineral skins covering walls of caves have been shown to have layers of paint within them, dated by AMS on calcium oxalate back to 25 ka and 28 ka ago at different sites, but of course the details of the motifs themselves have also been obscured (Watchman 1993; 1997, 32), and the technology in this research field is difficult (Gillespie 1997). Plant fibres incorporated into the pigment as binders have been directly dated, and in this case the identity of the picture itself can be recognized (Watchman & Cole 1993). A new technique is the dating of fossilized mud-wasp nests, which when old, have the look and texture of small blobs of cement. Sand grains within these nests, absorbing radiation from the rock on which they had been stuck, can be dated by OSL, using small sample and single-grain techniques (Roberts *et al.* 1997). In the Kimberley an early phase representation of a Wandjina stylized human face, associated with cults still actively being practised in the area during the 1930s, has been dated to more than 600 years old. An extremely faded, deep purple coloured, small human figure with a head-dress, had a cemented nest on it dated to 17 ka (ibid., 697). Field observations suggest that the faded figure may be considerably older than the nest, and in turn, there is an even more faded pale violet coloured hand stencil under the human figure.

Distributed widely across the continent are panels of pecked rocks, typically depicting tracks of bird, macropod, and sometimes human, together with geometric designs. Sometimes referred to as the Panaramittee style, from a site in South Australia, these panels are often covered with mineral skins. In northern Australia at least, these skins contain calcium oxalate, and can potentially be dated (Watchman 1997). At the Early Man Site in Cape York, a panel of such engravings was found stratified beneath deposit dated to 13 ka, indicating a minimum age for such art (Rosenfeld *et al.* 1981). High quality haematite, often with striations indicating their having been ground to produce pigment, are ubiquitous within Australian sites down to the very basal levels. One such piece was directly associated with a 50 ka OSL date from Nauwalabila (Jones & Johnson 1985; Roberts *et al.* 1994b). Now that the initial techniques have been developed, they need to be applied systematically on key sites. These manifestations of art, part of the cultural inheritance of the first Australians, were, to paraphrase Clark, 'symbols of excellence', the surviving evidence of the conceptual worlds of ancient Aboriginal societies.

Concluding remarks

Grahame Clark's inspiration for the concept of world prehistory sprang from despair in the depth of the Second World War, as a response to the racialist thinking of the time. He wrote then that

> To the peoples of the world generally, the peoples who willy nilly must in future co-operate and build, or fall out and destroy, I venture to think that palaeolithic man has more meaning than the Greeks. (There must be) an over-riding sense of human solidarity such as can come only from a consciousness of common origins.
>
> (Clark 1943, 410, 416)

And in another essay, written towards the end of his life, he returned to this universalist theme:

> In the final resort, archaeology—and prehistoric archaeology in particular—is concerned with nothing less than the identity of man.
>
> (Clark 1979, 3)

The past 40 years of archaeological research in Australia has placed the continent and the deep prehistory of its indigenous peoples into the forefront of knowledge about the global spread of modern sapient people and of the unique economic and symbolic adaptation that they made to the new continent. Amongst Aboriginal people themselves, there is a special interest and a sense of pride at the demonstrated fact of an antiquity of occupation that is recognized and celebrated by the wider community. This has become a potent symbol for cultural autonomy and emancipation. A key Aboriginal response to the bicentenary celebrations in 1988 of the first British settlement at Port Jackson, was a slogan saying 'You have been here for 200 years, we for 40,000'. Australia is at present in the throes of a profound analysis of itself and of its past as a 'settler nation' and of the possibilities of an equable reconciliation between the descendants of the indigines and colonists. To the extent that the archaeological discoveries of Australia's deep past can serve to induce a 'convergent' identity in the nation, to quote the poet Les Murray, it will be a vindication of the universalist message of Grahame Clark's world prehistory.

References

AITKEN, M.J. 1990. *Science-Based Dating in Archaeology*. London: Longmans.

ALLEN, J. 1989. When did humans first colonize Australia? *Search* 20, 149–54.

ALLEN, J. 1994. Radiocarbon determinations, luminescence dating and Australian archaeology. *Antiquity* 68, 339–43.

ALLEN, J., & HOLDAWAY, S. 1995. The contamination of Pleistocene radiocarbon determinations in Australia. *Antiquity* 69, 101–12.

ALLEN, J., GOSDEN, C. & WHITE, J.P. 1989. Human Pleistocene adaptations in the tropical island Pacific: recent evidence from new Ireland, a great Australian outlier. *Antiquity* 63, 548–61.

ANDERSON, D.D. 1990. *Lang Rongrien Rockshelter: a Pleistocene–Early Holocene Archaeological Site from Krabi, Southwestern Thailand.* University Museum Monograph 71. Philadelphia: The University Museum, University of Pennsylvania.

ARNOLD, J.R. & LIBBY, W.F. 1949. Age determinations by radiocarbon content: checks with samples of known age. *Science* 110, 678–80.

BAHN, P.G., 1996. Further back down under. *Nature* 383, 577–8.

BARD, E., ARNOLD, M., FAIRBANKS, R.G. & HAMELIN, B. 1993. 230 Th-234 Ur and 14C ages obtained by mass spectrometry on corals. *Radiocarbon* 35, 191–9.

BEDNARIK, R.G. 1997. The initial peopling of Wallacea and Sahul. *Anthropos* 92, 355–67.

BELLWOOD, P. 1997. *Prehistory of the Indo-Malaysian Archipelago* (Revised edn). Honolulu: University of Hawaii Press.

BIRD, M.I. & GROCKE, D.R. 1997. Determination of the abundance and carbon isotope composition of elemental carbon in sediments. *Geochimica et Cosmochimica Acta* 61, 3413–23.

BOWDLER, S. 1989. Australian colonization: a comment. *Search* 20, 173.

BOWDLER, S. 1990. 50,000 year-old site in Australia- is it really that old? *Australian Archaeology* 31, 93.

BOWDLER, S. 1993. Sunda and Sahul: a 30 kyr culture area? In M.A. Smith, M. Spriggs & B. Fankhauser (eds), *Sahul in Review: Pleistocene Archaeology in Australia, New Guinea and Island Melanesia*, 60–70. Canberra: Department of Prehistory, Research School of Pacific Studies, The Australian National University.

BOWLER, J.M. 1976. Recent developments in reconstructing late Quaternary environments in Australia. In R.L. Kirk and A. G. Thorne (eds), *The Origin of the Australians*, 55–77. Canberra: Australian Institute of Aboriginal Studies.

BOWLER, J.M., JONES, R., ALLEN, H. & THORNE, A.G. 1970. Pleistocene human remains from Australia: a living site and human cremation from Lake Mungo, western New South Wales. *World Archaeology* 2, 39–60.

BOWLER, J.M. & THORNE, A.G. 1976. Human remains from Lake Mungo: discovery and excavation of Lake Mungo 111. In R.L. Kirk and A.G. Thorne (eds), *The Origin of the Australians*, 127–38. Canberra: Australian Institute of Aboriginal Studies.

BULMER, S. 1964. Prehistoric stone implements from the New Guinea highlands. *Oceania* 34, 246–68.

CHALOUPKA, G. 1985. Chronological sequence of Arnhem Land plateau rock art. In R. Jones (ed.), *Archaeological Research in Kakadu National Park*, 269–80. Canberra: Australian National Parks and Wildlife Service, Special Publication no. 13.

CHALOUPKA, G. 1993. *Journey in Time: The World's Longest Continuing Art Tradition*. Sydney: Reed.

CHAPPELL, J., HEAD, J. & MAGEE, J. 1996. Beyond the radiocarbon limit in Australian archaeology and Quaternary research. *Antiquity* 70, 543–52.

CHILDE, V.G. 1956. *Piecing Together the Past: The Interpretation of Archaeological Data*. London: Routledge & Kegan Paul.

CHILDE, V.G. 1957. 'Valediction', reprinted in S. Green 1981. *Prehistorian: A Biography of V. Gordon Childe*. Bradford-on-Avon, Wilts, UK: Moonraker Press.

CHIPPINDALE, C. & TAÇON, P. 1993. Two old painted panels from Kakad: variation and sequence in Arnhem Land rock art. In J. Steinbring and A. Watchman (eds), *Time and Space: Dating and Spatial Considerations in Rock Art Research*, 32–56. Melbourne: Australian Rock Art Research Association, Occasional AURA Publication no. 8.

CLARK, J.G.D. 1943. Education and the study of man. Reprinted in *Economic Prehistory: Papers on Archaeology by Grahame Clark* (1989). Cambridge: Cambridge University Press.

CLARK, J.G.D. 1961. *World Prehistory: An Outline*. Cambridge: Cambridge University Press.

CLARK, J.G.D. 1968. Australian stone age. In K. Jazdzewski (ed.), *Liber Iosepho Kostrzewski Octogenario A Veneratoribus Dicatus*, 17–28. Warsaw: Zaklad Narodowy Im Ossolinskich.

CLARK, J.G.D. 1977. *World Prehistory in New Perspective*. Cambridge: Cambridge University Press.

CLARK, J.G.D. 1979. Archaeology and human diversity. *Annual Review of Anthropology* 8, 1–20. Palo Alto.

CLARK, J.G.D. 1980. World prehistory and natural science. A J.C. Jacobsen Memorial Lecture. *Det Kongelige Danske Videnskabernes Selskab Historisk-filosofiske Meddelelser*, 50. Copenhagen.

CLARK, J.G.D. 1989. *Prehistory at Cambridge and Beyond*. Cambridge: Cambridge University Press.

COLE, N.A., WATCHMAN, A. & MORWOOD, M.J. 1995. Chronology of Laura rock art. In M.J. Morwood and D.R. Hobbs (eds), *Quinkan Prehistory: The Archaeology of Aboriginal Art in S. E. Cape York Peninsula, Australia. Tempus* 3, 147–60. St Lucia, Queensland: Anthropology Museum, University of Queensland.

COLHOUN, E.A., VAN DE GEER, G. & MOOK, W.G. 1982. Stratigraphy, pollen analysis and palaeoclimatic interpretation of Pulbeena Swamp, northwestern Tasmania. *Quaternary Research* 18, 108–26.

DANIEL, G. 1950. *A Hundred Years of Archaeology*. London: Duckworth.

DAVID, B., ROBERTS, R.G., TUNIZ, C., JONES, R. & HEAD, J. 1997. New optical and radiocarbon dates from Ngarrabullgan Cave, a Pleistocene archaeological site in Australia: implications for the comparability of time clocks and for the human colonization of Australia. *Antiquity* 71, 183–8.

DAVID, T.W.E. 1924. Geological evidence of the antiquity of man in the Commonwealth, with special reference to the Tasmanian Aborigines. *Paps and Procs of the Royal Society of Tasmania for 1923*, 114–50.

DAVID, T.W.E. & WILSON, J.T. 1915. Preliminary communication on an Australian cranium of probable Pleistocene age. *Report of the Eighty-fourth Meeting of the British Association for the Advancement of Science, Australia, 1914*, 144. London: John Murray.

DAYTON, L. & WOODFORD, J. 1996. Australia's date with destiny. *New Scientist* 152, 28–31.

DIAMOND, J. 1997. *Guns, Germs and Steel*. London: Jonathan Cape.

EVANS, N. & JONES, R. 1997. The cradle of the Pama-Nyungans: archaeological and linguistic speculations. In P. McConvell and N. Evans (eds), *Archaeology and Linguistics: Aboriginal Australia in Global Perspective*, 385–417. Oxford: Oxford University Press.

FLOOD, J. 1995. *Archaeology of the Dreamtime*. Revised edn. Sydney and London: Collins.

FOLEY, R. & LAHR, M.M. 1997. Mode 3 technologies and the evolution of modern humans. *Cambridge Archaeological Journal* 7, 3–36.

FOX, R.B. 1970. *The Tabon Caves*. Manila: National Museum Monograph 1.

FRANKEL, D. 1990. Time inflation. *New Scientist* 7 July, 52–3.

FRAYER, D.W., WOLPOFF, M.H., THORNE, A.G., SMITH, F.H. & POPE, G.G. 1994. Getting it straight. *American Anthropologist* 96, 424–38.

FULLAGAR, R.L.K., PRICE, D.M. & HEAD, L.M. 1996. Early human occupation of northern Australia: archaeology and thermoluminescence dating of Jinmium rock-shelter, Northern Territory. *Antiquity* 70, 751–73.

FURBY, J.H.R., FULLAGAR, J., DODSON, R. & PROSSER, I. 1993. The Cuddie Springs bone bed revisited, 1991. In M.A. Smith, M. Spriggs and B. Fankhauser (eds), *Sahul in Review: Pleistocene Archaeology in Australia, New Guinea and Island Melanesia*, 204–12. Canberra: Department of Prehistory, Research School of Pacific Studies, The Australian National University.

GILLESPIE, R. 1997. On human blood, rock art and calcium oxalate: further studies on organic carbon content and radiocarbon age of material relating to Australian rock art. *Antiquity* 71, 430–7.

GILLESPIE, R., MAGEE, J.W., LULY, J.G., DLUGOKENCKY, E., SPARKS, R.J. & WALLACE, G. 1991. AMS radiocarbon dating in the study of arid environments: examples from Lake Eyre, South Australia. *Palaeogeography, Palaeoclimatology, Palaeoecology* 84, 333–8.

GOLSON, J. 1971. Both sides of the Wallace Line: Australia, New Guinea, and Asian prehistory. *Archaeology and Physical Anthropology in Oceania* 6, 124–44.

GOLSON, J. 1972. The remarkable history of Indo-Pacific Man: missing chapters from every world prehistory. *Search* 3, 13–21.

GOLSON, J. 1986. Old guards and new waves: reflections on antipodean archaeology 1954–75. *Archaeology in Oceania* 21, 2–12.

GOLSON, J. 1989. The origins and development of New Guinea agriculture. In D.R. Harris and G.C. Hillman (eds), *Foraging and Farming: The Evolution of Plant Exploitation*, 678–87. London: Allen and Unwin.

GOLSON, J. 1993. The last days of Pompeii? In M.A. Smith, M. Spriggs and B. Fankhauser (eds), *Sahul in Review: Pleistocene Archaeology in Australia, New Guinea and Island Melanesia*, 275–80. Canberra: Department of Prehistory, Research School of Pacific Studies, The Australian National University.

GORE, R. 1997. The dawn of humans: expanding worlds. *National Geographic* 191, 84–109.

GREEN, S. 1981. *Prehistorian: A Biography of V. Gordon Childe*. Bradford-on-Avon, Wilts, UK: Moonraker Press.

GRIFFITHS, T. 1996. In search of Australian antiquity. In T. Bonyhady and T. Griffiths (eds), *Prehistory to Politics: John Mulvaney, the Humanities and the Public Intellectual*, 42–62. Melbourne: Melbourne University Press.

GROUBE, L. 1989. The taming of the rain forests: a model for Late Pleistocene forest exploitation in New Guinea. In D.R. Harris and G.C. Hillman (eds), *Foraging and Farming: The Evolution of Plant Exploitation*, 292–304. London: Allen Hyman.

GROUBE, L., CHAPPELL, J., MUKE, J. & PRICE, D. 1986. A 40,000 year old occupation site at Huon Peninsula, Papua New Guinea. *Nature* 324, 453–5.

HABERLE, S.G., HOPE, G.S. & DEFRETES, Y. 1990. Environmental change in the Baliem Valley, Montane Irian Jaya, Indonesia. *Journal of Biogeography* 18, 25–40.

HALE, H.M. & TINDALE. N.B. 1930. Notes on some human remains in the Lower Murray Valley, South Australia. *Recs South Australia Museum* 4, 145–218.

HISCOCK, P. 1990. How old are the artefacts in Malakunanja II? *Archaeology in Oceania* 25, 122–4.

HOLDEN, C. 1996. Art stirs uproar down under. *Science* 274, 33–4.

HOOIJER, D.A. 1972. Stegodon trigonocephalus florensis Hooijer and Stegodon timorensis Sartono from the Pleistocene of Flores and Timor, I. *Procs of the Koninklijke Nederlandse Akademie van Wetenschappen*, Ser. B 75, 12–26.

HOPE, G.S. 1982. Pollen from archaeological sites: a comparison of swamp and an open archaeological site pollen. spectra at Kosipe Mission, Papua New Guinea. In W. Ambrose and P. Duerden (eds), *Archaeometry: an Australasian Perspective*, 211–19. Canberra: Department of Prehistory, Research School of Pacific Studies, The Australian National University.

HOPE, J. 1993. Pleistocene archaeological sites in the central Murray-Darling. In M.A. Smith, M. Spriggs & B. Fankhauser (eds), *Sahul in Review: Pleistocene Archaeology in Australia, New Guinea and Island Melanesia*, 183–96. Canberra: Department of Prehistory, Research School of Pacific Studies, The Australian National University.

HORN, W.A. 1896. Introduction. In B. Spencer (ed.), *Report of the Work of the Horn Scientific Expedition to Central Australia*. London: Dulau and Co. and Melbourne: Melville, Mullen and Slade.

HORTON, D. 1991. *Recovering the Tracks: The Story of Australian Archaeology*. Canberra: Aboriginal Studies Press,

HUNTLEY, D.J., GODFREY-SMITH, D.I. & THEWALT, M.L.W. 1985. Optical dating of sediments. *Nature* 313, 105–7.

HUXLEY, T.H. 1869. On the distribution of the races of mankind and its bearing on the antiquity of mankind. *International Congress of Prehistoric Archaeology, Third Session (1868)*, 39–48. London: Longmans, Green and Company.

JOHNSON, F. 1951. *Radiocarbon Dating Mem 8, Society of American Archaeology*, Supplement to *American Antiquity* 17.

JONES, R. 1973. Emerging picture of Pleistocene Australians. *Nature* 246, 278–81.

JONES, R. 1975. The neolithic, palaeolithic and the hunting gardeners: man and land in the Antipodes. In R.P. Suggate and M.M. Cresswell (eds), *Quaternary Studies*, 21–34. Wellington: The Royal Society of New Zealand.

JONES, R. 1979. The fifth continent: problems concerning the human colonization of Australia. *Annual Review of Anthropology* 8, 445–66. Palo Alto.

JONES, R. 1982. Ions and eons: some thoughts on archaeological science and scientific archaeology. In W. Ambrose and P. Duerden (eds), *Archaeometry, an Australasian Perspective*, 22–35. Canberra: Department of Prehistory, Research School of Pacific Studies, The Australian National University.

JONES, R. 1984. Hunters and history: a case study from western Tasmania. In C. Schrire (ed.), *Past and Present in Hunter Gatherer Studies*, 27–65. Orlando: Academic Press.

JONES, R. 1989. East of Wallace's Line: issues and problems in the colonisation of the Australian continent. In P. Mellars and C. Stringer (eds), *The Human Revolution: Behavioural and Biological Perspectives on the Origins of Modern Humans*, 743–82. Edinburgh: Edinburgh University Press.

JONES, R. 1993. A continental reconnaissance; some observations concerning the discovery of the Pleistocene archaeology of Australia. In M. Spriggs, D.E. Yen, W. Ambrose, R. Jones, A. Thorne & A. Andrews (eds), *A Community of Culture: The People and Prehistory of the Pacific*, 97–122. Canberra: Department of Prehistory, Research Schoool of Pacific Studies, The Australian National University.

JONES, R. 1995. Tasmanian archaeology: establishing the sequences. *Annual Review of Anthropology* 24, 423–46. Palo Alto.

JONES, R. & BOWLER, J. 1980. Struggle for the savanna: northern Australia in ecological and prehistoric perspective. In R. Jones (ed.), *Northern Australia: Options and Implications*, 3–31. Canberra: Research School of Pacific Studies, The Australian National University.

JONES, R. & JOHNSON, I. 1985. Deaf Adder Gorge: Lindner Site, Nauwalabila I. In R. Jones (ed.), *Archaeological Research in Kakadu National Park*, 165–227. Canberra: Australian National Parks and Wildlife Service, Special Publication no. 13.

KAMMINGA, J. & ALLEN, H. 1973. Report of the archaeological survey. *Alligator Rivers Environmental Fact-Finding Study*. Canberra.

KLEIN, R.G. 1995. Anatomy, behavior, and modern human origins. *Journal of World Prehistory* 9, 167–98.

LINSLEY, B. K. 1996. Oxygen-isotope record of sea level and climate variations in the Sulu Sea over the past 150,000 years. *Nature* 380, 234–7.

MACINTOSH, N.W.G. 1967. Recent discoveries of early Australian man. *Annals of the Australian College of Dental Surgeons* 1, 104–26.

MACINTOSH, N.W.G. 1969. The Talgai cranium: the value of archives. *Australian Natural History* 16, 189–95.

MCNIVEN, I.J. 1994. Technological organisation and settlement in southwest Tasmania after the glacial maximum. *Antiquity* 68, 75–82.

MAGEE, J.W., BOWLER, J.M., MILLER, G.H. & WILLIAMS, D.L.G. 1995. Stratigraphy, sedimentology, chronology and palaeohydrology of Quaternary lacustrine deposits at Madigan Gulf, Lake Eyre, South Australia. *Palaeogeography, Palaeoclimatology, Palaeoecology* 113, 3–42.

MARINGER, J. & VERHOEVEN, T. 1970. Die steinartefakte aus der Stegodon-Fossilschicht von Mengeruda auf Flores, Indonesien. *Anthropos* 65, 229–47.

MEEHAN, B. 1982. *Shell Bed to Shell Midden.* Canberra: Australian Institute of Aboriginal Studies.

MESTON, A.L. 1937. The problem of the Tasmanian Aborigines. *Paps and Procs of the Royal Society of Tasmania for 1936*, 85–92.

MILLER, G., MAGEE, J.W. & JULL, A.J.T. 1997. Low-latitude glacial cooling in the Southern hemisphere from amino-acid racemization in emu eggshells. *Nature* 385, 241–4.

MOORE, J. 1997. Wallace's Malthusian moment: The common context revisited. In B. Lightman (ed.), *Victorian Science in Context*, 290–311. Chigago: University of Chicago Press.

MORWOOD, M.J., AZIZ, F., BERGH, G.G. VAN DEN, SONDAAR, P.Y. & VOS, J. DE 1997. Stone artefacts from the 1994 excavation at Mata Menge, west central Flores, Indonesia. *Australian Archaeology* 44, 26–34.

MORWOOD, M.J., L'OSTE-BROWN, S. & PRICE, D.M. 1995. Excavations at Mushroom Rock. In M.J. Morwood and D.R. Hobbs (eds), *Quinkan Prehistory: The Archaeology of Aboriginal Art in S.E. Cape York Peninsula, Australia. Tempus*, vol. 3, 133–46. St Lucia, Queensland: Anthropology Museum, University of Queensland.

MORWOOD, M.J., O'SULLIVANT, P.B., AZIZ, F. & RAZA, A. 1998. Fission-track ages of stone tools and fossils on the east Indonesian island of Flores. *Nature*, 392, 173–6.

MOUNTAIN, M.-J. 1983. Preliminary report of excavations at Nombe Rockshelter, Simbu Province, Papua New Guinea. *Bulletin of the Indo-Pacific Prehistory Association* 4, 84–99. Canberra: The Australian National University.

MOUNTAIN, M.-J. 1991. Bulmer Phase1: environmental change and human activity through the late Pleistocene into the Holocene in the highlands of New Guinea: a scenario. In A. Pawley (ed.), *Man and a Half: Essays in Pacific Anthropology and Ethnobiology in Honour of Ralph Bulmer*, 510–20. Auckland: The Polynesian Society.

MULVANEY, D.J. 1961. The Stone Age of Australia. *Proceedings of the Prehistoric Society* 27, 56–107.

MULVANEY, D.J. 1962. Advancing frontiers in Australian archaeology. *Oceania* 33, 135–8.

MULVANEY, D.J. 1964. The Pleistocene colonization of Australia. *Antiquity* 38, 263–7.

MULVANEY, D.J. 1975. *The Prehistory of Australia*, revised edn. Harmondsworth, UK: Penguin Books.

MULVANEY, D.J. 1993. From Cambridge to the bush. In M. Spriggs, D.E. Yen, W. Ambrose, R. Jones,

A. Thorne & A. Andrews (eds), *A Community of Culture: The People and Prehistory of the Pacific*, 18–26. Canberra: Department of Prehistory, Research Schoool of Pacific Studies, The Australian National University.

MULVANEY, D.J. 1996. 'A splendid lot of fellows': achievements and consequences of the Horn Expedition. In S.R. Morton and D.J. Mulvaney (eds), *Exploring Central Australia: Society, the Environment and the 1894 Horn Expedition*, 3–12. Chipping Norton, N.S.W.: Surrey Beatty and Sons.

MULVANEY, D.J. & JOYCE, E.B. 1965. Archaeological and geomorphological investigations on Mt Moffatt Station, Queensland, Australia. *Proceedings of the Prehistoric Society* 31, 147–212.

MURRAY, A.S. & ROBERTS, R.G. 1997. Determining the burial time of single grains of quartz using optically stimulated luminescence. *Earth and Planetary Science Letters* 152, 163–80.

NELSON, D.E., CHALOUPKA, G., CHIPPINDALE, C., ALDERSON, M.S. & SOUTHON, J.R. 1995. Radiocarbon dates for beeswax figures in the prehistoric rock art of northern Australia. *Archaeometry* 37, 151–6.

O'CONNELL, J.F. & ALLEN, J. 1998. When did humans first arrive in Greater Australia and why is it important to know? *Evolutionary Anthropology* 6, 132–46.

O'CONNOR, S. 1995. Carpenter's Gap Rockshelter I: 40,000 years of Aboriginal occupation in the Napier Ranges, Kimberley, WA. *Australian Archaeology* 40, 58–9.

OYSTON, B. 1996. Thermoluminescence age determinations for the Mungo III human burial, Lake Mungo, southeastern Australia. *Quaternary Science Reviews* 15, 739–49.

PAIN, S. 1997. Cooking up a storm. *New Scientist*, 8 November, 36–40.

PAVLIDES, C. & GOSDEN, C. 1994. 35,000-year-old sites in the rainforests of West New Britain, Papua New Guinea. *Antiquity* 68, 604–10.

READHEAD, M. L. 1982. Extending thermoluminescence dating to geological sediments. In W. Ambrose and P. Duerden (eds), *Archaeometry: An Australasian Perspective*. Occasional Papers in Prehistory 12, 276–81. Canberra: Department of Prehistory, Research School of Pacific Studies, The Australian National University.

ROBERTS, R.G. & JONES, R. 1994. Luminescence dating of sediments: new light on the human colonisation of Australia. *Australian Aboriginal Studies* 2, 2–17. Canberra.

ROBERTS, R.G., JONES, R. & SMITH, M.A. 1990a. Thermoluminescence dating of a 50,000 year-old human occupation site in northern Australia. *Nature* 345, 153–6.

ROBERTS, R.G., JONES, R. & SMITH, M.A. 1990b. Stratigraphy and statistics at Malakunanja II: reply to Hiscock. *Archaeology in Oceania* 25, 125–9.

ROBERTS, R.G., JONES, R. & SMITH, M.A. 1994a. Beyond the radiocarbon barrier in Australian prehistory. *Antiquity* 68, 611–16.

ROBERTS, R.G., JONES, R., SPOONER, N.A., HEAD, M.J., MURRAY, A.S. & SMITH, M.A. 1994b. The human colonisation of Australia: optical dates of 53,000 and 60,000 years bracket human arrival at Deaf Adder Gorge, Northern Territory. *Quaternary Science Reviews* 13, 575–83.

ROBERTS, R.G., SPOONER, N.A., JONES, R., CANE, S., OLLEY, J.M., MURRAY, A.S. & HEAD, M.J. 1996. Preliminary luminescence dates for archaeological sediments on the Nullarbor Plain, South Australia. *Australian Archaeology* 42, 7–16.

ROBERTS, R.G., WALSH, G., MURRAY, A., OLLEY, J., JONES, R., MORWOOD, M., TUNIZ, C., LAWSON, E., MACPHAIL, M., BOWDERY, D. & NAUMANN, I. 1997. Luminescence dating of rock art and past environments using mud-wasp nests in northern Australia. *Nature* 387, 696–9.

ROBERTS, R.G., BIRD, M., OLLEY, J., GALBRAITH, R., LAWSON, E., LASLETT, G., YOSHIDA, H., JONES, R., FULLAGAR, R., JACOBSEN, G. & HUA, Q. 1998a. Optical and radiocarbon dating at Jinmium rock shelter in northern Australia. *Nature* 393, 358–62.

ROBERTS, R.G., YOSHIDA, H., GALBRAITH, R., LASLETT, G., JONES, R. & SMITH, M.A. 1998b. Single-aliquot and single-grain optical dating confirm thermoluminescence age estimates at Malakunanja II rock shelter in northern Australia. *Ancient T.L.*, June.

ROSENFELD, A., HORTON, D. & JOHN WINTER, D. 1981. *Early Man in North Queensland. Terra Australis* 6. Canberra: Department of Prehistory, Research School of Pacific Studies, The Australian National University.

SCHRIRE, C. 1982. *The Alligator Rivers: Prehistory and Ecology in Western Arnhem Land. Terra Australis* 7. Canberra: Department of Prehistory, Research School of Pacific Studies, The Australian National University.

SHAWCROSS, F.W. & KAYE, M. 1980. Australian archaeology: implications of current interdisciplinary research. *Interdisciplinary Science Reviews* 5, 112–28.

SINGH, G. & GEISSLER, E.A. 1985. Late Cainozoic history of vegetation, fire, lake levels and climate, at Lake George, New South Wales, Australia. *Phil Trans of the Royal Society of London*, ser. B 311, 379–477.

SMITH, M.A. & SHARP, N.D. 1993. Pleistocene sites in Australia, New Guinea and island Melanesia: geographic and temporal structure of the archaeological record. In M.A. Smith, M. Spriggs and B. Fankhauser (eds), *Sahul in Review: Pleistocene Archaeology in Australia, New Guinea and Island Melanesia*, 37–59. Canberra: Department of Prehistory, Research School of Pacific Studies, The Australian National University.

SMITH, M.A., PRESCOTT, J.R. & HEAD, M.J. 1997. Comparison of 14 C and luminescence chronologies at Puritjarra Rock Shelter, Central Australia. *Quaternary Science Reviews* 16, 299–320.

SONDAAR, P.Y., BERGH, G.D. VAN DEN, MUBROTO, B., AZIZ, F., VOS, J. DE & BATU, U.L. 1994. Middle Pleistocene faunal turnover and colonization of Flores (Indonesia) by *Homo erectus. Comptes Rendus de L'Académie des Sciences* 319, 1255–62. Paris.

SPENCER, B. & GILLEN, F. 1899. *The Native Tribes of Central Australia*. London: Macmillan.

SPOONER, N.A. 1994. On the optical dating signal from Quartz. *Radiation Measurements* 23, 593–600.

SPOONER, N.A. 1998. Human occupation at Jinmium, northern Australia: 116,000 years ago or much less? *Antiquity* 72, 173–8.

STRINGER, C.B. & BRAUER, G. 1994. Methods, misreading and bias. *American Anthropologist* 96, 416–24.

TAYLOR, W.W. 1948. *A Study of Archaeology. Mem. Series*, 69, American Anthropological Association. Reprinted 1967. Carbondale: Southern Illinois University Press.

THORNE, A.G. & WOLPOFF, M.H. 1992 The multiregional evolution of humans. *Scientific American*, April, 76–83.

TINDALE, N.B. 1957. Culture succession in south eastern Australia from late Pleistocene to the present. *Recs South Australian Museum* 13, 1–49.

TISHKOFF, S.A., DIETZSCH, E., SPEED, W., PAKSTIS, A.J., KIDD, J.R., CHEUNG, K., BONNE-TAMIR, B., SANTACHIARA-BENERECETTI, A.S., MORAL, P., KRINGS, M., PAABO, S., WATSON, E., RISCH, N., JENKINS, T. & KIDD, K.K. 1996. Global patterns of linkage disequilibrium at the CD4 locus and modern human origins. *Science* 271, 1380–7.

VETH, P., SPRIGGS, M. & O'CONNOR, S. in press. After Wallace: preliminary results of the first season's excavation of Liang Lemdubu, Aru Islands, Maluku. *Proceedings of the 6th International Conference of the European Association of Southeast Asian Archaeologists.* Leiden: Rijks Universiteit.

VOS, J. DE 1994. Dating hominid sites in Indonesia. *Science* 266, 1726–7.

WALLACE, A.R. 1865. On the varieties of man in the Malay Archipelago. *Trans. Ethnological Soc. of London*, n.s. 3, 209–12.

WALLACE, A.R. 1869 [my 10th edn 1894] *The Malay Archipelago, the Land of the Orang-Utan and the Bird of Paradise: a Narrative of Travel with Studies of Man and Nature*. London and New York: Macmillan and Co.

WALLACE, A.R. 1888. *Australasia*. London: Stanford's Compendium of Geography and Travel.

WALSH, G. 1994. *Bradshaws: Ancient Rock Paintings of North-West Australia*. Carouge-Geneva: The Bradshaw Foundation.

WATCHMAN, A. 1993. Evidence of a 25,000 year old pictograph in northern Australia. *Geoarchaeology* 8, 465–73.

WATCHMAN, A. 1997. Paleolithic marks: archaeometric perspectives. In M. Conkey, O. Soffer, D. Stratmann & N.G. Jablonski (eds), *Beyond Art: Pleistocene Image and Symbol*, 19–36. San Francisco: Mems of the California Academy of Science, No. 23.

WATCHMAN, A. & COLE, N. 1993. Accelerator radiocarbon dating of plant fibres binders in rock paintings from northeastern Australia. *Antiquity* 67, 355–8.

WEBB, R.E. & RINDOS, D.J. 1997. The mode and tempo of the initial human colonisation of empty landmasses: Sahul and the Americas compared. In C.M. Barton & G.A. Clark (eds), *Rediscovering Darwin: Evolutionary Theory and Archaeological Explanation*. Washington: Archaeological Papers of the American Anthropological Association 7, 233–50.

WHITE, C. 1967. Early stone axes in Arnhem Land. *Antiquity* 41, 149–52.

WHITE, J.P. 1977. Crude colourless and unenterprising? Prehistorians and their views on the stone age of Sunda and Sahul. In J. Allen, J. Golson & R. Jones (eds), *Sunda and Sahul: Prehistoric Studies in Southeast Asia, Melanesia and Australia*, 13–30. London: Academic Press.

WHITE, J.P., CROOK, K.A.W. & RUXTON, B.P. 1970. Kosipe: a late Pleistocene site in the Papuan Highlands. *Proceedings of the Prehistoric Society* 36, 152–70.

WILFORD, J.N. 1996. In Australia, signs of artists who predate *Homo sapiens*. *New York Times*, 29 September.

WILLEY, G.R. & PHILLIPS, P. 1958. *Method and Theory in American Archaeology*. Chigago: University of Chicago Press.

WINTLE, A.G. & HUNTLEY, D.J. 1979. Thermoluminescence dating of a deep-sea sediment core. *Nature* 279, 710–12.

WINTLE, A.G., SHACKLETON, N.J. & LAUTRIDOU, J. 1984. Thermoluminescence dating of periods of loess deposition and soil formation in Normandy. *Nature* 311, 363.

WOLPOFF, M.H., WU, X. & THORNE, A.G. 1984. Modern *Homo sapiens* origins: a general theory of hominid evolution involving the fossil evidence from east Asia. In F.H. Smith and F. Spencer (eds), 411–83. New York: Alan R. Liss.

WOOD, B. 1997. Ecce Homo—behold mankind. *Nature* 390, 120–1

WRIGHT, R. 1964. Probing Cape York's past. *Hemisphere* 8, 12–16.

Grahame Clark and American Archaeology

BRIAN FAGAN

GRAHAME CLARK ONLY VISITED THE AMERICAS on a few occasions, not out of a lack of interest in New World archaeology, but because he worked in a very different archaeological environment than that of today. Until the late 1950s, relatively few American archaeologists worked in the Old World or travelled widely to conferences or excavations far from home. By the same token, European prehistorians like Vere Gordon Childe tended to ignore American archaeology and confine their teaching and their syntheses to familiar turf. Today, we live in a different scholarly environment, where there is constant interchange between archaeologists all over the world. An explosion in higher education and in archaeology everywhere, in tourism and museums, and in international travel of all kinds, has led to a massive intellectual cross-fertilization between Old World and New since the advent of the jumbo jet and effortless electronic communication.

Grahame Clark did his most important work on the threshold of the jet and electronic era, at a time when multidisciplinary research was a new concept and radiocarbon dating a relative novelty. However, his influence on American archaeology was enormous, especially in the context of the theoretical furore and ardent debates of the 1960s, which catapulted New World archaeology and prehistory generally into a new, far more demanding paradigm.

Until the late 1950s, American archaeology was predominantly the study of culture history. To a great extent, this was a product of the direct historical method, pioneered by Alfred Kidder and others in the early years of this century (Willey and Sabloff 1990). The obsession with culture history also stemmed from a lack of accurate chronometric dating methods, except for dendrochronology, which provided a precise and reliable timescale for the last 2000 years of south-western archaeology. Elaborate seriations and complex stratigraphic sequences were the order of the day, many of them developed during the major river basin surveys in the 1930s. This preoccupation with culture history culminated in Gordon Willey and Philip Phillips' brilliant *Method and Theory in American*

Proceedings of the British Academy, **99**, 67–74

Archaeology (1958), which laid out a hierarchy of archaeological units that is still widely used today. However, *Method and Theory* was ultimately a work of descriptive rather than explanatory archaeology, a vital foundation for the new generation of researches that was to follow in the 1960s. Willey and Phillips themselves wrote: 'So little work has been done in American archaeology on the explanatory level that it is difficult to find a name for it' (1958, 5–6).

By the time Willey and Phillips wrote their classic work, a few voices were already expressing concerns about the sterile applications of culture history that had proliferated in North America. For example, Walter Taylor's *A Study of Archaeology* (1948) was a forthright critique of established methods, which evoked often strident criticism. Only a handful of American scholars were following developments in Europe and the Near East, notably Gordon Willey and Robert Braidwood. Willey had completed an ambitious settlement study in Peru's Virú Valley (1953), which showed the potential of aerial photographs and foot survey in the study of ancient settlement and landscape, an approach foreshadowed by the English archaeologist Cyril Fox before the Second World War. Fox developed settlement distributions for different prehistoric periods in the Cambridge region, chronicled in his *Archaeology of the Cambridge Region* (1925), which, however, could not take account of long-term environmental change, as there was no available evidence such as pollen diagrams from the Cambridgeshire Fens at the time. Braidwood organized one of the first multidisciplinary field projects in south-western Asia, where he caused a sensation with his skilled excavations and environmental researches in the Zagros Mountains of Iran (Braidwood & Braidwood 1983).

Willey and Braidwood's students were among the first American archaeologists to become aware of Grahame Clark's seminal work on human adaptations and subsistence in prehistoric Europe from the 1930s to 1950s. Everyone was familiar with Gordon Childe's culture historical syntheses of Europe and south-western Asia, where cultures acted like historical characters, and the Neolithic and Urban Revolutions became archaeological and historical canon (Childe 1936; 1952). Grahame Clark's researches were accessible to a far smaller audience. While Clark was gifted with a relatively fluent pen, his works did not cater to the kind of global readership Childe enjoyed, to the point that his syntheses became part of the world history of the 1930s to 1960s. Nevertheless, Clark wrote for both a specialized and wider archaeological audience, with a deep intellectual passion for both the minutiae of environmental adaptations and subsistence and the broad sweep of European prehistory. Until the 1950s, his pioneering work on the British Mesolithic and his seminal *The Mesolithic Settlement of Northern Europe* (1936) were known only to a handful of American scholars, notably Cambridge-trained Hugh Hencken of Harvard University, whom Clark (1989) himself credited with introducing him to the potential of wet sites with his research in Ireland. Then two books, published within two years of one another, established Grahame Clark in the American archaeological mind. The first was *Prehistoric Europe: The Economic Basis* (1952), the second *Star Carr* (1954), one of the classic monographs of twentieth-century archaeology.

To most European archaeologists of the 1950s, prehistoric archaeology was a form of history that used unwritten sources. Clark, after more than a quarter century of Mesolithic research, and strongly influenced by Scandinavian wet sites, espoused a multidisciplinary perspective, an anthropological approach which advocated the interpretation of archaeological finds in social, economic, and environmental terms. In all his post-Second World War work, he placed a strong emphasis on subsistence instead of artefacts and chronological sequences, calling *Prehistoric Europe* 'essentially an act of propaganda' (Clark 1989, 90). This remarkable book, which is still of value today, placed anthropology, ecology, and subsistence at the heart of archaeological research about a decade before this became a mainstream concern in American archaeology.

Prehistoric Europe was widely read in American universities, both because it offered a convenient and readable account of European prehistory from other than a Gordon Childe perspective, and also because it advocated research into environment, exchange, and subsistence using a multidisciplinary approach and carefully controlled ethnographic and folkloric analogy. The messages of the book were not lost on many American scholars, who were grappling with more than 10,000 years of pre-Columbian archaeology that unfolded against what appeared to be a highly complex backdrop of major, but still little understood, environmental change.

Clark wrote *Prehistoric Europe* when his Star Carr researches weighed heavily on his mind. In retrospect, he was probably one of the few archaeologists in the world who could have done justice to the Star Carr site in the late 1940s. This was because of his earlier work with the Fenland Research Committee, which had taken him across disciplinary boundaries in the early days of palynology at Cambridge University (Clark 1989). A Cambridge research team shouldered much of the Star Carr research and produced a portrait of a tiny hunter-gatherer site that was a model of its kind, right down to its emphasis on seasonality and identification of charcoals and pollens. Few American archaeologists were, or are, interested in the British or European Mesolithic. However, the Star Carr excavation transcended this narrow speciality, with its brilliant reconstructions and cogently argued descriptions not just of a tiny hunting stand, but of a 10,000 year-old site (one of the first ever radiocarbon dated) set in a wider environmental setting. The minute detail of the Star Carr excavations came as a revelation not only to European archaeologists, but to Americanists, many of whom had not fully realized the enormous value of palynology to archaeology, nor of wet sites to a fuller understanding of ancient native American societies. The methodologies employed at Star Carr exercised a profound influence on such important North American excavations as the Ozette village in Washington State's Olympia Peninsula (Kirk 1974).

The direct historical method, working back from the present into the past, and the strong intellectual foundations of American archaeology, have always placed the judicious use of ethnographic analogy at centre stage in the New World. An enormous literature surrounded the subject in the 1950s (Thompson 1956; Wylie 1985), and still proliferates in the 1990s. *Prehistoric Europe*, with its controlled use of such analogies, appeared at a time of renewed interest in both primate studies and hunter-gatherer research, which culminated in the famous 'Man the Hunter' conference at the University of Chicago in 1966 (Lee & DeVore 1968). This now-legendary meeting stemmed in part from Richard Lee and Irven DeVore's precedent-setting researches among the Kung San of the Kalahari Desert (Lee 1970), which influenced an entire generation of palaeoanthropological and hunter-gatherer research. The combination of controlled ethnographic analogy, the study of living societies ('ethnoarchaeology'), and Clark's ecological researches were important catalysts for the theoretical ferment that burst on American archaeology in the 1960s. Clark's Star Carr monograph and his writings on ecological archaeology were essential reading to anyone interested in the canons of the new archaeology, with its insistence on ecological thinking and cultural systems.

Grahame Clark's most important work came at a time of quiet despair in many archaeological circles. In 1965, Stuart Piggott was moved to write: 'We have lost the confidence of the nineteenth century, and are children of an age of doubt . . . We must recognize that in archaeology . . . there are facts other than those which are . . . observational data' (1965, 4–5), a point that Grahame Clark had long realized. However, by this time both David Clarke in Britain and Lewis Binford and others in North America were moving archaeology in new directions. Grahame Clark's anthropological and ecological approaches played an inconspicuous, but critical, role in these new directions, in what became known, inaccurately, as the 'new archaeology'.

Lewis Binford's thinking about a 'new archaeology' developed from a matrix of anthropological, sociological, and scientific thinking that appeared in the late 1950s (Binford, 1983). Central to his ideas were the writings of Julian Steward and Leslie White, who were proponents both of multilinear cultural evolution and of cultural ecology. Steward in particular was a powerful theoretical force, for he added the environment to what had always been an essentially cultural evolutionary equation. He developed the notion of cultural ecology, which argued that similar adaptations could be found in different cultures in broadly similar environments, that cultures change in response to environmental change, differences and changes that can lead to great societal complexity or completely new cultural patterns. In many respects, Steward's ideas (1955) ran parallel to those of Grahame Clark, whose Mesolithic and more general European researches provided first-hand examples of how multidisciplinary field research could produce fine-grained reconstructions of exactly the kinds of environmental adaptations that Julian Steward observed in living societies. They had both done the same thing, Steward at a largely theoretical level, Clark by adding the environmental perspective to the researches of Cyril Fox and early Mesolithic scholars.

One can only call Grahame Clark's influence on processual archaeology enormous. However, Clark's thinking moved far beyond the frontiers of environmental adaptations. He always considered ancient humans social beings, who lived not by universal cultural rules, but by their own wits and decisions about situations that confronted them. Clark was strongly opposed to the mechanistic, often anonymous cultural processes which soon masqueraded as explanations of the past in the most ardent processual literature. In his own writings, he foreshadowed the concerns of the post-processualists. 'There remain spheres of knowledge or awareness which . . . have been of supreme importance to individual men and as matter of fact, through their influence on social life have ultimately served to enhance biological effectiveness' (Clark 1961, 256).

As any of his former students will testify, Grahame Clark had a refreshingly eclectic perspective on archaeology. He himself had widened the horizons of Mesolithic research far beyond the narrow confines of Britain and worked closely with Scandinavian archaeologists. He also taught students for an undergraduate degree in Archaeology and Anthropology that had a long tradition of preparing Cambridge people for a career in the British Colonial Service, where, as another Cambridge lecturer, Miles Burkitt, would put it, 'your hand might by chance alight on a perfect Acheulian handaxe as you administered justice under a pawpaw tree' (Burkitt, pers. comm.). His predecessor as the Disney Professor, Dorothy Garrod of Mt Carmel fame, was the first to teach a course at the university entitled 'world prehistory' in 1946. Nevertheless the perspective of the Cambridge curriculum was still narrow and largely restricted to Europe and south-western Asia. Clark had developed a much broader vision as a direct result of many years of teaching undergraduates destined for administrative, and sometimes archaeological, careers overseas. His students included J. Desmond Clark and John Mulvaney, pioneers of African and Australian archaeology respectively. Once he was appointed to the Disney Chair in 1953, he strongly encouraged Cambridge archaeological graduates to find work in museums and universities overseas at a time when such opportunities abounded. As he himself has shown (Clark 1989), these Cambridge exports resulted in a quantum jump in new archaeological data from hitherto neglected parts of the Old World. Many of these graduates received a perspective on American archaeology from Clark's colleague Geoffrey Bushnell, which was to stand them in good stead in later years.

With the notable exceptions of Warwick Bray and Norman Hammond, few Cambridge graduates of the Clark years specialized in the Americas, so the influence of the Cambridge diaspora (and it is not exaggerating to call it this) was more indirect in the New World. However, more than a few Cambridge graduates began their careers far from the Cam, then moved across the Atlantic to teach in Canada and the United States during the massive expansion of higher education in the 1960s, notably J. Desmond Clark and Glynn Isaac. They brought with them refined versions of Clark's anthropological and ecological approach and their own researches in Africa, Central America, and Australia, to influence not only their American colleagues but new generations of fledgling archaeologists who would themselves specialize in hitherto little known or arcane aspects of world prehistory. Many of the Cambridge newcomers, this writer among them, arrived serendipitously just as the 'new archaeology' was rippling across the Americas and the world.

The development of radiocarbon dating was a seminal event in the history of archaeology, the more so because several eminent archaeologists of the day realized the enormous potential of the method as soon as Libby and Arnold published their famous paper in *Science* in 1949 (Libby 1955). Robert Braidwood, Grahame Clark, and Gordon Willey, among others, were in the forefront of the radiocarbon revolution. With characteristic zeal, Clark realized the potential of radiocarbon dating and worked hard both at Cambridge and elsewhere to foster the establishment of dating laboratories. He was also one of the first to comprehend how carbon 14 would transform our ability to develop global chronologies, to date, for example, the origins of agriculture in different parts of the world and to embark on comparative studies at a level of complexity unimaginable at the time. Clark used radiocarbon dating himself—at Peacock's Farm, Star Carr, Hurst Fen, and other Mesolithic and Neolithic excavations of the 1940s and 1950s. But he also used the scatter of new dates and his increasingly far-flung travels as the blueprint for a seminal book, which finally established him on the international stage—*World Prehistory*, published by Cambridge University Press in 1961. It is no exaggeration to say that archaeology has never been the same since, for Grahame Clark drew archaeological researches in every corner of the world into a simple, easy-to-read synthesis of human prehistory that was accessible to specialist and general reader alike. Not only did he provide the first truly scientific framework for world prehistory, he drew Old World and New together archaeologically for the first time.

American archaeologists, like everyone else, tend to be specialists, a condition brought upon them by the long distances that separate them and the very nature of their work—a small trench in a remote part of Alaska or Illinois, a lifetime spent investigating a single Maya ruin, or an arcane specialization in zooarchaeology or ethnobotany. Inevitably, such narrow scientific perspectives a generation ago spilled over into thinking about the first settlement of the Americas or the rise of state-organized societies in Mesoamerica. *World Prehistory* took a much broader view. For example, Clark insisted that one could not understand the issue of the first settlement of the New World without looking at the controversy on a much wider cultural canvas. Thus, *World Prehistory* thought of Paleo-Indian phenomena like Clovis and Folsom as cogs in a much wider web of late Ice Age cultural interconnections, which stretched deep into Asia, perhaps as far as Eurasia. Clark firmly espoused a relatively late settlement date, opting for a crossing over the Bering Land Bridge 'during an interstadial of the late Ice Age' (1961, 212). With his encyclopaedic knowledge of northern latitudes and glacial phenomena, he rejected any thought of a migration during the height of the last glaciation. In the 1969 edition, he still argued for relatively late settlement, while taking note of putative earlier discoveries, which did not hold scientific water. While his discussion of the 'ice-free corridor' and of the High Plains as a focus of big-game hunting is somewhat dated, one of Clark's most important contributions was his insistence that the New World was part of world prehistory, not a prehistoric world unto itself.

Along the same lines, he argued convincingly that both Mesoamerican and Andean civilizations were of indigenous, native American origin, while keeping open the door to some cultural innovations from Asia (such as the celebrated, and now discredited, Jomon/Valdivia connection). A wealth of new data since the 1960s has resulted in universal consensus as to the indigenous origins of pre-Columbian states. The sheer brevity of Clark's synthesis prevented him from giving anything more than a very generalized summary of New World civilizations, but the influence of his brief synthesis helped bring American archaeology into much wider focus.

Clark's world prehistories were exercises in comparative archaeology, an insistence that ancient civilizations in widely separated parts of the world shared many general similarities. *World Prehistory* is judicious in its comparisons, but leaves us in no doubt of the general similarities between, say, Maya and Mesopotamian civilization. These broad similarities came to the fore in a series of important researches conducted by American archaeologists in Mesopotamia and Mesoamerica in the 1960s, notably those by Robert Adams in ancient landscapes in Iraq (1966) and by William Sanders and others in the Basin of Mexico (1979). Adams (1966) in particular attempted comparisons between early civilizations in widely separated geographical areas. He pointed out that both early Mesopotamian and American civilizations followed a basically similar course of development in which the communal ownership of land by kin groups gave way to the growth of private estates owned by noble families. The eventual result was a stratified form of social organization rigidly divided along class lines.

Such comparions would have been unthinkable in an era dominated by local archaeologies and culture history. Adams' work, inspired in part by Clark's syntheses, is a foundation of most modern theorizing on the origins of states. Clark himself called his global prehistory a concern 'not with bricks and mortar so much as with the building' (1961, 3). Thirty years later, we know that the building he tentatively erected was indeed a priceless starting point for people 'to view the histories of their own cultures in the broad perspective of world prehistory' (1961, 5). His vision of a global past influenced a generation of American archaeologists.

Grahame Clark was an anthropological archaeologist, who placed the study of culture at the forefront of all archaeological research. To culture he added adaptation and ecology, just as Julian Steward (1955) did at a theoretical level in the United States. The difference between Clark and Steward was that the former was already practising in the field on a day-to-day basis what only a handful of American scholars of the day saw as important. The 'new archaeology' was a startling confirmation that Grahame Clark in ecological archaeology, as in so many other things, was ahead of his time. More than anyone else, he placed American archaeology on a truly global stage. His legacy is the concept of world prehistory which is the ultimate conceptual foundation of all contemporary prehistoric archaeology.

Acknowledgement

I am grateful to the Academic Senate Research Committee, University of California, Santa Barbara, for providing travel funds for me to attend the Grahame Clark Memorial Conference.

References

ADAMS, R.M. 1966. *The Evolution of Urban Society*. Chicago: Aldine.

BINFORD, L.R. 1983. *In Pursuit of the Past*. London: Thames and Hudson.

BRAIDWOOD, R.C. & BRAIDWOOD, L.S. (eds) 1983. *Prehistoric Archaeology Along the Zagros Flanks*. Chicago: Oriental Institute.

CHILDE, V.G. 1936. *Man Makes Himself*. London: Watts.

CHILDE, V.G. 1952. *New Light on the Most Ancient East*. London: Routledge and Kegan Paul.

CLARK, J.G.D. 1936. *The Mesolithic Settlement of Northern Europe*. Cambridge: Cambridge University Press.

CLARK, J.G.D. 1952. *Prehistoric Europe: The Economic Basis*. Cambridge: Cambridge University Press.

CLARK, J.G.D. 1954. *Excavations at Star Carr*. Cambridge: Cambridge University Press.

CLARK, J.G.D. 1961. (Second edn 1969, third edn 1977.) *World Prehistory: An Outline*. Cambridge: Cambridge University Press.

CLARK, J.G.D. 1989. *Prehistory at Cambridge and Beyond*. Cambridge: Cambridge University Press.

FOX, C. 1925. *The Archaeology of the Cambridge Region*. Cambridge: Cambridge University Press.

KIRK, R. 1974. *Hunters of the Whale*. New York: William Morrow.

LEE, R. 1970. *The !Kung San*. Cambridge: Cambridge University Press.

LEE, R. & DeVORE, I. (eds) 1968. *Man the Hunter*. Chicago: Aldine.

LIBBY, W. 1955. *Radiocarbon Dating*. Chicago: University of Chicago Press.

PIGGOTT, S. 1965. *Approach to Archaeology*. Cambridge, Mass.: Harvard University Press.

SANDERS, W., PARSONS, J.R. & SANTLAY, R.S. 1979. *The Basin of Mexico: Ecological Processes in the Evolution of a Civilization*. New York: Academic Press.

STEWARD, J. 1955. *A Theory of Culture Change*. Urbana: University of Illinois Press.

TAYLOR, W.W. 1948. *A Study of Archaeology*. Menasha, Wis.: American Anthropological Association.

THOMPSON, R.H. 1956. The subjective element in archaeological inference. *Southwestern Journal of Anthropology* 12, 327–32.

WILLEY, G.R. 1953. *Prehistoric Settlement Patterns in the Virú Valley, Peru*. Washington DC: Smithsonian Institution, Bureau of American Ethnology.

WILLEY, G.R. & PHILLIPS, P. 1958. *Method and Theory in American Archaeology*. Chicago: University of Chicago Press.

WILLEY, G.R. & SABLOFF, J.A. 1990. *A History of American Archaeology*. London: Thames and Hudson.

WYLIE, A. 1985. The reaction against analogy. *Advances in Archaeological Method and Theory* 8, 63–111.

Recent Advances in the Prehistory of South-east Asia

C.F.W. HIGHAM

THIRTY YEARS AGO, when I was seeking my first rung on a professional ladder, I asked Grahame Clark if he thought I should apply for a provincial post in England. His Delphic response was immediate: 'Higham', he said, 'do you want to be a porter or a station master?' He had recently returned from a term as visiting professor at the University of Otago in New Zealand (Figure 1), and before long I joined the diaspora of Cambridge prehistorians which in my case involved the world's most southerly university. I hope that my placement as far from Cambridge as it is possible to be did not reflect his personal preference, but one fact is undeniable: I found myself in a very large station, with tracks leading to many potential destinations.

It is difficult now to impress on a younger generation of archaeologists, the opportunities then presented as we found our feet in Australasia. There were very few departments of Archaeology and virtually no graduate programmes. Serious prehistoric research was only then gathering momentum in Australia; the Pacific was at best only sketchily documented and south-east Asia was hardly explored. My chosen route, quite by chance, took me to the mainland of Asia and by degrees, it has been possible to identify the main elements of its prehistoric past.

South-east Asia, broadly defined, includes the monsoon lands which stretch from the valley of the Yangzi River south and west to Burma (Figures 2 and 3). The present diversity of people, environments, languages, and human societies defies quick synthesis: within a matter of hours, you can leave some of the world's largest cities and enter rainforests still populated by hunter gatherers, or from a tourist hotel you can rub shoulders with the sea gypsies, who move by boat from base to camp over hundreds of leagues, living from the resources provided by the sea and coastal fringe.

There are several reasons why this area merits attention from anyone interested in world prehistory. It sustains approximately one-sixth of humanity, and was the springboard for three of the major expansionary movements in human history. The first involved the

Proceedings of the British Academy, **99**, 75–86

Figure 1. Sir Grahame Clark during his tenure of a visiting chair at the University of Otago, New Zealand.

settlement of greater Australia, the second the expansion of Austronesian-speaking people to Easter Island in one direction and Malagasy in the other. It saw the transition to rice agriculture in the Yangzi Valley, which resulted in a third expansion, involving the movement of proto-Austroasiatic speakers south to a broad tract from Guangdong to Bengal. South-east Asia then saw the development of a distinctive bronze age, it participated in the trade network which linked the Roman and Chinese empires, and produced one of the most singular civilizations known, that of Angkor.

The hunter-gatherer societies of south-east Asia have received rather a bad press. In the interior, there are numerous small rock shelters which reveal intermittent occupation over the past 40,000 years. The range of material culture is unexciting and the canopied forest habitat laced with streams did not encourage innovation. The broad spectrum gathering and hunting undertaken from such sites is best illustrated at Spirit Cave, located on a hill slope in northern Thailand. Typical of the widespread Hoabinhian tradition, it was a base for hunting and the collection of a wide range of plants. At nearby Banyan Valley Cave, rice has been recovered, but only in late contexts and according to Yen (1977), it was almost certainly a wild variety.

Such sites, however, provide only a partial picture. South-east Asia is surrounded by

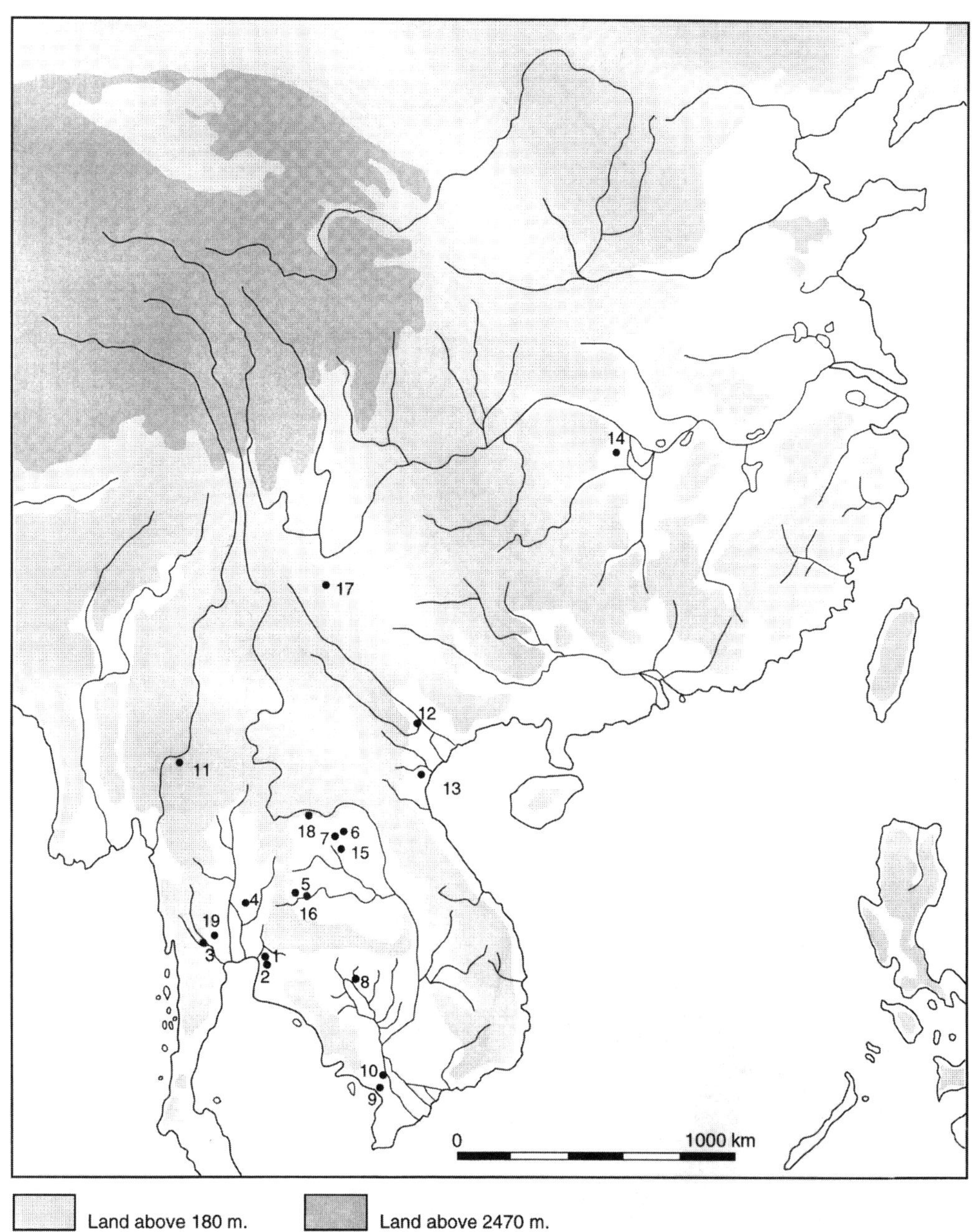

Figure 2. East and south-east Asia, showing sites mentioned in the text: 1. Khok Phanom Di; 2. Nong Nor; 3. Ban Kao; 4. Non Pa Wai; 5. Noen U-Loke, Non Muang Kao; 6. Ban Chiang; 7. Ban Phak Top; 8. Angkor; 9. Oc Eo; 10. Angkor Borei; 11. Spirit Cave, Banyan Valley Cave; 12. Phung Nguyen; 13. Dong Son; 14. Pengtoushan; 15. Ban Na Di; 16. Ban Lum Khao; 17. Shizhaishan, Lijiashan; 18. Phu Lon; 19. Ban Don Ta Phet.

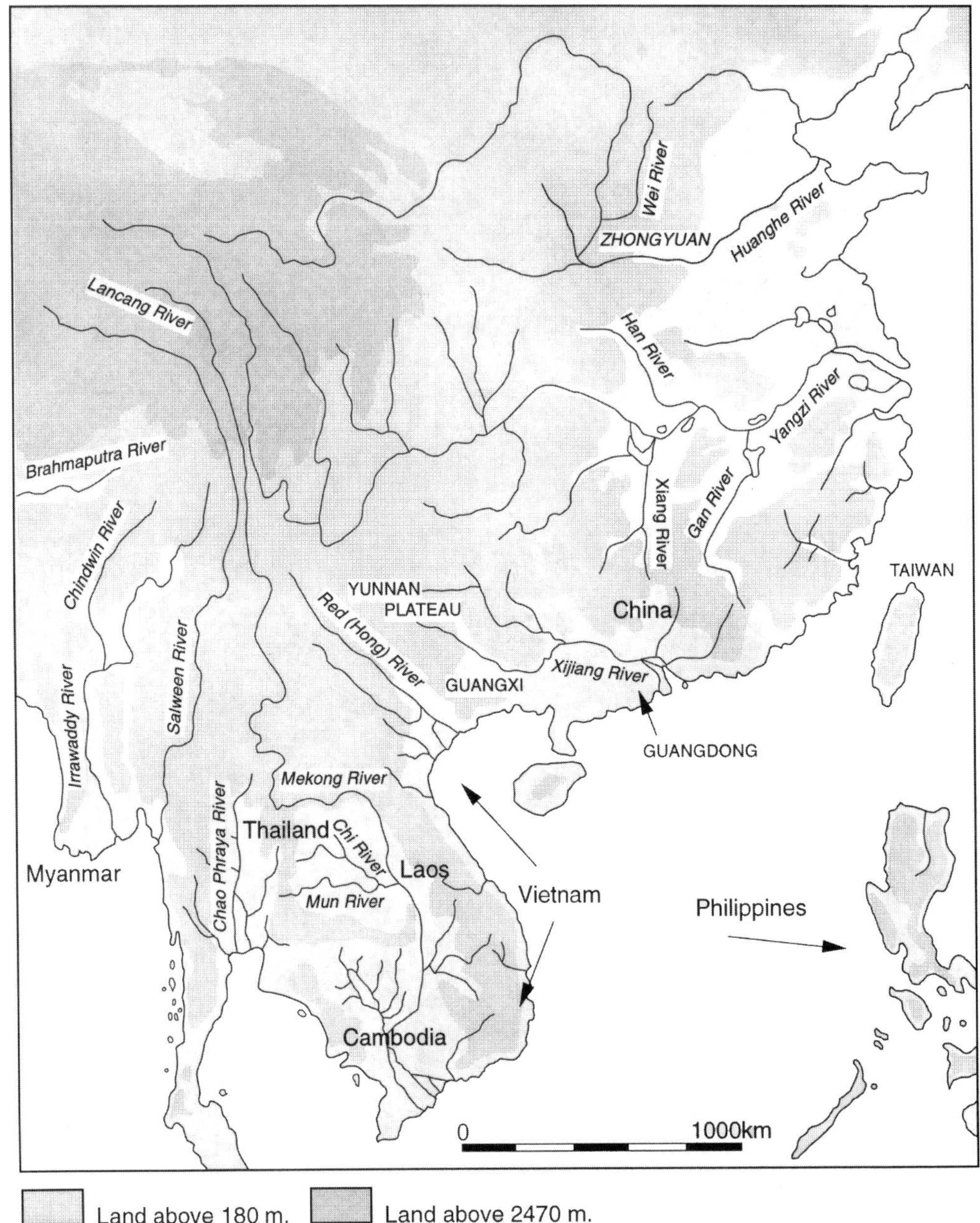

Figure 3. East and south-east Asia, showing the countries and major rivers.

broad continental shelves, and we have lost to the rising sea much evidence for the marine adaptation. From Japan to northern Australia, old shorelines formed during the Holocene high sea level, which date from about 4000 BC, harbour prehistoric settlements. While preceding sites have been drowned, two excavations behind the present Gulf of Siam have given us a glimpse of the richness and variety of such maritime hunter gatherers. Nong Nor was occupied for little more than a season, about 2500 BC (Higham & Thosarat 1998). It covers about 0.1 of a hectare, and may have harboured 30 or 40 people at most. The site was located on or very near a mangrove-fringed marine embayment, from which the occupants fished for tiger and bull sharks, eagle rays, and hunted dolphins. They collected millions of shellfish and made a variety of decorated pottery vessels as well as polished stone adzes. There is no evidence for any form of cultivated plant or domestic animal. People who could bring in some of the most ferocious sharks known must have been able sailors and this is to be expected: their ancestors crossed to Australia over 50,000 years previously.

Similar coastal settlements in south-east Asia have often been described as the 'Coastal Neolithic'. If this implies the domestication of plants or animals, then it is a serious misnomer, for no evidence for a transition to agriculture has yet been identified. The continuous heat, and low impact of seasonality conferred by proximity to the sea encourage great biological vigour, a situation which does not engender deep-seated economic innovation.

This continuity can be seen at Khok Phanom Di, located only 14 km to the north of Nong Nor. Similar pottery vessels and other items of material culture were present in the lowest layers, and again the occupants took advantage of the wealth to be found on the edge of a major estuary. On this occasion, however, settlement endured for five centuries, beginning in about 2000 BC. Rachanie Thosarat and I excavated this site in 1985, and we are still discovering new aspects of the kaleidoscopic set of variables which come from the cultural and biological remains. The occupants lived in one of the world's richest habitats, the tropical estuary. Its wealth in terms of biological vigour had a darker side: the environment was subject to change, which at times could be rapid and unpredictable. It was also, we think, shared with malarial mosquitoes. This site was, nevertheless, occupied through five centuries of change, and we can trace how the successive generations adapted. They began living near or within a mangrove belt backed by saline flats, collected shellfish from the mudflats and fished in the estuary and open sea beyond. Somehow, they obtained rice, but not, we think, through local cultivation for the environment was not supportive. By degrees, the mound accumulated and the dead were interred in tight clusters. The forest of post-holes surrounding groups of graves, and complementary distribution of shellfish deposits, suggest communal mortuary structures. Locally made pots of considerable beauty were placed with the dead, along with shell and fish-bone jewellery. Within an asbestos shroud, the bodies were laid out on wooden biers. We find that men, women, children, and infants, many infants, were grouped together in death. With time, the dead accumulated over their predecessors until the cemetery reached a depth of 5 m. By tracing genetically determined skeletal characteristics, and one day we hope, the sequencing of DNA, it seems that these people were related. We can count about 17 generations (Higham & Bannanurag 1990).

At first, there was very high infant mortality. The people suffered from anaemia linked to a haemoglobinopathy such as thalassaemia. Men, however, had robust upper body musculature associated perhaps with seafaring. By the fourth mortuary phase, freshwater lakes had formed near the site, men became weaker physically and we find shell-harvesting knives and granite hoes. We think that people began cultivating rice, but not for long: soon saline conditions returned, and artefacts indicating cultivation ceased to be found. Yet we find a burst of mortuary wealth associated with new exotic goods, as if exchange relationships intensified. We think that women made the pots which could have been fed into an exchange network, certainly some women were buried with extraordinary mortuary finery, including in one case over 120,000 shell beads (Figure 4). It was also at this period that a woman was interred within a rectangular mortuary structure featuring clay wall foundations and a plastered clay floor. In front of her tomb lay a row of less wealthy burials which included men, women, children, and two newly-born infants, probably twins, entwined in a single grave.

Given his lifelong dedication to the European Mesolithic, Grahame Clark showed considerable interest in Khok Phanom Di, and encouraged the Society of Antiquaries of London to publish the seven-volume report in its Research Report series.

As these coastal communities continued in their time-honoured way, major changes had already occurred in the middle Yangzi Valley which were to influence the course of prehistory over a very considerable area. At about the same time as in the Levant, and perhaps influenced by the same climatic changes centred on the Younger Dryas period, we find the establishment of settled villages such as Pengtoushan, in which rice was prominent in the diet (Yan Wenming 1991). In my view, one of the most interesting recent departures in Old World prehistory has been the proposed link between the expansion of agriculturists and the dispersal of related languages. I do not wish to enter the debate on the Indo-European languages, but in east and south-east Asia, two linguists have proposed that Austronesian and Austroasiatic languages share in the Austric phylum, a common origin (Reid 1993; Blust 1996). They have placed the Austric homeland in the Yangzi Valley. Austroasiatic languages are distributed from eastern India to southern China, and include languages spoken in Vietnam, Cambodia, Thailand, and Burma. Robert Blust has suggested that they were brought into south-east Asia by expansive rice farmers. Going a stage further, Peter Bellwood (1993) has further proposed that the people in question were southern Mongoloid.

If the climatic vagaries and extensive marshland bordering the Yangzi conspired to favour the transition to agriculture, the hot monsoonal lowlands of the Mekong, Chao Phraya, and Red River basins were receptive to intrusive settlement by farmers. I am reminded of the distribution of Danubian 1 settlement in the European loess which Grahame Clark used to show his undergraduates. Many south-east Asian agricultural settlements have been excavated, and we have the image of small, segmentary communities, cutting

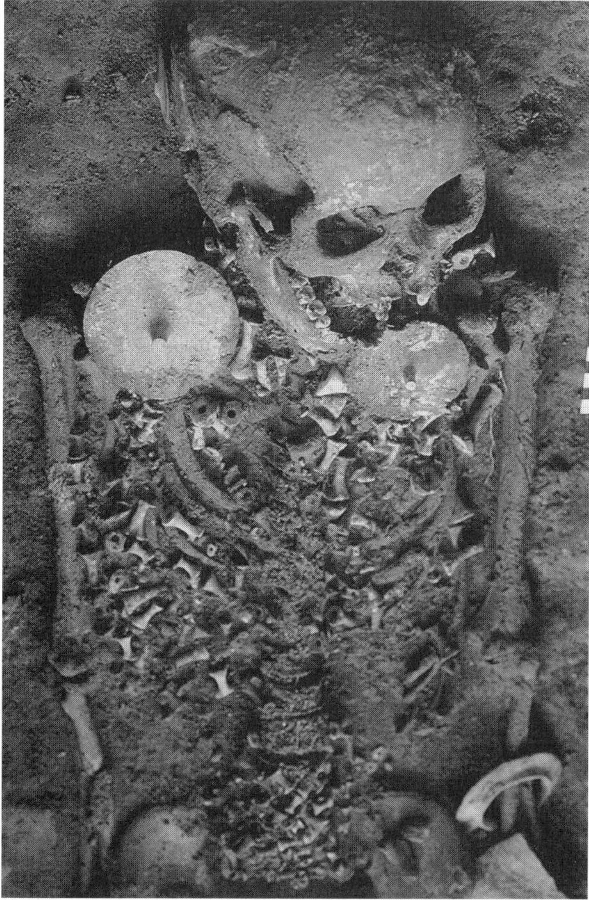

Figure 4. Burial 15 at Khok Phanom Di included over 120,000 shell beads, and illustrates the wealth of this coastal hunter-gatherer community.

back the forest in the margins of tributary streams, planting out some rice, and, to judge from the faunal remains, eating virtually anything that moved, from elephant, rhinoceros, and crocodile to a host of fish and shellfish species. These people introduced the domestic dog, descended from the Chinese wolf, and herded cattle and pigs.

In the lower Red River Valley above Hanoi, we encounter a network of sites ascribed to the Phung Nguyen culture (Ha Van Tan 1980). The well-watered Sakhon Nakhon Basin of north-east Thailand bore witness to early agricultural settlement at Ban Phak Top and Ban Chiang (Gorman & Charoenwongsa 1976; Schauffler 1976; Bannanurag & Bamrungwongse 1991). In central Thailand, the excavations of Ban Kao and Non Pa Wai have revealed the establishment of Neolithic communities. In each of these areas, it would be hard to argue in favour of initial settlement before the later third millennium BC. This date also applies to the early establishment of rice farming in eastern India (Glover & Higham 1996).

This new departure in south-east Asia prehistory with its widespread manifestation and initial settlement of the inland tributary river margins, it is argued, best explains the widespread distribution of Austroasiatic languages. Blust has suggested that the speakers of proto-Vietnamese languages travelled down the Red River, while proto-Khmer speakers used the Mekong, proto-Mon the Chao Phraya and Salween, and proto-Munda speakers, the Brahmaputra. This implies that the upper Yangzi region was the hub or centre of dispersal. While still speculative, this model best harmonizes with the available evidence.

Some time after 1500 BC, these people began to smelt and cast copper and tin, and alloy the two metals into bronze. We do not know yet whether this technique developed locally, or was introduced through the system of exchange in goods and ideas which linked the Yangzi homeland with Lingnan and Vietnam. The recovery of Chinese jades in late Neolithic burials in Vietnam and southern China certainly indicates a form of contact linking the two regions. Whichever the case, south-east Asia sustained a bronze age which, over a millennium, displays individuality in its techniques and the items cast. We can now trace the stages in this industry, from the mines to the processing floor, from the smelting furnace to the ingot moulds. In the production centres, there is some evidence that activity was seasonal, continuing over many centuries. Non Pa Wai and Phu Lon are mining centres, where the copper was concentrated and cast into ingots and a variety of implements or ornaments (White & Pigott 1996). Most finished artefacts at the former were cast from unalloyed copper, while the ingots must presumably have entered pre-existing exchange systems. At villages remote from the mines, such as Ban Na Di, we can pick up the story: ingots of copper and tin were mixed and brought to melting point in small clay furnaces, then cast into bivalve sandstone moulds into axes, spears, or arrowheads, or by using the lost wax technique and clay moulds, into ornaments.

Sites like Ban Na Di, Nong Nor in its second phase, Ban Chiang, and Ban Lum Khao reveal intimate details of the mortuary ritual and way of life of these bronze age communities. They displayed an interest in ornaments made of exotic substances: slate, marble, carnelian, nephrite, talc, serpentine, marine shell, and tin and copper as well as bronze. Pottery vessels and parts of animals, perhaps sacrificial in origin, were invariably included in mortuary rituals. When sufficient areas are exposed, we find that some groups of individuals were somewhat richer than others; there may have been some competitive ranking, but it was not marked. Bronzes were always relatively rare, and not associated with people otherwise rich in terms of mortuary offerings. At Ban Lum Khao, not one of 110 graves included a bronze grave good, and in no other site are more than one in five graves accompanied by bronzes.

From 500 BC, there were a series of deep and pervasive changes. Iron was smelted, and forged into ornaments, tools, and weapons. South-east Asia became a vital component of an exchange network which linked the Roman and Chinese empires. The Han Empire bore down on the defeated state of Chu in the Yangzi Valley, and in an imperial expansion no less dramatic in its consequences than in Europe under the Caesars, absorbed south-east Asian chiefdoms up to the Truong Son Cordillera. In Yunnan and Vietnam, we can appreciate the vigour of such chiefdoms through the cemeteries of the Dian and Dong Son cultures. The mastery of bronze casting, exemplary evidence for warfare, ritual, feasting, the chase, and accumulation of exotic valuables and the wealth of certain individuals provide one of the best reflections of a chiefdom known. At Shizhaishan and Lijiashan in Yunnan, royal tomb furniture included exquisite models of houses and scenes of ritual, feasting, warfare, and the chase. The Dong Son drums from northern Vietnam likewise reveal in their decoration, opulent warrior aristocrats directing operations from war pirogues. We can admire the plumed warriors and the decorated weaponry with which they were interred, often in sealed wooden boat coffins. It is intriguing to speculate what such societies might have become had they not been enveloped by the homogenizing hand of Han imperialism.

South of the Fortress of the Sky, as the Han described the Truong Son range, we encounter contemporary trends to complexity without quite the same degree of emphasis on warfare. At Ban Don Ta Phet, Ian Glover has uncovered a most important Iron Age cemetery (Glover 1989; 1996). Again, we encounter rich graves containing exotic valuables, such as carnelian, nephrite, glass, and agate ornaments. And once more, we find a surge in the local production of masterpieces in bronze. At this site, there was a special emphasis on high tin bronze bowls bearing languid scenes of animals, plants, and elaborately coiffured women. One particular ornament, a carnelian lion, stands out as an early representation of the Buddha. Radiocarbon dates suggest a date early in the fourth century BC for this, the earliest indication of new religious currents which were soon to dominate.

The Mun Valley during this period saw an extraordinary rash of large settlements ringed by earthworks. We are now in the midst of investigating such a site at Noen U-Loke, and our first season revealed a mortuary sequence divided into five phases all covering the Iron Age from about 300 BC to AD 400. The burial ritual changed with time. The earliest grave incorporated bronze torcs, tiger teeth pendants, an iron spearhead and two of bronze, and pottery vessels containing fish. Later, we found that people were partially cremated in beds of burning rice, along with glass, agate and carnelian beads, bronze bells, and ornaments. One individual was buried with more bronze artefacts than have come from the entire assemblage of hundreds of preceding bronze age graves: three belts, about 150 bangles, finger and toe rings, and silver earcoils bearing gold foil. Burial 113 included a necklace of 66 gold beads, as well as many fashioned from agate and glass (Figure 5). These people of Noen U-Loke represent the societies which were to establish, in due course, the early civilizations of south-east Asia. At the nearby site of Non Muang Kao, elaboration of the mortuary ritual during this period is seen in the provision of clay-lined and lidded graves.

Many states developed from about AD 200. The earliest is found in the deltaic plains of the lower Mekong, where Oc Eo has long been known, while Miriam Stark is currently

Figure 5. The Iron Age cemetery of Neon U-Loke included many very rich burials. This person was interred with a necklace incorporating gold, agate, and glass beads.

excavating at the 1100 ha walled city of Angkor Borei. The state of Dvaravati developed in central Thailand, that of Angkor in Cambodia and the adjacent Mun Valley in Thailand. The Cham state was found on the coastal plain of Vietnam. All have in common the selective adoption by local overlords of exotic Hindu or Buddhist religions, the Sanskrit or Pali languages, and the notion of the divine ruler. All were sustained by that most responsive of plants, rice. Rice today is the staple for half of humanity. This, alone, surely gives south-east Asia a prominent place in any consideration of human prehistory.

Some years ago, Grahame Clark was the prime mover in urging the British Academy to encourage research in south-east Asia. First taking the form of a physical presence, and later as a committee charged to disburse research funds, this initiative has seen the expansion of British activity in this vital region. Throughout my 30 years of research in south-east Asia, I have been regularly in touch with Sir Grahame and his responses have always been full of interest and incisive advice. Few have commanded his capacity to identify the significant and set a course for research.

No one has covered more miles than I to attend this day of celebration for his career, for to travel further would be to start my return journey to New Zealand. Grahame would have delighted in the irony that on this very day, the All Blacks are playing England but the sacrifice of not watching is willingly made in order to salute the memory of Sir Grahame Clark, teacher, mentor, friend.

References

BANNANURAG, R. & BAMRUNGWONGSE, A. 1991. A site survey of Ban Chiang culture sites in the Sakhon Nakhon Basin, Northeast Thailand, (in Thai). *Silpakon Journal*, 34, 38–60.

BELLWOOD, P. 1993. Cultural and biological differentiation in peninsular Malaysia: the last 10,000 years. *Asian Perspectives*, 32, 37–60.

BLUST, R. 1996. Beyond the Austronesian homeland: the Austric hypothesis and its implications for archaeology. In W. Goodenough (ed.), *Prehistoric Settlement of the Pacific. Transactions of the American Philosophical Society* 86, 117–40.

GLOVER, I.C. 1989. *Early Trade Between India and Southeast Asia: a Link in the Development of a World Trading System*. The University of Hull Centre for South-East Asian Studies, Occasional Paper No. 16, Hull.

GLOVER, I.C. 1996. The southern Silk Road: archaeological evidence for early trade between India and Southeast Asia. In A. Srisuchat (ed.), *Ancient Trades and Cultural Contacts in Southeast Asia* 57–94. National Culture Commission, Bangkok.

GLOVER, I.C. & HIGHAM, C.F.W. 1996. New evidence for early rice cultivation in South, Southeast and East Asia. In D.R. Harris (ed.), *The Origins and Spread of Agriculture and Pastoralism in Eurasia* 413–41. University College London Press.

GORMAN, C.F. & CHAROENWONGSA, P. 1976. Ban Chiang: a mosaic of impressions from the first two years. *Expedition* 8, 14–26.

HA VAN TAN 1980. Nouvelles recherches préhistoriques et protohistoriques au Viet Nam, *Bull. École Franç. d'Extrême Orient* 68, 113–54.

HIGHAM, C.F.W. & BANNANURAG, R. 1990. *The Excavation of Khok Phanom Di, a Prehistoric Site in Central Thailand. Volume I: The Excavation, Chronology and Human Burials*. Society of Antiquaries of London, Research Report no. XLVII.

HIGHAM, C.F.W. & THOSARAT, R. (eds), 1998. *The Excavation of Nong Nor, a Prehistoric Site in Central Thailand*. Oxbow Books, Oxford and University of Otago Studies in Prehistoric Anthropology no. 18.

REID, L.A. 1993. Morphological evidence for Austric. *Oceanic Linguistics* 33, 323–44.

SCHAUFFLER, W. 1976. Archaeological survey and excavation of Ban Chiang culture sites Northeast Thailand. *Expedition* 18, 27–37.

WHITE, J.C. and PIGOTT, V.C. 1996. From community craft to regional specialization: intensification of copper production in pre-state Thailand. In B. Wailes (ed.), *Craft Specialization and Social Evolution: in Memory of V. Gordon Childe* 151–76. University of Pennsylvania.

YAN WENMING 1991. China's earliest rice agriculture remains. *Bulletin of the Indo-Pacific Prehistory Association* 10, 118–26.

YEN, D. E. 1977. Hoabinhian horticulture? The evidence and the questions from Northwest Thailand. In J. Allen, J. Golson and R. Jones, (eds), *Sunda and Sahul. Prehistoric Studies in Southeast Asia, Melanesia and Australia* 567–99. London: Academic Press.

Settlement and Palaeoecology in the Scandinavian Mesolithic

LARS LARSSON

IN PROFESSOR GRAHAME CLARK'S research, which was both thematically and geographically wide-ranging, he showed a special interest in the Scandinavian Mesolithic. With books such as *The Mesolithic Settlement of Northern Europe* from 1936 and *The Earlier Stone Age Settlement of Scandinavia* from 1975, he made research and finds from Scandinavia accessible to archaeologists elsewhere. These books were not just a presentation of the Scandinavian Mesolithic but also contained extensive research findings of his own, demonstrating his thorough familiarity with the material, together with a marvellous capacity for innovative thinking.

These books, like Grahame Clark's investigations in Star Carr (Clark 1954) and further analyses of the results (Clark 1972), were to serve as models for several generations of Mesolithic scholars in northern Europe and an encouragement to extend the forms of analysis. His ability to incorporate new patterns of thought, several generated by Clark himself, into the study of the Mesolithic showed that previously excavated settlement sites contained a constantly accumulating information potential. Clark's global vision (1961) also meant that archaeologists came into contact with new reference interfaces, and he personally helped Scandinavians to link their network of contacts to a larger archaeological community. I would also emphasize his significance as a source of inspiration in contacts with young scholars—a characteristic that I had the privilege of experiencing.

My aim here is to follow up certain themes that Grahame Clark considered to be of particular interest, and also to add data from some current research efforts of relevance to the subject of this article, settlement and palaeoecology in the Scandinavian Mesolithic.

Proceedings of the British Academy, **99**, 87–106

The Late Palaeolithic–Mesolithic transition

In his research concerning the Scandinavian Stone Age, Grahame Clark devoted special attention to the Late Palaeolithic and its relation to the Mesolithic (1975). New research findings have produced an image of a much more dynamic pattern than previously suspected. I therefore choose this transitional phase as my starting-point.

Detailed studies in the areas of quaternary geology and biology have been carried out over the last two decades in relation to Late Glacial conditions in southern Sweden. This means that we now have a good idea of deglaciation and palaeoecology (Berglund 1979; Berglund & Rapp 1988; Björck *et al.* 1988).

Scania, the southernmost province of Sweden, was the first part of southern Sweden from which the ice disappeared about 13,500 BP (all dates are uncalibrated). The deglaciation process during the Late Glacial can be monitored to Middle Sweden, where the melting of the ice ceased as the temperature fell during the Younger Dryas period (Figure 1). The Swedish west coast became ice-free earlier than the eastern Baltic coast. A certain delay in the melting of the ice occurred in the central area included in the South Swedish Upland, an area of primary rocks at about 300 m above sea level. Very rapid melting occurred mainly during the late Bølling period, at a rate that is estimated at its maximum to be about 50 km per century.

After a temporary advance of the ice sheet during the Younger Dryas there was continued deglaciation. Clay varve chronology suggests that the central part of northern Sweden was deglaciated around 8500 BP and that the whole of northern Sweden was free of ice around 8000 BP (Forsberg 1996).

The data which are actually available to us with regard to our interpretation of the palaeoecological conditions prevailing during the deglaciation phase are disparate. Insect studies give a picture that differs noticeably from the pollen analysis as far as the oldest chronozones are concerned.

Pollen analysis from the south-west of Sweden points to an ice-free Bølling period, with vegetation consisting of steppe tundra with elements of birch and sallow (Björck *et al.* 1988; Berglund & Rapp 1988). An increase in temperature is indicated as well as a rapid decrease during the Younger Dryas period. On the other hand, an analysis of the insect fauna in the Late Glacial deposits in Scania indicates that southern Sweden was subject to a noticeable rise in temperature at the end of the Bølling period (Lemdahl 1988). There is evidence of a certain decrease in temperature during the Allerød period and a distinct minimum temperature during the Younger Dryas period, and also of a sharp increase in temperature during the transition to the post-glacial period (Lemdahl 1991).

The earliest settlement of Scandinavia belongs to the Hamburgian cultures with sites in western as well as eastern Denmark (Holm 1996; Petersen & Johansen 1996) and somewhat later in southernmost Sweden (Larsson 1996). The Bromme culture is well represented in south-western Scandinavia (Fischer 1991; Larsson 1991b; 1996; Johansson 1996), as the formation of a land bridge at about 11,200 BP between present-day eastern Denmark

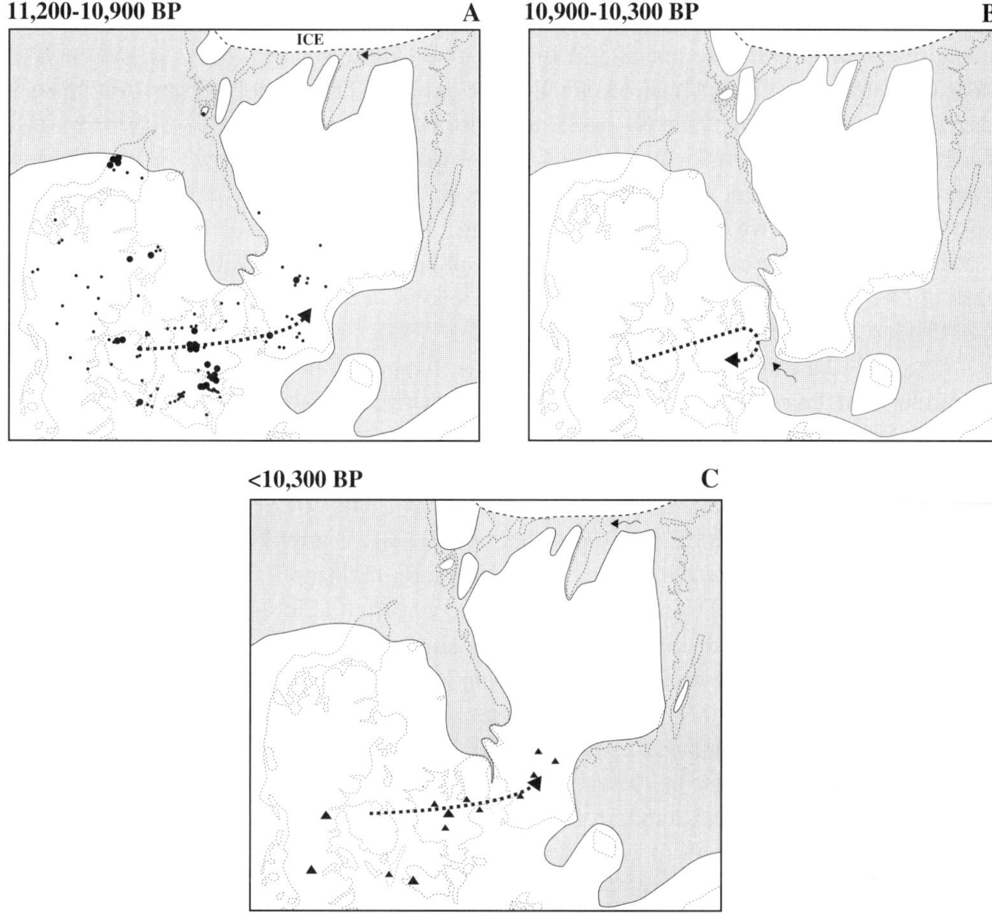

Figure 1. Different stages of the relation between land and water during the Late Palaeolithic and Early Mesolithic.

and southernmost Sweden made the movement of migrating animals from continental Europe much easier (Petersen & Johansen 1996) (see Figure 1A).

The development from the Late Palaeolithic into the Mesolithic has often been assigned to the start of the Holocene. How does this agree with new investigations?

The introduction of the Younger Dryas at about 10,900 BP was characterized by a sharp fall in temperature. The mean temperature during the summer may have fallen by as much as eight degrees over just a short period, perhaps within the course of a few decades (Lemdahl 1988). The former outflow of water in central Sweden was stopped by an advance of the ice at 10,800 BP (Björck 1996) (see Figure 1B). A new breakthrough of flowing water in Öresund, the sound that today separates Denmark and Sweden, may have had drastic or, more likely, catastrophic consequences for the fauna. A fall in temperature combined with the opening of the Öresund would probably have caused the total disappearance of the Boreal species which immigrated over the land bridge from present-day Denmark during the Alleröd interstadial. Reindeer and horse populations may have been severely reduced, reflected by the fact that datings of reindeer finds from southernmost Sweden are absent from this period. The ability to maintain continuous settlement east of the Öresund was very probably impaired.

During the latter part in the Younger Dryas, an increase in temperature initiated a withdrawal of the ice, a new outflow of the Baltic in central Sweden, and the formation of a land bridge at about 10,300 BP (see Figure 1C).

The increase in temperature might be linked to the establishment of the Ahrensburg culture in Scandinavia. Datings from northern Germany fall within the range 10,200–9,800 BP (Fischer & Tauber 1986). This coincides closely with the re-establishment of a land bridge in the Öresund.

Radiocarbon dates have shown that in Scania and part of eastern Denmark the reindeer survived into Pre-Boreal times until about 9600 BP (Aaris-Sørensen 1988; Liljegren & Ekström 1996). As a matter of fact, most radiocarbon dates of reindeer relate to a very late part of the Younger Dryas and early Pre-Boreal. That period saw the immigration of bison, wild horse, elk, red deer, wild boar, and aurochs (Liljegren & Ekström 1996). It is likely that a combination of Late Glacial fauna and new arrivals existed during the first half of the Pre-Boreal period. This should have given excellent conditions for human settlement. However, the remains of settlement from this timespan are very limited in south-western Scandinavia (Larsson 1996; Petersen & Johansen 1996).

In western Sweden and southern Norway the oldest coastal zone is located high above today's shoreline as a result of isostasy. Sites have been excavated which show a development from the Late Palaeolithic to the Mesolithic that has not yet been detected in southernmost Scandinavia (Schmitt 1994; Kindgren 1996). Several settlement sites along the former coast have proved to contain remains from the Ahrensburg culture. The Galta site at Stavanger in south-west Norway shows a typical and rich inventory of finds from this culture (Bang-Andersen 1996; Prøsch-Danielsen & Høgestøl 1995). But the traditions from the Ahrensburg culture extend much further than this. According to ^{14}C datings, the oldest settlement in northern Norway, 1600 km towards the north-east, took place shortly after the first colonization of southern Norway (Bjerck 1995; Thommessen 1996) (Figure 2). This occurred in areas with a rich marine environment but along a coast from which the land ice still was fully visible. This shows that colonization took place very quickly and shortly after the coast had been freed from land ice. The terrestrial resources were thus not considered interesting.

The Ahrensburgian is the first north European culture from which coastal as well as inland sites are known. This makes it a culture of special interest for detailed study.

The question is whether the rapid colonization was the result of new adaptation to the special coastal conditions in connection with deglaciation (Bjerck 1995), or derived from

Figure 2. Sites marking the earliest settlement along the coast of western Scandinavia.

a coastal settlement going back much further in time (Fischer 1996a). We cannot answer this question at the moment, owing to the unfortunate lack of remains of coastal settlement from the Upper Palaeolithic in other parts of western Europe. This is because there have been no deliberate searches in marine environments.

In inland sites of south-west Norway, a mixture of small tanged points, single-edge points, and microliths has been found. Radiocarbon dates cluster between 9600 and 9400 BP for samples from all the encampments (Bang-Andersen 1990). This can probably be taken as the time during which traditions from the Ahrensburg culture were replaced by a material culture corresponding to that of the Early Mesolithic, not only in western Norway but in most of Scandinavia too. In south-west Scandinavia the introduction of a new material culture appears to coincide with the disappearance of the last reindeer. In northern continental Europe a conscious replacement of the material culture can be linked to a change of fauna and flora. In Scandinavia the ecological shift is not as clear as it used to seem, with a much longer succession phase than has previously been claimed.

In Denmark the oldest settlement sites with unequivocal Mesolithic tool-kits are dated around 9400 BP, while the well-known aurochs from Vig, which was perforated by points fitted with microliths, is dated to 9500 BP (Fischer 1996a). The oldest evidence of the bog sites so familiar from the southern Scandinavian Mesolithic is found at Barmosen in southern Zealand, dated to 9300 BP (Johansson 1990; Fischer 1996a).

Submerged settlement during the Early Mesolithic

Although the number of Pre-Boreal sites in southernmost Scandinavia has increased in recent years, they are surprisingly few in relation to the Boreal sites. As is evident from the remains from further north in western Sweden, the coast appears to have exerted a great attraction to the settlers, borne out by the large number of sites (Kindgren 1995; Nordqvist 1995). But was the inland as empty as the finds suggest? The lack of finds is probably due to the unrepresentative source material. One explanation may be that precipitation was low and that several lakes had a very low water level. Sites beside the lake shore or on layers where lakes were becoming filled in, may today be covered with later sediment deposited at higher water levels and thus very difficult to detect (Larsson 1993).

Settlement during a somewhat later stage is characterized in southern Scandinavia chiefly by the inland bog sites well known because of the good preservation of organic material (Larsson 1990), as Clark showed very well in his research. At this time large areas of south-west Scandinavia were inundated. The melting of the land ice over northern Scandinavia combined with rapid isostatic uplift resulted in large parts of the present-day southern Baltic becoming under water (Björck 1995).

Especially in Late Boreal times there was a large rise in sea level which brought the surface of the water from a position of more than 20 m below present level to only a few metres below this in just a few centuries (Christensen 1995). To shed light on coastal settlement during this phase, attention may be directed to Öresund. During the Early Mesolithic this sound was a deep and narrow bay of the North Sea (Figure 3). It is evident from the topography of the sea bed that the bay contained a true archipelago. A rapid rise in the water level caused the bay to enlarge, at the same time as islands were submerged. A number of submerged areas with layers of peat and gyttja on the bottom of the Öresund show that this area, before it became a marine bay, contained a number of freshwater basins, which were gradually transformed into lagoons before finally being inundated (Mörner 1969; Larsson 1978). The area contained several biotopes which made it attractive for settlement.

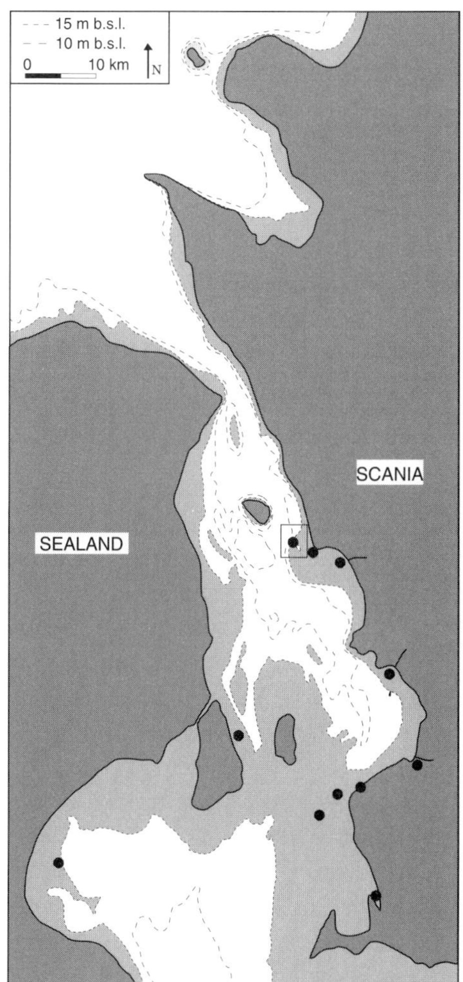

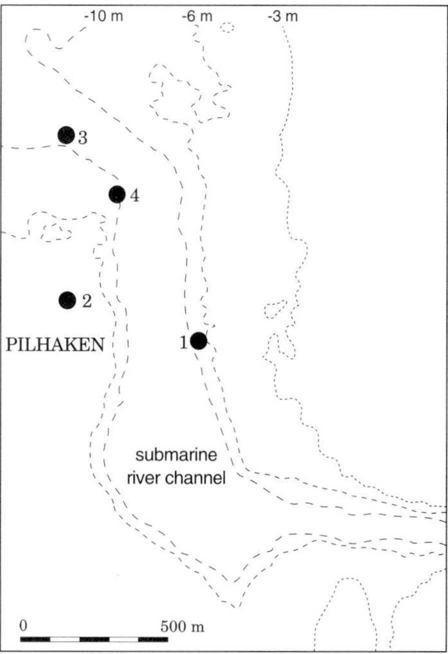

Figure 3. Submerged Late Palaeolithic and Early Mesolithic settlement sites in Öresund, the sound between present-day Denmark and Sweden.

Due to considerable rises in sea level during the Late Boreal and Atlantic, very little evidence of coastal settlement during the Early Post-Glacial in southern Scandinavia remains. It is only during a later part of the Boreal, about 8000 BP, that our knowledge of the southernmost part of Sweden improves. In order to obtain information on coastal settlement forms during the Early Mesolithic, marine archaeological investigations have been carried out on the Swedish side. They were concentrated on what is now a submarine furrow corresponding to the prehistoric course of the river Saxån (Figure 3). Along this river, both surveys and investigations have revealed a number of Late Mesolithic sites close to the present shoreline. From the study of sea charts, it was possible to trace the former course of the river, as well as submarine elevations and depressions. Areas of particular interest in a submarine context were noted. These were sampled, both from on board ship and with the aid of divers. During this phase of our tentative investigations, at least four Early Mesolithic sites were recorded, the depths of which varied between 20 and 6 m below surface level (Larsson 1983; Larsson in print). The best preserved site, Pilhaken 4 (Figure 3), which is partially stratified in peat, is situated at a depth of 7 to 8 m and has been dated to about 8000 BP. The muddy layer could be observed as a horizon in the steeply sloping submarine course of the river. The part nearest the course of the river channel is exposed to continuous erosion. With large-capacity nozzles and the resulting back-suction, small trenches were dug. The stratigraphy consisted of alternate layers of mud and sand. The find material consists of flint artefacts from the Late Maglemose Culture, and bones from roe deer, red deer, and aurochs were found (Larsson in print). The layers of peat were deposited in a comparatively well-protected basin, possibly in a part of the delta that may have included the former mouth of the river Saxån.

Surveys of the sea bed in the southern part of the sound, in the vicinity of the location of the former land bridge between Denmark and Sweden, were carried out in 1992–94 in conjunction with prospecting for the bridge to be built over the Öresund. Flint artefacts were found in a significant number of test pits, pointing to the fact that the area had been occupied (Larsson in print). None of these flints could be confirmed with certainty as *in situ* finds. Most also bore traces of rolling and saltwater patination. Such traces were absent from a small number of flints, however. These finds indicate that undisturbed find-bearing layers had been eroded quite recently, or that they may still exist in particularly well-protected areas. We were unable to identify any such find location, however, during the trial investigation.

The find material includes artefacts from a late part of the Boreal and the earlier part of the Atlantic, that is, a late part of the Maglemose Culture. The finds emerged at a depth of between 9 and 5 m (Fischer 1995). Roots of trees descending into the clay at the base of trial pits to a depth of approximately 6 m have been dated to 7800 BP (Fischer 1996b). The ingression threshold in the Öresund lies just below this level, which indicates that significant quantities of saltwater found their way into the Baltic Basin at that time.

There are several attested examples of inundated coastal settlement. During dredging work to extend the harbours, surveying for sites in the vicinity of the line of the proposed

Öresund Bridge, together with marine archaeological research focused on much younger barriers and unloading places, traces of settlement have been found at a depth of between 5 m and 1 m below present-day sea level (Fischer 1995; Larsson in print).

The results of these investigations provide the basis for an argument that coastal settlement during the Boreal was just as intensive as that which is well documented for the hinterland. The location in the outer parts of the course of a river or in bays points to a position entirely in accordance with the position in which settlements from the Late Mesolithic are found. This indicates that the choice of settlement site was dictated by the same factors as those which governed Late Mesolithic man. Whether these Early Mesolithic settlements were as extensive and of as permanent a character as that attributed to their later variants is a question to which we are still unable to provide a satisfactory answer. The sites investigated have suffered erosion, which has partially or totally disturbed the original find picture.

The fact that organic material is almost entirely absent rules out the possibility of using these find locations to provide an indication of the importance of marine food in the subsistence strategy. In this context, values from analyses of the ^{13}C content may give some indication of the composition of the diet. A human skull found at a depth of 10 m in the southern part of Öresund, dated to the Late Boreal, showed a ^{13}C value of –14.7‰ (Tauber 1989). In this case the dominance of a marine diet is obvious. However, ^{13}C analyses of human skeletal material from a small Danish cemetery found in the vicinity of a site dating from the Late Maglemose Culture in the Holmegaard Mose bog on Zealand, situated about 30 km inland, show low ^{13}C values, which means that the inhabitants of the site had no great contact with the coast and marine resources (Tauber 1986). This may be taken as an indication of specific resource structures typical of the coast and inland areas.

New results of ^{13}C analyses of dog bones from the Late Mesolithic, from Jutland in western Denmark, give further support for this view (Noe-Nygaard 1988). It turns out that dogs from the inland area had low ^{13}C values, indicating a terrestrial diet, while coastal dogs had high values from a diet of marine sources (Larsson 1991a).

We have to re-examine the frequently used settlement model for the Mesolithic. This includes a social exploitation system where base camps are situated on the coast and the inland area is used only temporarily (Larsson 1978). Perhaps it is the case that both in the latter part of the Early Mesolithic and in the Late Mesolithic there were two separate ethnic groups, one on the coast and one at least 30 km further inland (Larsson 1980).

Late Mesolithic—graves in the society

The Late Atlantic transgressions and their effect in southern Scandinavia on remains of settlement above the present-day sea level have been well known for a long time, not least as a result of Grahame Clark's publications. The shell middens in western Denmark have been a noted phenomenon for more than 150 years. However, new, goal-directed investigations have shown that they contain a great deal of previously unrecognized information about, for example, duration of use, resource utilization, and settlement structure (Andersen & Johansen 1987; Enghoff 1987; Brock & Bourget 1991; Andersen 1993; 1995). Several examples show that one must be very attentive in dealing with relations between settlement patterns and palaeoecological factors. The choice of settlement site may be influenced by conditions that cannot be related to the immediate environment of the site. For instance, a predominant proportion of the fishing reflected in the shell midden at Ertebølle was done in freshwater in the inland, not in the nearby marine environment.

Our knowledge of Late Mesolithic coastal settlement has been further expanded thanks to the results obtained from marine archaeological investigations of coastal sites in southwest Denmark which have been submerged as a result of later isostatic subsidence (Andersen 1987; Skaarup 1995). The exceptional preservation conditions here have given us a deeper knowledge of the material culture, exemplified in organic material.

Figure 4. Grave from the Late Mesolithic cemetery Skateholm II, in southernmost Sweden.

Cemeteries in eastern Denmark, Bøgebakken (Albrethsen & Petersen 1977), and southernmost Sweden, on three sites at Skateholm (Larsson 1984) (Figure 4), are a Late Mesolithic phenomenon whose implications for research into the transition to the Neolithic have been emphasized by several archaeologists (Chapman 1981; Price 1985; Price & Petersen 1987). It should be pointed out, however, that Clark already stressed the significant role of the graves in Mesolithic society for the study of the same phenomenon (Clark 1980).

The number of attested cemeteries has increased in recent years, which shows that they were common in the Late Mesolithic (Figure 5). One or more graves have been found at other sites at the mouth of the lagoon at Vedbæk in eastern Zealand, on which Bøgebakken is situated; examples of these include a couple of previously known graves at Vedbæk Boldbaner (Mathiassen 1946) or at Gøngehusvej, which have been investigated in more recent years (Petersen 1990; Petersen *et al.* 1993). These show that the cremation burial practice predominated in the oldest cemeteries which can be dated to the period 7000–6000 BP (Petersen 1990). A mass grave containing eight people at Støby Egede (Petersen 1988) on the east coast of Denmark completes our picture of Mesolithic burial practices. The interred were divided up by sex into two groups of the same size, which had been deposited at opposite ends of the grave.

Individual graves, or groups comprising a small number of graves, have also been found in the shell middens in east Jutland (Rasmussen 1990). Recent years have seen investigations of several graves in a shell midden at Nederst in east Jutland (Petersen 1988; 1989).

The Danish material is quite extensive if one adds previously known graves such as Korsør Nor on the west coast of Zealand (Hansen *et al.* 1972) and Blokbjerg (Westerby 1927) and new finds at Nivaagård on the east coast (Nielsen & Petersen 1993) and at the submarine sites of Tybrind Vig (Andersen 1987) and Møllegabet II on Funen (Grøn & Skaarup 1993). Individual graves occur in Sweden, such as Uleberg on the west coast (Wigforss 1968) and Stora Bjärs and Lummelunda on the island of Gotland (Arwidsson 1949; 1979; Larsson 1982). Only in the latter case, dated to around 7000 BC, can the three people identified be regarded as having been buried in a cemetery of any size. Investigations in conjunction with the individual grave finds, in both Denmark and Sweden, were far too limited to permit a reliable conclusion to be reached as to whether the graves were isolated or were included in actual cemeteries.

In parts of southern Scandinavian about two-thirds of the landscape disappeared beneath the water during the Late Boreal and the Early Atlantic period. This should not be regarded as ecologically critical for the hunter-gatherer societies. New, abundant fishing environments are formed just as quickly as old ones disappear. The social aspect ought to be far more interesting to study. These changes were so drastic that their effects must have been clearly identifiable in the landscape. Being forced to change one's physical map from one generation to the next probably also had consequences for the mental map. Fishing on a shallow bank on which previous generations were known to have lived must have produced a significant effect on the conceptual world. Stresses were thus of both a physical and a mental nature.

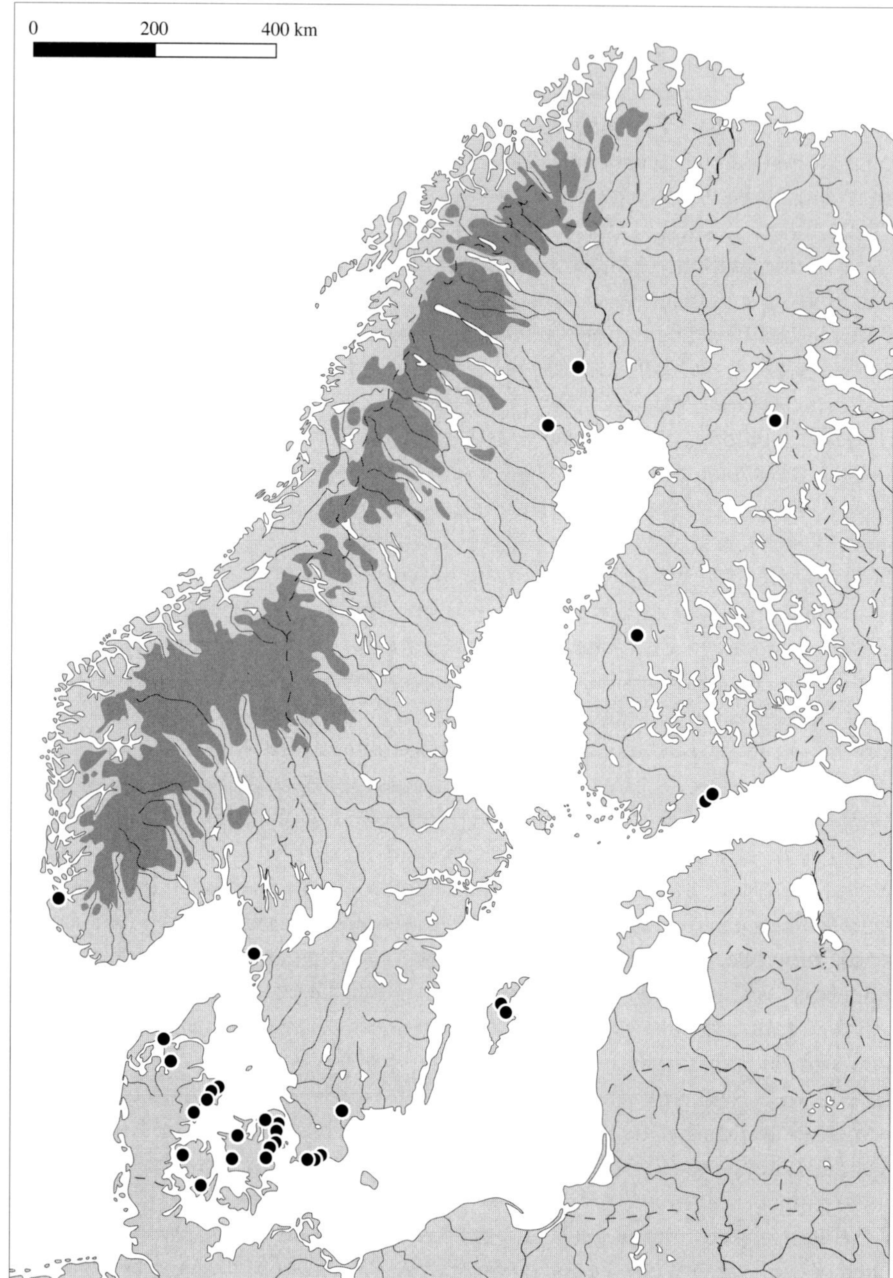

Figure 5. Sites with cemeteries or indications of cemeteries in the Mesolithic of Scandinavia.

The territorial perspective which we so often associate with stress symptoms between groups of people may also have had another dimension. The conceptual world in the Mesolithic no doubt contained various oppositions, with a clear dualism between the tame and the wild being an important element (Hodder 1990). In most examples of Neolithization in continental Europe, change takes place in mainland environments and involves relatively small alterations to the environment. The greatest changes that take place are thus the consequence of human activity. In southern Scandinavia, on the other hand, the greatest environmental changes take place in the natural environment. Perhaps we are dealing with a form of territorial marking here, which may be aimed less obviously against other societies and more against the changeability of nature which threatens the social and mental situation of mankind. Could it be that the establishment of cemeteries quite simply represents an attempt to halt changing nature—an attempt to bring about a *status quo*? Greater consideration must be given in future analyses to the mental relationship between the people and the environment, in order to fully appreciate the Late Mesolithic coastal societies.

A northern perspective

Findings concerning the southern Scandinavian Mesolithic have by tradition been more widely known than the results of investigations from further north. In his book *The Earlier Stone Age Settlement of Scandinavia* (1975) Grahame Clark helped to rectify this imbalance. In recent years, knowledge of the Mesolithic in northernmost Scandinavia has increased significantly (Nygaard 1989; Woodman 1993; Olsen 1994; Forsberg 1996; Hesjedal *et al.* 1996).

In northern Sweden this is due to increased archaeological activity combined with extensive surveys (Forsberg 1996; Halén 1994). A better understanding of isostatic uplift has also contributed to the surer identification of Mesolithic coastal levels, which today can lie more than 100 km from the present-day coast.

Several distinct house structures have been excavated at sites in northern Scandinavia. They consist of sunken house foundations surrounded by a rim with dug-up soil and waste. In northern Sweden house foundations with a length of 11 m have been excavated, yielding evidence of complex heating systems with smoke ducts under the floor (Loeffler & Westfal 1985). Accumulations of house remains with village-like structure have also been observed (Halén 1994).

At roughly the same time as the art of ceramic fabrication reached southern Scandinavia and resulted in the so-called Ertebølle pottery, ceramics appeared in northern Sweden through the spread of combed ware with rich decoration from Finland and north-west Russia. In recent years, graves, in a few cases in cemetery-like assemblages beside settlement sites belonging to the Late Mesolithic, have also been documented in northernmost Sweden (Halén 1994; 1995) (Figure 5). In certain cases they are furnished with a marking in the form of stone paving above ground. In a grave from Manjärv in north-east

Norrland there were two burials in the same pit, strewn with rich quantities of red ochre (Liedgren 1993). The grave is dated to 6000 BP. This form of grave is linked to similar phenomena at several places in Finland (Edgren 1993) (Figure 5). The northern Scandinavian Mesolithic is quickly on its way to becoming at least as rich in information as the Mesolithic further south.

On the margin

In the study of the Mesolithic, our perspective on society and environment has been broadened by creative efforts in both theory and method. In some cases, new points of view can

Figure 6. A flake deposit from Rönneholm moor, southernmost Sweden.

Figure 7. (*Above*) Stone with rock carvings and (*below*) an example of the illustrations from stones found between sunken house foundations at Slettnes, northern Norway. (*Source*: Hesjedal *et al.* 1996.)

be obtained by choosing new ways to excavate a settlement site. The importance of excavating on the periphery of the site will be illustrated by two interesting finds, one from the south and one from the north. In the central part of Scania, Sweden's southernmost province, excavations were conducted in summer 1997, occasioned by peat-cutting within the central part of a 12 km^2 area of the Ageröd and Rönneholm bog (Larsson 1978). In Early Atlantic times, around 7500 BP, there was a small island here which was used temporarily as a camp. Several small accumulations of flint material—the chemical composition of the peat does not allow the preservation of bone but wood does survive—have been attested. We are dealing with short-term visits which resulted in hearths with traces of activity around them. In one case the spread of flint clearly marks the limit of a hut structure which is moreover attested by means of surviving posts. On the periphery of the flint concentrations there are special accumulations of large, worked flint cores—often combined with a couple of knapping stones. In one case an assemblage of blades was dug up. There was a total of 106 blades, of which the longest is 16 cm (Figure 6). The blades can be refitted onto four cores and it is evident that the blades were placed beside each other in the cluster as they were struck. Was it the intention to use the blades later, or are they an offering to higher powers?

The northern example comes from Slettnes, a long-term settlement site on an island in northernmost Norway (Hesjedal *et al.* 1996). Here too there are sunken house foundations from the Late Mesolithic, of the kind previously mentioned from northern Sweden. To obtain a better insight into the relations between different house foundations, not only these were excavated but also the area between them. This yielded five large rocks with extensive carvings which were covered with littoral gravel from a later transgression (Figure 7). Although the place was in an archipelago setting, the carved motifs, which can be dated around 8500 BP, contain only examples of forest animals. These finds show what an enlargement of the excavated area may reveal, and also that out here on an island in the archipelago, with a rich marine fauna, people ate fish but thought about elk and bear.

References

AARIS-SØRENSEN, K. 1988. *Danmarks forhistoriske Dyreverden. Fra Istid til Vikingetid.* København: Gyldendal.

ALBRETHSEN, S.E. & PETERSEN, E.B. 1977. Excavation of a Mesolithic cemetery at Vedbæk, Denmark. *Acta Archaeologica* 47, 1–28.

ANDERSEN, S.H. 1987. Tybrind Vig: a submerged Ertebølle settlement in Denmark. In J.M. Coles & A. J. Lawson (eds), *European Wetlands in Prehistory*, 253–80. Oxford: Clarendon Press.

ANDERSEN, S.H. 1993. Bjørnsholm. A stratified Køkkenmødding on the Central Limfjord, North Jutland. *Journal of Danish Archaeology* 10 (1991), 59–96.

ANDERSEN, S. H. 1995. Coastal adaptation and marine exploitation in Late Mesolithic Denmark—with special emphasis on the Limfjord region. In A. Fischer (ed.), *Man and Sea in the Mesolithic. Coastal settlement above and below present sea level*, 41–66. Oxford: Oxbow Monograph 53.

ANDERSEN, S.H. & JOHANSEN, E. 1987. Ertebølle revisited. *Journal of Danish Archaeology* 5 (1986), 31–61.

ARWIDSSON, G. 1949. Stenåldersfynden från Kams i Lummelunda. *Gotländskt Arkiv* XX, 147–67.

ARWIDSSON, G. 1979. Stenåldersmannen från Stora Bjärs i Stenkyrka. *Arkeologi på Gotland*, 17–23. Visby: Gotlandica 14.

BANG-ANDERSEN, S. 1990. The Myrvatn Group, a Preboreal find-complex in Southwest Norway. In P.M. Vermeersch & P. Van Peer (eds), *Contributions to the Mesolithic in Europe. Papers presented at the Fourth International Symposium 'The Mesolithic in Europe', Leuven 1990*, 215–26. Leuven: Studia Praehistorica Belgica 5.

BANG-ANDERSEN, S. 1996. The colonization of Southwest Norway. An ecological approach. In L. Larsson (ed.), *The Earliest Settlement of Scandinavia and its Relationship with Neighbouring Areas*, 220–34. Lund: Acta Archaeologica Lundensia 8:24.

BERGLUND, B. 1979. The deglaciation of southern Sweden 13,500–10,000 B.P. *Boreas* 8, 89–118.

BERGLUND, B. & RAPP, A. 1988. Geomorphology, climate and vegetation in NW Scania, Sweden, during the Late Weichselian. *Geographia Polonica* 55, 13–35.

BJERCK, H.B. 1995. The North Sea and the pioneer settlement of Norway. In A. Fischer (ed.), *Man and Sea in the Mesolithic. Coastal settlement above and below sea level*, 131–44. Oxford: Oxbow Monograph 53.

BJÖRCK, S. 1995. Late Weichselian to early Holocene development of the Baltic Sea—with implications for coastal settlement in the southern Baltic region. In A. Fischer (ed.), *Man and Sea in the Mesolithic. Coastal settlement above and below present sea level*, 23–34. Oxford: Oxbow Monograph 53.

BJÖRCK, S. 1996. Late Weichselian/Early Preboreal development of the Öresund Strait; a key area for northerly mammal migration. In L. Larsson (ed.), *The Earliest Settlement of Scandinavia and its Relationship with Neighbouring Areas*, 123–34. Lund: Acta Archaeologica Lundensia 8:24.

BJÖRCK, S., BERGLUND, B. & DIGERFELDT, G. 1988. New aspects on the deglaciation chronology of South Sweden. *Geographia Polonica* 55, 37–49.

BROCK, V. & BOURGET, E. 1991. Analyses of shell increment and microgrowth band formation to establish seasonality of Mesolithic shellfish collection. *Journal of Danish Archaeology* 8, 7–12.

CHAPMAN, R. 1981. The emergence of formal disposal areas and the 'problem' of the megalithic tombs in prehistoric Europe. In R. Chapman, R. Kinnes & K. Randsborg (eds), *The Archaeology of Death*, 71–81. Cambridge: Cambridge University Press.

CHRISTENSEN, C. 1995. The littorina transgressions in Denmark. In A. Fischer (ed.), *Man and Sea in the Mesolithic. Coastal settlement above and below present sea level*, 15–22. Oxford: Oxbow Monograph 53.

CLARK, J.G.D. 1936. *The Mesolithic Settlement of Northern Europe*. Cambridge: Cambridge University Press.

CLARK, J.G.D. 1952. *Prehistoric Europe: The Economic Basis*. London: Methuen.

CLARK, J.G.D. 1954. *Excavations at Star Carr. An early Mesolithic Site at Seamar near Scarborough, Yorkshire*. Cambridge: Cambrige University Press.

CLARK, J.G.D. 1961. *World Prehistory: An Outline*. Cambridge: Cambridge University Press.

CLARK, J.G.D. 1972. *Star Carr: a Case Study in Bioarchaeology*. Reading, Mass.: Addison-Wesley Modular Publications. Module 10.

CLARK, J.G.D. 1975. *The Earlier Stone Age Settlement of Scandinavia*. Cambridge: Cambridge University Press.

CLARK, J.G.D. 1980. *Mesolithic Prelude. The Palaeolithic–Neolithic Transition in the Old World*. Edinburgh: Edinburgh University Press.

EDGREN, T. 1993. Den förhistoriska tiden. In *Finlands historia. Del 1*, 11–270. Ekenäs.

ENGHOFF, I.B. 1987. Freshwater fishing from a sea-coast settlement—the Ertebølle *locus classicus* revisited. *Journal of Danish Archaeology* 5 (1986), 62–76.

FISCHER, A. 1991. Pioneers in deglaciated landscapes: The expansion and adaptation of Late Palaeolithic societies in Southern Scandinavia. In N. Barton, A.J. Roberts & D.E. Roe (eds), *The Late Glacial in North-West Europe: Human Adaptation and Environmental Change at the End of the Pleistocene*, 100–21. London: CBA Research Report 77.

FISCHER, A. 1995. An entrance to the Mesolithic world below the ocean. Status of ten years' work on the Danish sea floor. In A. Fisher (ed.), *Man and Sea in the Mesolithic. Coastal settlement above and below present sea level*, 371–84. Oxford: Oxbow Monograph 53.

FISCHER, A. 1996a. At the border of human habitat. The Late Palaeolithic and Early Mesolithic in Scandinavia. In L. Larsson (ed.), *The Earliest Settlement of Scandinavia and its Relationship with Neighbouring Areas*, 157–76. Lund: Acta Archaeologica Lundensia 8:24.

FISCHER, A. 1996b. Rødder og stubbe af havsoplugte treer. *Marinarkæologiske rekognosceringer efter fredede vrag og fortidsminder i højbrotraceet* 41–43. København: Miljø- og Energiministeriet, Skov- og Naturstyrelsen.

FISCHER, A. & TAUBER, H. 1986. New C-14 datings of the Late Palaeolithic cultures from Northwestern Europe. *Journal of Danish Archaeoogy* 5, 7–13.

FORSBERG, L. 1996. The earliest settlement of Northern Sweden—problems and perspectives. In L. Larsson (ed.), *The Earliest Settlement of Scandinavia and its Relationship with Neighbouring Areas*, 241–50. Lund: Acta Archaeologica Lundensia 8:24.

GRØN, O. & SKAARUP, J. 1993. Møllegabet II—a submerged Mesolithic site and a 'boat burial' from Ærø. *Journal of Danish Archaeology* 10 (1991), 38–50.

HALÉN, O. 1994. *Sedentariness during the Stone Age of Northern Sweden. In the light of the Alträsket site, c.5000 B.C., and the Comb Ware site Lillberget, c.3900 B.C. Source Critical Problems of Representativity in Archaeology.* Lund: Acta Archaeologica Lundensia. 4:20.

HALÉN, O. 1995. Alträsket—a Mesolithic coastal site in the northernmost Sweden, 25 km inland, and 100 m above the present sea. In A. Fischer (ed.), *Man and Sea in the Mesolithic. Coastal settlement above and below present sea level*, 229–39. Oxford: Oxbow Monograph 53.

HANSEN, U.L., VAGN NIELSEN, O. & ALEXANDERSEN, V. 1972. A Mesolithic grave from Melby in Zealand, Danmark. *Acta Archaeologica* XLIII, 239–49.

HESJEDAL, A., DAMM, C., OLSEN, B. & STORLI, I. 1996. *Arkeologi på Slettnes. Dokumentasjon av 11.000 års bosetning.* Tromsø: Tromsø Museums Skrifter XXVI.

HODDER, I. 1990. *The Domestication of Europe. Structure and Contingency in Neolithic Societies.* Oxford: Basil Blackwell.

HOLM, J. 1996. The earliest settlement of Denmark. In L. Larsson (ed.), *The Earliest Settlement of Scandinavia and its Relationship with Neighbouring Areas*, 43–59. Lund: Acta Archaeologica Lundensia 8:24.

JOHANSSON, A.D. 1990. *Baremose-gruppen. Skiveokser i tidligmesolitiske fundkomplekser.* Århus.

JOHANSSON, A.D. 1996. A base camp and kill sites from the Bromme Culture on South Zealand, Denmark. In L. Larsson (ed.), *The Earliest Settlement of Scandinavia and its Relationship with Neighbouring Areas*, 89–97. Lund: Acta Archaeologica Lundensia 8:24.

KINDGREN, H. 1995. Hensbacka-Hogen-Hornborgasjön: Early Mesolithic coastal and inland settlements in western Sweden. In A. Fischer (ed.), *Man and Sea in the Mesolithic. Coastal settlement above and below present sea level*, 171–84. Oxford: Oxbow Monograph 53.

KINDGREN, H. 1996. Reindeer or seals? Some Late Palaeolithic sites in central Bohuslän. In L. Larsson (ed.), *The Earliest Settlement of Scandinavia and its Relationship with Neighbouring Areas*, 191–205. Lund: Acta Archaeologica Lundensia 8:24.

LARSSON, L. 1978. *Ageröd I:B—Ageröd I:D. A Study of Early Atlantic Settlement in Scania.* Lund: Acta Archaeologica Lundensia 4:12.

LARSSON, L. 1980. Aspects of the Kongemose Culture of Southern Sweden. *Papers of the Archaeological Institute of Lund* 3 (1979–1980), 5–22.

LARSSON, L. 1982. De äldsta gutarna. *Gotländskt Arkiv* 54, 7–14.

LARSSON, L. 1983. Mesolithic settlement on the sea floor in the Strait of Öresund. In P.M. Masters & N.C. Flemming (eds), *Quaternary Coastlines and Marine Archaeology*, 283–301. New York: Academic Press.

LARSSON, L. 1984. The Skateholm Project. A Late Mesolithic settlement and cemetery complex at a south Swedish bay. *Papers of the Archaeological Institute University of Lund* 1983–1984, 5–38.

LARSSON, L. 1990. The Mesolithic of Southern Scandinavia. *Journal of World Prehistory* 4:3, 257–309.

LARSSON, L. 1991a. Coastal adaptation in the Early and Middle Holocene of Southern Scandinavia. *Journal of Korean Ancient Historical Society Hanguk Sanggosa Hakbo* 8, 93–118.

LARSSON, L. 1991b. The Late Palaeolithic in southern Sweden: investigation in a marginal region. In N. Barton, A.J. Roberts & D.A. Roe (eds), *The Late Glacial in North-West Europe: Human Adaptation and Environmental Change at the End of the Pleistocene*, 122–7. Oxford: CBA Research Report no. 77.

LARSSON, L. 1993. Review of Johansson, A. D. Barmosegruppen. Præboreale bopladsfund i Sydsjælland. *Journal of Danish Archaeology* 10 (1991), 215–17.

LARSSON, L. 1996. The colonization of South Sweden during the Deglaciation. In L. Larsson (ed.), *The Earliest Settlement of Scandinavia and its Relationship with Neighbouring Areas*, 141–55. Lund: Acta Archaeologica Lundensia 8:24.

LARSSON, L. 1998. Submarine settlement remains on the bottom of the Öresund Strait, Southern Scandinavia. *Epipaléolithique et Mésolithique en Europe. Paléoenvironnement, peuplements et systèmes culturels.* Grenoble. In print.

LEMDAHL, G. 1988. *Palaeoclimatic and Palaeoecological Studies based upon Subfossil Insects from Late Weichselian Sediments in Southern Sweden.* Lund: Lundqua Thesis 22.

LEMDAHL, G. 1991. A rapid climatic change at the end of the Younger Dryas in south Sweden—palaeoclimatic and palaeoenvironmental reconstructions based on fossil insect assemblages. *Palaeogeography, Palaeoclimatology, Palaeoecology* 83, 313–31.

LIEDGREN, L. 1993. Rödockragravar från stenåldern. *Populär Arkeologi* 1993:2, 28–9.

LILJEGREN, R. & EKSTRÖM, J. 1996. The terrestrial Late Glacial fauna in South Sweden. In L. Larsson (ed.), *The Earliest Settlement of Scandinavia and its Relationship with Neighbouring Areas*, 135–9. Lund: Acta Archaeologica Lundensia 8:24.

LOEFFLER, D. & WESTFAL, U. 1985. A well-preserved Stone Age dwelling site. Preliminary presentation of the investigation at Vuollerim, Lapland, Sweden. *Archaeology and Environment* 4, 425–34.

MATHIASSEN, T. 1946. En boplads fra ældre stenalder ved Vedbæk Boldbaner. *Søllerødbogen* 1946, 19–35.

MÖRNER, N.-A. 1969. *The Late Quaternary History of the Kattegatt Sea and the Swedish West Coast. Deglaciation, Shorelevel Displacement, Chronology, Isostasy and Eustasy.* Stockholm: Sveriges Geologiska Undersökning Ser. C. Nr 640.

NIELSEN, E.K. & PETERSEN, E.B. 1993. Grave, mennesker og hunde. In S. Hvass & B. Storgaard (eds), *Da klinger i muld . . . 25 års arkæologi i Danmark*, 76–81. Aarhus: Konglige Nordiske Oldskriftselskabet.

NOE-NYGAARD, N. 1988. 13 C values of dog bones reveal the nature of changes in Man's food resources at the Mesolithic–Neolithic transition, Denmark. *Isotope Geoscience* 73, 87–96.

NORDQVIST, B. 1995. The Mesolithic settlement of the west coast of Sweden—with special emphasis on chronology and topography of coastal settlements. In A. Fischer (ed.), *Man and Sea in the*

Mesolithic. Coastal settlement above and below present sea level, 185–96. Oxford: Oxbow Monograph 53.

NYGAARD, S.E. 1989. The Stone Age of Northern Scandinavia: a review. *Journal of World Prehistory* 1989:3, 71–116.

OLSEN, B. 1994. *Bosetning og samfunn i Finnmarks forhistorie.* Oslo: Universitetsforlaget.

PETERSEN, E.B. 1988. Ein mesolithisches Grab mit acht Personen von Strøby Egede, Seeland. *Archäologisches Korrespondenzblatt* 18, Heft. 2, 121–5.

PETERSEN, E.B. 1989. Late Palaeolithic and Mesolithic. *Arkæologiske udgravninger i Danmark 1988*, 73–5. København: Det Arkæologiske Nævn.

PETERSEN, E.B. 1990. Nye graver fra Jægerstenalderen. Strøby Egede og Vedbæk. *Nationalmuseets Arbejdsmark*, 19–33.

PETERSEN, E.B., ALEXANDERSEN, V. & MEIKLEJOHN, C. 1993. Vedbæk, graven midt i byen. *Nationalmuseets Arbejdsmark* 1993, 61–9.

PETERSEN, P.V. & JOHANSEN, L. 1996. Tracking Late Glacial reindeer hunters in eastern Denmark. In L. Larsson (ed.), *The Earliest Settlement of Scandinavia and its Relationship with Neighbouring Areas*, 75–88. Lund: Acta Archaeologica Lundensia 8:24.

PRICE, D.T. 1985. Affluent foragers of Mesolithic Southern Scandinavia. In D.T. Price & J.A. Brown (eds), *Prehistoric Hunter-Gatherers. The Emergence of Cultural Complexity*, 341–63. New York: Academic Press.

PRICE, D.T. & PETERSEN, E.B. 1987. Prehistoric coastal settlement in Mesolithic Denmark. *Scientific American* 112–21.

PRØSCH-DANIELSEN, L. & HØGESTØL, M. 1995. A coastal Ahrensburgian site found at Galta, Rennesøy, Southwest Norway. In A. Fischer (ed.), *Man and Sea in the Mesolithic. Coastal settlement above and below present sea level*, 123–30. Oxford: Oxbow Monograph 53.

RASMUSSEN, G.H. 1990. Okkergrave fra ældre stenalder på Djursland. *Kuml* 1988–89, 31–41.

SCHMITT, L. 1994. The Hensbacka: A subsistence stategy of continental hunter-gatherers, or an adaptation at the Pleistocene-Holocene boundary? *Oxford Journal of Archaeology* 13:3, 245–63.

SKAARUP, J. 1995. Hunting the hunters and fishers of the Mesolithic—twenty years of research on the sea floor south of Funen, Denmark. In A. Fischer (ed.), *Man and Sea in the Mesolithic. Coastal settlement above and below present sea level*, 397–401. Oxford: Oxbow Monograph 53.

TAUBER, H. 1986. Analysis of stable isotopes in prehistoric populations. In B. Herrmann (ed.), *Innovative Trends in der prähistorischen Anthropologie,* 31–8. Göttingen: Mitteilungen der Berliner Gesellschaft für Anthropologie Ethnologie und Urgeschichte, Band 7.

TAUBER, H. 1989. Danish radiocarbon datings of archaeological samples 1988. *Arkæologiske udgravninger i Danmark* 1988, 212–28.

THOMMESSEN, T. 1996. The early settlement of Northern Norway. In L. Larsson (ed.), *The Earliest Settlement of Scandinavia and its Relationship with Neighbouring Areas*, 235–40. Lund: Acta Archaeologica Lundensia 8:24.

WESTERBY, E. 1927. *Stenaldersbopladser ved Klampenborg. Nogle Bidrag til Studiet af den Mesolitiske Periode.* København.

WIGFORSS, J. 1968. Gamla vänner daterade. *Fyndmeddelanden* 1968, 1–4.

WOODMAN, P. 1993. The Komsa Culture. A re-examination of its position in the Stone Age of Finnmark. *Acta Archaeologica* 63, 1992, 57–76.

Shippea Hill and after: Wetlands in North European Prehistory and the Case of the *Donken*

LEENDERT P. LOUWE KOOIJMANS

Wetland qualities

WHAT WOULD OUR PICTURE of the North European prehistoric past be without the wonders of the wetlands, without the miracles of the mires, without the beauty of the bog bodies? What would it be without Ezinge and Biskupin, without Friesack and Grahame Clark's Star Carr? It was the wet sites that in the early days of prehistoric archaeology opened our eyes to the people behind the prehistoric objects at Robenhausen and Obermeilen, at Svaerdborg and Mullerup, at Glastonbury and La Tène. Wetlands are found all over Europe, in extensive areas or small pockets and they set the stage for our image of the past because of their many qualities for archaeological research.

First of all their organic preservation offers us objects made of perishable materials, bone and antler tools, wooden utensils, basketry, woven fabrics, and fishing gear like the Bergschenhoek fish trap (Figure 1). Of equal importance from a scientific point of view is their palaeoecological and palaeoeconomical potential: the treasury of pollen, botanical macro remains, wood, insects, bones of mammals, birds and fishes, and—at the apex of preservation—prehistoric people themselves (Van der Sanden 1996). While organic artefacts can correct our upland stone and pottery bias of prehistory, demonstrated in every museum, we are endangered by a potential wetland distortion of the ecological and economic past, because of this dominant source (Coles & Coles 1989; 1995).

A second specific wetland quality is the sealed-in condition of the embedded remains, like the native Roman and Iron Age structures in the peat deposits near Rotterdam and Assendelft (Trierum 1992; Trierum *et al.* 1988; Brandt *et al.* 1987). The sites have a restricted time depth, there is no older or later contamination, everything is packed in a perfect 'time capsule' and potentially well dated. This can all be the work of nature, but

Proceedings of the British Academy, **99**, 107–124

Figure 1. Bergschenhoek, Netherlands, 1981. Early Neolithic fish trap embedded in Calais II deposits, *c.*4200 cal BC. (Photo: National Museum of Antiquities, Leiden)

we should realize that prehistoric men, by placing offerings in bogs and rivers, intentionally anticipated the untouchable context of the wet subsoil.

Within these deposits original archaeological deposition patterns are hardly disturbed. Self-evidently there has been some distortion in the timespan covered by the period of use and embedding, but from then on all patterns have been fully fossilized, whether we speak of Middle Palaeolithic river plain sites like Maastricht-Belvédère, or those from the end of prehistory, like Flag Fen (Roebroeks 1988; Pryor 1992).

But not only spatial patterns are preserved, the same holds for the vertical, for relative chronology and time resolution, on many scales. At one end of the scale is the full sedimentary landscape, like the British Fenland or the Dutch Rhine delta, where geology offers a basic stratigraphic framework on a geographical scale, governed by a natural deposition rate, in these cases linked to post-glacial sea level rise. At the other end are time sequences, established by means of the micro-stratigraphy of individual sites, with a potential resolution up to the individual year or season, as at Glastonbury or Dutch Bergschenhoek (Coles & Minnitt 1995; Louwe Kooijmans 1987). House floor micro-stratigraphy can be preserved under specific conditions, as in the case of peat fissures in Midden-Delfland (Abbink 1993).

We should also value the wealth of absolute dating opportunities in the wetlands. Radiocarbon material is all around, and dendrochronology in western Europe is fully dependant on wet conservation. Its potential is demonstrated by the spectacular results and time resolution of Hornstaad Hörnle, Bodensee (Billamboz 1990).

Wetland diversity

Talking about wetlands in a general sense we become more and more aware of their diversity. First, in a long diachronic view, they are unstable factors in the landscape. They come and go. Land may be gradually submerged, or overgrown by peat as in Ireland and large tracts of the North German Plain. Reclamation has made many low wetlands dry, as all over the western Netherlands and the British Fenland, and upland bogs have disappeared on regional scales as a result of unrestricted peat cutting. We now realize that wetlands are a phenomenon of all times and that wetlands from more remote times may have turned to dry conditions by uplift and fluvial erosion, as is the case in most Palaeolithic terrace sites.

So a whole range of wetland types should be distinguished from an archaeological point of view, each with its specific qualities and restrictions. There are, in my view, three main categories:

- peat bogs
- sedimentation basins
- drowned land.

Peat bogs

The peat bogs—with all their variations from small *Kesselmoore* (Behre & Kucan 1986) to the cover of full landscapes with extensive raised bogs—offer us mainly trackways and hoards. The bog offerings reflect a sacredness, the relationship with 'the other world' of these specific wetlands, but what do the trackways say? They give us a second prehistoric view. Corduroy roads, like those from Lower Saxony (Hayen 1987) and Corlea (Raftery 1996) and foot tracks, like Sweet track in the Somerset Levels (Coles & Coles 1986), can be perfectly understood in a secular, profane way as a means of crossing an unsafe, damp zone. Bog offerings show us the belief in spirits in this landscape, wooden tracks the secular use of it, a combination plausible for all 'animated' landscapes, but preserved—visible for us—so clearly in the wet.

Sedimentation basins

More important from a Dutch point of view are the sedimentation basins, ranging from minor inland lakes and brook valleys to river valley floors, estuaries, and deltas. They offered rich natural environments with a wide range of plant and game resources. Sites from the later (Mesolithic) foragers concentrate strategically along the basin edges, from where both the wetland and upland zones could be exploited, as around lake Dümmer (Lower Saxony). Quite often archaeology profits from the wet dump zones of these margin locations, at Star Carr, Tybrind Vig, and Ringkloster (Clark 1954; Andersen 1974; 1985). Occasionally sites are discovered from the wetlands themselves: Duvensee (Bokelmann 1991) and Bedburg (Street 1992), and structures or equipment reflect the exploitation of the wetlands as at Kunda and Noyen-sur-Seine (Mordant & Mordant 1992).

Middle Palaeolithic wetland sites have become archaeologically accessible by the intersection of the rivers in their valley floors and the resulting formation of terraces. In the same way, valley edge sites have been fully eroded and so disappeared. For the Mesolithic the situation is exactly the reverse. Valley floor sites are very problematical in respect of discovery. They are almost beyond archaeological reach, since they have been covered by metres of sediment. They are only recovered by mere accident: deep quarrying or dredging (Bedburg, Noyen). Valley edges and basin margins have, in contrast, not yet been eroded. The archaeological *site* patterns are not representative—to say the least—of the original *occupation* patterns.

These major differences in preservation might even be used to question whether there was really a 'Mesolithic wetland revolution' in the sense of a first full exploitation of aquatic resources, including the development of the necessary equipment. It is true that the Mesolithic sites present us for the first time with the full equipment of dugout canoes, paddles, fish weirs, traps, nets, leisters, hooks, and so on, but we should realize that preservation plays a dominant role and we should not exclude earlier roots. We are warned by the recently discovered sophisticated Palaeolithic lances of Schöningen (Thieme 1996) and the early Mediterranean obsidian networks which provide indirect evidence of maritime mobility.

While one can understand in a simple functionalistic way how hunting and gathering societies with a broad-spectrum exploitation strategy settled in and around low and wet basins, this is more problematical for the later, agrarian societies. Their lake margin, valley floor, and basin settlement preferences might be better explained in a social and/or defensive approach, than in an economic/functionalistic one, taking the protective structures, especially palisades, into account, with the presumed population densities and territorial pressure. Valley floors and coastal plains are included in models of territorial exploitation, because of their rich and full year grazing, but in the same period people also put their offerings in the lowlands. Hoards of axes are especially found in 'low and damp areas', the rivers themselves being locations for intentional deposition of arms, either in relation to funeral ceremonies of specific groups in society, as Bradley (1990) argued, or as a ritual related to ascribed spiritual concepts linked to the animated landscape. We see in the lowlands a similar double value of practical/economic use and ritual sacrifice as we do in the bogs with their trackways and offerings: Glastonbury Lake Village versus the

Battersea shield, Manching versus La Tène. Again we should not consider this as incompatible. It is just a reflection of that complex, manifold attitude to the natural world around in general.

Drowned land

The third category of wetland types is the drowned or submerged dryland sites. These are often upland or wetland margin locations covered by encroaching sedimentation or peat growth. Examples are Tybrind Vig and other coastal Ertebølle sites in southern Denmark, parts of Runnymede on the Thames, and Etton and Haddenham in the Fenland (Andersen 1985; Needham 1992; Shand & Hodder 1990). A considerable part of British estuarine archaeology, including submerged forests, the famous 'Lyonesse Surface' of the Essex coast, and discoveries in the Severn estuary and Langstone harbour near Southampton falls into this category (Fulford *et al.* 1997). These are locations close to the upland–wetland interface, covered over and later washed free. Other 'drowned land' sites are those covered by blanket bogs, like the famous Neolithic field systems of Glenulra, county Mayo (Caulfield 1983) or the megaliths reappearing now from below drained bogs in northern Germany.

Settling in the wetlands

We might wonder why pre-industrial farmers settled themselves in extensive wetlands like the coastal deposits around the southern North Sea, especially in the extensive Rhine delta plain. Our surprise reflects our ethnocentric attitude to and our modern agrarian depreciation of marshland, and also our modern opposition to the dry and the wet, the high and the low. This might be obvious around the Wash or the Thames estuary, but is less so in Holland. At any rate the wetland–upland distinction is ours, based on our geological erudition, separating the Holocene from the Pleistocene geology. Prehistoric people were no geologists and in prehistory the landscape of Holland certainly showed far fewer contrasts. Land was split up by many wide and marshy brook valleys, while on the other hand the delta held more solid stream deposits, salt marshes, and dunes. To prehistoric eyes the differences would have been more gradual and not as fundamental as in our view. Farmers made the deliberate choice to settle on the few and slight elevations in the fertile, rich wet environment to profit from its wealth and to avoid the soil exhaustion and sand drift of the poor and acid coversand landscape. In other words, the wetland way of life should not be seen as aberrant, but—if not fully representative—at any rate reflecting the wet side of the range of acceptable life styles. For Early Neolithic Swifterbant this range was apparently wide, as was the case for the later Vlaardingen group, whereas for the Middle Bronze Age the range was very narrow (Louwe Kooijmans 1997; 1998b).

Start of modern research

Britain: Grahame Clark

Although recognized for their informative value in the early days of prehistoric research, I have the feeling that wetland values have only been fully discovered, recognized, and exploited in the more recent past, not only in Great Britain, but in Denmark, Holland, and the Alpine area as well. For this modern research tradition Grahame Clark, no doubt, was a pioneer. His Mesolithic, together with his anthropological, interest must have opened his eyes to the crucial role of wetland research conditions for constructing images of the past. He lectured on his excavations at Plantation Farm, Shippea Hill for the London Society of Antiquaries at the surprisingly young age of 25, on 11 November 1932, the same year in which his *Mesolithic Age in Britain* appeared. The Fenland Research Committee had

Figure 2. Peacock's Farm, Shippea Hill, 1934. The excavations show Grahame Clark in the cutting and Gordon Fowler sitting on the edge. (Photo: Department of Archaeology, University of Cambridge)

been founded earlier, in June of the same year, and Shippea Hill was one of its first formal projects. The report combined Quaternary geology with prehistoric archaeology, palynology, and reports on molluscs, forams, and animal remains. Profit was derived from the discoveries and knowledge of Major Gordon Fowler (Figure 2). New concepts were introduced into traditional archaeology: Buttery Clay, roddons, and so on. It was the start of a research period in which the Mesolithic and the wet were intimately combined: the Meso/Neolithic stratigraphy at Peacock's Farm (1935), *The Mesolithic Settlement of Northern Europe* in the same year, and later, in post-war times, the excavation of Star Carr (1949–50) and the papers that together would form Clark's famous *Prehistoric Europe: the Economic Basis* (Clark 1936; 1952; 1954; Clark *et al.* 1935; Clark & Godwin 1962).

Wetland archaeology was reactivated in Britain by John Coles' involvement in the Somerset Levels in 1962, ultimately resulting in the Somerset Levels Project in 1973 (Coles & Coles 1986). Work in the Fenland was reopened with the Fenland surveys of 1978–88 (Hall & Coles 1994) and then Francis Pryor's prospections and excavations, culminating in his Flag Fen excavation (Pryor 1992). Now a full series of coastal and wetland projects has been or still is being executed all around Britain (Fulford *et al.* 1997). The crusade for more wetland archaeology was and still is successfully led by both John and Bryony Coles. This means good discussion partners on both sides of the North Sea.

The Netherlands

Grahame Clark's research was particularly inspiring for archaeologists on the other side of the North Sea, in the Netherlands. It might surprise those who know that 50 per cent of the Netherlands consist and consisted of Holocene sedimentation, that the discovery and research on prehistoric wetland settlement started that late. It is true that the *terpen* were well known early in the nineteenth century but their full archaeological potential was only demonstrated by Van Giffen in his excavations of the *terp* at Ezinge in 1931–34 (Van Giffen 1936). The *terpen* were, however, considered to be a special case: that of the brave Frisians living on—by Dutch standards—high and dry mounds. Surprisingly for a population spending its full life below sea level, occupation of the 'true' wetlands in prehistory was considered both impossible and improbable. This must have to do with negative perceptions held by educated and civilized intellectuals of the wild and uncontrolled wetlands, where these were not drained and reclaimed (Louwe Kooijmans 1997). So, the discovery of Bronze Age barrows on the Westfrisian clay in 1937 was a very great surprise and even more so the discovery of the first true wetland settlement, the Late Neolithic site of Hekelingen on the levees of an Early Subboreal tidal gully. Modderman's excavation in 1948 and his report of 1953 were very much inspired by his personal contacts with Grahame Clark, and by Clark's work in the Fenland and at Star Carr (Modderman 1953).

While the Fenland research was not continued after the Second World War, wetland research in Holland grew very rapidly. Underlying it were the new, widespread and detailed soil surveys and the growth of organized amateur archaeology in post-war times. Both meant an intensive prospection, not only of the surface, but especially of the subsoil, and intensive monitoring of the increasing number of public works.

The *donken* and the Meso–Neolithic transition

Hazendonk

Grahame Clark also guided me into the wetlands in a type of distance learning *avant la lettre*. As a student in geography I chose to write my MA essay on the Holocene of East England as a reference for the Dutch case and ultimately I found myself in the 1960s in a Ph.D. project inspired by prehistoric sites, newly discovered, and fully unexpected, on the Dutch equivalents of roddons and on outcropping hills in the Rhine/Meuse delta, not dissimilar to the Shippea Hill case 30 years before. In this case the outcrops are the very tops of extensive complexes of Late Glacial dunes, locally called *donken*. I would like to present a first comment on the present research on these *donken* as an *hommage* to Grahame Clark.

The dune tops provided small dry spots in the immense wetlands, attracting prehistoric people who exploited the marshes. The camp sites themselves on the dune tops are deeply disturbed by post-depositional processes, but the refuse levels extending into the surrounding marshland have been covered over and preserved. The Hazendonk (excavated 1974–6) appeared to have been used as a base for over two millennia, from *c*.4000 cal BC until the very end of the Neolithic, *c*.2000 cal BC. Phases of more intensive use were separated by periods of occasional visits or even disuse. Main activities were fishing and hunting, predominantly beaver and otter, but also of some large game such as red deer, roe deer, and wild boar in different ratios according to the various phases. Most surprising is the presence of agrarian domestic animals (cattle and pig) in low percentages and of charred cereals, grain, and chaff in all phases. This, together with the presence of pottery and polished axes from the lower level onward, make the site fully Neolithic, albeit that its function cannot have been a permanent agrarian settlement, in view of the dimensions of the outcrop, the palaeogeography, and the archaeozoology. It must have been a special camp site, supporting fishing, fowling, specialized hunting, and herding by societies in an evolved but very long-lasting stage of 'substitution', that is, transition to a fully agrarian subsistence (Bakels 1981; Louwe Kooijmans 1987; Zeiler 1997).

Since the Hazendonk excavation my interest in the *donken* has persisted. They proved to be a perfect example of wetland potential in archaeology, in this case related to the Mesolithic–Neolithic transition in north-western Europe, the fifth and fourth millennia cal BC, which occurred in societies presently archaeologically known as the Swifterbant Culture. It is the western counterpart of Ertebølle, but related only in some general characteristics of its pottery style. Hardly any upland evidence for these interesting communities between the Elbe and the Scheldt is known, except for some flint surface assemblages, many of them mixed up with earlier or later material. Every field of knowledge is problematical on the upland: dating, non-flint material culture, subsistence, environmental impact. The main upland information is from a spread of unassociated imported adzes and axes. Only the phase and its internal processes are known, and there in great detail, from some local wetlands and their specific archaeological values: the famous Dümmer depression in Lower Saxony, the sites in the Dutch central lake district, and the *donken* between Rhine and Meuse (Louwe Kooijmans 1993a; 1998a).

In this perspective relevant questions were: in what sense could the Hazendonk site be considered as representative and could the results of that single and singular site be generalized? How are the results related to the more general process of Neolithization in this corner of the North European Plain? What about the more than 100 other dune tops, some of which had already produced Neolithic remains?

General survey

It was decided to execute a detailed coring prospection. This work was done as a Ph.D. project by Marten Verbruggen (Leiden University) in the period 1990 to 1996. On 20 out of a selection of 25 *donken*, 65 distinct Neolithic 'occupation levels' were found, that is, surfaces in the surrounding peat containing archaeological indicators, like sand, charcoal, burnt and unburnt bone, and pottery fragments (Figure 3). The ages of the levels range from 5500 to 2000 cal BC. The extent and expression of the levels change upward, becoming wider and more intense, possibly reflecting a gradual change from more ephemeral to a more intensive use. The deepest levels are under-represented because of their depth below the general coring routine. Apparently the sandhills were fully used as a group to support the exploitation of this delta district up to the general establishment of fully agrarian societies in Beaker times. The fluctuating intensity, reflected in a cumulative radiocarbon graph, might reflect changing environmental conditions together with the shift in site character mentioned.

Most intriguing are the earlier levels in the district. We see at the Hazendonk and Brandwijk (a test excavation in 1991) the late stages of a longer tradition that started well back in the Mesolithic. It seems to be the continuation of a mobile settlement system, with extraction camps on the dunes in the middle of the wetlands, or perhaps even temporary base camps.

Excavations at Hardinxveld, 1997–1998

We recently had an opportunity to dig to some of these deep levels at two sites near the village of Hardinxveld: 'site 4' in 1997, 'site 3' in 1998. A new railway connecting Rotterdam harbour with the German industrial centres, is planned through the river district and will disturb two of these dunes that have traces of occupation. They are not visible at the surface, since their tops are at 6 and 5 m, respectively, below mean sea level

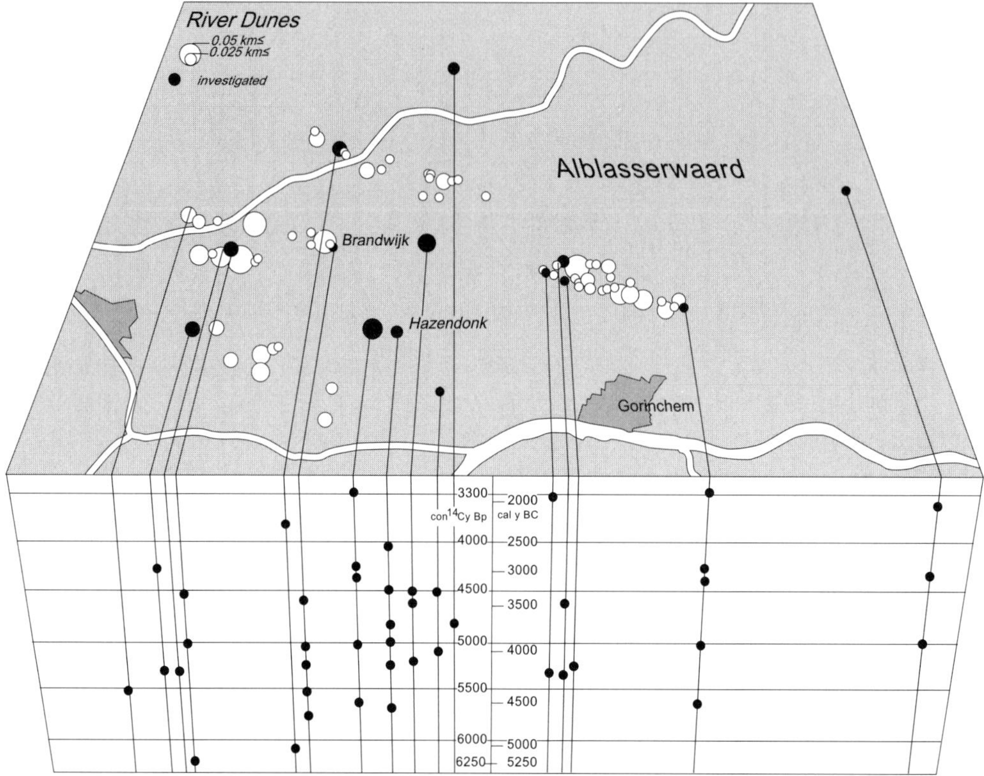

Figure 3. Diagram showing the Alblasserwaard region in the western Netherlands with its *donken*. Those in black have been surveyed by hand coring. C14-dated Late Mesolithic and Neolithic refuse levels indicated in the section. (Published by kind permission of drs M. Verbruggen)

and they disappeared below the delta peat and clay as early as 4600 and 4200 cal BC. Dutch Rail has accepted responsibility for this archaeological heritage, and is freely financing the necessary archaeological work ahead of the new railway, including both these excavations.

The attested occupation of 'site 4' dates from 5300 to 4700 cal BC. A trench of 18 × 30 m has been dug, reinforced with steel planking, kept dry by an advanced drainage system, and covered by a huge tent because of the autumn and winter weather conditions (Figure 4). The refuse levels on the slope of the dune are over 1 m in depth and reach down to –10 m as a result of later compaction. They are recorded in twenty thousand 50 × 50 cm units of 5 cm thickness, giving us full control over horizontal and stratigraphic patterning.

The finds at present comprise a flint blade and flake industry on river pebbles, antler axes in a wide range of forms and their production refuse, a socketed axe made out of an

Figure 4. Hardinxveld site 4 'Polderweg' 1997. Trench dug down to the top of a river dune with Late Mesolithic settlement refuse layers at 6–10 m below mean sea level. (Photo: Faculty of Archaeology, Leiden University)

aurochs' metapodial, an elm bow, and several paddles made of ash. An original aspect of the antler work is the range of unperforated axe blades, apparently inserts for shaft-hole handles. There are quantities of bones of fish, birds, and mammals (beaver, otter, small predators, wild boar, red deer, but *no* agrarian animals). The botanical work attests *no* cereal remains at present. This apparently is an assemblage fully in a Late Mesolithic north European tradition, except for one new aspect: a modest number of sherds of point-based pottery in a (very) early Swifterbant tradition, found in the uppermost level only. At the edge of the dune four burials were discovered, two of humans and two of dogs, all firmly dated before 4700 cal BC. One human interment and one dog are seriously disturbed, but the other human and dog are both fully intact. The human is a woman of more than 40 years of age, buried on her back in a stretched position (Figure 5). The burials together form a section of the first Mesolithic cemetery in the Netherlands and its wider surroundings, a cemetery modest in extent but with its dogs an important comparison for Skateholm, and by its very presence important for site function interpretation and our image of Mesolithic society.

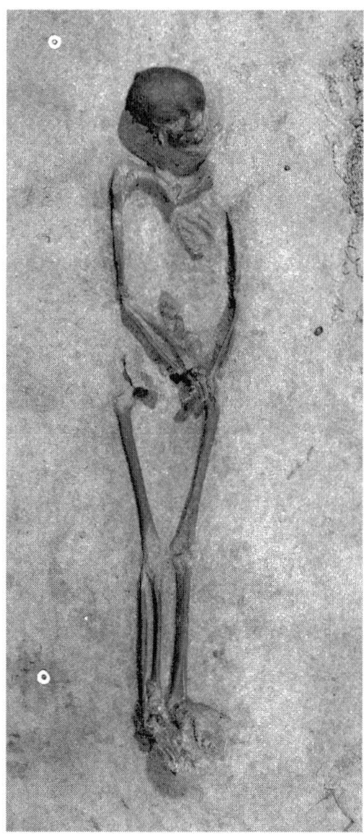

Figure 5. Hardinxveld site 4 'Polderweg' 1997. Late Mesolithic burial at 7 m below mean sea level. (Photo: Faculty of Archaeology, Leiden University)

Contemporaneous with the upper levels, *c*.4700 cal BC, is a site situated further north at Hoge Vaart in the central Dutch lake district. It was dug a few years ago by the State Service for Archaeological Investigations (Amersfoort) and offers a similar picture. The site is at –5 m, in a submerged upland margin situation, located on a coversand ridge along a former course of the river Vecht. In spite of large-scale sieving, no cereals have been found and the few indications for domestic animals other than dog seem to be questionable, but there is characteristic early Swifterbant pottery in combination with a Late Mesolithic broad blade trapeze flint complex (Hogestijn & Peters 1996).

Both sites represent the very earliest contacts of the latest native hunter gatherers with the Late bandkeramik (LBK) and early Rössen farmers in the loess zone, 100–150 km to the south. The sites give us a wealth of information, thanks to their wetland conditions, for a crucial and interesting phase in social evolution, a period we could not approach until now—the early fifth millennium.

The exploitation of a drowning landscape, 9000–2500 cal BC

We are looking at a landscape and a society that were changing considerably over a period of several millennia, between *c.*9000 and 2500 cal BC, the Early and Middle Holocene, the Late Meso, and Early Neolithic. We can now give a hypothetical view on the changing man–land relations in this area (Figure 6). The occupation sequence starts with numerous Late Palaeolithic and Early Mesolithic barbed points dredged up from below –20 m at Europoort, Rotterdam harbour (Verhart 1988). They fit into the same time slice as the bone implements from the Brown Bank, North Sea and Grahame Clark's famous barbed point from the Leman and Ower Bank in the southern North Sea.

The Late Glacial braided river plain, 30 km wide, had by now changed into more marshy conditions around the Preboreal–Boreal transition as a result of the more temperate climate, a meandering river regime, and ground water rise. The barbed points appear to indicate that the valley floor was an attractive hunting and fishing ground. We have no direct evidence for the location of camp sites, except very modest Mesolithic traces on some of the dunes. It is likely that the valley floor was exploited from sites along its margins, at the edges of a low terrace documented in the contour map of the subsoil Late Glacial surface. These presumed sites are, however, beyond the depth of regular prospection. The then still extensive dune complexes in the middle of the valley floor seem not to have had any special significance.

Their importance increased when the terrace edges disappeared below the accumulation of peat and river clays. The wetlands grew quickly in extent and their margins became wide apart and diffuse in the undulating coversand landscape. The dunes, although shrunken to small and isolated tips, still offered some firm ground in the middle of the swamps, at an increasing distance from the surrounding upland, and became intensively used. In the meantime society had changed by adopting cereal cultivation and the husbandry of cattle, pigs, and ovicaprids, introduced by the farmers of the loess zone. But these later, formally Neolithic, communities continued to include the traditional locations in their settlement system as a support not only of hunting and fishing but, at least from 4000 cal BC (Hazendonk, level 1) onward, of cattle herding as well. Archaeological indicators (clearings in the pollen diagrams, extensive dark levels full of refuse) point to more intensive and longer-lasting stays, that is, to a more lasting function in the settlement system. This continued to the very end of the Neolithic, that is, late Bell Beaker times, *c.*2000 cal BC. It seems that we only can speak from that time onward of fully settled farming communities on the surrounding uplands (Louwe Kooijmans 1993b).

We have the feeling—as we ever have with the north European wetlands—that nature made for us an experimental station in the *donken* district, a systematic sampling of forager societies, and packed the samples for us in their spatial and chronological patterns and under perfect conditions for organic preservation. They give us a minimum option for the degree of Neolithization and demonstrate an ongoing old mobile and foraging aspect of these communities. We have to learn how to extrapolate from these special activity data

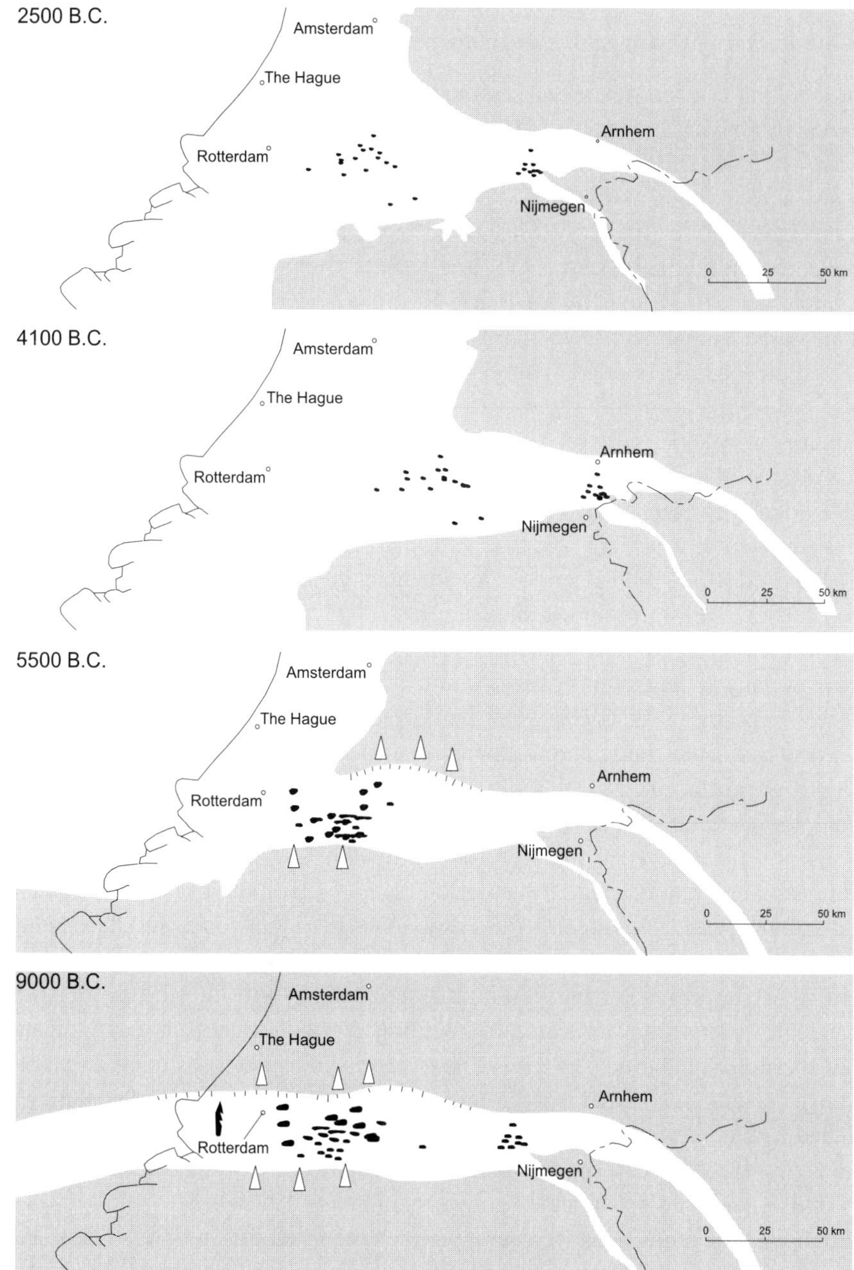

Figure 6(a). Palaeogeography (a) and sections (b) of the Rhine/Meuse river district in the Netherlands in several stages of submersion during the Holocene, showing the decrease of the number and dimensions of the *donken* and their increasing distance from the shifting upland margin. Site locations indicated with triangles (open = presumed, black = attested).

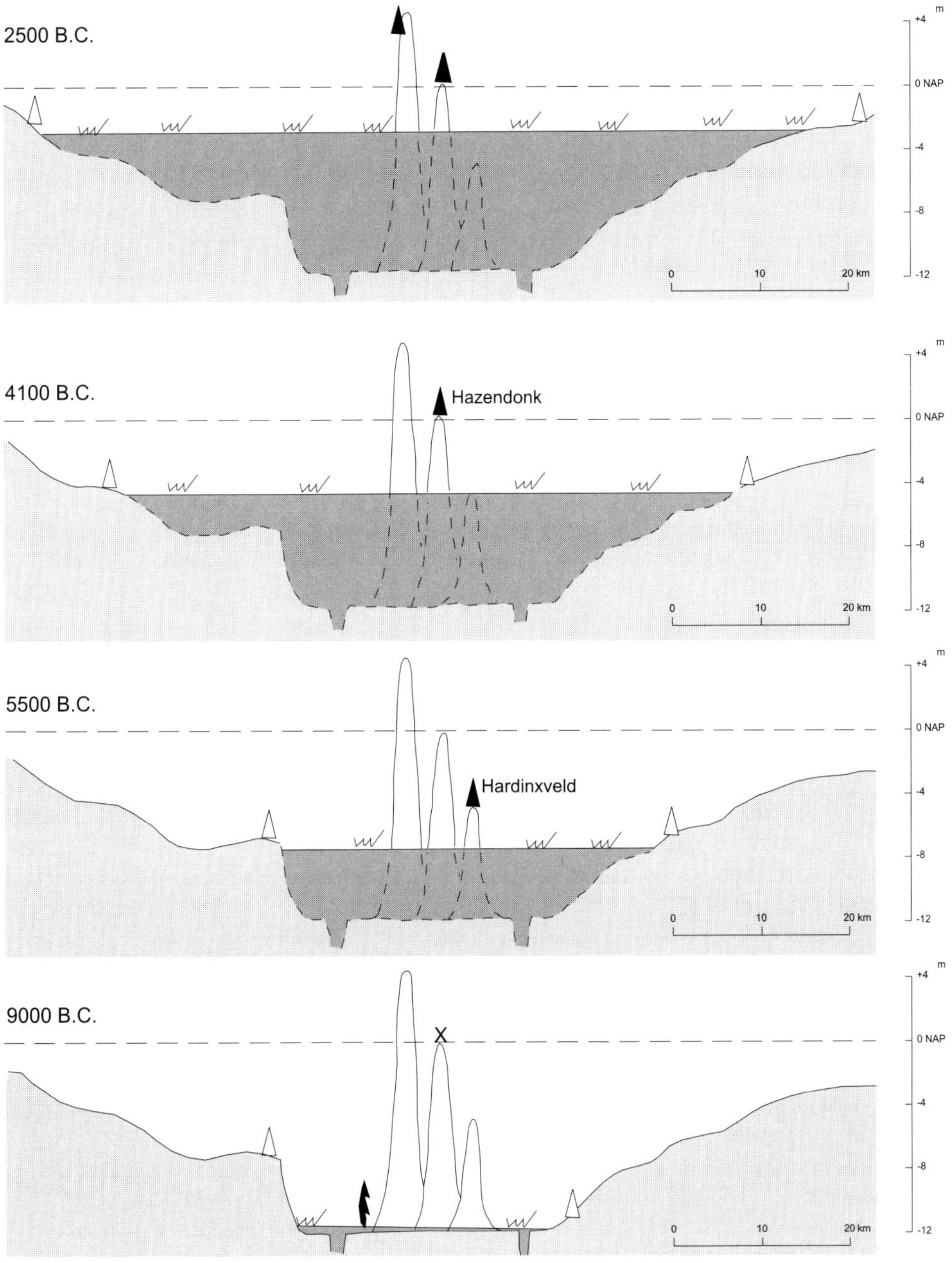
2500 B.C.
4100 B.C.
Hazendonk
5500 B.C.
Hardinxveld
9000 B.C.
X
m
+4
0 NAP
-4
-8
-12
0
10
20 km

Figure 6(b)

to models that cover the total of the communities in this part of the North European Plain. We feel that these special activity sites reflect a deliberate choice of the Swifterbant people, and are representative of the way their society was organized and of the choices made by them. Apparently the Swifterbant communities had made a deliberate choice to continue their traditional way of life beyond the fully agrarian societies to the south. The transition to farming occurred piecemeal, step by step, and, it seems to me, rather differently from the start of the British Early Neolithic and the Danish Ertebølle–TRB transition.

We may complain about this wetland bias, but we should realize that upland information is factually non-existent. What would our image of the past be without the wonders of those wetlands?

References

ABBINK, A. 1993. Dwelling on peat; fissures as a recurrent feature of prehistoric structures built on peat in the Western Netherlands. *Analaecta Praehistorica Leidensia* 26, 45–58.

ANDERSEN, S. 1974. Ringkloster, en Jysk inlandsplads med Ertebøllekultur. *Kuml*, 11–108.

ANDERSEN, S. 1985. Tybrind Vig. A preliminary report on a submerged Ertebølle settlement on the west coast of Fyn. *Journal of Danish Archaeology* 4, 52–69.

BAKELS, C.C. 1981. Neolithic plant remains from the Hazendonk, province of Zuid-Holland, The Netherlands. *Zeitschrift fur Archäologie* 15, 141–8.

BEHRE, K.-E. & KUCAN, D. 1986. Die Reflektion archäologisch bekannter Siedlungen in Pollendiagrammen verschiedener Entfernung – Beispiele aus der Siedlungskammer Flögeln, Nordwestdeutschland. In K.-E. Behre (ed.), *Anthropogenic Indicators in Pollen Diagrams*, 95–114. Rotterdam/Boston: Balkema.

BILLAMBOZ, A. 1990. Das Holz der Pfahlbausiedlungen Südwestdeutschlands. In *Siedlungsarchäologie im Alpenvorland II*, 87–207. Mainz: Philipp von Zabern.

BOKELMANN, K. 1991. Duvensee, Wohnplatz 9. Ein präborealzeitlicher Lagerplatz in Schleswig-Holstein. *Offa* 48, 75–114.

BRADLEY, R. 1990. *The Passage of Arms*. Cambridge: Cambridge University Press.

BRANDT, R.W., GROENMAN-VAN WAATERINGE, W. & VAN DER LEEUW, S.E. (eds), 1987. *Assendelver Polder Papers 1*. Amsterdam: Cingula 10.

CAULFIELD, S. 1983. Neolithic fields: the Irish evidence. In H.C. Bowen & P.J. Fowler (eds), *Early Land Allotment in the British Isles*, 137–43. Oxford: British Archaeological Reports 48.

CLARK, J.G.D. 1932. *The Mesolithic Age in Britain*. Cambridge: Cambridge University Press.

CLARK, J.G.D. 1933. Report on an early bronze age site in the south-eastern Fens. *The Antiquaries Journal* 13, 266–96.

CLARK, J.G.D. 1936. *The Mesolithic Settlement of Northern Europe*. Cambridge: Cambridge University Press.

CLARK, J.G.D. 1952. *Prehistoric Europe: The Economic Basis*. London: Methuen & Co.

CLARK, J.G.D. 1954. *Excavations at Star Carr*. Cambridge: Cambridge University Press.

CLARK, J.G.D. & GODWIN, H. 1962. The neolithic in the Cambridgeshire Fens. *Antiquity* 36, 10–23.

CLARK, J.G.D., GODWIN, H., GODWIN, M.E. & CLIFFORD, M.H. 1935. Report on recent excavations at Peacock's Farm, Shippea Hill, Cambridgeshire. *The Antiquaries Journal* 15, 284–319.

COLES, B. (ed.) 1992. *The Wetland Revolution in Prehistory*. Exeter: Warp Occasional Paper 6.

COLES, B. & COLES, J. 1986. *Sweet Track to Glastonbury, the Somerset Levels in Prehistory*. London: Thames and Hudson.

COLES, B. & COLES, J. 1989. *People of the Wetlands*. London: Thames and Hudson.

COLES, J. & COLES, B. 1995. *Enlarging the Past, the Contribution of Wetland Archaeology*. Society of Antiquaries of Scotland Monograph Series 11.

COLES, J. & MINNITT, S. 1995. *'Industrious and Fairly Civilized', the Glastonbury Lake Village*. Somerset Levels Project & Somerset County Council Museums Service.

FULFORD, M., CHAMPION, T. & LONG, A. 1997. *England's Coastal Heritage, a survey for English Heritage and the RCHME*. English Heritage Archaeological Report 15.

GIFFEN, A.E. VAN 1936. Der Warf in Ezinge, Provinz Groningen, Holland, und seine westgermanischen Häuser. *Germania* 20, 40–7.

HALL, D. & COLES, J. 1994. *Fenland Survey, an Essay in Landscape and Persistence*. London: English Heritage Archaeological Report 1.

HAYEN, H. 1987. Peat bog archaeology in Lower Saxony, West Germany. In J.M. Coles & A.J. Lawson (eds), *European Wetlands in Prehistory*, 117–36. Oxford: Clarendon Press.

HOGESTIJN, W.-J. & PETERS, H. 1996. De opgraving van de mesolithische en vroegneolithische bewoningsresten van de vindplaats 'Hoge Vaart' bij Almere (prov. Fl.): een blik op een duistere period van de Nederlandse prehistorie. *Archeologie* 7, 80–113.

LOUWE KOOIJMANS, L.P. 1987. Neolithic settlement and subsistence in the wetlands of the Rhine/Meuse delta of the Netherlands. In J.M. Coles & A.J. Lawson (eds), *European Wetlands in Prehistory*, 227–51. Oxford: Clarendon Press.

LOUWE KOOIJMANS, L.P. 1993a. The mesolithic/neolithic transformation in the Lower Rhine Basin. In P. Bogucki (ed.), *Case Studies in European Prehistory*. Boca Raton: CRC Press.

LOUWE KOOIJMANS, L.P. 1993b. Wetland exploitation and upland relations of prehistoric communities in the Netherlands. In J. Gardiner (ed.), *Flatlands and Wetlands: Current Themes in East Anglian Archaeology*, 71–116. Norwich: East Anglian Archaeology 50.

LOUWE KOOIJMANS, L.P. 1997. Denkend aan Holland. . . . Enige overwegingen met betrekkeing tot de prehistorische bewoning in de Nederlandse delta, aangeboden aan François van Regteren Altena. In D.P. Hallewas, G.H. Scheepstra & P.J. Woltering (eds), *Dynamisch Landschap, Archeologie en geologie van het Nederlandse kustgebied*, 9–25. Amersfoort: Rijksdienst voor het Oudheidkundig Bodemonderzoek.

LOUWE KOOIJMANS, L.P. 1998a. Understanding the Mesolithic/Neolithic frontier in the Lower Rhine Basin. In M. Edmonds & C. Richards (eds), *Social Life and Social Change: the Neolithic of Northwestern Europe*, 407–27. Glasgow.

LOUWE KOOIJMANS, L.P. 1998b. Bronzezeitliche Bauern in und um die niederländische Delta-Niederung. In B. Hänsel (ed.), *Mensch und Umwelt in der Bronzezeit Europas*, 327–39, Kiel.

MODDERMAN, P.J.R. 1953. Een neolithische woonplaats in de polder Vriesland onder Hekelingen (eiland Putten) (Zuid-Holland), *Berichten van de Rijksdienst voor het Oudheidkundig Bodemonderzoek* 4.2, 1–26.

MORDANT, M. & MORDANT, D. 1992. Noyen-sur-Seine: a mesolithic waterside settlement. In B. Coles (ed.), *The Wetland Revolution in Prehistory*, 55–64. Exeter: Warp Occasional Paper 6.

NEEDHAM, S. 1992. Holocene alluviation and interstratified settlement evidence in the Thames Valley at Runnymede Bridge. In S. Needham & M.G. Macklin (eds), *Alluvial Archaeology in Britain*, 249–60. Oxford: Oxbow Monographs 27.

PRYOR, F. (ed.) 1992. Current research at Flag Fen. *Antiquity* 66, 439–531.

RAFTERY, B. 1996. *Trackway Excavations in the Mountdillon Bogs, Co. Longford, 1995–1991*. Dublin: Transactions of the Irish archaeological wetland unit 3.

ROEBROEKS, W. 1988. *From Find Scatters to Early Hominid Behaviour*. Leiden: Analecta Praehistorica Leidensia 21.

SANDEN, W. VAN DER 1996. *Vereeuwigd in het veen, de verhalen van de Noordwest-Europese veenlijken*. Amsterdam: De Bataafsche Leeuw.

SHAND, P. & HODDER, I. 1990. Haddenham. *Current Archaeology* 10, 339–42.

STREET, M. 1992. Der Fundplatz Bedburg-Königshoven. In *Spurensicherung. Archäologische Denkmalpflege in der Euregio Maas-Rhein*, 427–31. Mainz: Philipp von Zabern.

THIEME, H. 1996. Altpaläolithische Wurfspeere aus Schöningen, Niedersachsen—ein Vorbericht. *Archäologisches Korrespondenzblatt* 26, 377–93.

TRIERUM, M.C. VAN 1992. Nederzettingen uit de ijzertijd en de Romeinse tijd op Voorne-Putten. *BOORbalans* 2, 15–102.

TRIERUM, M.C. VAN, DÖBKEN, A.B. & GUIRAN, A.J. 1988. Archeologisch onderzoek in het Maasmondgebied 1976–1986. *BOORbalans* 1, 11–107.

VERHART, L.B.M. 1988. Mesolithic barbed points and other implements from Europoort, the Netherlands. *Oudheidkundige Mededelingen uit het Rijksmuseum van Oudheden te Leiden* 68, 145–94.

ZEILER, J.T. 1997. *Hunting, fowling and stock-breeding at neolithic sites in the western and central Netherlands*. Ph.D. thesis Groningen.

Economic Prehistory in Southern Scandinavia

PETER ROWLEY-CONWY

THE WORK OF SCANDINAVIAN ARCHAEOLOGISTS on sites with organic remains was an inspiration to Grahame Clark from the start of his career. *The Mesolithic Settlement of Northern Europe* appeared in 1936, followed nearly 40 years later by *The Earlier Stone Age Settlement of Scandinavia* (Clark 1936; 1975). In between, Clark's perspective had broadened to encompass the world, but Scandinavia remained an area of major interest. It is probably no coincidence that his last three research students all worked in the region: Priscilla Renouf (Memorial University of Newfoundland) in northern Norway; Marek Zvelebil (University of Sheffield) in Finland; and the author of this contribution in Denmark.

This paper examines some recent developments in Scandinavian prehistory in two areas: (1) hunter-gatherer settlement and society, and (2) the appearance of agriculture. These topics, always of interest to Clark, will be approached principally via two methodologies championed by him: zooarchaeology, and radiocarbon dating. Clark was one of the first to realize that subsistence and chronology are not just pleasing cultural wallpaper; they often revolutionize the way we view the past.

The periods considered will be the Mesolithic and the earlier Neolithic. The chronology is set out in Figure 1. The Maglemosian forms the long early Mesolithic period. The Kongemose (middle Mesolithic) and Ertebølle (late Mesolithic) are each divided into early, middle, and late phases. The Neolithic is divided into four: early, middle, Single Grave (middle Neolithic B), and late. Contemporary sea level is crucial in any consideration of especially the Mesolithic; the curve in Figure 1 is from Christensen (1995).

Proceedings of the British Academy, **99**, 125–159

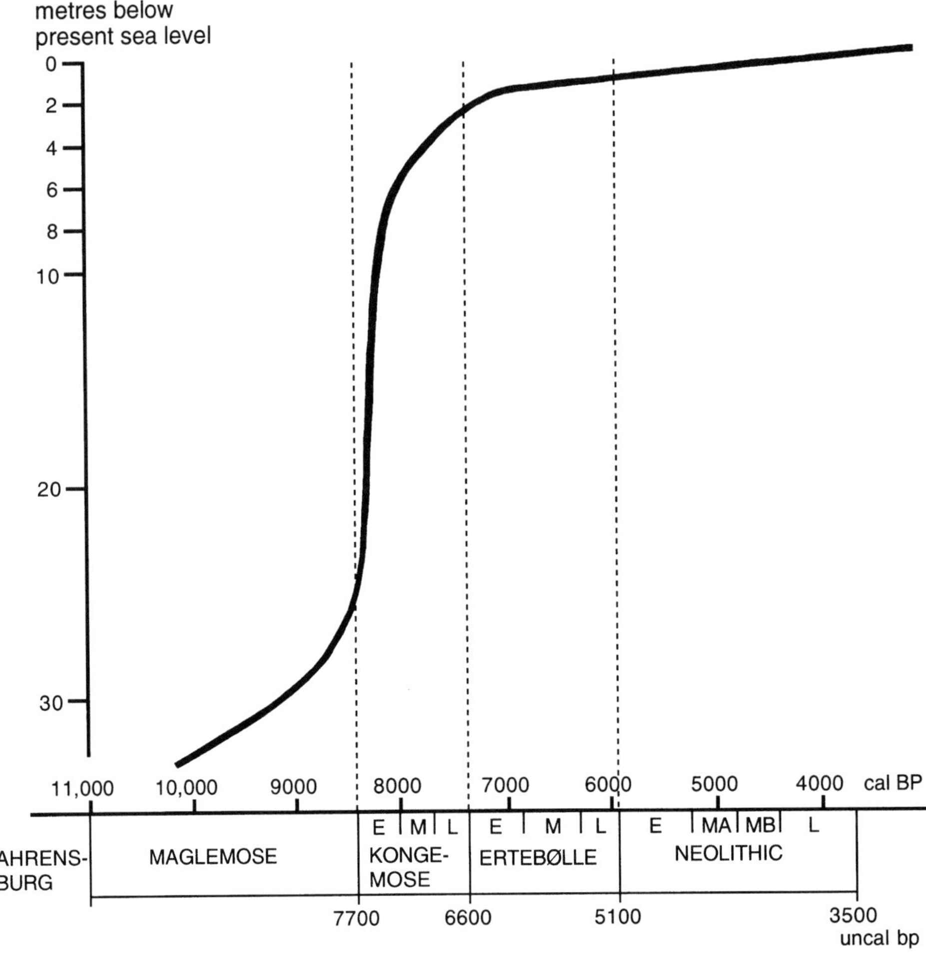

Figure 1. Sea level curve and chronology of the Danish Mesolithic and Neolithic. The sea level curve is for the Storebælt region, from Christensen (1995, Fig. 2). Dates for archaeological periods from Fischer (1997a, Fig. 1).

Hunter-gatherer settlement and society

The Danish early Mesolithic

The Maglemosian period is characterized by small lakeside settlements, often with good organic preservation (for recent reviews see Grøn 1995; Blankholm 1996). Clark's excavation of Star Carr (Clark 1954) was of a similar site in Britain, believed to be occupied in winter; this led to a settlement model involving winter sites such as Star Carr in the lowlands, and summer sites in the highlands (Clark 1972).

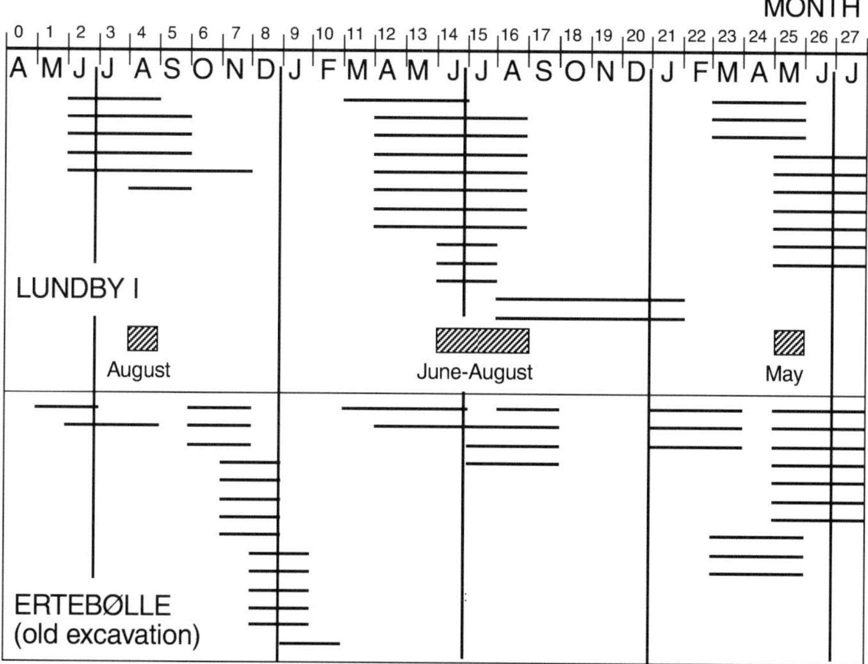

Figure 2. Season of death of wild boar at Mesolithic sites. Lundby I is Maglemosian, Ertebølle is the *locus classicus* of the late Mesolithic. Based on the method put forward by Rowley-Conwy (1993; in press a).

The Danish Maglemosian was, however, different. Zooarchaeology demonstrated from the very first that the sites were mostly occupied in summer (Winge 1903; Rosenlund 1980; Richter 1982). More recently, tooth eruption and bone growth of the large mammals, particularly wild boar, have confirmed that these animals too were killed in the summer (Rowley-Conwy 1993; in press a). Lundby I is an example (Figure 2). The site yielded numerous immature wild boar jaws which can be aged fairly precisely and thus allocated to a season of death assuming a restricted season of birth in late March or early April. Each line on Figure 2 represents one jaw, covering the period in which the animal could have been killed. Lundby I has three killing peaks; all fall in the summer, and there is no need to suggest any winter occupation.

Recently, a re-examination of Star Carr has indicated that this site was in fact also occupied in summer (Legge & Rowley-Conwy 1988). Only a single Danish Maglemosian site was claimed to be occupied in winter, namely Holmegaard V (Becker 1953; Brinch Petersen 1973). The argument was that unlike the other sites it lay on firm ground, not peat, and had no evidence for fishing. Neither of these arguments is particularly conclusive. No mandibular evidence of seasonality is available, but bone growth suggests that this site was also a summer occupation like the others (Rowley-Conwy 1993; in press a).

Thus no Maglemosian site is demonstrably a winter settlement. Some could remain unrecognized among the numerous undiagnosed findspots. Alternatively, the post-glacial marine transgression may have covered many settlements. During the Maglemosian, sea level was well below that of the present day (Figure 1). As a result the map of Denmark looked completely different to that of today (Figure 3): large areas of the modern North Sea bed and the straits between the islands were dry land. The Baltic Sea was a freshwater lake, draining into the North Sea through two rivers, one via the now-submerged Danish lowlands, the other via central Sweden.

Occasional hints of Maglemosian activity off the current land area are known, for example the grey seal mandible from Sværdborg I (Degerbøl 1933). A human bone found on the bed of the Øresund has been radiocarbon dated to the late Maglemosian; trace elements indicate a marine diet (Tauber 1989) although at this time the sea was probably still some way from the findspot. More recently, several submarine Maglemose findspots have been located by divers in the Øresund and the Storebælt waterways (Figure 3), some in connection with the extensive work preceding the construction of fixed links across them (L. Larsson 1983; Fischer 1997a; 1997b). These sites are at considerable depths and have

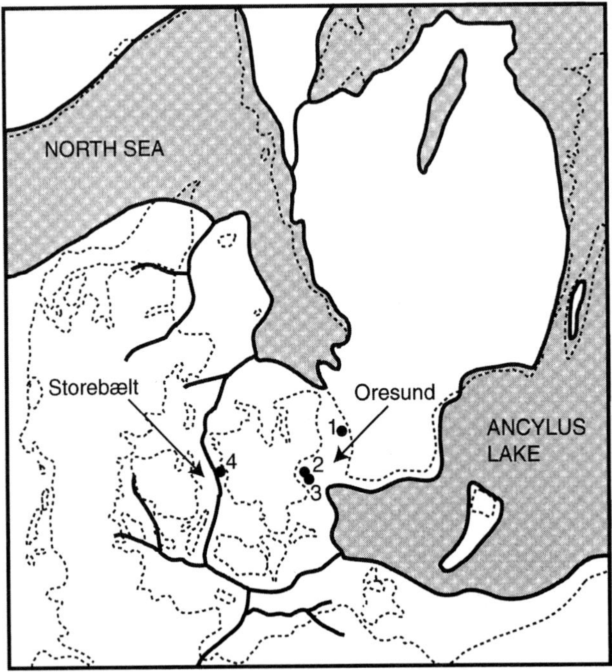

Figure 3. The Danish coastline at *c.*8400 BC, during the early Mesolithic. Submarine finds of Maglemose sites are marked in the Øresund and the Storebælt. 1. Pilhaken; 2. Juelsgrund; 3. Knaggen; 4. Tudeå.

not been excavated, so season and nature of occupation is unknown; but it is quite possible that much or all of the winter facies of the Maglemosian is below present sea level.

At the moment it is therefore not possible to describe the whole Maglemosian settlement system. It may be that the entire year was spent moving from campsite to campsite, exploiting seasonal resources in sequence; if so, the system would resemble the 'serial specialists' described by Binford (1980), and if little or no storage was practised the economy was of the 'immediate return' type (Woodburn 1982). Alternatively, the winter sites might have had a logistically organized delayed return economy. The logistic aspect could have been more pronounced if the summer sites were occupied by task groups involved in transporting stored resources back to the winter (or all year?) base camps. However, spatial studies suggest that the summer sites were occupied by family groups (Blankholm 1996; Grøn 1995), so unless these families formed the task groups this is less likely. In addition, initial zooarchaeological studies show that these sites did *not* resemble the late Mesolithic logistic hunting camp of Ringkloster (see below).

The South Scandinavian late Mesolithic

By the Ertebølle period, the sea had risen to near present levels (Figure 1). The isostatic rebound of central Scandinavia carried southern Sweden and northern Denmark with it, however, so these regions have risen further than the sea. As a result, late Mesolithic coastlines in these regions are above contemporary sea level. In Denmark south and west of the axis of tilt the coasts are now below sea level (Figure 4).

The middle and late Ertebølle is the era of the big shell middens (kitchen middens, Danish *køkkenmødding*). Much work has established that the settlement system was very different from that of the Maglemosian. The big shell middens are often on the interior parts of sheltered bays or fiords. Due to the low-lying topography, Danish fiords are not deep clefts like the Norwegian ones, but are broad shallow estuaries. Estuaries are among the most productive and reliable ecological systems (for example, Odum 1975; Whittaker 1975). If this ecological productivity is in forms exploitable by humans, it may provide all-year support for hunter-gatherer groups. Sedentary occupation based on the Danish fiords has been suggested for this reason (Paludan-Müller 1978; Rowley-Conwy 1983; Aaris-Sørensen 1988). The stable, long-term nature of the large settlements has been stressed (S.H. Andersen 1995). Zooarchaeological support for all-year settlement appeared early on, based on migratory birds (Winge, in Madsen *et al.* 1900). Tooth eruption in wild boar supports this; Ertebølle itself is an example (Figure 2) in which animals appear to be killed in all seasons of the year, in contrast to the Maglemosian pattern.

The big shell middens are not the only Ertebølle coastal settlements, however. Smaller sites, with or without shell middens, are also numerous. These are often in more exposed locations, and specialize on fewer resources than the large middens. Some contain large numbers of winter migrant waterfowl; these include Aggersund (Møhl 1978) and Sølager (Skaarup 1973). Ølby Lyng contains an unusual number of harp seal and porpoise (Møhl

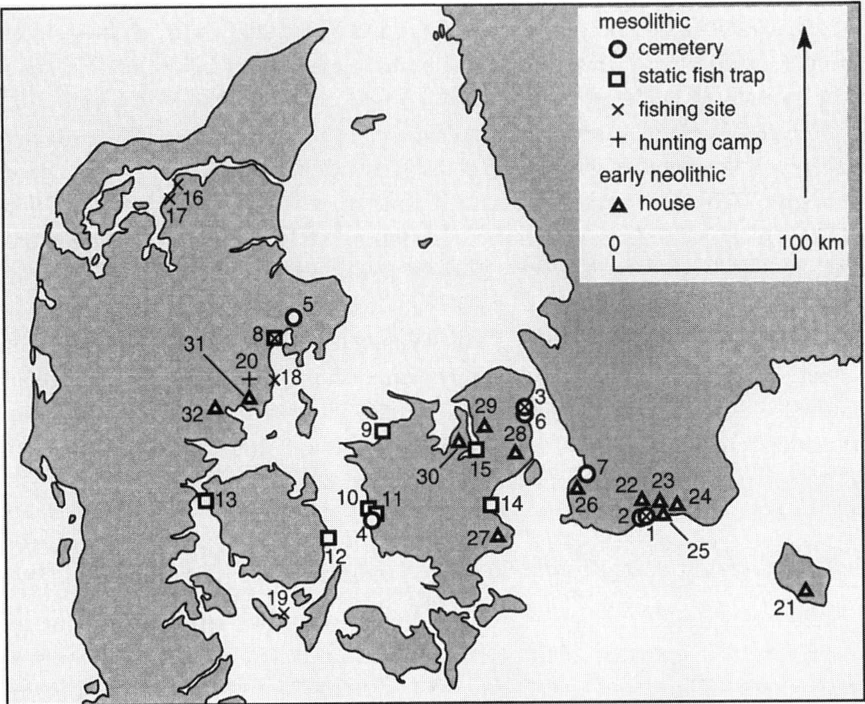

Figure 4. Mesolithic and early Neolithic in Denmark and southern Sweden. *Mesolithic cemeteries:* 1, 2: Skateholm I and II; 3: Vedbæk; 4: Korsør Nor; 5: Nederst; 6: Gøngehusvey; 7: Segebro. *Mesolithic static fish traps:* 8: Lystrup; 9: Nekselø; 10, 11: Halsskov Øst and Syd; 12: Lindholm; 13: Tybrind Vig; 14: Vedskølle Åmunding Nord; 15: Blak II. *Mesolithic fishing settlements:* 16: Bjørnsholm; 17: Ertebølle; 18: Norsminde; 19: Møllegabet II. *Mesolithic hunting camp:* 20: Ringkloster. *Early Neolithic houses:* 21: Limensgård; 22: Karlshem; 23: Karlsfält; 24: Mossby; 25: Rävgrav; 26: Bellevuegård; 27: Ornehus; 28: Albertslund; 29: Topperøgel; 30: Skæppekærgård; 31: Mosegården; 32: Bygholm Nørremark.

1970), while Hjerk Nor saw the specialized hunting of fur-bearing animals such as wild cat (Hatting *et al.* 1973). These smaller settlements are interpreted as seasonal hunting camps exploited by groups from the central large shell midden. The Danish Ertebølle settlement pattern was thus radial and logistic: the small settlements were visited from and supplied resources to the large central sites (Rowley-Conwy 1983; S.H. Andersen 1995).

The best example of a logistically organized hunting camp, however, lies inland. This is Ringkloster (S.H. Andersen 1975), a lakeside settlement with excellently preserved animal bones. Several zooarchaeological aspects mark the site out as a specialist hunting camp. Firstly, it is seasonally occupied; all indicators point to winter and spring. Secondly, there was specialized procurement of furs and skins: nearly 800 bones of pine marten were found, making this the second most common animal, while over 20 per cent of both red deer and roe deer are newborn or even foetal—presumably killed for their soft spotted skins. Thirdly, despite the superb conditions of preservation the bones of aurochs, red deer, and wild boar show peculiar patterns of skeletal representation. The red deer and aurochs are represented predominantly by neck vertebrae, the wild boar mostly by the head and upper forelimb. This cannot be explained by any process of natural taphonomy, but must represent human action. The most likely explanation is that animals were processed at Ringkloster, and much meat was then transported to some other location—perhaps the large sedentary settlements on the coast 14 km away (Rowley-Conwy 1993, in press b). The radial settlement pattern thus encompassed the interior hinterland as well as the coast; Ringkloster was not a base camp in a separate settlement system operating exclusively in the interior, as argued by Price (1993). Despite the lakeside location, 26 bones of marine fish and five oyster shells were found (Enghoff in press), as were three bones of bottle nosed dolphin (Rowley-Conwy in press b). These are best explained as food supplies brought along by hunters on logistic expeditions from the coast.

The radial system described above is based mostly on the middle and late Ertebølle of Jutland. It cannot automatically be applied to other areas and/or periods of the Ertebølle as though economy and settlement were cultural variables similar to artefact styles. The early Ertebølle in southern Sweden was apparently different. The major site of Skateholm I has yielded a cemetery and a settlement (L. Larsson 1988; 1989). Most of the migratory fish and marine mammals were available in winter, although the general productivity of the area was such that the faunal analyst argued that the site was probably occupied all year (Jonsson 1988). Re-examination of the large mammals leads, however, to the somewhat unexpected conclusion that Skateholm I was occupied seasonally, since the large mammals were also procured only in winter (Rowley-Conwy 1998a). It is not clear where the inhabitants spent the summer, but it does seem that the settlement pattern was not radial like the Jutland Ertebølle.

Skateholm I is further into the Baltic than the Jutland Ertebølle sites. The sea was more brackish and less productive in this region, and this may have contributed to the difference between the two cases. In between the two areas is the major Ertebølle settlement concentration around the Øresund, including the cemetery and settlements at Vedbæk. These have yielded rich faunal remains (Aaris-Sørensen 1980; Enghoff 1983) and it would be interesting to know more about their seasonality.

Ertebølle fishing

The most important recent development in Ertebølle archaeology is the realization of just how important fishing was. Developments have occurred on three fronts. Firstly, trace element analysis of human skeletons has revealed a strongly marine diet (Tauber 1982).

Secondly, several spectacular static fish traps have recently come to light. The remains consist of numerous sharpened stakes, mostly lying on the former sea bed but sometimes still standing *in situ*. The stakes originally formed a barrier projecting out at right angles to the shore; fish encountering the barrier swam along it, and entered a basket trap or catching chamber at the outer end. Such traps are passive, requiring (once built) no active human involvement beyond periodic emptying. People are thus free to undertake other activities while the trap is working. The traps have come to light because excavations have begun focusing on areas away from the settlements themselves, in areas formerly just offshore. North-east of Denmark's tilt axis the relevant areas may now be above sea level, the trap elements being preserved in waterlogged sediments. South of the line they remain under the sea and are studied by divers.

The largest and most spectacular is Lystrup. Excavation has encompassed over 3500 m^2 (part is reproduced in Figure 5). No fewer than 588 pointed stakes have been recovered, 67 of them *in situ*. They are up to 3 m long, and 1–4 cm in diameter. Two have

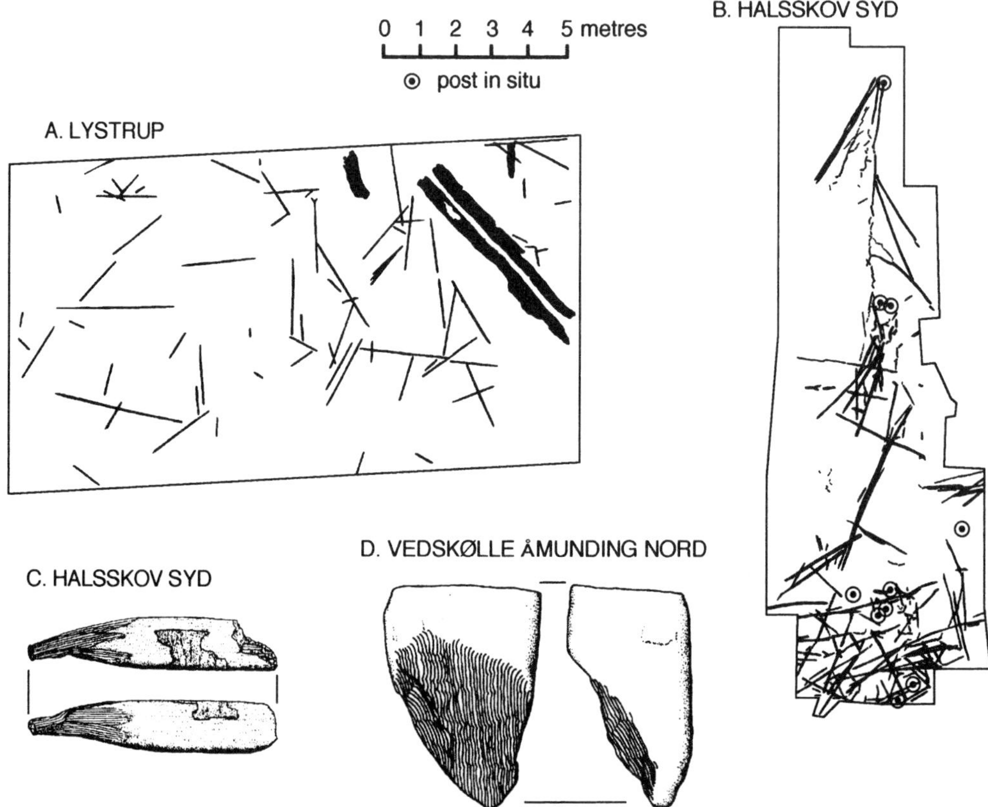

Figure 5. Static fish traps from the Danish middle and late Mesolithic. A: part of the very large exposure at Lystrup (redrawn from S.H. Andersen 1997, Fig. 3)—the large fragments are a 5 m dugout canoe; B: plan of Halsskov Syd (redrawn from Pedersen 1997, Fig. 20); C: pointed stake from Halsskov Syd (redrawn from Pedersen 1997, Fig. 21); D: pointed stake from Vedskølle Åmunding Nord (redrawn from Fischer 1997a, Fig. 17); this is truncated because the upper part was radiocarbon dated to 7880–7675 BP (T–11331) and is thus of Kongemose date.

been radiocarbon dated to 7210–6950 BP (K 4053) and 7200–6910 BP (K 4054); the trap is thus early Ertebølle (S.H. Andersen 1997). The large size of some of these traps is shown by the middle Ertebølle find at Nekselø, below present sea level. *In situ* stakes were found 100 m from the contemporary shoreline, and to function properly the trap would have had to extend this far (Pedersen 1995).

The remarkable work resulting from construction of the fixed link across the Storebælt has yielded three more examples. Halsskov Syd (Figure 5) is early Ertebølle, while Halsskov Øst is middle Ertebølle (Pedersen 1997). On the opposite side of the Storebælt an example was located at Lindholm, excavated by divers (Dencker 1997). The fact that intensive survey in a relatively small area has produced no fewer than three such structures is a good indication of how common they were. Finally, Tybrind Vig was excavated by divers, and has produced many pointed stakes testifying to yet another example (S.H. Andersen 1987a; 1987b).

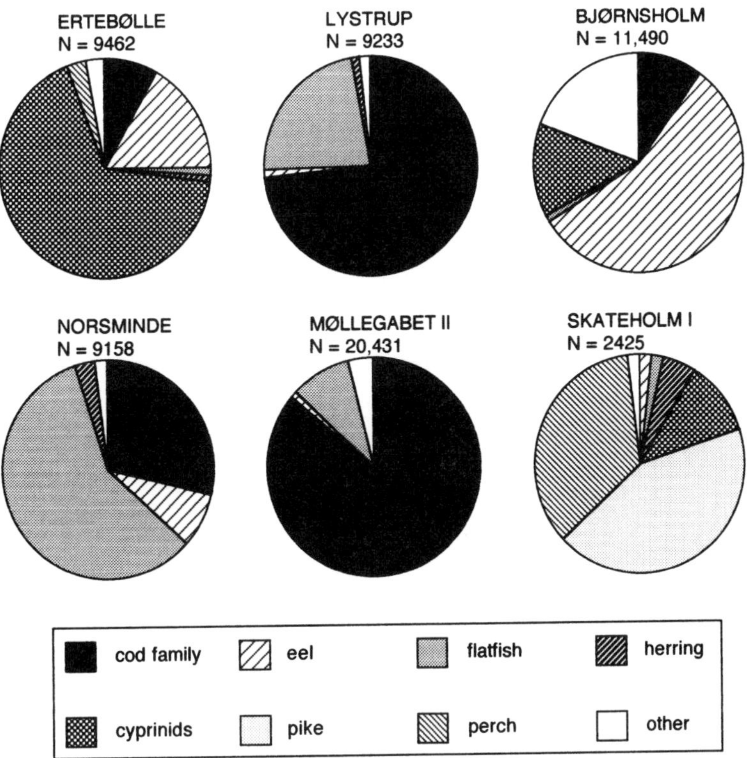

Figure 6. Proportions of fish species at Ertebølle sites. Ertebølle from Enghoff (1987, Table 1); Lystrup from Enghoff (1994, Table 1); Bjørnsholm from Enghoff (1993, Table 1); Norsminde from Enghoff (1993, Table 1); Møllegabet II from Cardell (in press, Table 1); Skateholm I from Jonsson (1988, Table 1). The true cod (*Gadus morhua*) is overwhelmingly predominant within the 'cod family' group.

Thirdly, fish remains have been recovered in quantity and well studied. Considering the material available at the time, Clark (1975) concluded that cod fishing using hook and line was the major activity. Recent work has altered this conclusion. The majority of fish caught were remarkably small, and fine sieving is vital if their bones are to be recovered during excavation. At Lystrup, most cod were below 50 cm in length (Enghoff 1994). This is significant because of the static fish trap at this site (see above and Figure 5): large numbers of small fish are evidently the typical catch using this technology. Cod were small everywhere in the Ertebølle—at Maglemosegårds Vænge the majority were between 25 and 35 cm, and at Norsminde they were even smaller—and Enghoff (op. cit.) states that these size ranges indicate the widespread use of static traps.

Static traps are indicated by the fish remains in another way as well. While cod was important, other fish predominate at some sites. Several examples of fish proportions are given in Figure 6. Cod predominate at Lystrup, but at Norsminde they are heavily outnumbered by flatfish, mostly plaice, flounder, and dab (Enghoff 1991). At Bjørnsholm, eel was the main catch; small freshwater cyprinids were also common, perhaps taken as a byproduct of the eel fishery (Enghoff 1993; 1995). At Ertebølle, the small cyprinids (mainly roach) were dominant despite the coastal location of the site; few were over 15 cm in length (Enghoff 1987). Further to the south, the early Ertebølle site of Møllegabet II, 4.5 m below present sea level, was excavated by divers using fine screening (Grøn & Skaarup 1991). The sample of over 20,000 identified fishbones is dominated by cod, mostly between 30 and 45 cm in length (Cardell in press); these were probably much more important than the far less numerous mammals and birds (Hodgetts & Rowley-Conwy in press). At Skateholm I, in less saline waters, freshwater pike and perch dominated; herring was the most common marine fish (Jonsson 1988). The small size of the fish, the local variation in predominant species, and the wide range of rarer species including some that are active only at night, are exactly the patterns expected from the use of static traps (Enghoff 1994).

Ertebølle complexity?

The Ertebølle has attracted attention regarding hunter-gatherer 'complexity'. Various definitions of this concept have been offered; that used here is based on a four-fold scheme for non-tropical hunter gatherers (Rowley-Conwy in press c):

1 Serial specialists moving from resource to resource in sequence, with little or no logistic movement of resources or food storage.

2 Logistic groups that *do not* defend territories.

3 Logistic groups that *do* defend territories.

4 Sedentary groups, who invariably defend territories and store resources.

These form a continuum from non-complex (type 1) to most complex (type 4). Other attributes are sometimes brought into the definitions, for example complex technology, hierarchical social organization, resource specialization and intensification, high population density, and so on (for example, Price 1985).

Some aspects of the Ertebølle have been linked to complexity. Perhaps the earliest was the sedentism of the large Jutland settlements. Although many of the other attributes could not be demonstrated archaeologically, it was argued that social and demographic factors would covary with sedentism; regional population would probably be relatively dense, and society might not be egalitarian (Rowley-Conwy 1983).

Another unusual archaeological feature is the presence of cemeteries. Those at Skateholm I and II (L. Larsson 1988; 1989) and Vedbæk (Albrethsen & Brinch Petersen 1976) are well known. Another at Korsør Nor, containing seven or eight graves, was destroyed during harbour works in 1945 (Schilling 1997; Bennike 1997). Nederst in Jutland is another likely candidate, and there may be more (L. Larsson 1995). Formal disposal of the dead was linked to territoriality by Saxe (1970), who argued that cemeteries containing ancestors legitimized territorial ownership by the living. This argument was extended and applied to other areas (see, for example, Goldstein 1981; Pardoe 1988; Chattopadhyaya 1996), and has been discussed in connection with Skateholm I (Rowley-Conwy 1998a).

The discussion has been taken further in two main ways. The first is archaeological: the recovery of the numerous static fish traps and the small fish they caught (see above). This adds complex technology to the Ertebølle attributes suggesting complexity. Such technology is one of the key features allowing recognition of food storage in the archaeological record, because it implies that more resources were taken than could be consumed on a day-to-day basis. Food storage has important implications for social stratification, because stores are privately owned and not accessible by all (Rowley-Conwy & Zvelebil 1989).

The second is ethnographic. A major cross-cultural survey of hunter gatherers by Keeley (1988; 1991) has revealed some interesting correlations (Figure 7). Degree of sedentism is closely linked to population density relative to ecological productivity; both charts in the figure show this. This suggests that the intuitive feeling of many archaeologists that the Ertebølle had a relatively high population density is in fact correct. The left-hand chart in Figure 7 plots the dependence of the various societies on stored food, and shows a strong trend for this to increase with sedentism and population—which fits well with the archaeological arguments mentioned above. The right-hand chart plots social variables, and again there is a strong trend for more stratified societies to correlate with sedentism and population—and thus with food storage, confirming Rowley-Conwy and Zvelebil (1989). This opens further connections: descent classes are common among territorial societies (Richardson 1982), and are thus linked to the use of cemeteries (Saxe 1970; Pardoe 1988); territorial exclusivity is thus mirrored by social exclusivity (Rowley-Conwy 1998a).

The upshot is that the early suggestions of Ertebølle complexity in areas not directly visible archaeologically may now be put forward with somewhat greater confidence. More connections between the various attributes have been established, to the point where Keeley (1988) felt able to distinguish between two major types of hunter gatherers—visible in both parts of Figure 7. Accordingly, the Jutland middle and late Ertebølle is interpreted as sedentary, territorial, and food storing (type 4, above), and therefore probably organized

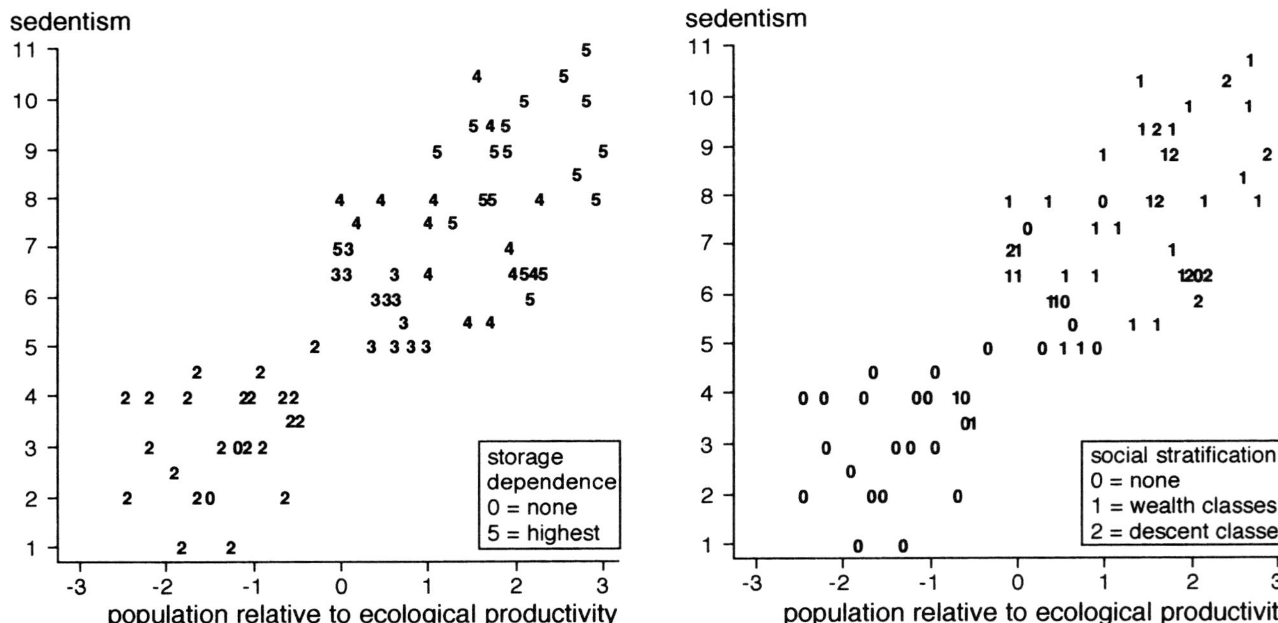

Figure 7. Correlations between various attributes of hunter-gatherer societies (redrawn from Keeley 1991, Figs. 17.1 and 17.6). Sedentism (Keeley's STAY) is the number of months for which the winter settlement is occupied. Population relative to ecological productivity (LNY) is calculated by Keeley (1988, 385). Each data point is one ethnographic hunter-gatherer group. Left: correlation with dependence on storage. Right: correlation with social stratification.

in descent classes. The South Swedish early Ertebølle was not sedentary but did establish cemeteries, and is accordingly interpreted as a type 3 group. It is not clear whether the Øresund groups were type 3 or 4.

Where does complexity come from?

We thus have an early Mesolithic in which complexity cannot be demonstrated, and a late Mesolithic in which (with increasing clarity) it can. Explanations for the appearance of complexity may be divided into developmental and adaptational (Rowley-Conwy in press c; cf. also Gould 1985; Bettinger 1991). Developmental views seek the cause of complexity in either internal sociocultural change or demographic increase; whichever is selected is put forward as an independent variable. Adaptational views, however, seek to embed these factors in a broader social and ecological context.

Developmental views assume slow unidirectional change in the variable selected for emphasis. Intensification of economic activities is sometimes apparently regarded as the normal and ubiquitous state of affairs during the Mesolithic (for example, Price 1996; J. Thomas 1996); sometimes this is seen as having quasi-agricultural results by the late Mesolithic (Clarke 1976; Zvelebil 1994; 1995). The concept of intensification is sometimes rather vague, however, and (if it is used at all) it is better placed in context. In the South Scandinavian case, the use of large static fish traps is an intensification, but it occurred in the ecological context of an approaching sea shore; in the early Mesolithic the sea was elsewhere. The social context was the increase in population resulting from the arrival of the sea and its resources. A subsequent intensification of terrestrial resources would occur in coastal hinterlands due to this greater population. This was probably why logistic hunting camps like Ringkloster were used (see above). There is currently no evidence for quasi-husbandry (Rowley-Conwy 1995a). Intensification is thus best seen as an economic adaptation within the changing ecological and social context, rather than an explanatory *deus ex machina*. The word 'intensification' is therefore redundant and potentially misleading, and best omitted from future discussions.

Demographic increase is the other variable sometimes regarded as independent (Cohen 1977). Cemeteries have been argued to result from the crossing of a 'demographic threshold' at the start of the late Mesolithic (Clark & Neely 1987, 124). Independent population growth has, however, been criticized (Rowley-Conwy in press c). Cemeteries should not be considered outside the context of territoriality (see above), which in turn has an ecological context. Territoriality arises when resources in a limited area are both productive and reliable (Dyson-Hudson & Smith 1978; D.H. Thomas 1981). In South Scandinavia the relevant resources were probably migratory fish such as cod and eel—whose routes could be interdicted by large fishtraps and whose meat could be stored. Keeley (1988; 1991) draws these ecological factors into his cross-cultural correlations: groups based on storage and arranged in descent classes are usually found in areas with less interannual variability. Descent classes are the common organization of territorial groups (Richardson 1982); reliable and productive resource nodes owned by territorial descent classes are thus directly linked to the establishment of cemeteries (Saxe 1970; Pardoe 1988; Rowley-Conwy 1998a).

'Intensification' and demography are thus elements in a complex contextual web rather than independent causative factors. In South Scandinavia the arrival of the rising sea and its resources was the most important element creating the differences between early and late Mesolithic. Change in response to this was apparently rapid—not long and slow as the developmental view implies. This emerges from a consideration of the middle Mesolithic Kongemose period, not considered so far. The period of most rapid sea level rise falls in the earlier Kongemose (Figure 1), but there are some signs that complexity was present. An outstanding result from the work in connection with the Storebælt fixed link has been the offshore extension of Ertebølle coastal settlement foci. Suitable settlement areas were occupied much earlier than the Ertebølle, when the sea was lower; as it encroached, so the settlements moved further into the bays or estuaries to locations above present sea level (Fischer 1997b). The earlier submarine settlements go back to the early Kongemose; at this time sea level rise was so rapid that it would have been discernible within a human generation (Aaris-Sørensen 1988). Despite this the settlements were substantial; discussing Stavreshoved, Fischer (1997b, 77) writes:

> These sites are from a time at which the rise in sea-level was at its most rapid. As a result there would have been significantly fewer years available for the accumulation of cultural traces here than on corresponding coastal sites from the end of the Ertebølle Culture. It is therefore remarkable that Stavreshoved does bear comparison, in terms of its extent and the density of cultural traces, with the richest known find places from the latest Ertebølle period. This site can thus hardly be the product of short, seasonal visits by small groups. It must reflect the more or less permanent settlement of a relatively large group of people.

Musholm Bay is another large site, at 8.5 m below sea level the deepest excavation yet conducted in Denmark. This has been radiocarbon dated to 8300–8100 BP, the very inception of the Kongemose period, and was in a good location for the erection of a static fish trap—although no trap was found (Fischer & Malm 1997). Probable traces of a static trap were however found in the Øresund at Vedskølle Åmunding Nord (Figure 4); a pointed stake (Figure 5) was dated to 7880–7675 BP (T–11331) and is thus of early Kongemose date (Fischer 1997a). Another probable site is Blak II, where several stakes were found driven into the sea bed. The stakes have not been dated, but bone and charcoal range between 7660–7390 BP (K 5836) and 8360–8120 BP (K 5834) and are thus also very early Kongemose (Sørensen 1996).

Kongemose complexity is hinted at in another way. Gøngehusvej 7 (Figure 4) in the town of Vedbæk has so far yielded four Kongemose graves containing several individuals, some interred, some cremated (Brinch Petersen *et al.* 1993). Segebro in Sweden yielded three grave-shaped features containing red ochre, although no bones were preserved; they were interpreted as graves (L. Larsson 1982, 30–1). Both these sites might be Kongemose cemeteries.

The Kongemose thus encompasses large sedentary settlements, large static fish traps, and possible cemeteries. These are all attributes indicating complexity, and we must now accept that the Kongemose was in this respect similar to the Ertebølle. This is a key point, because in the Storebælt the marine environment *was only formed around 9000 BP* as the sea inundated the former river valley; at this time it was still brackish and only attained

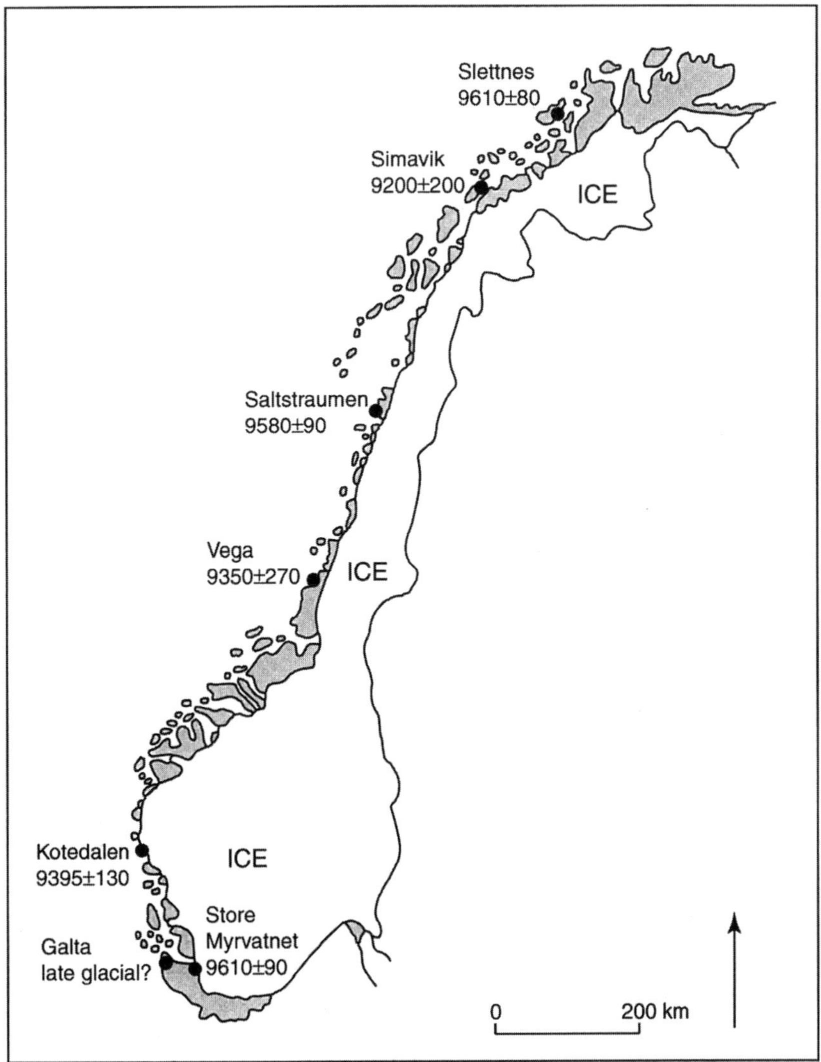

Figure 8. Radiocarbon ages in uncalibrated years BP for the early maritime occupation of Norway. Shaded: ice-free areas at Younger Dryas maximum glacial extension, 11,000–10,000 BP. Combined from Bjerck (1995, Figs. 5 and 7) with additions.

its modern form around 8000 BP (Mathiassen 1997). The Kongemose thus 'went complex' as soon as it was possible to do so. This is the clearest possible evidence that the change was an adaptation to the new environment and not the result of the independent operation of 'intensification' or demography.

The radiocarbon dating evidence thus indicates that complexity was a rapid adaptation, not a slow independently-generated process. Perhaps Maglemosian coastal settlements on the palaeoshore of the North Sea were complex, perhaps not. Either way, the developmental view of slow change from simple to complex can no longer be sustained; it must be seen in an adaptive context.

Speed of response: coast and mountain in Norway

Norway differs from South Scandinavia in a number of ways. The first is its sheer size: from Copenhagen to the North Cape is the same distance as from Copenhagen to Naples, and most of this is Norway, which extends to over 71°N. The deeply indented shoreline has a total length of 26,000 km. Unlike Denmark and South Sweden, the terrain is steep and rocky, not gentle and undulating; organic preservation is usually poor. Despite this, recent work in Norway provides two very good examples of fast hunter-gatherer responses to changed conditions.

The first concerns the initial occupation. The oldest potential site is Galta, which may be of late Glacial date (Prøsch-Danielsen & Høgestol 1995). It is, however, only dated by the beach level in which it is found, and some remain doubtful as to its date (Bjerck 1995). Good radiocarbon evidence is available from the early post-glacial (Bjerck op. cit.). This is plotted in Figure 8; note that the ages are in uncalibrated radiocarbon years, because of the problems of calibration in the 10th radiocarbon millennium BP (Becker & Kromer 1991). Two things stand out: firstly, occupation appears to have been extremely rapid, with no visible trend from south to north—although the 10th millennium BP radiocarbon wiggles may be an obscuring factor; and secondly, most of Norway was still under ice at this time, so the adaptation must have been strongly maritime. Animal bones do not survive, but there can be little doubt that marine resources would have been overwhelmingly important.

The second concerns the occupation of the very mountainous southern interior region. This is shown in Figure 9 (dates again uncalibrated). Again, there was rapid occupation as the ice melted (Bang-Andersen 1996). The nature of the exploitation of the highlands is not clear, but it does represent the rapid appearance of a new adaptation when the opportunity appeared.

The lack of organic remains makes these sites seem less spectacular than the South Scandinavian ones considered above, but the results are arguably at least as significant. The maritime adaptation is earlier than any documented further south, and must have been spread by boats peninsula-hopping along the coast. Its rapidity and antiquity contain important implications for other areas of the globe, and both coast and mountains reveal once again how fast hunter-gatherer communities can respond to new adaptive possibilities.

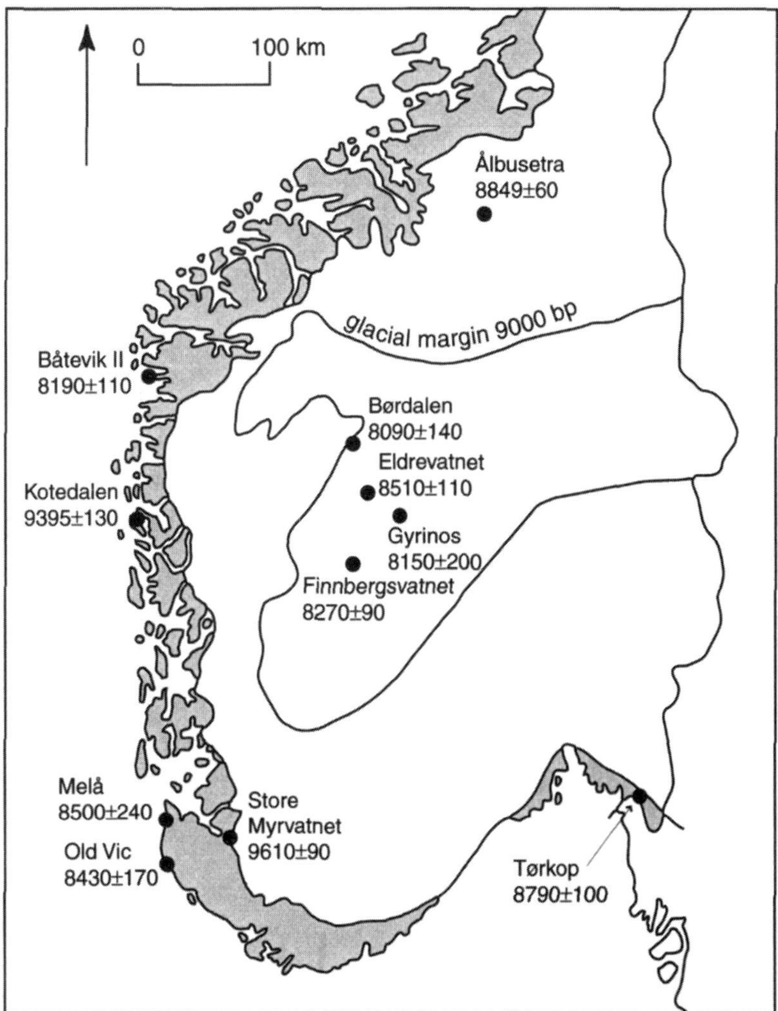

Figure 9. Radiocarbon ages in uncalibrated years BP for the early occupation of the mountains of southern Norway. Shaded: ice-free areas at 10,000 BP; glacial margin at 9000 BP also marked. Simplified from Bang-Andersen (1996, Figs. 3 and 5).

The appearance of agriculture

Denmark: radiocarbon dating and the demise of tribal explanations

Radiocarbon dating has had a fundamental effect on theories concerning the appearance of agriculture in Denmark. It was the major cause of the change from tribal to processual views. Many archaeological explanations changed in this way in the late 1960s and early 1970s, but the impact of radiocarbon dating in Denmark was earlier than this. The theoretical change in Denmark was thus a direct result of the application of archaeological science.

The tribal view was the result of relative stratigraphic dating. The chronological scheme was put forward by Iversen (1937), who distinguished four marine transgressions which he linked to vegetational changes (Figure 10 left). He used the elm decline as the border between pollen zones VIIb and VIII (Iversen 1941). Jessen (1937) correlated two marine layers at the Ertebølle midden of Klintesø with two layers in a bog 2 km away; these latter could be dated by their pollen to transgressions III and IV. The Klintesø midden was contemporary with the upper marine layer, and was thus placed in transgression IV, in pollen zone VIII. Troels-Smith (1937) pollen dated the major Ertebølle site of Brabrand to the time of transgression IV, and Dyrholm phase III (also regarded as Ertebølle) to the same transgression (1942). There were thus three major Ertebølle sites in the early part of pollen zone VIII (Figure 10).

This dating was crucial because Jessen (1938) pollen dated Troldebjerg and Bundsø to the same period. These are Neolithic sites with full domestic economies, contemporary with the megalithic passage graves. Therefore coastal hunter gatherers and inland farmers, economically and culturally distinct, were apparently living alongside each other. This tribal separation formed the basis for the next round of debate: Becker (1954) believed that the Neolithic was ethnically intrusive in its entirety, while Troels-Smith (1953) believed that phase A of the early Neolithic was an integral part of the Ertebølle, while phases B and C were the immigrants.

This scheme unravelled as radiocarbon dates accumulated. Figure 10 shows the process (using uncalibrated dates, because this is the form in which they had their impact). Dates are plotted from the datelists quoted by Tauber (1972), although the pattern had become clear well before 1972. Ertebølle dates preceded the elm decline, while Neolithic dates fell at or after it. The large series of dates from the stratified site of Norsminde (S.H. Andersen 1989) confirms this neatly (Figure 10). Troels-Smith (1966) retracted the stratigraphic dates: the correlation between Klintesø and the bog 2 km away may have been spurious, and Brabrand might have been disturbed by ice action; certainly both equate typologically with Dyrholm II, not Dyrholm III. Dyrholm III is typologically Neolithic, and remains in pollen zone VIII where Troels-Smith placed it; it is now regarded as a hunting or fishing camp used by Neolithic farmers (Skaarup 1973; Rowley-Conwy 1983).

Denmark and South Sweden: rate of change

The speed of the appearance of agriculture in Denmark and South Sweden is debated. Some take a gradualist perspective, stating that developments began in the Ertebølle while full agriculture appeared only quite late in the Neolithic (for example, Price 1996; J. Thomas 1996). This paper, however, argues the opposite view, that the change was relatively fast.

The site of Löddesborg in South Sweden (Jennbert 1984) is often quoted as evidence

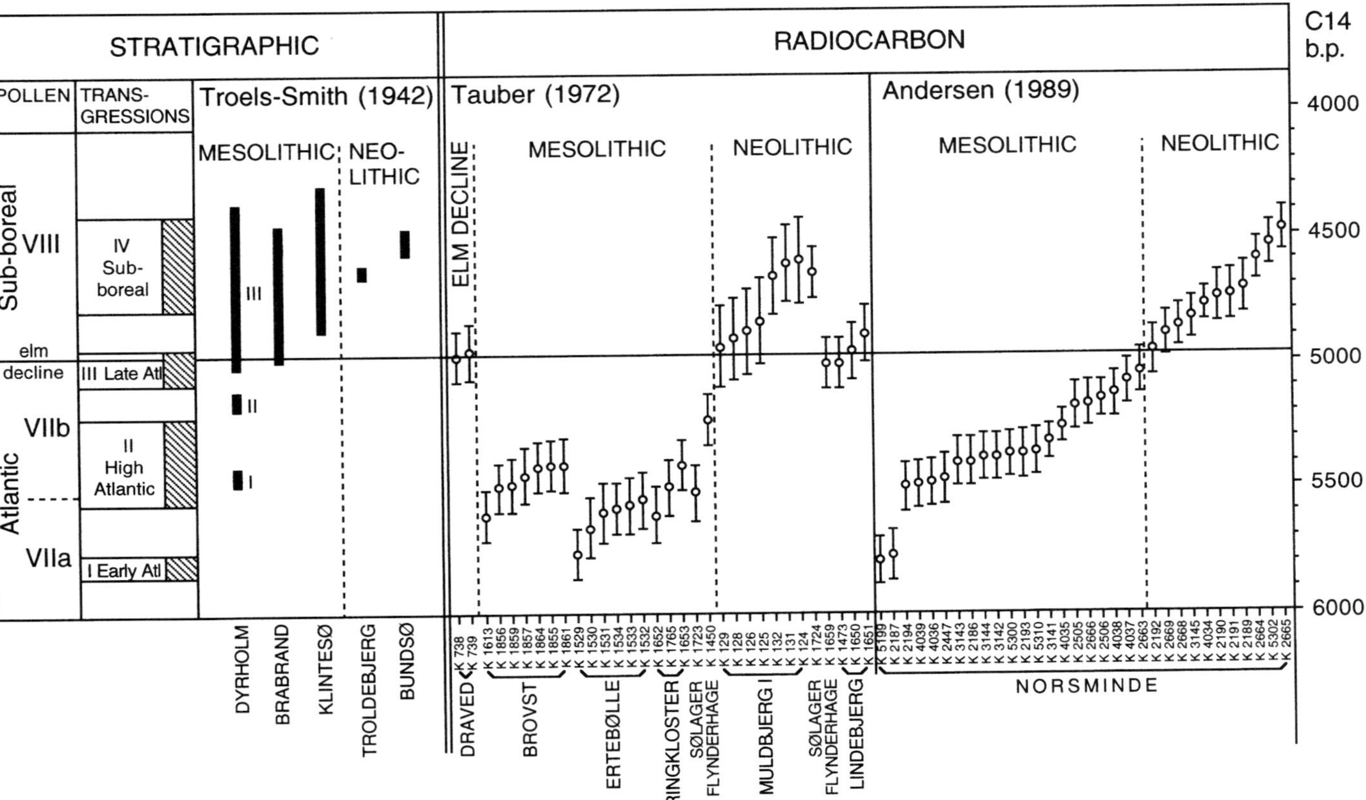

Figure 10. Changing chronological views of the Mesolithic–Neolithic transition in Denmark. Left: relative scheme based on stratigraphic correlations (simplified from Troels-Smith 1942, Fig. 5). Right: absolute scheme based on accumulating radiocarbon ages (in uncalibrated years BP); dates from Tauber (1972) and S.H. Andersen (1989). Note that the radiocarbon scale applies only to the right-hand part of the figure; the only chronological marker common to both parts is the elm decline. The pollen and transgressions columns are now known to cover substantially more time than is covered by the radiocarbon scale on the right.

of Ertebølle cereal cultivation, but the original report makes it clear that the typological attribution of the sherds with cereal impressions to Mesolithic or Neolithic was problematic; the Mesolithic and Neolithic ceramics were not stratigraphically separated, raising questions about the stratigraphic integrity of the site (M. Larsson 1984; Nielsen 1985). There is in fact no convincing evidence for any Ertebølle cereals or domestic animals except dogs (Rowley-Conwy 1995a; 1995b; 1998b).

The claim that the earlier Neolithic was nomadic and mainly based on hunting and gathering ignores the evidence from trace element analysis that there was an abrupt change to a terrestrial diet at the start of the Neolithic (Tauber 1982); this is matched by an abrupt shift of settlement into the interior (Nielsen 1985; M. Larsson 1984). It also ignores no fewer than 43 Danish sets of preserved Neolithic ard marks, 14 of which date to the early or the start of the middle Neolithic (Thrane 1982); these suggest permanent fields. Finally, it ignores a major recent development: the appearance of early Neolithic longhouses. Earlier claimed residential houses at Barkær (Glob 1949) and Stengade (Skaarup 1975) are now regarded as funerary monuments (Madsen 1979; Liversage 1992). A new series of residential longhouses has, however, appeared in Denmark; Ornehus measures 16 × 6 m, Skæppekærgård 14 × 4.5 m, and the best preserved of two at Limensgård on Bornholm 18.5 × 5.5 m (Eriksen 1992). Two indeterminate post-hole structures were found at Mosegården, stratigraphically older than 5940–5730 BP (K 3463), the earliest good Neolithic date in Denmark (Madsen & Pedersen 1984). In South Sweden Mossby measures 12 × 6 m, Karlshem 7 × 3 m (Larsson & Larsson 1986). Probable examples are known from Bellevuegård (M. Larsson 1984), Karlsfält (L. Larsson 1985), and Rävgrav (L. Larsson 1992). Three house plans are reproduced in Figure 11; the substantial and consistent nature of the constructions do not mesh well with the notion of nomadism.

Grahame Clark (1965a; 1965b) was probably the first to see that radiocarbon showed that agriculture spread across Europe not slowly and evenly, but in a series of rapid jumps punctuated by pauses. The longest pause occurred at the southern margin of Scandinavia, where for well over a millennium there was a fairly stable boundary between hunter gatherers and farmers—but, as argued, when the change came it was rapid. The rapidity of the change argues against developmental explanations. This writer's suggestion that the oyster was seasonally important, so that its disappearance at the end of the Ertebølle caused problems (Rowley-Conwy 1984a), has not met much favour (for example, Blankholm 1987; Price & Gebauer 1992) and social explanations have been more in vogue (for example, Blankholm 1996; Hodder 1990). However, the end of the late Ertebølle remains contemporary with a marine regression; shell midden accumulation declined drastically and the oyster virtually disappeared (S.H. Andersen 1995, Figs 9a and b). Whether the oyster was an important seasonal resource or not, it acts as an index of high marine salinity; its disappearance thus testifies to a substantial decline in ecological productivity. The appearance of agriculture in Denmark is likely therefore to have an ecological context.

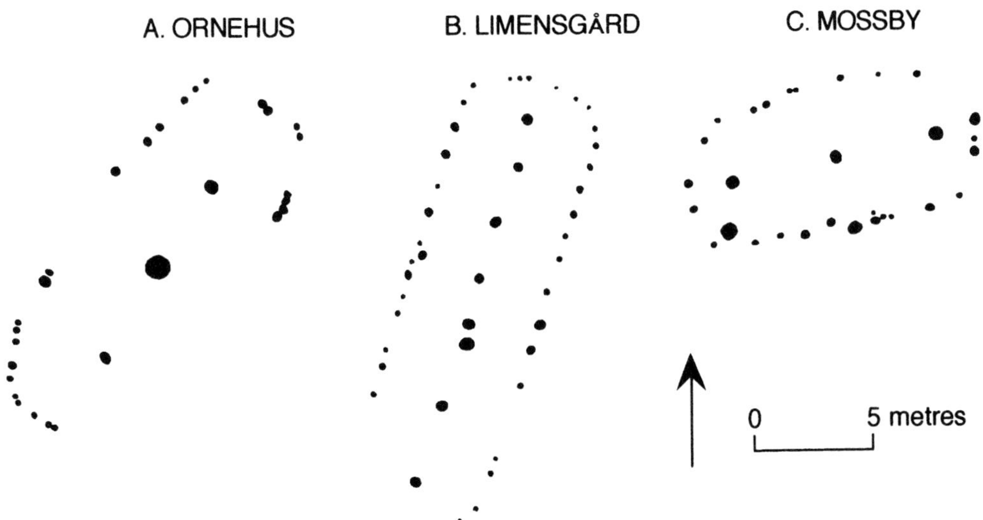

Figure 11. Early Neolithic houses from southern Scandinavia, reproduced to the same scale and orientation. Ornehus and Limensgård redrawn from Eriksen (1992, Figs. 3 and 8); Mossby redrawn from Larsson and Larsson (1986, Fig. 35). See Figure 4 for locations.

Norway: another stable boundary?

The spread of farming far to the north up the Scandinavian coasts is sometimes seen as an early development. This could be so, but the rarity of preserved organic remains makes the picture far from straightforward and an alternative picture is emerging.

In coastal Norway, the later layers at the important site of Kotedalen (Figure 12) are of Neolithic age, with 29 radiocarbon dates falling around 5800–5000 BP (A.B. Olsen 1992). These layers produced a few traces of cereal-type pollen (Hjelle 1992), perhaps evidence for agriculture. However, the macrobotanical assemblages contained no cereals at all (Soltvedt 1992). Exceptionally, bone was preserved. The very large combined Neolithic assemblage is shown in Figure 13 (right). Fragments of fish and birds between them outnumbered those of mammals, something not unexpected in view of the site's location on a narrow strait between the open sea and an interior basin (Figure 13, left); tidal movements through the strait make fishing highly productive. The overwhelming majority of mammal bones were unfortunately pulverized beyond recognition. No domestic animals at all were observed in the identified sample, and the faunal analyst states that non-native species such as sheep, goat, and cattle are quite different to the native large terrestrial species. Had domestic mammals been present in any numbers it is therefore likely they would have been spotted despite the degree of fragmentation (Hufthammer 1992; 1995).

The few cereal-type pollen grains thus remain the only source of agricultural evidence. This is not the only place in Scandinavia with claimed cereal pollen but an absence of

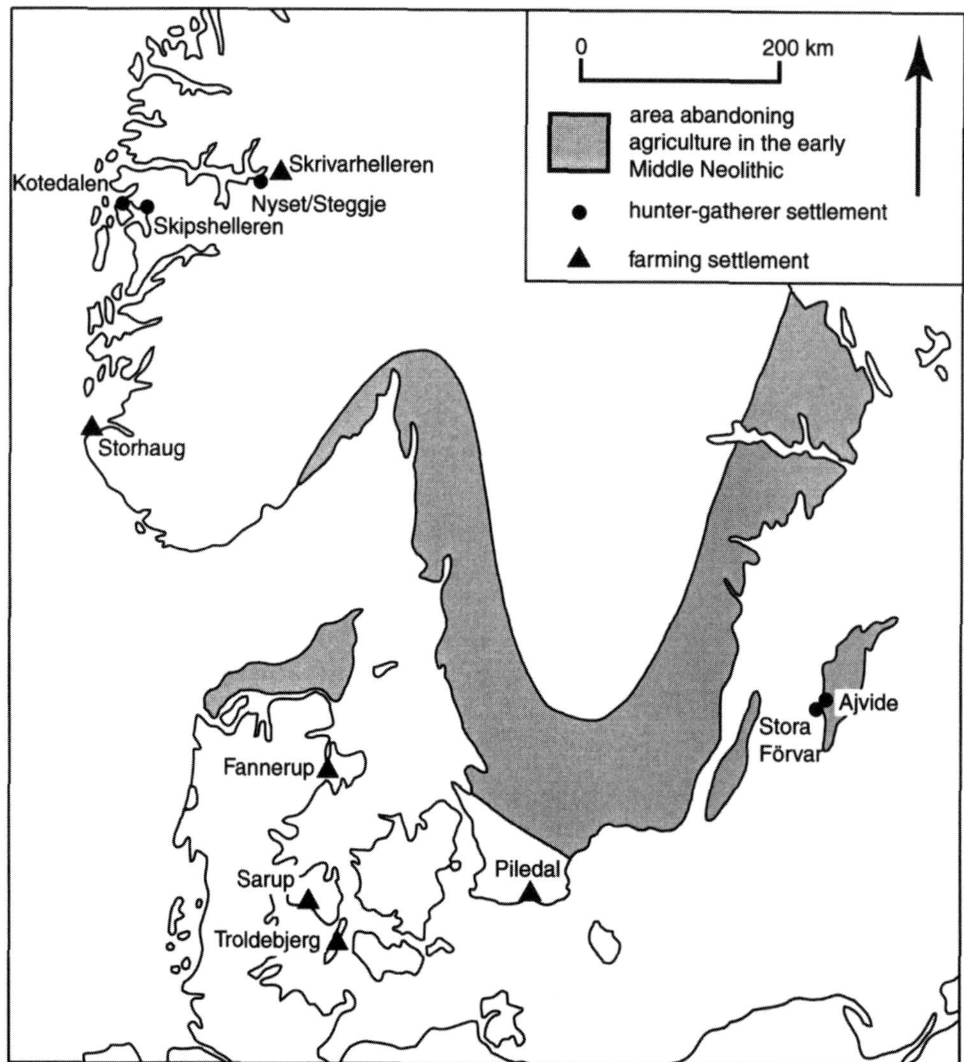

Figure 12. Southern Scandinavia at the start of the middle Neolithic period (except Storhaug and Skrivarhelleren, which are late Neolithic). Area abandoning agriculture after Zvelebil (1996, Fig. 18.3).

domestic animals or cereals (Rowley-Conwy 1995b). In view of the problems in identifying such pollen (Edwards 1989), the claims for agriculture are by no means certain unless and until backed up by domestic animals and plants. This is certainly true for Kotedalen in view of the situation at other nearby sites. The earliest domestic animal bones in the stratified cave of Skipshelleren (see Figure 12) were directly dated to 4820–4350 BP (H. Olsen 1976). These remain the oldest domestic animal bones from anywhere in Norway (Hufthammer 1995), and even this date is not without its problems (Prescott 1996, 81). At

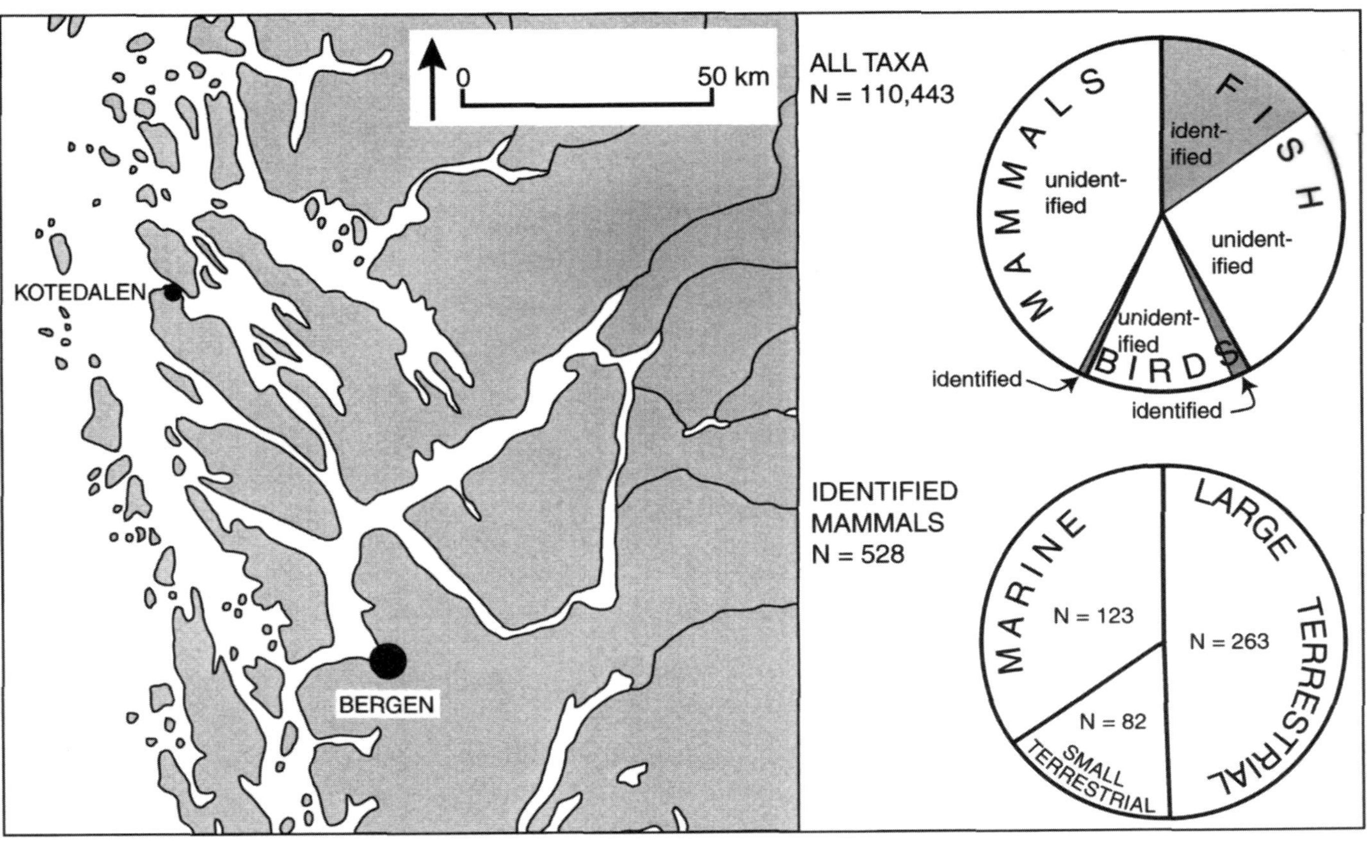

Figure 13. The south-west Norwegian site of Kotedalen, near the city of Bergen. Left: map showing site location on entry to interior marine basin, redrawn from A.B. Olsen (1992, Fig. 1). Right: faunal proportions in Neolithic layers 12–15; top, major groupings including unidentified fragments; bottom, identified mammals only. Information from Hufthammer (1992, Tables 20, 22, 26, and 31).

Skrivarhelleren, the earliest domestic animals and cereals are in late Neolithic layers dated after 4050–3850 BP (T 7686—Prescott 1991; Soltvedt 1991). The earliest directly dated cultivated cereals are from late Neolithic Storhaug, dated to 3850–3690 BP (Soltvedt & Mydland 1995). A major shift in late Neolithic settlement location in the Nyset and Steggje regions is believed to reflect the appearance of agriculture (Bjørgo *et al.* 1992; Prescott 1995). Bones are not preserved on the island of Flatøy, but early Neolithic sites are in the same locations as Mesolithic ones, optimally placed for fishing and sea mammal hunting; the 50,000 artefacts are linked to the manufacture and repair of hunting and fishing gear (Simpson 1992). The same is true of the island of Kollsnes except that the sites continue through the middle Neolithic; all sites appear small and temporary and are probably fishing camps. The only exception is Budalen 17 whch has a larger post-hole structure; one post-hole contained pellets of sheep dung, one of which was dated to 4200–3945 BP (Ua-2456), at the transition from middle to late neolithic (Nærøy 1994).

This suggests that agriculture was not adopted in south-west Norway until the (artifactually defined) late Neolithic. At least for the present it can be argued that there was a stable boundary between hunter gatherers and farmers somewhere south of Skipshelleren. Where the boundary lay is not known because organic preservation is very poor. In the highlands of the Hardanger (Figure 12) 13 Neolithic sites yielded a total of only 38 identifiable bones, none of them from domestic animals (Indrelid 1994). Further south in Telemark the many Neolithic sites have produced no bone at all, and pollen remains the only basis for claims of agriculture (Mikkelsen 1989). Even in Østfold, Norway's south-eastern extremity, the only evidence for early Neolithic agriculture is that some sites are on sandy soils suitable for cultivation (Østmo 1988). It is legitimate to ask: was there *really* a Neolithic in Norway? (Prescott 1996).

Gotland: middle Neolithic re-adoption of hunting and gathering

Agriculture spread through South Sweden in the early Neolithic, coming to a halt near the northern edge of the temperate zone (Hulthén & Welinder 1981, 156–61). Denmark and southernmost Sweden remained agricultural in the middle Neolithic; for example, domestic animal bones come from Troldebjerg (Higham & Message 1968) and Fannerup (Rowley-Conwy 1984b); cereals were found at Piledal (Hjelmqvist 1985) and the major causewayed camp at Sarup (N.H. Andersen 1997). In much of coastal Sweden, however, there was a re-adoption of hunting and gathering (Figure 12).

The island of Gotland (see Figure 12) is perhaps the best place to examine this. The key sequence is from Stora Förvar cave, on an islet 6.5 km off Gotland's west coast, excavated in the last century in horizontal 30 cm spits. The basal spits were aceramic but thought to date from the later part of the early Neolithic, while the rest of the sequence was middle Neolithic (Schnittger & Rydh 1940, 78–9). Grahame Clark used the sequence as a case study in bioarchaeology (1976); his chart based on Schnittger and Rydh's chronology is reproduced in Figure 14, annotated with recent results.

		PHOCINAE				ARTEFACTS		
	Layers	GREY SEALS %	RINGED SEALS %	HARP SEALS %	Numbers	HARPOONS %	FISH-HOOKS	CERAMICS
	B 1	100			6			STONE CIST
	H 2		100		1			
	B 2	75	25		4			
	H 3	666	33		3			
Iron Age	G^H 3	100			1			
	B 3	100			2			
Late Neolithic/ Early Bronze Age	I 4		89	11	9	3		
	G 4		86	14	14	3		
	I 5	14	71	14	14	3		SÄTER IV
Middle Neolithic no sheep or cattle	G 5	11	76	13	38	32	▮	
	B 6		86	14	43	53		SÄTER III
cattle, sheep, pigs	H 7	57	42	1	74	53		
	G 7	37	54	9	59	53		
2000 year hiatus	G 8	71	29		55	3		SÄTER II
	G 9	73	27		86			
Early Mesolithic no large terrestrial mammals	F10	88	12		32			
	G11	94	6		34			
	A11	75	25		40	3		
	F12	92	8		38			
9500 BP	F13	85	15		39	Total 34		

Figure 14. Right: table correlating seals and artefacts at Stora Förvar cave, after Clark (1976, Fig. 1), based on dating from Schnittger and Rydh (1940). Left: revisions resulting from radiocarbon dating and zooarchaeological analysis (Lindqvist 1997; Lindqvist & Passnert 1997).

Recent work has demonstrated that the chronology is much longer than formerly envisaged (Lindqvist 1997; Lindqvist & Possnert 1997). Radiocarbon reveals that the basal aceramic spits are in fact early Mesolithic, separated from later deposits by a 2000-year hiatus. During the Mesolithic, no large terrestrial mammals were present; accelerator dating demonstrates that 'mesolithic' pigs are intrusive, thus resolving a problem that has plagued the archaeology of Gotland for a century. Domestic species were introduced in the early Neolithic; these, along with a change from a marine to a terrestrial diet (and a token megalith), link Gotland with the early farmers in Denmark and South Sweden (Lindqvist & Possnert op. cit.).

Many sites are known from Gotland proper, and their distributions reflect the economic changes: a coastal Mesolithic is followed by an interior early Neolithic (Österholm 1989). The middle Neolithic is of crucial interest: diet is strongly marine, and sheep and cattle disappear (Lindqvist & Possnert 1997). Sites move back to the coast; many are large, and associated with cemeteries (Österholm op. cit.). The major site of Ajvide D is a good example, with a settlement and 50 graves (Burenhult 1997). In the late Neolithic, domestic sheep and cattle reappear at Stora Förvar (Lindqvist & Possnert op. cit.).

The evidence thus supports a re-adoption of coastal hunting and gathering during the middle Neolithic. One problem, however, remains. Pigs must have been introduced by human agency. Initially they were part of the early Neolithic agricultural suite, but they continue to be found when the other domestic animals disappear and settlement moves back to the coast in the middle Neolithic. They are often regarded as domestic, both because they are a human import (Jonsson 1986; Lindqvist & Possnert 1997) and because many mandibles are found in some graves; it would be difficult to hunt so many pigs to order when required for a funerary ritual (Österholm 1989). The issue is far from clear, however; killing was seasonal, which suggests they could have been wild (Ekman 1974; Rowley-Conwy & Storå 1997). Wild as well as domestic animals may be carried to islands as an economic resource. The specimens in the graves were killed over several months of the year, not all at once; they *could* therefore be trophied jaws from hunted specimens. More work is needed; but one may ask what niche a domestic pig would fill in an economy that was not producing agricultural waste.

Conclusions

The economic prehistory of Scandinavia is a truly massive subject, something shown not least by the size of the bibliography accompanying this contribution. The number of references published in the last few years testifies that work is increasing, and the last decade has transformed our views of many issues.

Clark's favourite archaeological sciences, zooarchaeology and radiocarbon dating, have played crucial roles in this transformation. Changes in theoretical perspective are vital for the future of archaeology, and the most useful ones emerge simply from an improved knowledge of what happened in prehistory. Archaeology is, fortunately, a discipline that can be (and frequently is) surprised by unexpected findings. The production of new theories to account for such surprises is the basic method of disciplinary advance; much more fruitful than merely basing them on whim.

An aspect stressed throughout this contribution has been the speed of change (with regard to Danish Mesolithic complexity, Norwegian maritime and mountain adaptations, and the appearance of agriculture) and the punctuated and sometimes reversible nature of the spread of agriculture (with regard to stable boundaries between hunter gatherers and farmers in Denmark and Norway, and the re-adoption of hunting and gathering in middle Neolithic Gotland). These are aspects argued on the basis mainly of zooarchaeological and radiocarbon results, but they conform to theoretical changes in neighbouring disciplines such as ecology. Here we find rapid and contingent change replacing unilinear succession and climax (Blumler 1996); the conflict between adaptational and developmental views is not unique to archaeology.

Given the wealth of its well-preserved archaeological record and its long history of research, Scandinavia is probably unique in its ability to contribute to such theoretical issues. No wonder Grahame Clark liked the place so much.

Acknowledgements

I would like to thank the numerous Scandinavian colleagues who have made this half-Scandinavian welcome whenever he has returned there, and kept me well supplied with copies of their work. They include Kim Aaris-Sørensen, Niels Andersen, Søren Andersen, Sveinung Bang-Andersen, Knut Andreas Bergsvik, Lisa Bostwick Bjerck, Hans Peter Blankholm, Göran Burenhult, Annica Cardell, Inge Bødker Enghoff, Anders Fischer, Ole Grøn, Randi Haaland, Anne Karin Hufthammer, Kristina Jennbert, Lars Larsson, Mats Larsson, Christian Lindqvist, Torsten Madsen, Arne Johan Nærøy, Inger Österholm, Erik Brinch Petersen, Christopher Prescott, Knud Rosenlund, David Simpson, Jørgen Skaarup, Jan Storå, Henrik Thrane, and many others—and outside Scandinavia, Rupert Housley, Chris Meiklejohn, Kristian Pedersen, and Marek Zvelebil. Most will disagree with at least parts of the above, and should not be held responsible for any of the contents.

Thanks also to the organizers of the Grahame Clark and World Prehistory conference for organizing such a memorable event.

And finally, thanks to Grahame Clark himself for introducing me to Scandinavian economic prehistory.

References

AARIS-SØRENSEN, K. 1980. Atlantic fish, reptile and bird remains from the mesolithic settlement at Vedbæk, North Zealand. *Videnskabelige Meddelelser fra Dansk Naturhistorisk Forening* 142, 139–49.

AARIS-SØRENSEN, K. 1988. *Danmarks Forhistoriske Dyreverden*. Copenhagen: Gyldendal.

ALBRETHSEN, S.E. & BRINCH PETERSEN, E. 1976. Excavations of a mesolithic cemetery at Vedbæk, Denmark. *Acta Archaeologica* 47, 1–28.

ANDERSEN, N.H. 1997. *The Sarup Enclosures*. Aarhus: Jysk Arkæologisk Selskab. (Jutland Archaeological Society Publications 33:1).

ANDERSEN, S.H. 1975. Ringkloster: en jysk inlandsboplands med Ertebøllekultur. *Kuml* 1973–4, 11–108.

ANDERSEN, S.H. 1987a. Mesolithic dug-outs and paddles from Tybrind Vig, Denmark. *Acta Archaeologica* 57, 87–106.

ANDERSEN, S.H. 1987b. Tybrind Vig: a submerged Ertebølle settlement in Denmark. In J.M. Coles and A.J. Lawson (eds), *European Wetlands in Prehistory*, 253–80. Oxford: Clarendon.

ANDERSEN, S.H. 1989. Norsminde. A køkkenmødding with late mesolithic and early neolithic occupation. *Journal of Danish Archaeology* 8, 13–40.

ANDERSEN, S.H. 1995. Coastal adaptation and marine exploitation in late mesolithic Denmark—with special emphasis on the Limfjord region. In A. Fischer (ed), *Man and Sea in the Mesolithic*, 41–66. Oxford: Oxbow Books. (Oxbow Monograph 53).

ANDERSEN, S.H. 1997. Ertebøllebåde fra Lystrup. *Kuml* 1993/94, 7–38.

BANG-ANDERSEN, S. 1996. Coast/inland relations in the Mesolithic of southern Norway. *World Archaeology* 27, 427–43.

BECKER, B. & KROMER, B. 1991. Dendrochronology and radiocarbon calibration of the early Holocene. In N. Barton, A.J. Roberts and D.A. Roe (eds), *The Late Glacial in North-West Europe*, 22–4. London: Council for British Archaeology. (Research Report 77).

BECKER, C.J. 1953. Die Maglemosekultur in Dänemark. Neue Funde und Ergebnisse. In E. Vogt (ed.), *Actes de la IIIe Session, Zurich 1950*, 180–3. Congrès International des Sciences Préhistoriques et Protohistoriques.

BECKER, C.J. 1954. Stenalderbebyggelsen ved Store Valby i Vestsjælland. *Aarbøger for Nordisk Oldkyndighed og Historie* 1954, 127–97.

BENNIKE, P. 1997. Death in the mesolithic. Two old men from Korsør Nor. In L. Pedersen, A. Fischer and B. Aaby (eds), *The Danish Storebælt since the Ice Age*, 99–105. Copenhagen: A/S Storebælt Fixed Link.

BETTINGER, R.L. 1991. *Hunter-Gatherers: Archaeological and Evolutionary Theory*. New York: Plenum.

BINFORD, L.R. 1980. Willow smoke and dogs' tails: hunter-gatherer settlement systems and archaeological site formation. *American Antiquity* 45, 4–20.

BJERCK, H.B. 1995. The North Sea continent and the pioneer settlement of Norway. In A. Fischer (ed.), *Man and Sea in the Mesolithic*, 131–44. Oxford: Oxbow Books. (Oxbow Monograph 53).

BJØRGO, T., KRISTOFFERSEN, S. & PRESCOTT, C. 1992. *Arkeologiske Undersøkelser i Nyset-Steggjevassdragene 1981–87*. Bergen: Historisk Museum.

BLANKHOLM, H.P. 1987. Late mesolithic hunter-gatherers and the transition to farming in southern Scandinavia. In P. Rowley-Conwy, M. Zvelebil and H.P. Blankholm (eds), *Mesolithic Northwest Europe: Recent Trends*, 155–62. Sheffield: Department of Archaeology and Prehistory, University of Sheffield.

BLANKHOLM, H.P. 1996. *On the Track of a Prehistoric Economy. Maglemosian Subsistence in Early Postglacial South Scandinavia*. Aarhus: Aarhus University Press.

BLUMLER, M.A. 1996. Ecology, evolutionary theory, and agricultural origins. In D.R. Harris (ed.), *The Origins and Spread of Agriculture and Pastoralism in Eurasia*, 25–50. London: UCL Press.

BRINCH PETERSEN, E. 1973. A survey of the late palaeolithic and the mesolithic of Denmark. In S.K. Kozlowski (ed.), *The Mesolithic in Europe*, 77–127. Warsaw: Warsaw University Press.

BRINCH PETERSEN, E., ALEXANDERSEN, V. & MEIKLEJOHN, C. 1993. Vedbæk, graven midt i byen. *Nationalmuseets Arbejdsmark* 1993, 61–9.

BURENHULT, G. 1997. *Ajvide och den moderna arkeologin*. Stockholm: Natur och Kultur.

CARDELL, A. in press. Fish bones from the late Atlantic Ertebølle settlement Møllegabet II, Ærø, Denmark. In J. Skaarup and O. Grøn (eds), *The Underwater Settlement at Møllegabet II*.

CHATTOPADHYAYA, U.C. 1996. Settlement pattern and the spatial organisation of subsistence and mortuary practices in the Mesolithic Ganges Valley, North-Central India. *World Archaeology* 27, 461–76.

CHRISTENSEN, C. 1995. The littorina transgressions in Denmark. In A. Fischer (ed.), *Man and Sea in the Mesolithic*, 15–22. Oxford: Oxbow Books. (Oxbow Monograph 53).

CLARK, G.A. & NEELY, M. 1987. Social differentiation in European mesolithic burial data. In P. Rowley-Conwy, M. Zvelebil and H.P. Blankholm (eds), *Mesolithic Northwest Europe: Recent Trends*, 121–7. Sheffield: University of Sheffield, Department of Archaeology and Prehistory.

CLARK, J.G.D. 1936. *The Mesolithic Settlement of Northern Europe*. Cambridge: Cambridge University Press.

CLARK, J.G.D. 1954. *Excavations at Star Carr*. Cambridge: Cambridge University Press.

CLARK, J.G.D. 1965a. Radiocarbon dating and the expansion of farming culture from the Near East over Europe. *Proceedings of the Prehistoric Society* 31, 58–73.

CLARK, J.G.D. 1965b. Radiocarbon dating and the spread of farming economy. *Antiquity* 39, 45–8.

CLARK, J.G.D. 1972. *Star Carr: a Case Study in Bioarchaeology*. Reading, Mass.: Addison-Wesley.

CLARK, J.G.D. 1975. *The Earlier Stone Age Settlement of Scandinavia*. Cambridge: Cambridge University Press.

CLARK, J.G.D. 1976. A Baltic cave sequence: a further study in bioarchaeology. In H. Mitscha-Marheim, H. Friesinger and H. Kerchler (eds), *Festschrift für Richard Pittioni zum siebzigsten Geburtstag*, 113–23. *Archaeologia Austraica* Beiheft 13.

CLARKE, D.L. 1976. Mesolithic Europe: the economic basis. In G. de G. Sieveking, I.H. Longworth and K.E. Wilson (eds), *Problems in Economic and Social Archaeology*, 449–81. London: Duckworth.

COHEN, M.N. 1977. *The Food Crisis in Prehistory*. Yale: Yale University Press.

DEGERBØL, M. 1933. *Danmarks Pattedyr i Fortiden i Sammenligning med recente Former*. Copenhagen: C.A. Reitzel. (Videnskabelige Meddelelser fra Dansk Naturhistorisk Forening 96).

DENCKER, J. 1997. Stone-age settlements in the middle of nature's larder. In L. Pedersen, A. Fischer and B. Aaby (eds), *The Danish Storebælt since the Ice Age*, 87–92. Copenhagen: A/S Storebælt Fixed Link.

DYSON-HUDSON, R. & SMITH, E.A. 1978. Human territoriality: an ecological reassessment. *American Anthropologist* 80, 21–41.

EDWARDS, K.J. 1989. The cereal pollen record and early agriculture. In A. Milles, D. Williams and N. Gardner (eds), *The Beginnings of Agriculture*, 113–47. Oxford: British Archaeological Reports. (International Series 496).

EKMAN, J. 1974. Djurbensmaterialet från stenålderslokalen Ire, Hangvar sn, Gotland. In G. Janzon (ed.), *Gotlands Mellanneolitiska Gravar*, 212–46. Stockholm: Almqvist and Wiksell. (Acta Universitatis Stockholmiensis, Studies in North-European Archaeology 6).

ENGHOFF, I.B. 1983. Size distribution of cod (*Gadus morhua* L.) and whiting (*Merlangius merlangius* (L.) (Pisces, Gadidae) from a mesolithic settlement at Vedbæk, Denmark. *Videnskabelige Meddelelser fra Dansk Naturhistorisk Forening* 144, 83–97.

ENGHOFF, I.B. 1987. Freshwater fishing from a sea-coast settlement—the Ertebølle *locus classicus* revisited. *Journal of Danish Archaeology* 5, 62–76.

ENGHOFF, I.B. 1991. Fishing from the stone age settlement Norsminde. *Journal of Danish Archaeology* 8, 41–50.

ENGHOFF, I.B. 1993. Mesolithic eel-fishing at Bjørnsholm, Denmark, spiced with exotic species. *Journal of Danish Archaeology* 10, 105–18.

ENGHOFF, I.B. 1994. Fishing in Denmark during the Ertebølle period. *International Journal of Osteoarchaeology* 4, 65–96.

ENGHOFF, I.B. 1995. Fishing in Denmark during the mesolithic period. In A. Fischer (ed.), *Man and Sea in the Mesolithic*, 67–74. Oxford: Oxbow Books. (Oxbow Monograph 53).

ENGHOFF, I.B. in press. Freshwater fishes at Ringkloster, with a supplement of marine fishes. *Journal of Danish Archaeology*.

ERIKSEN, L.B. 1992. Ornehus på Stevns—en tidligneolitisk hustomt. *Aarbøger for Nordisk Oldkyndighed og Historie* 1991, 7–19.

FISCHER, A. 1997a. *Marinearkæologiske forundersøgelser forud for etablering af en fast Øresundsforbindelse*. Copenhagen: Miljø- og Energiministeriet, Skov- og Naturstyrelsen.

FISCHER, A. 1997b. People and the sea—settlement and fishing along the mesolithic coasts. In L. Pedersen, A. Fischer and B. Aaby (eds), *The Danish Storebælt since the Ice Age*, 63–77. Copenhagen: A/S Storebælt Fixed Link.

FISCHER, A. & MALM, T. 1997. The settlement in the submerged forest in Musholm Bay. In L. Pedersen, A. Fischer and B. Aaby (eds), *The Danish Storebælt since the Ice Age*, 78–86. Copenhagen: A/S Storebælt Fixed Link.

GLOB, P.V. 1949. Barkær: Danmarks ældste landsby. *Fra Nationalmuseets Arbejdsmark* 1949, 5–16.

GOLDSTEIN, L. 1981. One-dimensional archaeology and multi-dimensional people: spatial organization and mortuary analysis. In R. Chapman, I. Kinnes and K. Randsborg (eds), *The Archaeology of Death*, 53–69. Cambridge: Cambridge University Press.

GOULD, R.A. 1985. 'Now let's invent agriculture ... ': a critical review of concepts of complexity among hunter-gatherers. In T.D. Price and J.A. Brown (eds), *Prehistoric Hunter-Gatherers*, 427–34. New York: Academic Press.

GRØN, O. 1995. *The Maglemose Culture*. Oxford: Tempus Reparatum. (BAR International Series 616).

GRØN, O. & SKAARUP, J. 1991. Møllegabet II—a submerged Mesolithic site and a 'boat burial' from Ærø. *Journal of Danish Archaeology* 10, 38–50.

HATTING, T., HOLM, E. & ROSENLUND, K. 1973. En pelsjægerboplads fra stenalderen. *Kaskelot* 10, 13–21.

HIGHAM, C.F.W. & MESSAGE, M. 1968. An assessment of a society's attitude towards bovine husbandry. In D. Brothwell and E.S. Higgs (eds), *Science in Archaeology*, 315–30. London: Thames and Hudson.

HJELLE, K.L. 1992. Pollenanalytiske undersøkelser innenfor boplassen i Kotedalen. In K.L. Hjelle, A.K. Hufthammer, P.E. Kaland, A.B. Olsen and E.C. Soltvedt (eds), *Kotedalen—en Boplass gjennom 5000 År (vol. 2)*, 91–122. Bergen: Historisk Museum.

HJELMQVIST, H. 1985. Economic plants from two stone age settlements in southernmost Scania. *Acta Archaeologica* 54 (1983), 57–63.

HODDER, I. 1990. *The Domestication of Europe*. Oxford: Blackwell.

HODGETTS, L. & ROWLEY-CONWY, P. in press. Mammal and bird remains from the underwater excavations at Møllegabet II. In J. Skaarup and O. Grøn (eds), *The Underwater Settlement at Møllegabet II.*

HUFTHAMMER, A.K. 1992. De osteologiske undersøkelsene fra Kotedalen. In K.L. Hjelle, A.K. Hufthammer, P.E. Kaland, A.B. Olsen and E.C. Soltvedt (eds), *Kotedalen—en Boplass gjennom 5000 År (vol. 2)*, 9–64. Bergen: Historisk Museum.

HUFTHAMMER, A.K. 1995. Tidlig husdyrhold i Vest-Norge. *Arkeologiske Skrifter fra Arkeologisk Institutt, Bergen Museum* 8, 203–19.

HULTHÉN, B. & WELINDER, S. 1981. *A Stone Age Economy*. Stockholm: University of Stockholm, Department of Archaeology. (Theses and Papers in North European Archaeology 11).

INDRELID, S. 1994. *Fangstfolk og Bønder i Fjellet. Bidrag til Hardangerviddas Førhistorie 8500–2500 År før Nåtid.* Oslo: Universitetets Oldsaksamling. (Universitetets Oldsaksamlings Skrifter, ny rekke, 17).

IVERSEN, J. 1937. Undersøgelser over Litorinatransgressioner i Danmark. *Meddelelser fra Dansk Geologisk Forening* 9, 223–32.

IVERSEN, J. 1941. Land occupation in Denmark's stone age. *Danmarks Geologiske Undersøgelse* II, 66, 1–68.

JENNBERT, K. 1984. *Den Produktiva Gåvan*. Lund: University of Lund. (Acta Archaeologia Lundensia, series in 4°, 16).

JESSEN, K. 1937. Litorinasænkninger ved Klintesø i pollenfloristisk belysning. *Meddelelser fra Dansk Geologisk Forening* 9, 232–6.

JESSEN, K. 1938. Some west Baltic pollen diagrams. *Quartär* 1, 124–39.

JONSSON, L. 1986. From wild boar to domestic pig—a reassessment of Neolithic swine of northwestern Europe. In L.-K. Königsson (ed.), *Nordic Late Quaternary Biology and Ecology*, 125–9. Striae 24.

JONSSON, L. 1988. The vertebrate faunal remains from the Late Atlantic settlement Skateholm in Scania, South Sweden. In L. Larsson (ed.), *The Skateholm Project I. Man and Environment*, 56–88. Stockholm: Almqvist and Wiksell. (Skrifter utgivna av Kungliga Humanistiska Vetenskapssamfundet i Lund 74).

KEELEY, L.H. 1988. Hunter-gatherer economic complexity and 'population pressure': a cross-cultural analysis. *Journal of Anthropological Archaeology* 7, 373–411.

KEELEY, L.H. 1991. Ethnographic models for late glacial hunter-gatherers. In N. Barton, A.J. Roberts and D.A. Roe (eds), *The Late Glacial in Northwest Europe*, 179–90. London: Council for British Archaeology. (Research Report 77).

LARSSON, L. 1982. *Segebro. En Tidigatlantisk Boplats vid Sege Ås Mynning*. Malmö: Malmö Museum (Malmöfynd 4).

LARSSON, L. 1983. Mesolithic settlement on the sea floor in the Strait of Öresund. In P.M. Masters and N.C. Flemming (eds), *Quaternary Coastlines and Marine Archaeology*, 283–301. New York: Academic Press.

LARSSON, L. 1985. Karlsfält. A settlement from the early and late Funnel Beaker culture in southern Scania, Sweden. *Acta Archaeologica* 54 (for 1983), 3–63.

LARSSON, L. 1988. *The Skateholm Project I. Man and Environment*. Stockholm: Almqvist and Wiksell. (Skrifter utgivna av Kungliga Humanistiska Vetenskapssamfundet i Lund 74).

LARSSON, L. 1989. Big dog and poor man. Mortuary practices in mesolithic societies in southern Sweden. In T.B. Larsson and H. Lundmark (eds), *Approaches to Swedish Prehistory*, 211–23. Oxford: British Archaeological Reports. (International Series 500).

LARSSON, L. 1992. Neolithic settlement in the Skateholm area, southern Scania. *Meddelanden från Lunds Universitetets Historiska Museum* 1991–1992, 5–44.

LARSSON, L. 1995. Man and sea in southern Scandinavia during the Late Mesolithic. The role of cemeteries in the view of society. In A. Fischer (ed.), *Man and Sea in the Mesolithic*, 95–104. Oxford: Oxbow Books. (Oxbow Monograph 53).

LARSSON, L. & LARSSON, M. 1986. Stenåldersbebyggelse i Ystadområdet. En presentation av fältverksamhet och bearbetning hösten 1984–våren 1986. *Ystadiana* 1986, 9–78.

LARSSON, M. 1984. *Tidigneolitikum i Sydvästskåne*. Lund: University of Lund. (Acta Archaeologica Lundensia, series in 4°, 17).

LEGGE, A.J. & ROWLEY-CONWY, P.A. 1988. *Star Carr Revisited. A Re-Analysis of the Large Mammals*. London: University of London, Centre for Extra-Mural Studies.

LINDQVIST, C. 1997. Ansarve hage-dösen. Tvärvetenskapliga aspekter på kontext ochden neolitiska förändringen på Gotland. In A. Åkerlund, S. Bergh, J. Nordbladh and J. Taffinder (eds), *Till Gunborg. Arkeologiska Samtal*, 361–78. Stockholm: Stockholms Universitet. (Stockholm Archaeological Reports 33).

LINDQVIST, C. & POSSNERT, G. 1997. The subsistence economy and diet at Jakobs/Ajvide, Eksta parish and other prehistoric dwelling and burial sites on Gotland in long-term perspective. In G. Burenhult (ed.), *Remote Sensing vol. I*, 29–90. Stockholm: Institute of Archaeology, University of Stockholm. (These and Papers in North European Archaeology 13a).

LIVERSAGE, D. 1992. *Barkær. Long Barrows and Settlements*. Copenhagen: Akademisk Forlag. (Arkæologiske Studier 9).

MADSEN, A.P., MÜLLER, S., NEERGAARD, C., PETERSEN, C.G.J., ROSTRUP, E., STEENSTRUP, K.J.V. & WINGE, H. 1900. *Affaldsdynger fra Stenalderen i Danmark*. Copenhagen: C.A. Reitzel.

MADSEN, T. 1979. Earthen long barrows and timber structures: aspects of the early neolithic mortuary practice in Denmark. *Proceedings of the Prehistoric Society* 45, 301–20.

MADSEN, T. & PETERSEN, J.E. 1984. Tidligneolitiske anlæg ved Mosegården. Regionale og kronologiske forskelle i tidligneolitikum. *Kuml* 1982/83, 61–120.

MATHIASSEN, D.R. 1997. The changing landscapes of the Storebælt, from the retreat of the ice to the sea flood. In L. Pedersen, A. Fischer and B. Aaby (eds), *The Danish Storebælt since the Ice Age*, 22–8. Copenhagen: A/S Storebælt Fixed Link.

MIKKELSEN, E. 1989. *Fra Jeger til Bonde. Utviklingen av Jordbrukssamfunn i Telemark i Steinalder og Bronsealder*. Oslo: Universitetets Oldsaksamling. (Universitetets Oldsaksamlings Skrifter, ny rekke, 11).

MØHL, U. 1970. Oversigt over dyrknoglerne fra Ølby Lyng. *Aarbøger for Nordisk Oldkyndighed og Historie* 1970, 43–77.

MØHL, U. 1978. Aggersund-bopladsen zoologisk belyst. Svanejagt som årsag til bosættelse? *Kuml* 1978, 57–76.

NIELSEN, P.O. 1985. De første Bønder. Nye fund fra den tidligste Trægtbægerkultur ved Sigersted. *Aarbøger for Nordisk Oldkyndighed og Historie* 1984, 96–126.

NÆRØY, A.J. 1994. *Troll-Prosjektet. Arkeologiske undersøkelser på Kollsnes, Øygarden K. Hordaland, 1989–1992*. Bergen: Arkeologisk Institutt, Universitetet i Bergen. (Arkeologiske Rapporter 19).

ODUM, E.P. 1975. *Ecology*. (second edn). London: Holt, Rinehart and Winston.

OLSEN, A.B. 1992. *Kotedalen—en Boplass gjennom 5000 År (vol. 1)*. Bergen: Historisk Museum.

OLSEN, H. 1976. *Skipshelleren. Osteologisk Materiale*. Bergen: Zoologisk Museum.

ÖSTERHOLM, I. 1989. *Bosättningsmönstret på Gotland under Stenåldern*. Stockholm: University of Stockholm, Institute of Archaeology. (Theses and Papers in Archaeology 4).

ØSTMO, E. 1988. *Etablering av jordbrukskultur i Østfold i steinalderen*. Oslo: Universitetets Oldsaksamling. (Universitetets Oldsaksamlings Skrifter, ny rekke, 10).

PALUDAN-MÜLLER, C. 1978. High Atlantic food gathering in northwestern Zealand, ecological conditions and spatial representations. In K. Kristiansen and C. Paludan-Müller (eds), *New Directions in Scandinavian Archaeology*, 120–57. Copenhagen: National Museum of Denmark.

PARDOE, C. 1988. The cemetery as symbol. The distribution of prehistoric Aboriginal burial grounds in southeastern Australia. *Archaeology in Oceania* 23, 1–16.

PEDERSEN, L. 1995. 7000 years of fishing: stationary fishing structures in the mesolithic and afterwards. In A. Fischer (ed.), *Man and Sea in the Mesolithic*, 75–86. Oxford: Oxbow Books. (Oxbow Monograph 53).

PEDERSEN, L. 1997. They put fences in the sea. In L. Pedersen, A. Fischer and B. Aaby (eds), *The Danish Storebælt since the Ice Age*, 124–43. Copenhagen: A/S Storebælt Fixed Link.

PRESCOTT, C. 1991. *Kulturhistoriske Undersøkelser i Skrivarhelleren*. Bergen: Historisk Museum.

PRESCOTT, C. 1995. *From Stone Age to Iron Age. A Study from Sogn, western Norway*. Oxford: Hadrian Books. (British Archaeological Reports, International Series 603).

PRESCOTT, C. 1996. Was there *really* a neolithic in Norway? *Antiquity* 70, 77–87.

PRICE, T.D. 1985. Affluent foragers of mesolithic southern Scandinavia. In T.D. Price and J.A. Brown (eds), *Prehistoric Hunter-Gatherers*, 341–63. New York: Academic Press.

PRICE, T.D. 1993. Issues in palaeolithic and mesolithic research. In G.L. Peterkin, H. Bricker and P. Mellars, *Hunting and Animal Exploitation in the Later Palaeolithic and Mesolithic of Eurasia*, 241–4. Archaeological Papers of the American Anthropological Association no. 4.

PRICE, T.D. 1996. The first farmers of southern Scandinavia. In D.R. Harris (ed.), *The Origins and Spread of Agriculture and Pastoralism in Eurasia*, 346–62. London: UCL Press.

PRICE, T.D. & GEBAUER, A.B. 1992. The final frontier: foragers to farmers in southern Scandinavia. In A.B. Gebauer and T.D. Price (eds), *Transitions to Agriculture in Prehistory*, 97–116. Madison:

Prehistory Press. (Monographs in World Archaeology 4).

PRØSCH-DANIELSEN, L. & HØGESTOL, M. 1995. A coastal Ahrensburgian site found at Galta, Rennesøy, Southwest Norway. In A. Fischer (ed.), *Man and Sea in the Mesolithic*, 123–30. Oxford: Oxbow Books. (Oxbow Monograph 53).

RICHARDSON, A. 1982. The control of productive resources on the northwest coast of North America. In N. Williams and E. Hunn (eds), *Resource Managers: Australian and North American Hunter-Gatherers,* 93–112. Canberra: Australian Institute of Aboriginal Studies.

RICHTER, J. 1982. Faunal remains from Ulkestrup Lyng Øst. In K. Andersen, S. Jørgensen and J. Richter (eds), *Maglemose Hytterne ved Ulkestrup Lyng*, 141–77. Copenhagen: Det Kongelige Nordiske Oldskriftselskab.

ROSENLUND, K. 1980. Knoglematerialet fra bopladsen Lundby II. In B.B. Henriksen (ed.), *Lundby-holmen. Pladser af Maglemose-type i Sydsjælland*, 120–42. Copenhagen: Det Kongelige Nordiske Oldskriftselskab.

ROWLEY-CONWY, P. 1983. Sedentary hunters: the Ertebølle example. In G.N. Bailey (ed.), *Hunter-Gatherer Economy in Prehistory*, 111–26. Cambridge: University Press.

ROWLEY-CONWY, P. 1984a. The laziness of the short-distance hunter: the origins of agriculture in Denmark. *Journal of Anthropological Archaeology* 3, 300–24.

ROWLEY-CONWY, P. 1984b. Mellemneolitisk økonomi i Danmark og Sydengland. Knoglefundene fra Fannerup. *Kuml* 1984, 77–111.

ROWLEY-CONWY, P. 1993. Season and reason: the case for a regional interpretation of mesolithic settlement patterns. In G.L. Peterkin, H. Bricker and P. Mellars (eds), *Hunting and Animal Exploitation in the Later Palaeolithic and Mesolithic of Eurasia,* 179–88. Archaeological Papers of the American Anthropological Association no. 4.

ROWLEY-CONWY, P. 1995a. Wild or domestic? On the evidence for the earliest domestic cattle and pigs in South Scandinavia and Iberia. *International Journal of Osteoarchaeology* 5, 115–26.

ROWLEY-CONWY, P. 1995b. Making first farmers younger: the West European Evidence. *Current Anthropology* 36, 346–53.

ROWLEY-CONWY, P. 1998a. Cemeteries, seasonality and complexity in the Ertebølle of Southern Scandinavia. In M. Zvelebil, L. Domanska and R. Dennell (eds), *Harvesting the Sea, Farming the Forest: the Emergence of Neolithic Societies in the Baltic Region*, 193–202. Sheffield: Sheffield Academic Press.

ROWLEY-CONWY, P. 1998b. On the origins and spread of agriculture and pastoralism—are the grey horses dead? *International Journal of Osteoarchaeology* 8, 218–24.

ROWLEY-CONWY, P. in press a. Determination of season of death in European wild boar (*Sus scrofa ferus*): a preliminary study. In A.R. Millard (ed.), *Archaeological Sciences 1997*, Oxford: British Archaeological Reports.

ROWLEY-CONWY, P. in press b. Meat, furs and skins: mesolithic animal bones from Ringkloster, a seasonal hunting camp in Jutland. *Journal of Danish Archaeology.*

ROWLEY-CONWY, P. in press c. Complexity in the mesolithic of the Atlantic façade: development or adaptation? In M.G. Morales and G.A. Clark, *The Mesolithic of the Atlantic Façade*. Oxford: Oxbow Books.

ROWLEY-CONWY, P. & STORÅ, J. 1997. Pitted Ware seals and pigs from Ajvide, Gotland: methods of study and first results. In G. Burenhult (ed.), *Remote Sensing, vol. I*, 113–27. Stockholm: Institute of Archaeology, University of Stockholm. (Theses and Papers in North European Archaeology 13a).

ROWLEY-CONWY, P. & ZVELEBIL, M. 1989. Saving it for later: storage by prehistoric hunter-gatherers in Europe. In P. Halstead and J. O'Shea (eds), *Bad Year Economics*, 40–56. Cambridge: Cambridge University Press.

SAXE, A. 1970. *Social Dimensions of Mortuary Practices*. Unpublished Ph.D. thesis, University of Michigan.

SCHILLING, H. 1997. The Korsør Nor site. The permanent dwelling place of a hunting and fishing people in life and death. In L. Pedersen, A. Fischer and B. Aaby (eds), *The Danish Storebælt since the Ice Age*, 93–8. Copenhagen: A/S Storebælt Fixed Link.

SCHNITTGER, B. & RYDH, H. 1940. *Grottan Stora Förvar på Stora Karlsö*. Stockholm: Wahlström and Widstrand. (Kungliga Vitterhets Historie och Antikvitets Akademien).

SIMPSON, D.N. 1992. *Archaeological Investigations at Krossnes, Flatøy 1988–1991*. Bergen: Historisk Museum, Universitetet i Bergen. (Arkeologiske Rapporter 18).

SKAARUP, J. 1973. *Hesselø-Sølager. Jagdstationen der südskandinavischen Trichterbecherkultur*. Copenhagen: Akademisk Forlag.

SKAARUP, J. 1975. *Stengade. Ein Langeländischer Wohnplatz mit Hausresten aus der Frühneolithischen Zeit*. Rudkøbing: Langelands Museum.

SOLTVEDT, E.C. 1991. Makrofossiler i Skrivarhelleren. In C. Prescott (ed.), *Kulturhistoriske Undersøkelser i Skrivarhelleren*, 130–2. Bergen: Historisk Museum.

SOLTVEDT, E.C. 1992. Makrofossilundersøkelserne fra Kotedalen. In K.L. Hjelle, A.K. Hufthammer, P.E. Kaland, A.B. Olsen and E.C. Soltvedt (eds), *Kotedalen—en Boplass gjennom 5000 År (vol. 2)*, 123–37. Bergen: Historisk Museum.

SOLTVEDT, E.C. & MYDLAND, L. 1995. Kornfunn fra to neolitiske/eldre bronsealder boplasser på Rennesøy, Rogaland, SV Norge. *Arkeologiske Skrifter fra Arkeologisk Institutt, Bergen Museum* 8, 220–32.

SØRENSEN, S.A. 1996. *Kongemosekulturen i Sydskandinavien*. Jægerspris: Egnsmuseet Færgegården.

TAUBER, H. 1972. Radiocarbon chronology of the Danish mesolithic and neolithic. *Antiquity* 46, 106–10.

TAUBER, H. 1982. Carbon-13 evidence for the diet of prehistoric humans in Denmark. *PACT* 7, 235–7.

TAUBER, H. 1989. Danske arkæologiske C-14 dateringer. *Arkaeologiske Udgravninger i Danmark 1988* (1989), 210–28.

THOMAS, D.H. 1981. Complexity among Great Basin Shoshoneans: the world's least affluent hunter-gatherers? In S. Koyama and D.H. Thomas (eds), *Affluent Foragers*, 19–52. Osaka: National Museum of Ethnology. (Senri Ethnological Studies 9).

THOMAS, J. 1996. The cultural context of the first use of domesticates in continental Central and Northwest Europe. In D.R. Harris (ed.), *The Origins and Spread of Agriculture and Pastoralism in Eurasia*, 310–22. London: UCL Press.

THRANE, H. 1982. Dyrkningsspor fra yngre stenalder i Danmark. In H. Thrane (ed.), *Om Yngre Stenalders Bebyggelseshistorie*, 20–8. Odense: Odense University Press. (Skrifter fra Historisk Institut, Odense Universitet, 30).

TROELS-SMITH, J. 1937. Pollen-analytisk datering af Brabrand-fundet. *Danmarks Geologiske Undersøgelse IV* 2 (16), 5–21.

TROELS-SMITH, J. 1942. Geologisk datering af Dyrholm-fundet. In T. Mathiassen, M. Degerbøl and J. Troels-Smith (eds), *Dyrholm. En Stenalderboplads på Djursland*, 137–212. Copenhagen: Det Kongelige Dansk Videnskabernes Selskab. (Arkæologisk-Kunsthistorisk Skrifter 1, 1).

TROELS-SMITH, J. 1953. Ertebøllekultur-Bondekultur. *Aarbøger for Nordisk Oldkyndighed og Historie* 1953, 5–62.

TROELS-SMITH, J. 1966. The Ertebølle culture and its background. *Palaeohistoria* 12, 505–25.

WHITTAKER, R.H. 1975. *Communities and Ecosystems*. New York: Macmillan.

WINGE, H. 1903. Oversigt over knoglematerialet fra Mullerup-pladsen. *Aarbøger for Nordisk Oldkyndighed og Historie* 1903, 194–8.

WOODBURN, J. 1982. Egalitarian societies. *Man* 17, 431–51.

ZVELEBIL, M. 1994. Plant use in the mesolithic and its role in the transition to farming. *Proceedings of the Prehistoric Society* 60, 35–74.

ZVELEBIL, M. 1995. Hunting, gathering, or husbandry? Management of food resources by the late Mesolithic communities of temperate Europe. *MASCA Research Papers in Science and Archaeology* 12 (Supplement), 79–104.

ZVELEBIL, M. 1996. The agricultural frontier and the transition to farming in the circum-Baltic region. In D.R. Harris (ed.), *The Origins and Spread of Agriculture and Pastoralism Eurasia*, 323–45. London: UCL Press.

Twenty Thousand Years of Palaeolithic Cave Art in Southern France

JEAN CLOTTES

ABOUT 350 PALAEOLITHIC SITES with rock art are now known in Europe, most of them in France and Spain, with a scattering in Italy and Sicily, and a few sites as far as Romania and even the Urals in Russia. They are not all deep caves. Shallow shelters at the foot of a cliff, inhabited cave entrances, and even outside rocks in Spain and Portugal have also been painted and engraved. In France, nearly 160 Palaeolithic rock art sites have so far been discovered, of which fewer than a dozen are situated in the northern half of France. This means that the majority of the sites—including some very major ones, such as Lascaux, Chauvet, Cosquer, Trois-Frères, Niaux, and Font-de-Gaume—are located in Southern France. This paper will therefore have to be highly selective and will primarily be based on the research and findings of the past few years. Three aspects will be covered: the progress in dating and the consequences for our understanding of Palaeolithic cave art; some temporal and regional specificities in the cave art of Southern France; and finally, the question: what overall view—if any—is it now possible to have about the art?

Dating cave art

Within the past few years, numerous radiocarbon dates of charcoal directly lifted from paintings have been obtained from French and Spanish caves. For the Chauvet cave these dates were very early, ranging between 30,000 and more than 32,000 BP (Clottes *et al.* 1995). They created quite a stir. If there had been one single date with such a result, it would no doubt have been set aside and considered to be 'too early' and too far off the range to be accepted. However, at Chauvet there were four direct dates from three samples coming from three different animal representations (two rhinos (see Plate 1) and one

Proceedings of the British Academy, **99**, 161–175

bison). In addition, they were confirmed on the one hand by the dating of a large piece of charcoal found among many others on the ground (29,000±400 BP, Ly-6878), and on the other hand by the dating of a torch mark (26,120±400 BP, GifA-95127) superimposed on a thin veil of calcite that covered some earlier paintings in the vicinity of the two dated rhinos. Another identical torch mark in a different chamber gave two dates (26,980±410 BP, GifA-95129 and 26,980±420 BP, GiFA-95130) (Clottes *et al.* 1995) that tallied with the other one. A veritable stratigraphy on the wall thus yielded a coherent set of dates and destroyed the possibility that the earliest dates for the art could have been due to the use of fossil wood or to the picking up and reuse of early charcoal by latecomers to the cave (Züchner 1996).

Other very early dates going back to the Aurignacian or to the early Gravettian have been obtained in a few other caves, such as Cosquer (Clottes & Courtin 1994; Clottes *et al.* 1997), Grande Grotte at Arcy-sur-Cure (Girard *et al.* 1995), and Gargas (Clottes *et al.* 1992). Others were older than presumed at Pech-Merle (Lorblanchet *et al.* 1995) and Cougnac (Lorblanchet 1994). On the other hand, at Niaux (Clottes *et al.* 1992) and Portel (Figure 1) (Igler *et al.* 1994), in the Ariège, several dates fell within the Late Magdalenian, somewhat later than was expected by applying the existing set of stylistic criteria.

Figure 1. The most recent date for an Upper Palaeolithic painting was obtained for this horse in Portel. (Photo: J. Clottes)

All this drastically changes the rather simple landscape of Palaeolithic art in the caves which, since Leroi-Gourhan's work (1965), had been considered as firmly set. At this stage, three main consequences can be established and discussed.

1 The direct dates for Palaeolithic paintings range from Chauvet for the earliest one (Plate 1) (32,410±720 BP, GifA-95132) to Portel for the latest one (Figure 1) (11,600±150 BP, AA-9466). It is a timespan of at least 20,000 years, with possibilities for still earlier dates since the Aurignacians had reached western Europe by 38,000 BP at least (Delporte 1998). For such an enormous timespan, the 350 or so sites known from the tip of the Iberian Peninsula to the Urals are far too few to have allowed a proper transmission of cultural traditions and practices. Thousands of sites have probably been destroyed or have not yet been discovered (Bednarik 1994). As we have no means of reaching any degree of certainty as to whether the painted sites that have reached us constitute a representative sample of what there used to be, we must expect changes and even upheavals in our knowledge of the art when major discoveries are made. We are very far from knowing all there is to know about the evolution of artistic techniques, themes, and practices over such a very long period.

Specialists are generally reluctant to admit such ignorance, obvious though it is, as was pointed out some years ago (Ucko & Rosenfeld 1967). Which is probably why, whenever an upsetting discovery is made, it may be rejected out of hand as being 'a fake' (see, for example, the Cosquer Cave, in Clottes & Courtin 1994). The dates at Chauvet elicited two kinds of adverse attitudes, both based on an implicit faith in the validity and intangibility of stylistic criteria. Züchner (1996) argued at length why they were contradictory with existing schemas (but see Clottes 1996a). Much more strangely, Brigitte and Gilles Delluc in a recent synthesis on the earliest European cave art did not change any of their theories—inherited from Leroi-Gourhan—and did not discuss the Chauvet dates. They simply remarked that 'those dates are notably more ancient than is indicated by the stylistic analysis of the works of art' (Delluc & Delluc 1996, 90). If they do not 'believe' in the Chauvet dates they should express their arguments against them. Or else, the dates must be accepted, in which case it becomes necessary to re-examine the validity of traditional conceptions about several stylistic conventions in cave art, as well as about its origins and its development.

2 One of the main advances made in the past few years is the realization that the Aurignacians had mastered all the artistic techniques that were supposed to have gradually developed over the following millennia. At Chauvet, for instance, they made great use of spatial perspective and they did so by different means, which shows that they deliberately tried to create certain effects: next to the Panel of Horses, a lion was made to look as though it were behind some horses by stopping the line of its contour next to the previously painted animals (Chauvet *et al.* 1995, Fig. 54); the horns of a group of rhinos (see Plate 2) have been drawn in decreasing perspective from the one in the foreground to those in the background (Chauvet *et al.* op. cit., Fig. 86); a bison was drawn on the angle of a wall, with its head facing us, on one plane, and its body on another plane at a 90° angle, which stresses its perspective (Chauvet *et al.* op. cit., Fig. 88). Still at Chauvet the Aurignacians made an extensive and very sophisticated use of stump-drawing to shade the inside of animal bodies, they scraped the walls to provide a blank space where their works would stand out, and they captured the vivid expressions of the animals they drew with an incredible accuracy.

Since the beginning of the twentieth century, the current paradigm has been that art had known crude beginnings in the Aurignacian—mostly in the Dordogne—and had then slowly and gradually improved up to the apogee of Lascaux. This argument is no longer tenable, but the problem of how early the development of art is still remains. For those who believe that the achievements of Chauvet must have been preceded by thousands (if not tens or hundreds of thousands) of years of artistic endeavours of various kinds, the origins of art are very early. Several authors have lately insisted on the taphonomy of visual art whether it be portable art or on cave walls: the earlier it is the less chance it would have of being preserved (Bednarik 1994; Bahn 1995). However, even if the Châtelperronians—the last of the European Neanderthals—are responsible for striated bones and stones and if they used beads and pendants, they did not make any portable or wall art, at least so far as we know. In their case, as they were contemporary with the Aurignacians, the taphonomic argument of the slow erosion of many millennia cannot hold. Even if one leaves aside the possibility of very early art forms, created by Neanderthals, or even by *Homo erectus*, it is still theoretically possible to contemplate an invention of art thousands of years before Chauvet and to hold to the idea of a gradual evolution and progress. After all, the earliest dates at Chauvet are a full 6000 years later than the earliest Aurignacian dates in western Europe, without even mentioning the presence of *Homo sapiens sapiens* in the Middle East nearly 100,000 years ago.

However, another possibility also exists, that the essential discoveries concerning the multitudinous techniques of visual art—portable or on walls—should not have taken many millennia but that from the moment humans decided—for whatever cultural reasons—to represent some aspects of their environment (essentially animal and human forms) in two or three dimensions, the progress was swift and that some forms of art developed within a few generations or even centuries. Ucko (1987, 18) has shown very clearly how Breuil, Luquet, and even Leroi-Gourhan refused to admit that art could thus emerge quickly under a perfectly accomplished form, even though many historical examples are available in Africa and elsewhere (Ucko op cit., 41).

3 Leroi-Gourhan's theories about the stylistic evolution of art throughout the Upper Palaeolithic are no longer tenable after the discoveries in Chauvet and Cosquer and the dates obtained in other caves. His Style I, that he equated with the Aurignacian, can now only apply to a few Dordogne sites. The new Ardèche cave (Chauvet) is totally outside of it because of its originality and sophistication. Lions and rhinos (see Plates 1 and 2) are given a great importance on the main panels where they are centrally situated. This is also contrary to Leroi-Gourhan's ideas about the organization and structure of Palaeolithic parietal art, because lions, for example, should have been either in the entrance or at the bottom of the cave in a secondary position. In addition, those animals are often represented in movement (Plate 1), which is contrary to Leroi-Gourhan's contention (1982, 42) that in Palaeolithic art, there was an 'ever increasing preoccupation with representing movement during the course of the evolution of Upper Palaeolithic art' with still figures at the beginning and many more 'animated' ones at the end.

More important still, after the discoveries of the past few years, it is no longer possible to hold to the idea that art slowly and gradually evolved from archaic crude beginnings in the Aurignacian to better and better representations in a kind of linear progress. The aesthetic quality of the Chauvet wall art can be compared with that of the contemporary portable art found in the Aurignacian shelters of the Swabian Jura in Germany. But for the same period no such successes are known either in the Périgord, the Spanish Cantabrian coast, or the Pyrenees. Occasionally, some sophisticated forms of art have been created. Under what kind of cultural, personal, or religious influences did they appear? Were there any further developments and continuations or did they remain local and short-lived? The data are not yet sufficient to be able to answer those questions. As Ucko and Rosenfeld (1967) surmised as early as 30 years ago, all along the Upper Palaeolithic there may have been all sorts of apogees and declines, as well as the temporal coexistence in different places of talented and poor artists (see also Ucko 1987). For a progressive linear evolution of early art, with the slow acquisition of more and more complex techniques (Leroi-Gourhan 1965; Delluc & Delluc 1991), must now be substituted the idea of a zigzag type of evolution, depending on local circumstances.

Some temporal and regional specificities

Given what has been said above, one of the most promising lines of research is probably to distinguish particular themes or techniques that can be solidly ascribed to a precise timespan and/or to a precise area. Leroi-Gourhan (1981) insisted on the value of some of those 'ethnical markers' as he called them. Among them were the tectiform signs in the Eyzies region and the so-called 'aviform' signs of Pech-Merle and Cougnac.

Our knowledge of the latter has lately progressed. They consist of a kind of thick horizontal bar topped in its middle by a chimney-like appendage; at each of its extremities the bar generally has one short extension more or less perpendicular to it, that is, pointing downwards. Even though they do not look much like a bird or a roof, they were called 'aviforms' and 'tectiforms' and even 'tectiforms with chimneys'. These very inadequate terms are still occasionally used, even though it is much preferable to call them Placard signs, from the cave where most have been found and the only one where they are well dated. Their discovery at Placard (Figure 2) was important for several reasons. First, both painted and engraved signs of the same type were found in the cave; previously only painted ones had been known at Cougnac (Figure 3) and Pech-Merle. That type of sign could thus be painted and/or engraved. Secondly, they could be dated to the Solutrean (ie

20,000 BP or slightly earlier) by using different methods (Clottes *et al.* 1990a; 1991). Thirdly, their discovery in the Charentes, 150 km from Pech-Merle and Cougnac, showed that the area in which they had been used was much more extensive than previously assumed. This was confirmed in a most unexpected way with the discovery of one of those very distinctive complex signs (see Plate 3) in the Cosquer Cave near Marseilles (Clottes *et al.* 1997, Fig. 2), which marks a remarkable extension of its range.

Claviforms are other very specific geometric signs present in caves which have been found distributed over a wide area, since they are known mostly in a number of caves in the French Pyrenees (Ariège region) (see Plate 4) but also in Quercy (Sainte-Eulalie) and even in Cantabria (La Cullalvera) and Asturias (Pindal). They were thought to be restricted to the Middle Magdalenian until paint analyses in the Niaux Cave showed that the Magdalenians there made use of different recipes for their paint. One of those recipes could be tied to the Late Magdalenian—in particular from similar analyses made of pigment covering artefacts found in a well-dated archaeological layer at La Vache, very close to Niaux. All the available claviforms in Niaux were analysed and it appeared that two had been made with the latest recipe (Clottes *et al.* 1990b, 191) whereas the other five had been made with the earlier type of recipe. Apparently, the symbols we call claviforms were used for longer than had been surmised, from the Middle Magdalenian to the Late

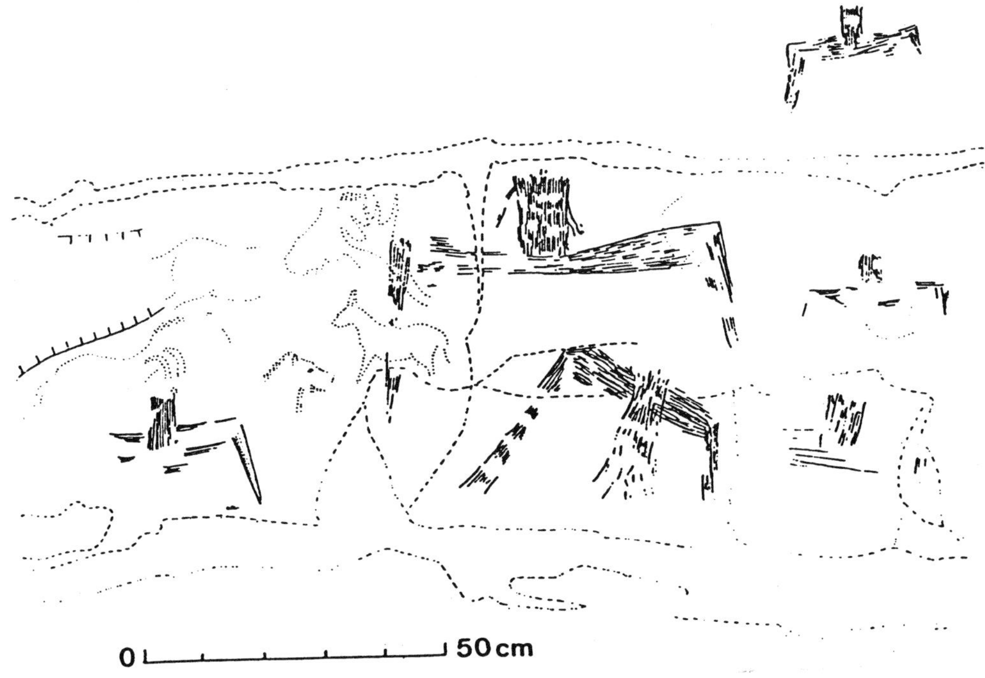

Figure 2. Engraved Placard signs in the Placard Cave (Charente). (Tracing: V. Feruglio)

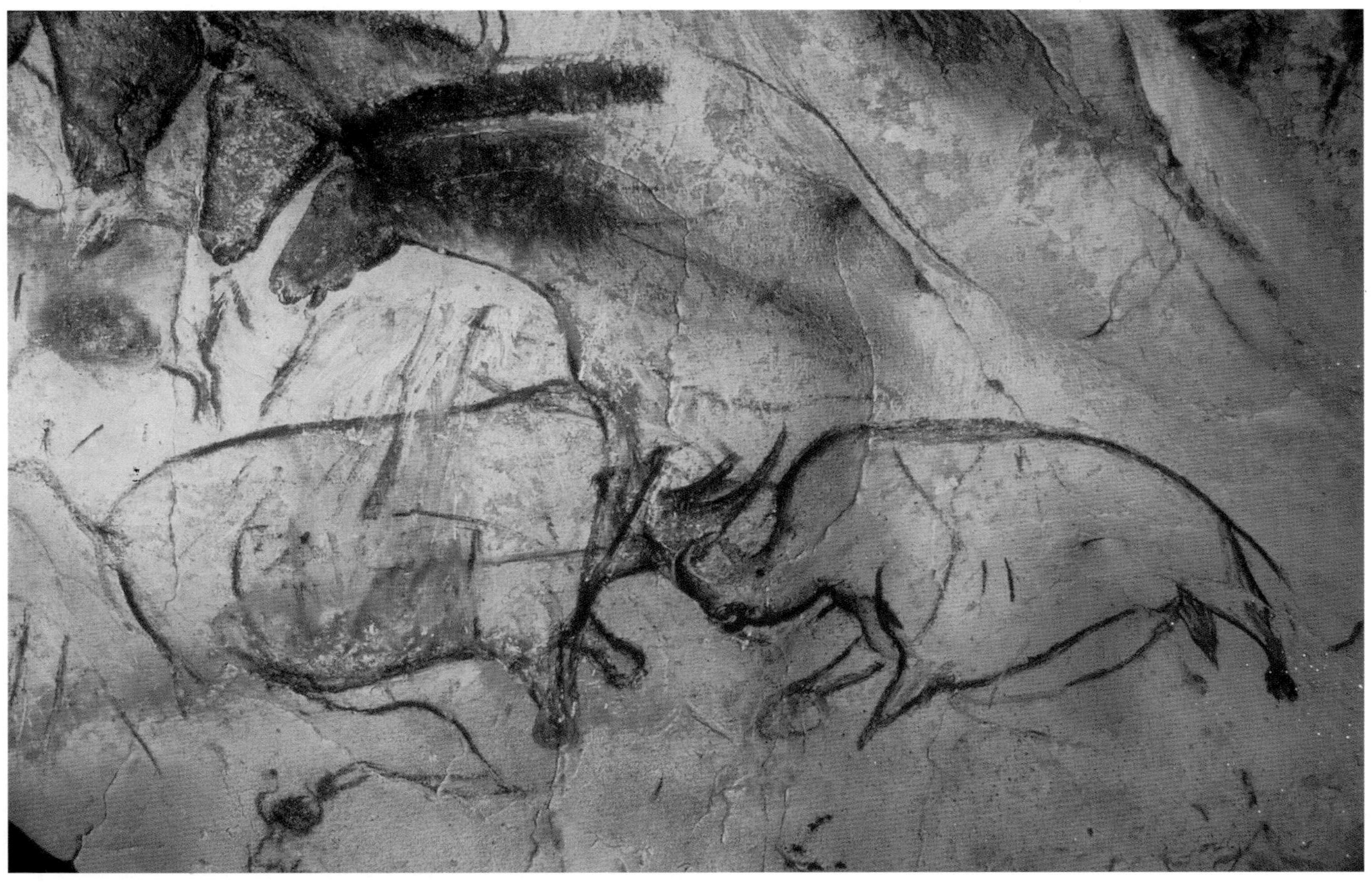

The oldest paintings directly dated in the world so far. Two rhinos in the Chauvet Cave. (Photo: J. Clottes)

PLATE 2

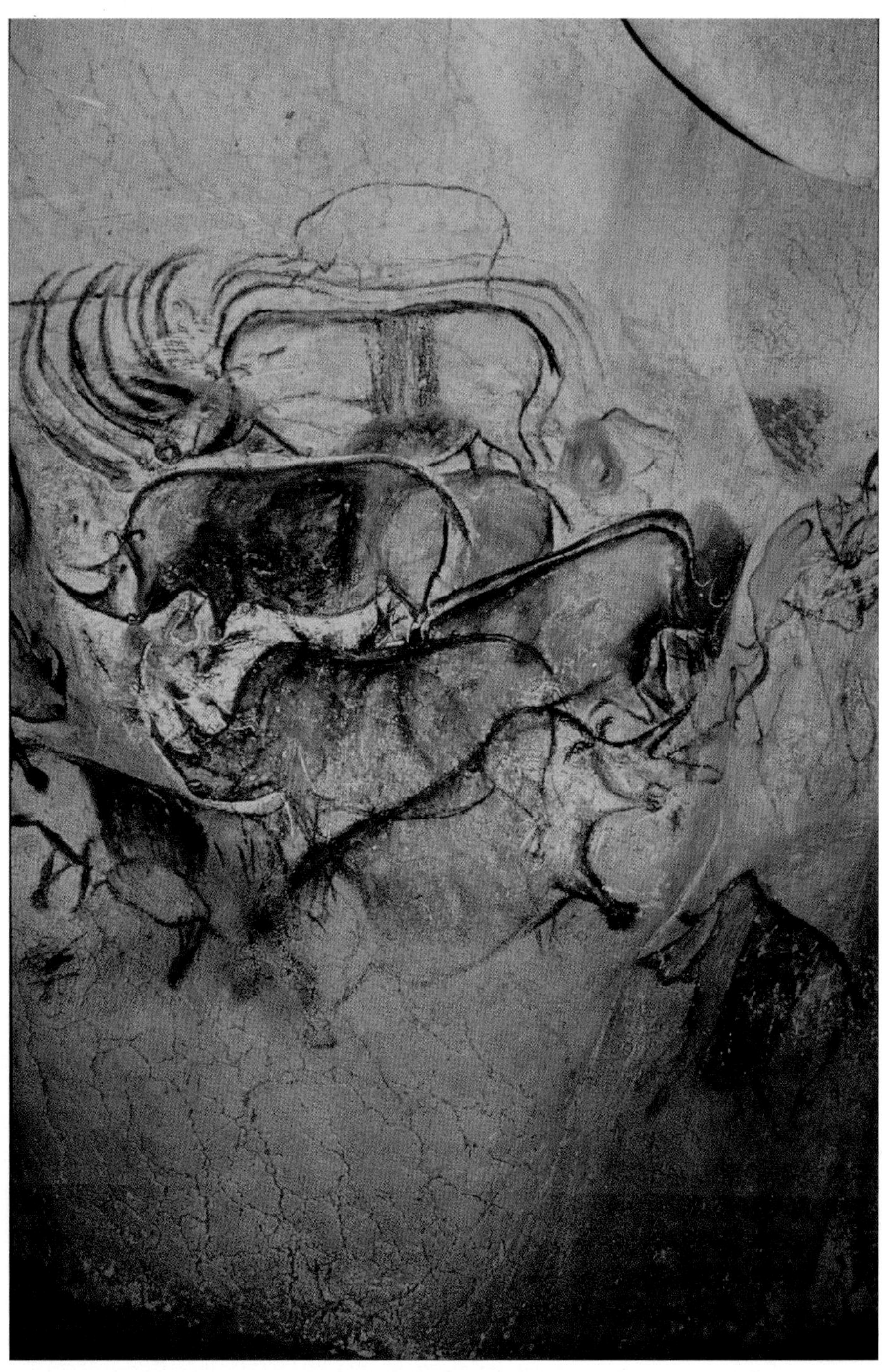

A number of rhinos shown in spatial perspective at Chauvet. (Photo: J. Clottes)

PLATE 3

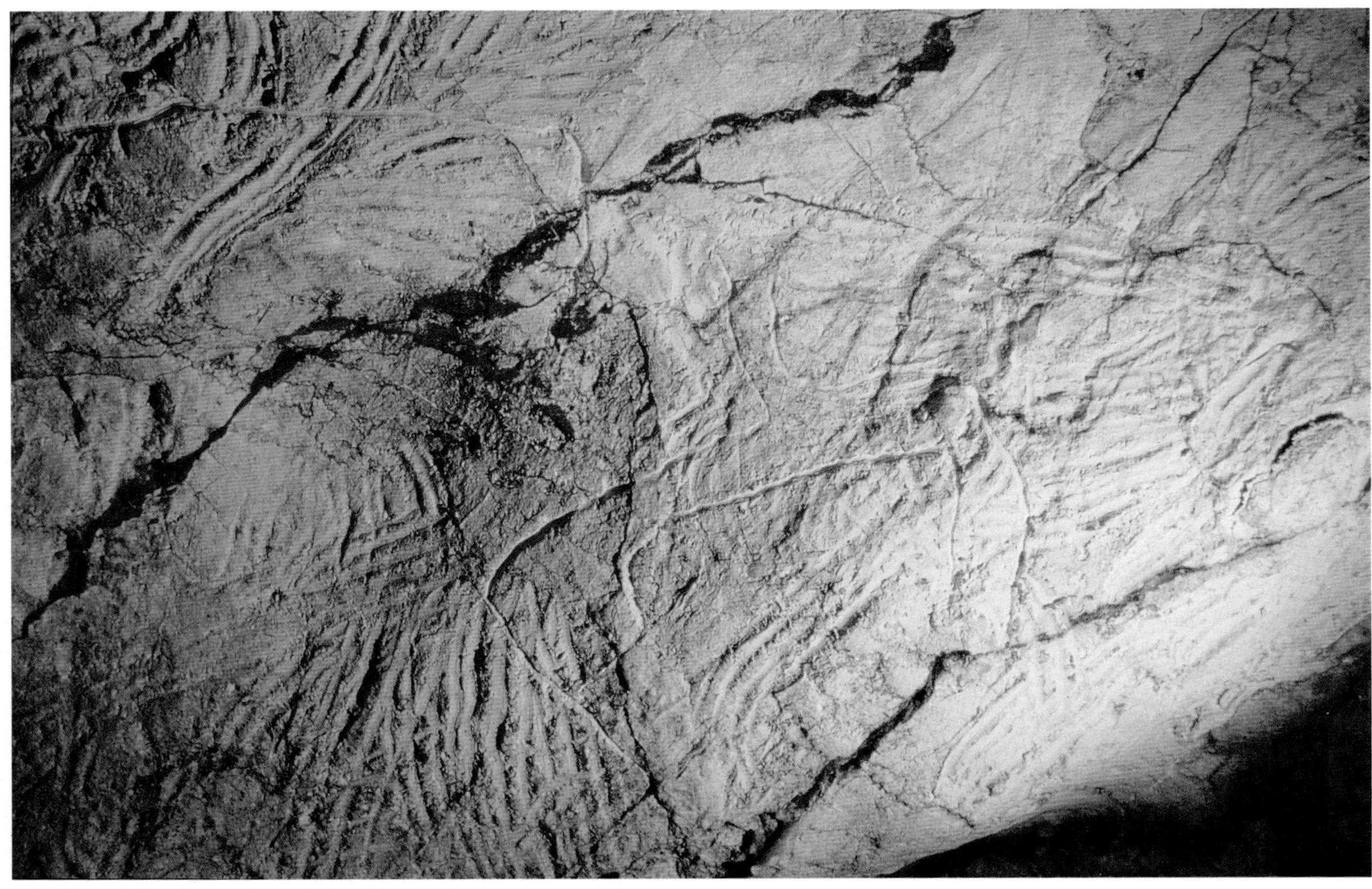

Engraved Placard sign in the Cosquer Cave (Photo: J. Collina-Girard)

PLATE 4

Red claviforms (top and lower right) in the Niaux Cave. (Photo: J. Clottes)

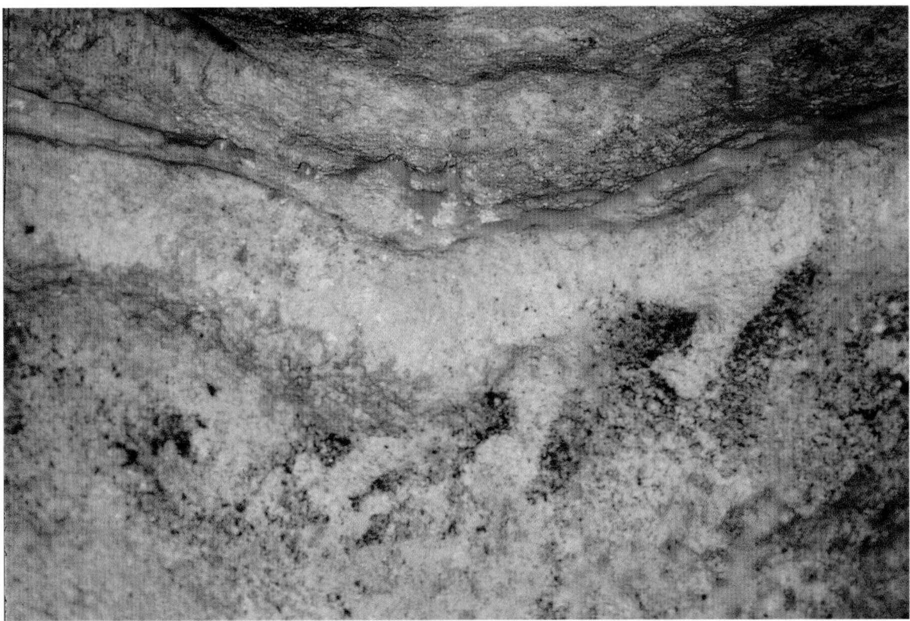

(a) A row of stencilled thumbs shown in profile at Gargas. (Photo: J. Clottes)

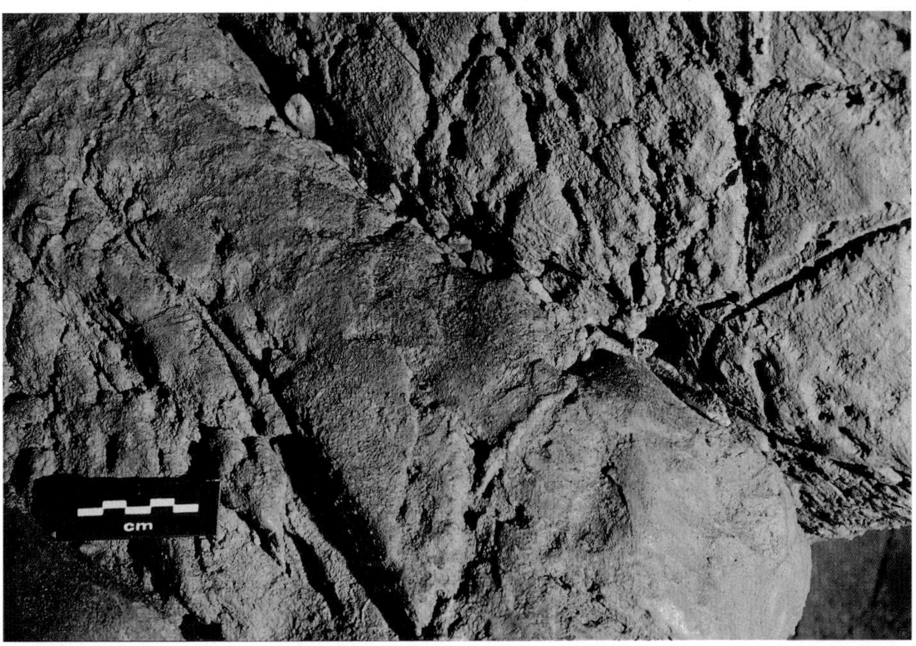

(b) Bone fragments stuck into cracks at Elène (Ariège). (Photo: R. Bégouën)

PLATE 6

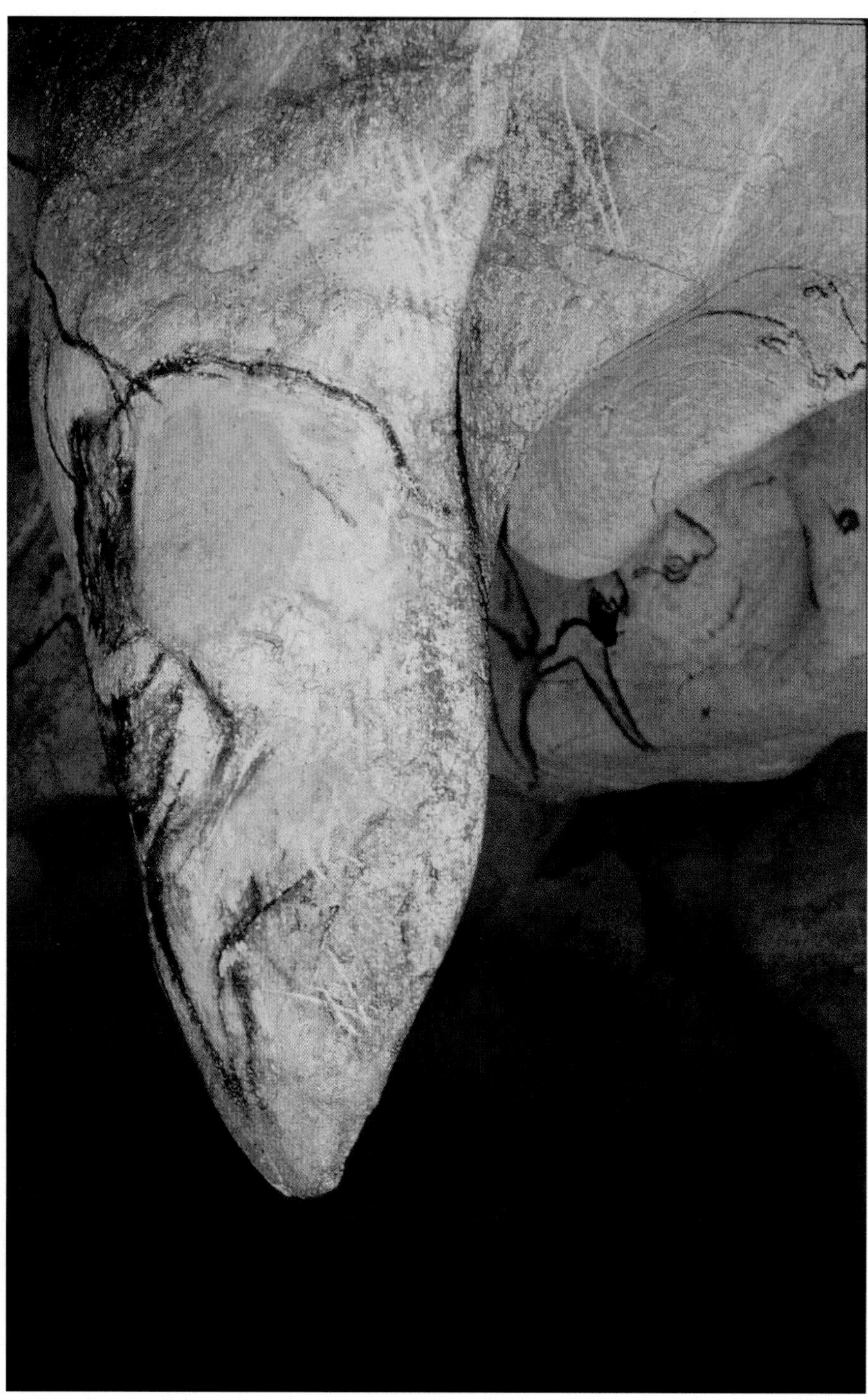

The Chauvet composite creature, part-human and part-bison. (Photo: J. Clottes)

An aurochs seeming to come out of the wall at Chauvet. (Photo: J. Clottes)

PLATE 8

Virtual reality reconstruction of Shrine 10 in Level VIB. (Courtesy Monique Mulder and Heinrich Klotz, Centre for Art and Media, Karlsruhe)

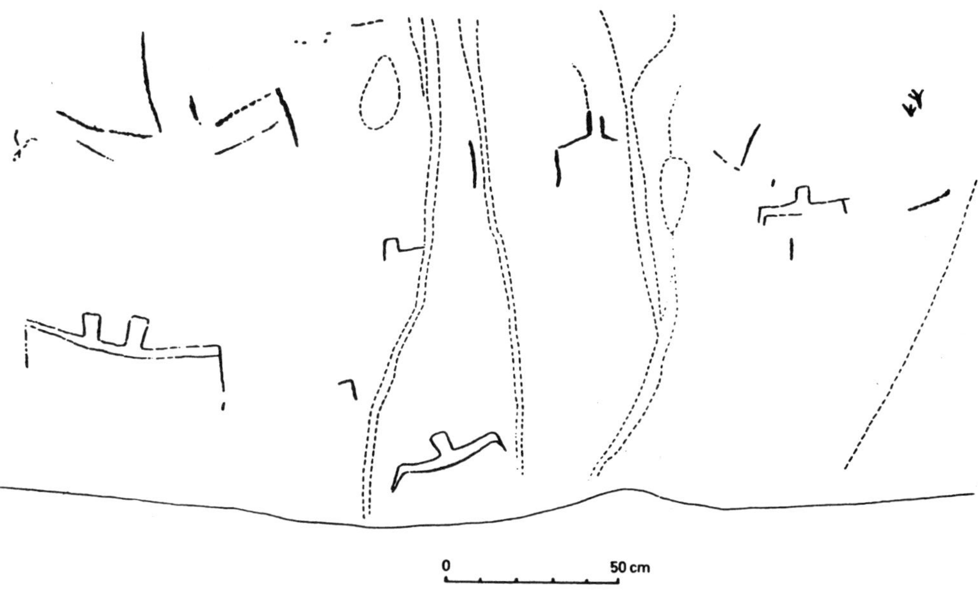

Figure 3. Painted Placard signs in the Cougnac Cave (Lot). (Tracing: M. Lorblanchet)

Magdalenian inclusive. The existence of paintings attributable to both periods in Niaux was confirmed by direct radiocarbon dating of three drawings (Valladas *et al.* 1992).

New data have also been obtained on hand stencils and handprints. They were traditionally attributed to the Gravettian (as in Labattut shelter in the Dordogne). This has been confirmed with a radiocarbon dating for an associated archaeological context at Fuente del Salín, in Cantabria, which gave a date of 22,340±510/480 BP (GrN 18.574) (Moure Romanillo & Gonzalez Morales 1992), the latest for that motif. The earliest ones are in Cosquer: 27,740±410 BP (GifA-96073) for hand stencil no. 19; 27,110±390 BP (GifA-92409) for hand stencil no. MR7; and 24,840±340 BP (GifA-95358) for hand stencil no. 12 (Clottes & Courtin 1994; Clottes *et al.* 1997). However, if the hand stencils and handprints in Chauvet are contemporary with the dated black paintings of the same cave, they could be Aurignacian and older than 30,000 BP. Two other radiocarbon dates, in Gargas and Pech-Merle, have given comparable results. At Gargas one of several bits of bones stuck into cracks next to some hand stencils was dated to 26,860±460 BP (GifA-92369). The Gargas and Cosquer dates reinforce each other all the more as the hand stencils in both caves show incomplete fingers, that is, they belong to a very special category. In Gargas two series (5 and 3) of stencilled bent thumbs shown in profile (Plate 5a) have long been known. The same extraordinary motif also exists in Trois-Frères and in Pech-Merle. As this is far too specific a theme for its repetition to be coincidental, when the Gargas date was published we had assumed that some of the oldest figures in Pech-Merle were probably Gravettian, contrary to traditional evaluations (Clottes *et al.* 1992). This was confirmed soon afterwards when one of the Pech-Merle spotted horses associated to hand stencils was dated to 24,640±390 BP (GifA-95357) (Lorblanchet *et al.* 1995). No evidence exists for later dates for hand stencils. They thus seem to have been essentially in use during all the Gravettian with a strong possibility of beginning in the Aurignacian, that is, for a timespan of nearly 10,000 years.

The duration of another very special theme must also be extended now for an extra number of millennia. Therianthropes, or composite creatures, are representations of beings with both animal and human features. They were supposed to belong only to the Magdalenian, with the Middle Magdalenian figures in Trois-Frères, and with the famous bird-man in the Well of Lascaux and the Sorcerer in Gabillou, both supposed to belong to the Early Magdalenian. The Cougnac and Pech-Merle figures, also with bird heads, were often forgotten. The recent dates obtained in Pech-Merle (see above) and in Cougnac (Lorblanchet 1994) make dates for them over 20,000 BP plausible. Two other cave art discoveries of therianthropes were made, one at Cosquer, the other at Chauvet. At Cosquer, there is an engraved figure of a supine man with the head of a seal; he seems to be dead on his back and a fearsome spear was drawn all over him (Clottes & Courtin 1994, Figs 157, 158). Now, in Cosquer, two sets of dates are centred around 19,000 BP and 27,000 BP respectively (Clottes *et al.* 1997) and we cannot be certain to which group the 'Killed Man' belongs. Whereas in Chauvet the chances are that the composite creature standing (see Plate 6), whose lower body is human and whose upper part is that of a bison (Chauvet *et al.* 1995, Fig. 93), dates to the same period as the other figures, that is, to the Aurignacian, between 30,000 and 32,000 BP. An ivory statuette of a man with a lion's head had been found in an Aurignacian layer at Hohlenstein-Stadel, in south-western Germany (Hahn 1986). Thus, the theme of a man partially transformed into an animal or that of creatures part-human and part-animal runs all through the Upper Palaeolithic. As the same idea is also to be found in all sorts of different cultural and chronological contexts all over the world, it is quite likely that it is part of the universals of the human mind.

On the other hand, the discovery of the Chauvet Cave has made it possible to pinpoint some deep thematic changes in the course of the early Upper Palaeolithic (Clottes 1996b). Leroi-Gourhan (1965, 137, 147) believed that Palaeolithic cave art represented one single symbolic view of the world from the Aurignacian to the Magdalenian with a continuity of the same themes and only minor variations, with the representation of male-female principles essentially embodied in horses and bison. The dominance in Chauvet of rhinos (Plates 1 and 2), lions, mammoths, and bears, that is, of fearsome, difficult to hunt, or even not-hunted animals (60.8 per cent of the identifiable animals in the cave), posed a problem. Was this a freakish local phenomenon or could those themes be found elsewhere on Aurignacian or other sites and thus testify to a major change in concepts at an unspecified date after the Aurignacian?

The well-dated Aurignacian sites of the Dordogne include about three times more 'dangerous' animals than those of the Gravettian in the same area (Delluc & Delluc 1991). Those animals are also dominant for the Aurignacian German statuettes (Riek 1934; Hahn

1986). In Gargas, the Gravettian cave with most figures, only a few mammoths are present and they represent a mere 4 per cent of the bestiary (Barrière 1976, 380). Other caves, belonging to early periods of parietal art but still undated (Grande Grotte at Arcy-sur-Cure, Grotte Bayol, and Baume-Latrone in the Gard), show that the enormous number of dangerous animals at Chauvet is not a unique phenomenon that would be isolated in time and space. Drastic thematic changes have occurred at the end of the Aurignacian or during the Gravettian in south-western France, though perhaps not everywhere at the same time. In central and eastern Europe, the same dangerous animals continued to be carved on the statuettes during all the Pavlov (62.6 per cent) and Kostienki-Avdeevo periods (60.4 per cent) (Kozlowski 1992), whereas in the same regions, they became far fewer in the Magdalenian (8.6 per cent; Hahn 1990).

A common way of thinking over 20,000 years

We have now seen that in the course of the Upper Palaeolithic changes did occur in the use of various themes, and recent research has brought precision as to their duration (hand stencils, claviforms, fearsome animals) or geographic extension (Placard signs). Other themes (such as therianthropes) have been used all through the period. For an art which lasted for more than 20,000 years over such immense distances it would be naive to expect a solid unity. Most specialists have stressed this point and direct all their efforts to determining the duration and extension of particular motifs and techniques, the influences from one group to another, and problems of chronological evolution.

However, many characteristics are common to all the Palaeolithic cultures that produced cave art. We can briefly sum them up, as a reminder, because they appear so commonplace now—after a century of studies of cave art—that they are no longer mentioned or even noticed because of the current focus on 'diversity' rather than on 'unity'.

The artists mostly represented animals and geometric signs. Humans were seldom depicted and when they were, they appeared deliberately sketchy or caricatural: they did not play the same part as the animals in the ceremonies, myths, and religious practices of the time. Composite beings, or therianthropes, constituted one of the minor—in numbers—but important, themes of Palaeolithic art. Among the available animals around them, Palaeolithic people chose to represent the large herbivores that they hunted, especially horses which are the dominant animal images by far. But they also represented bison and aurochs, ibex and all varieties of deer, even if the Aurignacians, as we have seen, seemed to favour the most fearsome species statistically. Birds and fish are only occasionally featured. Some animals are very rare, such as snakes, wolves, and foxes, or missing altogether like insects. Generally animals were painted or engraved without any understandable reference one to the other; explicit scenes are exceptional. The art does not give an accurate account of the world around the artists. The sun, stars, and moon are never drawn, nor the ground line. There are no mountains, no huts, no rivers, no recognizable representations of tools, weapons, or personal adornment. There was no finality, no inevitability either in the artists' choices or in the fact that they kept to them for thousands of years; they could have chosen to represent many other subjects which they did not, and they could have changed their choices every so often. There are a few exceptions but surprisingly few.

During the past ten years or so, new discoveries and research have revealed some more consistent types of behaviour that cover the whole Upper Palaeolithic. We shall mention three of them.

1 Going inside deep caves. Leroi-Gourhan has devoted much thought to what he considered to be two distinct categories of sanctuaries: those under shelters or in the entrances to caves, and those in the dark (Leroi-Gourhan 1965, 114). He wrote that the use of deep caves was one of the characteristics of his Early Style IV during the Middle Magdalenian. Then, with the Late Magdalenian and the Late Style IV, 'the great period of deep sanctuaries comes to an end and wall art can again be found next to the entrances' (Leroi-Gourhan 1965, 42; see also 1965, 73, 77, 156, 316, 319). He thus saw differences in the choice of location as being characterized both culturally and chronologically. The first period, from the Gravettian to Magdalenian III, and the last were examples of art in the open.

A recent review of the evidence (Clottes 1997) has caused two surprises. Art in the light is just slightly less frequent (42.5 per cent) than art inside deep caves (57.5 per cent). This runs counter to the prevailing impression that art in the open is far more rare than cave art because most of it has been destroyed by natural and other causes, and that what is left constitutes 'exceptions', however 'notable' (Bednarik 1993, 4). Bednarik even challenges the very idea of 'cave art' which is only prominent 'because it generally survived only there' (Bednarik op. cit.).

The taphonomy of European Upper Palaeolithic rock art is not a new area of interest. It has been considered by researchers working on the subject ever since Breuil (Breuil 1952, 24; Laming-Emperaire 1962, 186). In France (Campome), in Portugal (Mazouco, Foz Côa), and in Spain (Domingo García, Carbonero Mayor, Siega Verde, Piedras Blancas) (Ripoll López & Muncio Gonzalez 1994), recent discoveries of engravings not only in shelters or in caves but also on rocks out in the open, show that it is possible for Palaeolithic petroglyphs to have survived in fairly exposed locations. Obviously, paintings are a different proposition. They can only endure in sheltered locations, and so many were probably destroyed. On the other hand, caves are certainly not museum-like places where wall art was always perfectly preserved. Wall surfaces can be ravaged by natural causes such as flooding (for example, two-thirds of the Cosquer Cave near Marseille has been damaged), or by water seeping through cracks and dissolving pigments (Niaux in 1978–80), or by calcite covering huge surfaces, or even by draughts (one entire gallery in Lascaux). Many cave entrances have been blocked by scree or by collapses and so remain undiscovered unless modern speleologists find a roundabout way to get in (Fontanet, Réseau Clastres, Chauvet). To postulate then that rock art in the open must have been the norm, since most of it has disappeared, and that compared to this worldwide phenomenon, cave art was a sort of side-event, would mean taking the stance that the destruction of outside sites was far more frequent than that of caves. This is possible but it remains a gratuitous supposition until in-depth geological and taphonomical studies are undertaken, assuming they are feasible. If the rock art sites known today were to represent a hopelessly biased sample because of the destruction of a large number of open-air sites compared with the relative preservation of caves, one should find roughly the same proportion in each type of location whatever the period. This is not the case (Clottes 1997). The numbers of sites are about equal (13 and 12) for the earlier art (Leroi-Gourhan's Styles I–II, corresponding to the Aurignacian and Gravettian), for Style III (mostly Solutrean: 21 and 27), and for the Final Magdalenian (5 and 7), but change to a ratio of nearly one to three for Style IV (Middle and Upper Magdalenian), with 20 sites in the light (30 per cent) and 49 in the dark (70 per cent). As Leroi-Gourhan had argued, people during the Middle and perhaps the Final Magdalenian made a cultural choice to paint or engrave in deep caves more often than ever before or after. That choice is clearer in the Pyrenees where a larger number of deep caves were available.

Before the Magdalenian, however, deep caves were occasionally used, such as Chauvet in the Aurignacian, and that is the second surprise of the study. Gravettians left stencilled handprints, engravings, and finger tracings throughout fairly extensive caves such as Gargas and Cosquer. The Solutreans painted and engraved deep inside caves as well, for example at Cougnac, Pech-Merle, Cosquer, and Oulen. With the Middle Magdalenian, the main difference is that in a number of cases the creators of the art consistently explored mile-long caves, such as Niaux, Montespan, and Rouffignac. They also crawled along very narrow passages (Massat, Le Cheval at Arcy-sur-Cure—assuming the art in that cave is not earlier, as it might well be), climbed chimneys (Tuc d'Audoubert) and precipitously narrow ledges (Trois-Frères, Etcheberri-ko-karbia), and even went down shafts several metres deep (Fontanet). These speleological feats (Leroi-Gourhan 1992, 367) were accomplished again and again. Even if the Palaeolithic artists of western Europe were not the only humans to have dared to go far into the depths, as Leroi-Gourhan had supposed (Leroi-Gourham op. cit., 379) (see the Palaeolithic caves in Australia, such as Koonalda), they are unusual in that they did it habitually, whatever the difficulties, and in this they are unique in world history until much more recent times. The now established fact that, contrary to Leroi-Gourhan's observations, they did it from the Aurignacian (Chauvet) to the Late Magdalenian (Niaux) testifies to a most unusual—one might say 'unnatural'—way of behaving, that is, to a common way of thinking over 20 millennia at least.

Inside the caves other examples show that the cave walls and environment were considered with the same frame of mind from beginning to end.

2 Sticking bits of bones into cracks (see Plate 5b). Modern prehistorians entertain a deeply-rooted mistrust of the word 'ritual' and of whatever may be hidden behind it in the way of prejudice and ignorance. As a consequence, nothing is ritual any longer and as far as possible all traces and remains are explained in a utilitarian manner. However, we do know from ethnographic evidence that the making of rock art was often accompanied by ritual activities, at times quite important and elaborate ones. What is left of them in the archaeological record will probably be very tenuous and may easily be overlooked unless special (and critical) attention is paid to it. When facts resist all practical explanations, even by the most sceptical and materialistic observers, the most convincing one may be that there could have been some religious activity involved, bearing in mind that wall art is generally set in a religious or magical context.

Various deposits of objects in cracks of the walls such as bear teeth or teeth of other animals, shells, flints, or antlers, or even mere bits of bones stuck into wall fissures (Plate 5b) may testify to such practices because there is no way a practical use can be found for them. After attention had been drawn to them in some Pyrenean caves (Bégouën & Clottes 1981), such discoveries became common in painted or engraved caves. In Bernifal, for example, Archambeau found a flint blade stuck half way up in the Mammoth Gallery. This led him to a systematic exploration of the walls and the roof in the area and he then discovered some new paintings, in particular two superb representations of mammoths in a chimney. Now, bits of bones stuck into cracks are known at Enlène, Trois-Frères, Tuc d'Audoubert, Bédeilhac, Portel, Erberua, Troubat, Isturitz, Brassempouy, Montespan, Gargas, all caves with Palaeolithic art.

The most important discovery though was that bone fragments were stuck into a number of cracks in the vicinity of hand stencils at Gargas. One of them could be radiocarbon dated (see above) to 26,860±460 BP (GifA-92369). As most of the others are in Late or Middle Magdalenian contexts, the obvious inference is that this was a practice which lasted for at least 15,000 years.

3 Making animals come out of the walls. The lighting techniques used at the time—torches or grease lamps that would cast a dim and fluctuating light—help to explain this practice. When such conditions are replicated, or even when visiting a cave with a candle, the walls seem to come alive with the moving shadows cast by the flickering flame. It becomes very easy then to see animals in the shapes of the rocks. As with some modern hunter gatherers, perhaps shapes seen in this way were taken for real and the artists then drew animals exactly where they happened to see them, possibly believing that they were thus bringing them to life, controlling them, or gaining their good will (Lewis-Williams 1994; Clottes 1995). This was done through different means. It has long been known that Palaeolithic artists made a great use of natural shapes. The location of very important panels in relation to deep shafts or to the entrances to galleries has sometimes been mentioned (for example, at Rouffignac, see Nougier 1981; Barrière 1982), but much more rarely the fissures or passages out of which some animals seem to emerge, as at Covalanas, Chauvet (Plate 7), Cosquer, and many others (Clottes & Lewis-Williams 1996; 1997). In that case again, the practice—which testifies to a common attitude in relation to the cave itself—has lasted from the Aurignacian (Chauvet) to the Magdalenian (Rouffignac).

Conclusion

It is an astonishing fact that an essentially common way of behaving in the caves, and of considering them as receptacles for images that have not changed so much over the millennia, should have persisted little changed for such an immensity of time. Even in Christianity a mere two thousand years have seen a great number of changes both in the content of the religion itself and in its outward manifestations. From what is an established—if so far underplayed—fact it is possible to draw two main conclusions.

First, such continuity could not have been possible without a very strong framework of beliefs that passed from generation to generation through a strict educational system, perhaps for all or perhaps for those who would have to enact the rites and create the art.

Secondly, the framework of beliefs and the forms of behaviour they generated must have remained fairly consistent throughout the period. This makes it possible not to propose a 'global explanation' of the art where one would try to explain all the cave images in all their details—an obviously impossible endeavour—but to aim at a far more modest goal which is to decipher the essential elements of prehistoric people's beliefs through their tangible manifestations, that is, to provide a theory which constitutes an explanatory framework. So far as we can tell at this stage the best-fit theory is that of shamanism (Lewis-Williams & Dowson 1988; Clottes & Lewis-Williams 1996; 1997). Grahame Clark's interest in cave art is present in much of his writings about the Stone Age (eg Clark 1967), and his analytical mind would, I think, surely be stimulated by all of the recent developments in this field of enquiry.

References

BAHN, P.-G. 1995. Cave art without the caves. *Antiquity* 69 (263): 231–7.

BARRIÈRE, C. 1976. *L'art pariétal de la Grotte de Gargas*. Oxford: BAR Supplementary Series 14 (1).

BARRIÈRE, C. 1982. *L'art pariétal de Rouffignac*. Paris: Picard, Fondation Singer-Polignac.

BEDNARIK, R.G. 1993. European Paleolithic Art—typical or exceptional? *Oxford Journal of Archaeology* 12 (11) 1–8.

BEDNARIK, R. 1994. On the scientific study of palaeoart. *Semiotica* 100, 2/4, 141–68.

BÉGOUËN, R. & CLOTTES, J. 1981. Apports mobiliers dans les Cavernes du Volp (Enlène, Les Trois-Frères, Le Tuc d'Audoubert). *Altamira Symposium*, 157–88.

BREUIL, H. 1952. *Quatre cents siècles d'art pariétal*. Montignac: Centre d'Etudes et de Documentation préhistoriques.

CHAUVET, J.M., BRUNEL-DESCHAMPS, E., HILLAIRE, C. 1995. *La Grotte Chauvet à Vallon-Pont-d'Arc*. Paris: Le Seuil. *Postface* by J. Clottes.

CLARK, G. 1967. *The Stone Age Hunters*. London: Thames and Hudson.

CLOTTES, J. 1995. *Les Cavernes de Niaux. Art préhistorique en Ariège*. Paris: Le Seuil.

CLOTTES, J. 1996a. Les dates de la Grotte Chauvet sont-elles invraisemblables? *INORA* 13, 27–9.

CLOTTES, J. 1996b. Thematic changes in Upper Palaeolithic art: a view from the Grotte Chauvet. *Antiquity* 70, 268, 276–88.

CLOTTES, J. 1997. Art of the light and art of the depths. In M. Conkey, O. Soffer, D. Stratmann & N.-G. Jablonski (eds), *Beyond Art. Pleistocene Image and Symbol.* University of California Press, Memoirs of the California Academy of Sciences, no. 23, 1997, 203–16.

CLOTTES, J. & COURTIN, J. 1994. *La Grotte Cosquer. Peintures et gravures de la caverne engloutie.* Paris: Le Seuil.

CLOTTES, J. & LEWIS-WILLIAMS, D. 1996. *Les Chamanes de la Préhistoire. Transe et magie dans les grottes ornées.* Paris: Le Seuil.

CLOTTES, J. & LEWIS-WILLIAMS, D. 1997. Les Chamanes des Cavernes. *Archéologia* 336, 30–41.

CLOTTES, J., DUPORT, L. & FERUGLIO, V. 1990a. Les signes du Placard. *Bulletin Société Préhistorique Ariège-Pyrénées* 45, 15–49.

CLOTTES, J., MENU, M. & WALTER, P.H. 1990b. La préparation des peintures magdaléniennes des cavernes ariégeoises. *Bulletin Société Préhistorique française* 87, 6: 170–92.

CLOTTES, J., DUPORT, L. & FERUGLIO, V. 1991. Derniers éléments sur les signes du Placard. *Bulletin Société Préhistorique Ariège-Pyrénées* 46, 119–32.

CLOTTES, J., VALLADAS, H., CACHIER, H. & ARNOLD, M. 1992. Des dates pour Niaux et Gargas. *Bulletin Société Préhistorique française* 89, 9, 270–4.

CLOTTES, J., CHAUVET, J.-M., BRUNEL-DESCHAMPS, E., HILLAIRE, C., DAUGAS, J.-P., ARNOLD, M., CACHIER, H., EVIN, J., FORTIN, P., OBERLIN, C., TISNERAT, N. & VALLADAS, H. 1995. Les peintures paléolithiques de la Grotte Chauvet-Pont-d'Arc, à Vallon-Pont-d'Arc (Ardèche, France): datations directes et indirectes par la méthode du radiocarbone. *Comptes-rendus de l'Académie des Sciences de Paris*, 320:IIa, 1133–40.

CLOTTES, J., COURTIN, J., COLLINA-GIRARD, J., VALLADAS, H. & ARNOLD, M. 1997. News from Cosquer Cave: climate studies, recording, sampling, dates. *Antiquity* 71, no. 272, 321–6.

DELLUC, B. & DELLUC, G. 1991. *L'art pariétal archaïque en Aquitaine.* Paris: Ed. du CNRS, XXVIII° suppl. to *Gallia Préhistoire.*

DELLUC, B. & DELLUC, G. 1996. L'art paléolithique archaïque en France. In A. Beltrán & A. Vigliardi, (eds), *Art in the Palaeolithic and Mesolithic,* XIII International Congress of Prehistoric and Protohistoric Sciences, Forlì, Italy, 87–90.

DELPORTE, H. 1998. *Les Aurignaciens, premiers hommes modernes.* Paris: La Maison des Roches.

GIRARD, M., BAFFIER, D., VALLADAS, H. & HEDGES, R. 1995. Dates ^{14}C à la Grande Grotte d'Arcy-sur-Cure (Yonne, France). *INORA*, 12, 1–2.

HAHN, J. 1986. *Kraft und Aggression. Die Botschaft der Eiszeitkunst im Aurignacien Süddeutschlands?* Tübingen: Institut für Urgeschichte der Universität Tübingen, Verlag Archaeologica Venatoria.

HAHN, J. 1990. Fonction et signification des statuettes du Paléolithique supérieur européen. In J. Clottes (ed.), *L'Art des Objets au Paléolithique, t. 2: Les Voies de la Recherche*, 173–83.

IGLER, W., DAUVOIS, M., HYMAN, M., MENU, M. ROWE, M., VÉZIAN, J. & WALTER, P. 1994. Datation radiocarbone de deux figures pariétales de la grotte du Portel (Commune de Loubens, Ariège). *Bulletin Société Préhistorique Ariège-Pyrénées* 49, 231–6.

KOZLOWSKI, J.K. 1992. *L'art de la Préhistoire en Europe orientale.* Paris: CNRS.

LAMING-EMPERAIRE, A. 1962. *La signification de l'art rupestre paléolithique.* Paris: Picard.

LEROI-GOURHAN, A. 1965. *Préhistoire de l'art occidental.* Paris: Mazenod.

LEROI-GOURHAN, A. 1981. Les signes pariétaux comme 'marqueurs' ethniques. *Altamira Symposium*, 289–94.

LEROI-GOURHAN, A. 1982. *The Dawn of European Art—an introduction to Palaeolithic cave painting.* Cambridge: Cambridge University Press.

LEROI-GOURHAN, A. 1992. *L'art pariétal, langage de la Préhistoire.* Paris: Jérome Millon.

LEWIS-WILLIAMS, J.D. 1994. Rock art and ritual: Southern Africa and beyond. *Complutum* 5, 277–89.

LEWIS-WILLIAMS, J.D. & DOWSON, T.A. 1988. The signs of all times. Entoptic phenomena in Upper Palaeolithic art. *Current Anthropology* 29 (2), 201–45.

LORBLANCHET, M. 1994. La datation de l'art pariétal paléolithique. *Bulletin de la Société des Etudes Littéraires, Scientifiques et Historiques du Lot* CXV, 3, 161–82.

LORBLANCHET, M., CACHIER, H. & VALLADAS, H. 1995. Datation des chevaux ponctués du Pech-Merle. *INORA* 12, 2–3.

MOURE ROMANILLO, A. & GONZALEZ MORALES, M., 1992. Datation ^{14}C d'une zone décorée de la grotte Fuente del Salín en Espagne. *INORA* 3, 1–2.

NOUGIER, L.R. 1981. Art, magie, mythologie et religions. *Bulletin Société Préhistorique Ariège* 36, 77–92.

RIEK, G. 1934. *Die Eiszeitjägerstation am Vogelherd im Lonetal.* Tübingen: Bd. 1, Die Kulturen.

RIPOLL LÓPEZ, S. & MUNCIO GONZÁLEZ L.J. 1994. A large open air grouping of Paleolithic rock art in the Spanish Meseta. *INORA* 7, 2–5.

UCKO P.J. 1987. Débuts illusoires dans l'étude de la tradition artistique. *Bulletin Société Préhistorique Ariège-Pyrénées* XLII, 15–81.

UCKO, P.J. & ROSENFELD, A. 1967. *L'art paléolithique.* Paris: Hachette, Collection L'univers des Connaissances 9.

VALLADAS, H., CACHIER, H., MAURICE, P., BERNALDO DE QUIROS, F., CLOTTES, J., CABRERA VALDEZ, V., UZQUIANO, P. & ARNOLD, M. 1992. Direct radiocarbon dates for prehistoric paintings at the Altamira, El Castillo and Niaux caves, *Nature* 357, 68–70.

ZÜCHNER, C. 1996. La Grotte Chauvet. Radiocarbone contre Archéologie. *INORA* 13, 25–7.

Symbolism at Çatalhöyük

IAN HODDER

THE 9000 YEAR OLD SITE OF ÇATALHÖYÜK in central Turkey was first excavated by James Mellaart (1967) between 1961 and 1965. The importance of the site was quickly and widely recognized. In particular the great size of the mound was noted, remarkable for an early agricultural site. Grahame Clark (1977) estimated that it held a population of 5000 people. More recent estimates have suggested figures between 2000 and 10,000 (Hodder 1996). But it was not just the size of the site which hit the headlines. It was the art and symbolism which captured the imagination (see Plate 8). Commentators noted the bucrania (plastered bulls' heads) set on walls and pillars within buildings, plaster reliefs of leopards and 'Mother Goddess' figures, paintings of hunting scenes or of vultures stripping the flesh from headless human corpses, or of geometric designs.

New work began at the site in 1993, under the auspices of the British Institute of Archaeology at Ankara. The first three years of fieldwork concentrated on studies of the surface of the West (Chalcolithic) and East (Neolithic) mounds (published in Hodder 1996). Since 1995 excavation has been undertaken in the areas identified in Figure 1. One of the aims of this work is better to understand the art and symbolism at Çatalhöyük East.

It is often presumed that Grahame Clark focused his work mainly on ecology, environment, and long-term evolutionary trends. But it is important to recognize that he also gave due attention to social and symbolic factors. For example, in 1970 (95–6) he wrote '*Homo economicus* is a lay figure who never, in fact, walked the earth'. He can be used 'as a model, if only to point up the non-economic motivations of human behaviour' (ibid.). Back in 1939 (revised 1957, 219) he had emphasized that while the environment limits or constrains social choice it is social choice which determines cultural behaviour in its specific form. He argued that social factors are both a consequence and a cause of economic change (ibid., 221).

For Grahame Clark it was this social choice which, when released from environmental constraint, created the diversity of human culture which he celebrated in his 1982 book *The Identity of Man*. Changing patterns of subsistence associated with the shift to farming did not determine cultural diversity. Rather, the change to farming happened many

Proceedings of the British Academy, **99**, 177–191

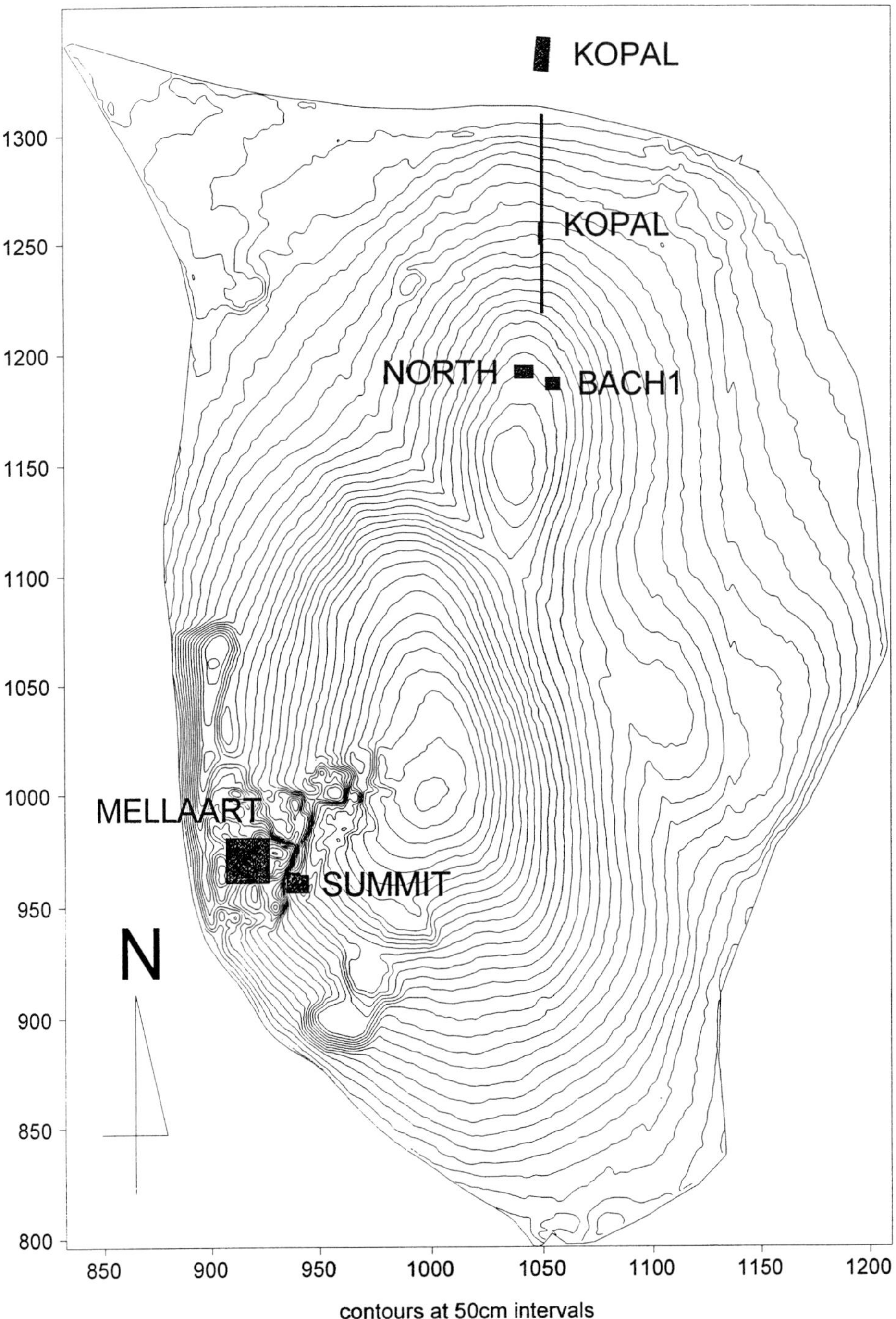

Figure 1. The excavation areas on the East mound at Çatalhöyük.

times in different parts of the world 'on each occasion under unique circumstances' (1982, 79). These circumstances included social factors such as craft specialization and the search for identity.

Çatalhöyük is a prime example of a unique response to farming—a prime example of the social creation of diversity of which Grahame Clark wrote. He recognized this himself and discussed the site at some length in his *World Prehistory* (1977), itself dedicated to 'the diversity of men'. In his description of the site he predicted, in a remarkably prescient way, many of the conclusions we have recently arrived at in the new work at the site. For example, he talked of the so-called 'shrines' at Çatalhöyük which we would now argue were used as domestic houses. Clark said of the 'shrines', 'but the number and small size of these argues for domestic family cults' rather than public temples with full-time priests (1977, 72). He also said the art was about 'the generative forces of nature' (ibid.) and with both these points I would substantially agree.

Clark argued in general for the 'social character of art' (1939, revised 1957, 224). For him, art mirrored and embodied social life and the physical environment. He saw art as systemically linked to society. It is this social character of art and its unique social character at Çatalhöyük that I wish to discuss in this paper. This is because Clark's view of art coincides very much with the primary aim of our own project which is to place the art into its full environmental, economic, and social context.

Building 1

I wish to provide an example of the social character of art at Çatalhöyük East by discussing the first building that we have excavated in detail: Building 1 in the North area of the site. I believe this discussion contributes to Grahame Clark's vision of art.

Scraping of the surface of the mounds at Çatalhöyük had earlier proved successful in establishing the overall arrangement of architecture on the Neolithic East mound. Despite some later (Hellenistic and Byzantine) occupation, in many areas on the top of the mound removal of the plough-soil immediately exposed plans of Neolithic buildings. These results and the supporting geophysical prospection are described by R. Matthews (1996) and Shell (1996). It became clear that the upper levels of occupation on the East mound consisted largely of densely packed small buildings and extensive midden areas. The small rectangular buildings recalled closely those excavated by Mellaart (1967) in the south-western part of the mound. Indeed, the scraping technique suggested that these buildings, even well away from the area excavated by Mellaart, included elaborate examples with complex internal fittings. This suggested that the so-called 'shrines' occurred in different parts of the site at a high density. Rather than envisaging a priestly elite in one quarter of the site, it became necessary to think of domestic cults widely spread.

Further study of the material excavated in the 1960s, including the artefacts housed in museums in Turkey, suggested a more complex picture (Hodder 1996). A continuum of variation could be identified between more and less architecturally complex buildings. The more complex buildings with more platforms, bins, pillars, sculpture, and painting also tended to have more bifacially flaked obsidian points and more obsidian cores. They also tended to be more innovative in the use of ceramic forms, and to have more figurines. It was also clear that the more elaborate buildings in one phase would often continue to be more elaborate when rebuilt in ensuing phases. There are many difficulties with the definition of such variation between more and less elaborate buildings because of the limitations of the surviving records. In any case, what variation occurs is within a narrow band, and micromorphological work (W. Matthews *et al.* 1996) indicated that even the more elaborate buildings (termed 'shrines' by Mellaart) had traces of a wide range of domestic activities on their floors.

In approaching Building 1, therefore, we were of the opinion that the art at Çatalhöyük had a domestic context but that certain buildings played a slightly more central role in the generation and transmission of cultural elaboration. Unfortunately, the preservation of Building 1 proved to be relatively poor since the walls and upper fills had been subject to millennia of erosion on the top of the North mound, and since the plasters on the surviving walls and floors (the latter only 50 cm from the surface of the mound) had been affected by roots, animal burrows, and freeze-thaw action. Nevertheless, the building yielded a large amount of information, resulting from detailed data collection. All soil from the site was dry-sieved, and 30 litres from each deposit were wet-sieved in a flotation system. The heavy residues from this were collected in a 0.5 mm mesh, were dried and then sieved through 4 mm, 2 mm, and 1 mm meshes before hand sorting. The resultant heavy residue plots from the floors in Building 1 will be discussed below. (The results from the organic and inorganic chemistry analyses of the floor samples are not available at the time of writing.) This work on micro-artefact distributions on the floors at Çatalhöyük is needed because the floors were carefully swept clean in antiquity. Macro-artefacts (above 4 mm) occur rarely on or beneath floors, and when they do they appear to be special foundation or abandonment deposits or material which has fallen from roofs or walls.

Up to 40 layers of replastering were found on the walls and floors of Building 1. We believe, on the basis of correlations with dendrochronological sequences, that these replasterings occurred annually (Kuniholm & Newton 1996). The use of the building has been divided into the eight phases summarized in Figure 2. The following is a brief summary of the story of these phases. During the construction of the building (phase one), clean foundation deposits were placed between the walls, and burials were placed within these deposits. In particular, a row of three neonate burials was placed just in front of what was to be the entrance from the western room (Space 70) into the main eastern room (Space 71). In the first occupation phase (phase two) a fire installation was constructed within the south wall of Space 71. Adjacent to this were the traces of a ladder which allowed access to the building, presumably through the same roof-hole through which the smoke from the fire escaped. The western room (Space 70) contained a fire installation in the south-west corner. In the centre of the west side of Space 71 sculpture was placed on the wall, although

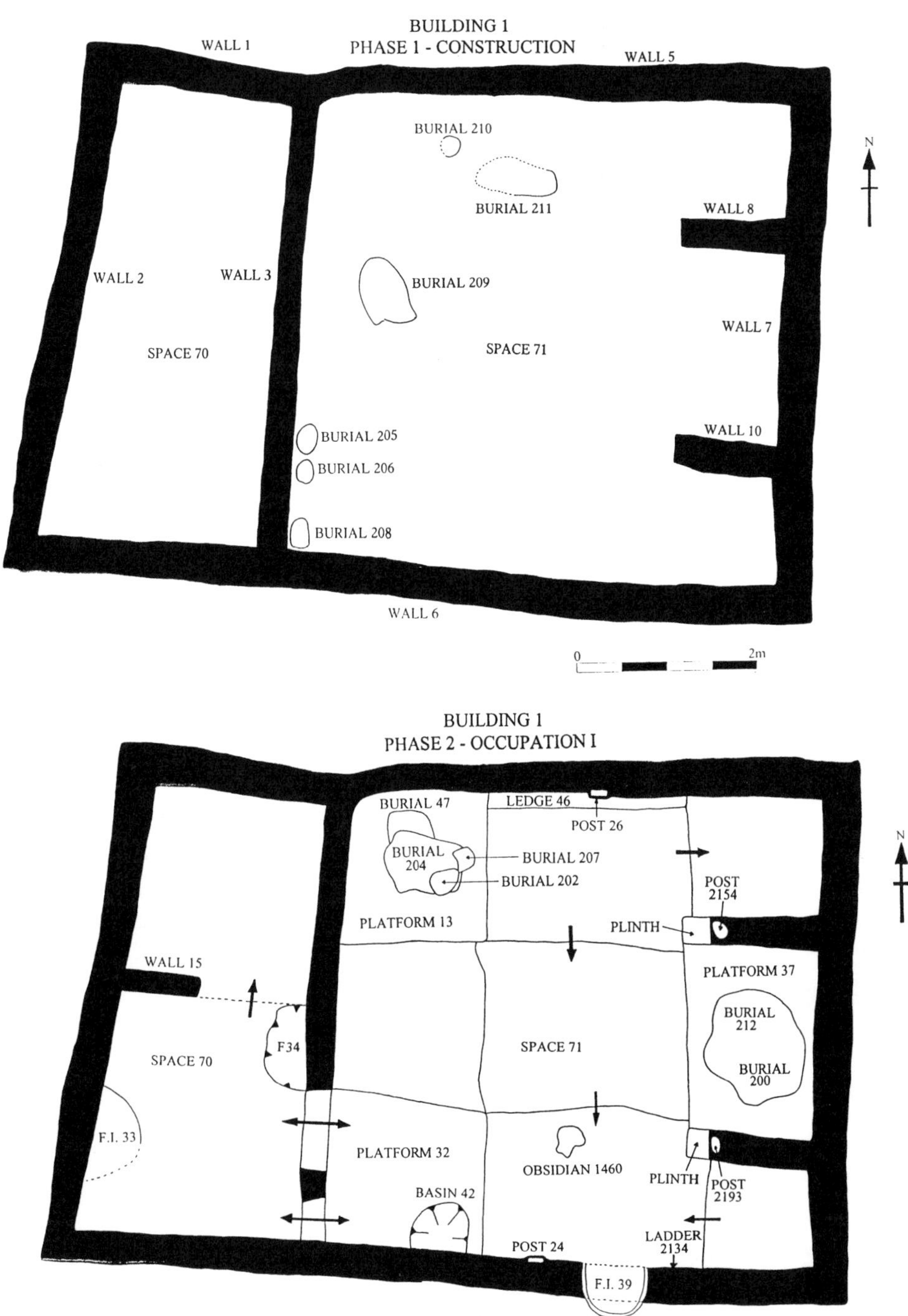

Figure 2. Building 1 at Çatalhöyük. The eight phases of use are summarized.

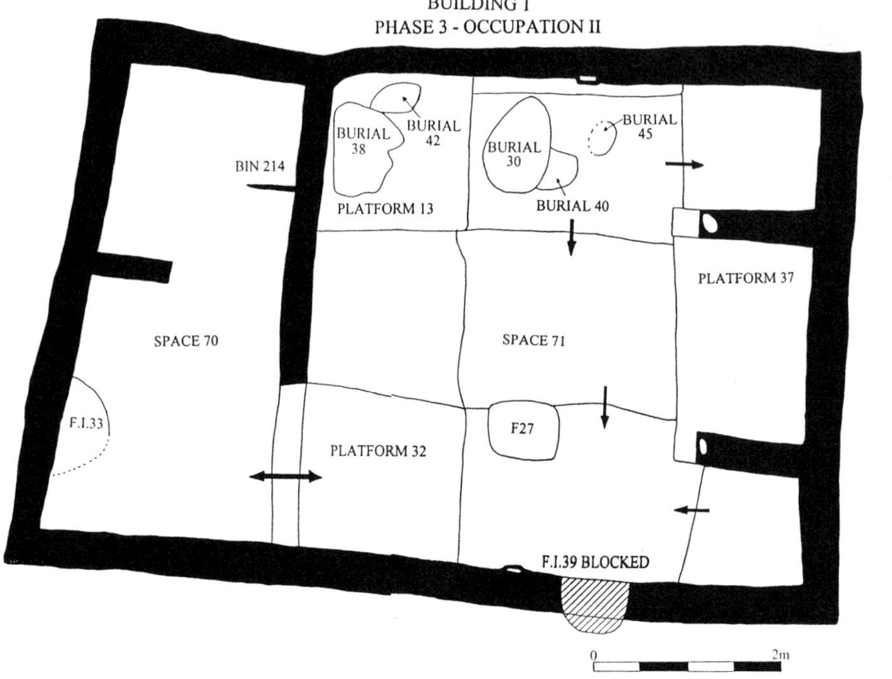

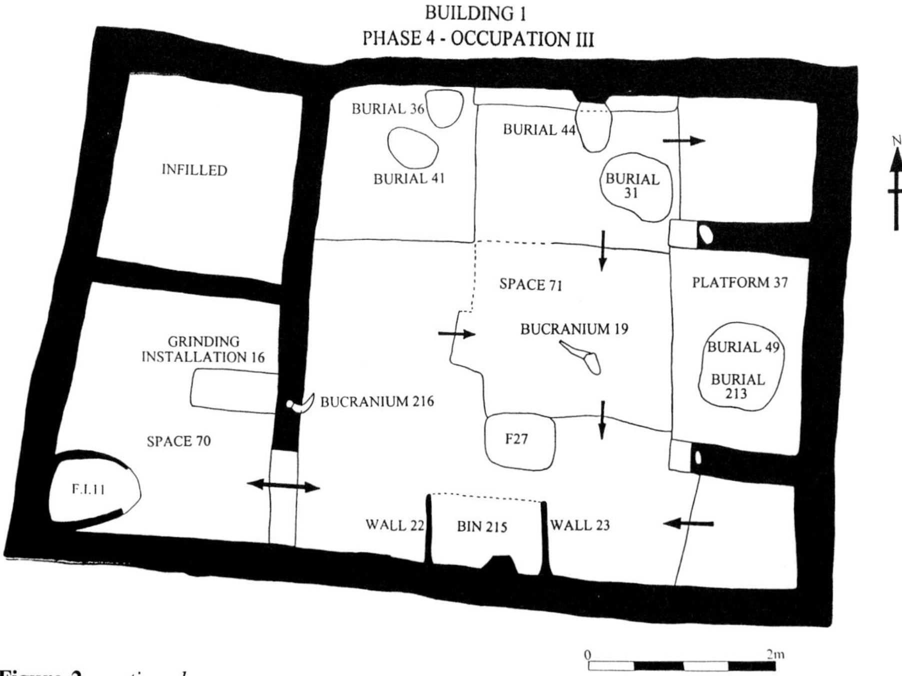

Figure 2. *continued*

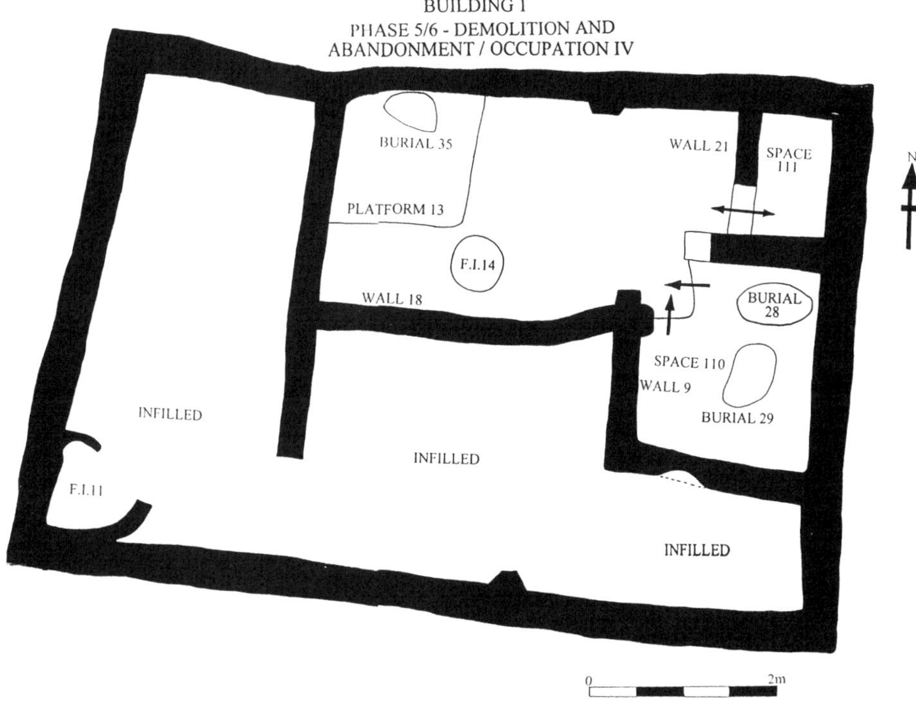

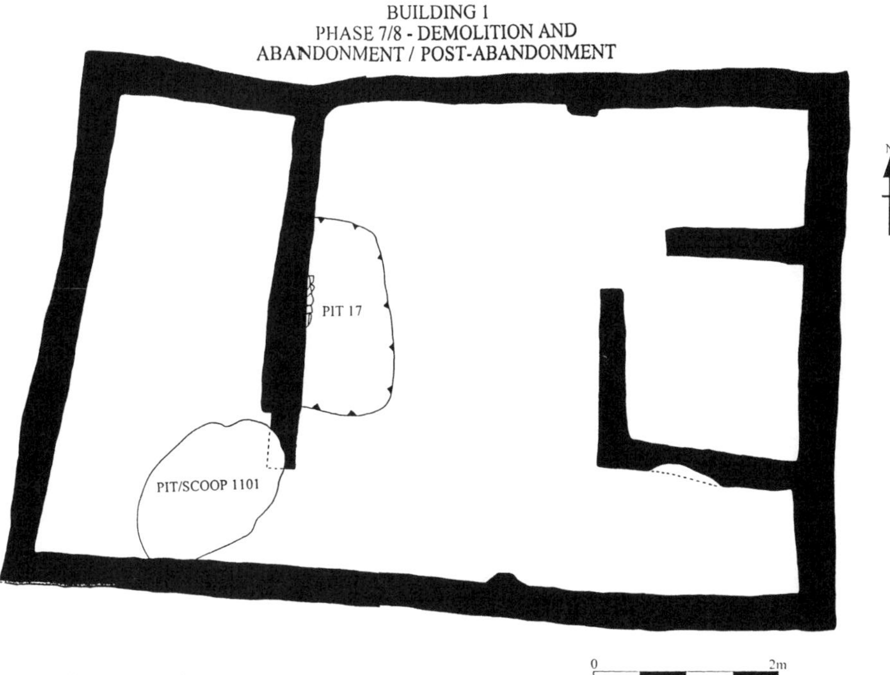

Figure 2. *continued*

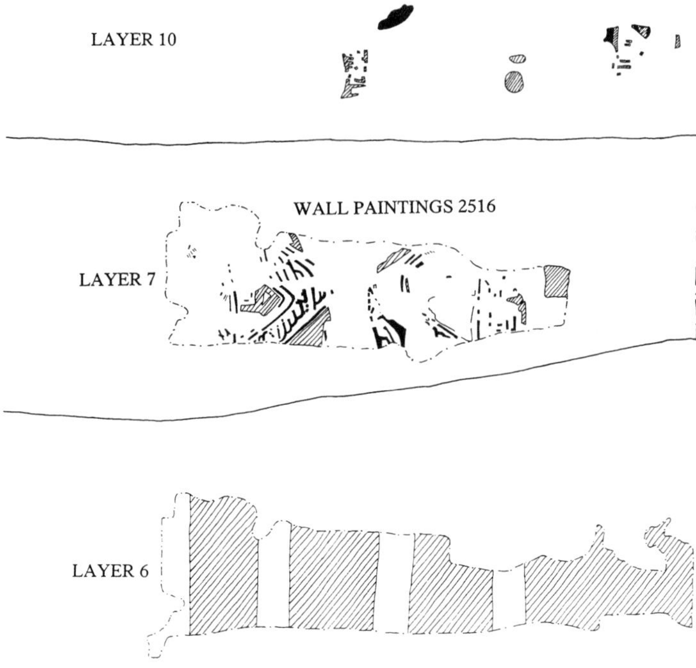

Figure 3. The painting on layers of wall plaster around the north-west platform in Building 1, Space 71.

since this was later removed (see phase eight) we do not know what this consisted of. Certainly there was a frame of vertical plaster edges within which the relief sculpture was placed. Although traces of red paint were found elsewhere on the walls of Spaces 70 and 71, the only concentration of painting and the only evidence of designs and motifs occurred around and on the north-western platform (Platform 13). Here some of the early layers of plaster were painted in geometric designs (Figure 3) in various hues of red and in black.

In order to understand the social role of painting in Building 1 we need to try and determine what activities were taking place in the building, particularly around the north-west platform. The micro-artefact distributions suggest a wide range of activities, as do the micromorphological studies by W. Matthews *et al.* (1996). It is clear that micro-traces survive of obsidian knapping, fish processing, wood-working, bone implement manufacture, hearth sweeping, and plant storage within the buildings at Çatalhöyük. There are indications of animal dung, even on the cleaner floors, although this may derive from dung used as fuel (ibid.). However, in Building 1 most of these activities occurred in the southern part of Space 71 and in the western room (Space 70), as is indicated by the micro-artefact plots (Figure 4). The floors in the north and east parts of Space 71 had thicker and cleaner plaster and fewer artefact residues. It is possible that this differentiation into 'clean' and 'dirty' floors resulted from the placing of carefully woven reed mats on the floors of parts of the building (the imprint of such mats having been recorded by Mellaart (1967)).

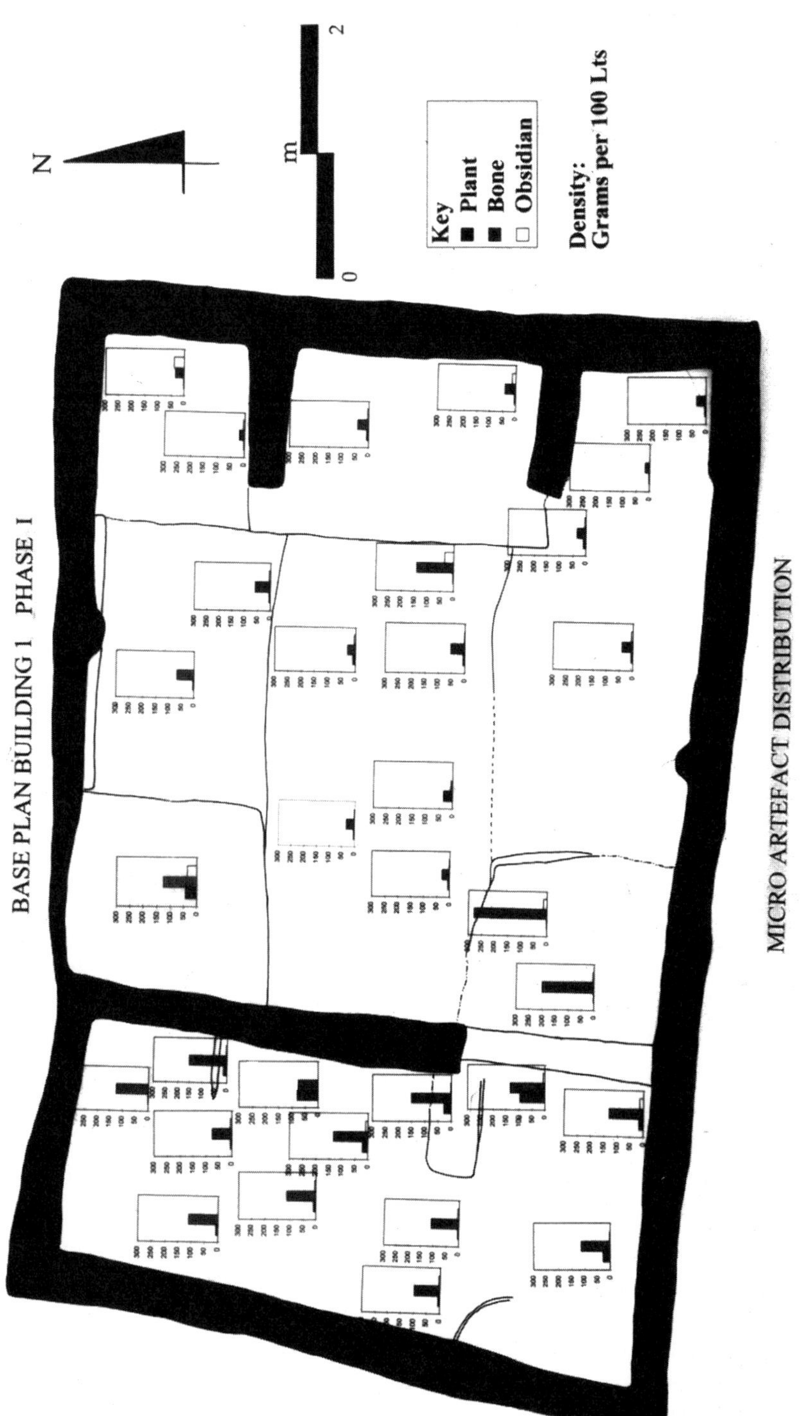

Figure 4. The distribution of micro-artefacts in Building 1.

The painting in Building 1 thus occurred, as Clark had suggested, in a domestic context. And in particular it occurred in the 'cleaner' parts of the building away from the main food preparation and storage areas. In order to understand these areas better, and in order to understand what particularly was happening on the north-west platform, we need to continue on to the second occupation phase (phase three). In this phase, the fire installation in the south wall of Space 71 was blocked up. A small basin (F27), perhaps used for grinding (grinding stones with traces of red ochre were found within it), was placed in the southern part of Space 71. A wooden bin, perhaps for storage, was built within Space 70. In this phase, the same division in the use of space between the south-west and the north-east parts of the building occurred, as seen in the micro-artefact distributions and micromorphological studies.

In phase four, the third phase of occupation, a substantial fire installation was built in the south-west corner of Space 70. A grinding installation was also constructed in this room. A storage bin used mainly for lentils was placed on the south wall of Space 71. The entrance between Spaces 70 and 71 was remodelled and a cattle horn set within the western wall of Space 71.

What activities were occurring in the 'cleaner' parts of Building 1 during these first three occupation phases? One important activity seems to have been burial. So far at least 64 individuals have been found in a series of graves beneath the north-western platform, beneath the floor immediately to the east of the north-western platform, and beneath the main eastern platform. Study of the human remains (Molleson & Andrews 1997) has indicated that most of the burials were placed in small graves while still fleshed, the bodies tightly flexed and often wrapped in cloth or braids. As later bodies were added into graves, earlier bones were disturbed, moved aside, or removed. This repeated cutting and recutting of graves has made phasing of the grave sequence difficult, as will be discussed below. But bodies seem to have been added to the building throughout the phases of occupation.

The spatial patterning of the ages of the individuals buried in different parts of the building is informative (Figure 5). The north-west platform has not only the highest concentration of burials, but also the highest proportion of young individuals. So the painting in Building 1 is associated with burial, especially of young people. If this spatial link can be established, what of the temporal link between the painting and the burials?

The fourth phase of occupation (phase six) occurs after a serious fire—perhaps deliberately controlled—had destroyed the southern half of the building. As a result, the building was remodelled (phase five). A wall was constructed to separate the rubble in the southern half of the building from the re-occupied northern half (Figure 2). The eastern platform was rebuilt as a separate small room (Space 110) and a small, perhaps storage room, was built in the north-east of the building (Space 111). A fire installation was placed near the north-west platform.

The micro-artefact distributions suggest that even in this remodelled space the west was kept for food processing and other 'dirty' activities, while the eastern spaces were kept 'clean'. Burial continued especially under the floor of the eastern room (Space 110),

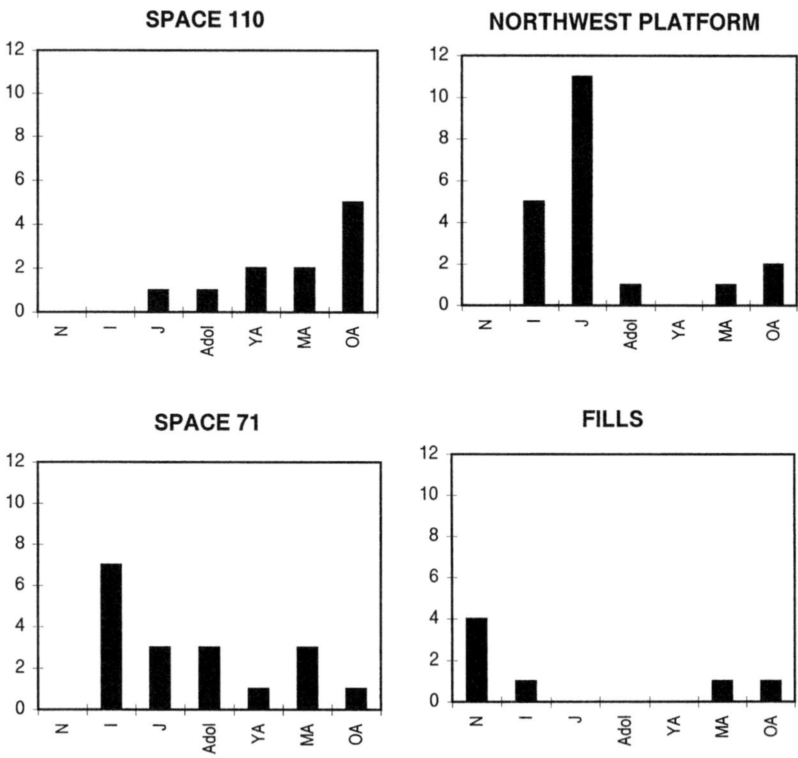

Figure 5. Histogram of the ages of individual skeletons buried beneath different parts of Building 1. Fills indicates phase one constructional deposits; Space 71 is immediately to the east of the north-west platform, and Space 110 is the eastern platform (see Figure 2). Ages are given as Neonate (N), Infant (I), Juvenile (J), Adolescent (Adol), Young Adult (YA), Medium Adult (MA), Old Adult (OA).

and declined beneath the north-western platform (Platform 13). Perhaps this was because this latter platform had come to be used for domestic activities. Indeed, the last floor surface on this platform was associated with a concentration of fish bones. It is thus of interest that the latest layers of plaster around this platform do not seem to have been painted.

There is thus both a spatial and a temporal link between the painting around the north-western platform in Building 1 and burial, especially of young people. What can we say about the traces of relief sculpture on the west wall of Space 71, including the cattle horn set into the wall here? In the first three phases of occupation the sculpture is not associated with a particular activity area. Instead it seems to be centrally located, looking out into Space 71 as a whole. Behind it is the food storage and preparation taking place in the smaller western room. Unlike the painting which has a short, annual cycle of use, the relief sculpture has a life cycle linked to the building itself. Fixed to the wall it is less easy to change and transform. As Mellaart often remarked (1967), the relief sculptures are integral to the architecture of the Çatalhöyük buildings, being attached to upright beams and pillars.

The sculpture in Building 1 is centrally placed in the building and it has a life cycle which spans the building as a whole. That 40 year cycle in Building 1 seems to follow the life of an extended family. There are too many individuals buried in Building 1 to have been produced by deaths within a small nuclear family in this time period. We assume that a larger, extended group had rights of burial in this building. However, the early burials are predominantly of young individuals and the later of older individuals (Figure 6). It would appear, therefore, that the building was constructed by a young family which suffered a high death rate among its young children. Most of these young deaths were accommodated beneath the north-western platform. But as the family matured, some individuals lived on within the building, they had fewer children, and the building was abandoned after the burial of the last old family head beneath the floor in Space 110.

The relief sculpture thus seems to be related to this longer family/house cycle. A specific relationship between this sculpture on the west wall of Space 71 and the house

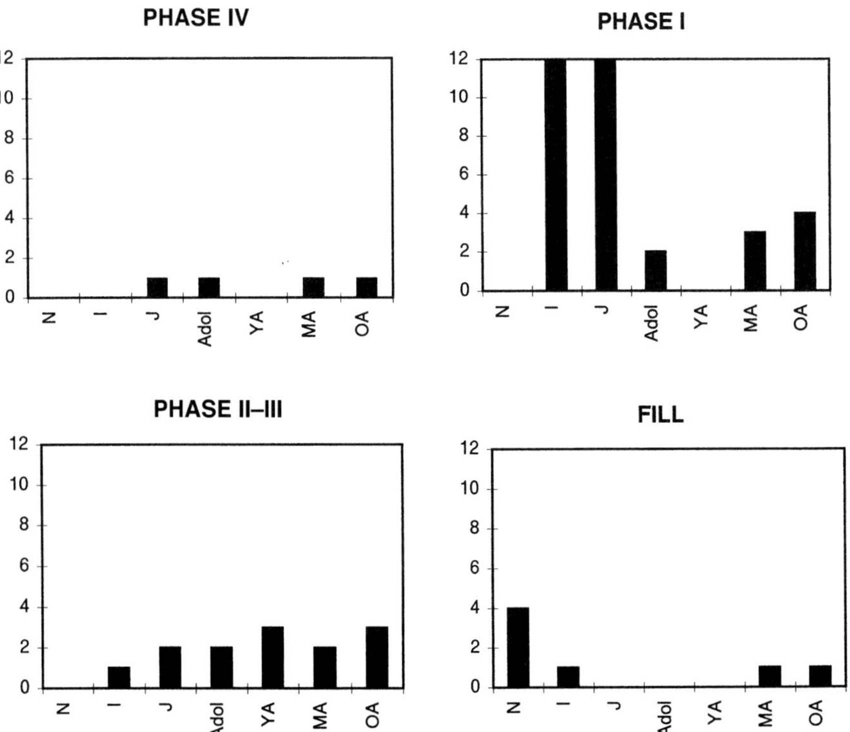

Figure 6. Histogram of the ages of individual skeletons buried in Building 1 in different occupation phases (see Figure 2). For ages see Figure 5.

cycle is indicated by the final phases of use of Building 1. We do not know what happened to the sculpture in the fourth occupation phase. This is because, after the abandonment and infilling (phase seven) of the fourth occupation in the building (phase six), a pit was dug down against the west wall of Space 71 and the sculpture removed (phase eight) leaving only traces and fragments. Small deposits of bone points and obsidian blades were left as offerings against the wall. The pottery from the robbing pit suggests that the removal of the sculpture occurred in the Neolithic, not long after the abandonment of the building.

This social concern with the sculpture on the west wall of Building 1 is reflected in numerous similar acts at Çatalhöyük. In Building 2 in the Mellaart area of the site (Hodder 1997), the west wall had been violently destroyed, and in the debris around the wall a very large wild bull's horn was found. Mellaart (1967) had noted a repeated pattern of destruction of the west walls of buildings. These actions can be seen as destructive, or as attempts made to recover sculptures of great social significance. Whatever the specific interpretation, it does seem that the end of the use of a building was often linked in some way to the relief sculptures within it. As already noted, the sculptures are often found integrated into the architecture of the buildings. And the buildings themselves are built and rebuilt as part of family cycles.

Conclusion

Clearly we do not yet have a full answer to questions regarding the meanings of the unique flowering of art at Çatalhöyük. So far we have made only short steps. But the approach being followed is to contextualize the art and by doing so we have seen that, as Grahame Clark would have it, the art had a social character.

The life of the houses in which the art occurred may relate to the life cycles of extended familes. Some of the art, especially the relief sculpture on the western walls, seems to be related to these longer cycles. It seems to have been used and destroyed as the house was used and abandoned, and as family heads grew from young to old. The destruction or recovery of relief sculpture from central points in abandoned buildings perhaps suggest a concern with the passing on of authority, rights of access, or ancestral ties.

Other aspects of the art, in this case the geometric wall painting, seem to be linked to shorter cycles of activity. The painting in Building 1 is placed on plaster which is annually renewed. Any particular painting is quickly covered over. Mellaart (1967) records examples of repeated repainting of similar motifs. But the best examples of this are on relief sculptures such as leopards and bulls' heads. Our own observations are that most walls have some painting but that this is infrequently applied, to different degrees in different parts of a building. The motifs painted are much more varied than the relief sculptures. It is thus of interest that in Building 1, the painting around the north-western platform seems to be related to specific events rather than to the life cycle of the building as a whole. The painting here seems to be related to concentrations of burials, especially the burials of young people. Perhaps this spatial and temporal link implies some generic association between painting and young people, say between painting and the initiation of young people. On the other hand, the painting may be related specifically to the death of young people.

Because of the link to young people under the north-western platform, it seems unlikely that the painting (perhaps in contrast to the relief sculpture) is associated with ancestors. Rather, the painting may have something to do with protecting the inhabitants of the building from negative spirits surrounding young death, or the painting itself may have helped directly to calm or control those spirits (as happens in many small-scale, shamanic societies—Humphrey & Onon 1996).

Jean Clottes (this volume) has pointed to the way in which animals in some south-western French Palaeolithic art seem to be 'coming through' the walls in the deep parts of caves. David Lewis-Williams, in his work with the Çatalhöyük project, has suggested that the bulls' heads and some other relief sculpture at the site may be seen as 'coming through' the membrane of the walls in the interior parts of buildings. Certainly, there is much evidence of vulture beaks, jaws of fox and weasel, and the tusks of wild boar protruding through the walls into the interior spaces at Çatalhöyük (Mellaart 1967). It is possible that much of the art and symbolism at Çatalhöyük has little to do with representation and symbolism at all. It may be more like a tool, used to control or communicate with animals, spirits, and ancestors. The common use of the hand motif at Çatalhöyük may suggest the idea of touching or reaching through the walls. The location of the images deep in buildings does not suggest a concern with communication or display to other people. Rather it suggests a concern to control or communicate with another world.

We must await further excavation at Çatalhöyük in order to see whether the patterns so far identified in Building 1 are repeated elsewhere. We still have little idea of the degree of conformity to social norms at the site. Hopefully further analyses in Building 1 and further excavation of other buildings will allow a fuller contextualization of the imagery. Only in this way can the social character of the 'art' that I have suggested here be further explored. Only in this way can the different types of 'art' be related to the differing social rhythms of life at Çatalhöyük, and perhaps to conceptualizations of the world very different from our own.

Acknowledgement

The work at the site is undertaken with a permit from the Turkish Ministry of Culture, and is funded by the British Academy, British Institute of Archaeology at Ankara, Newton Trust, and McDonald Institute. The main sponsors are Visa and KoçBank, the long-term sponsor is Merko, and the co-sponsors are British Airways, Shell, and GlaxoWellcome. The official tour operator is Meptur. I would personally like to thank and acknowledge all the project members whose collaborative efforts make articles like this possible. In particular I wish to thank Roger Matthews and Gavin Lucas for their painstaking work on Building 1.

References

CLARK, J.G.D. 1957 (first edn 1939). *Archaeology and Society*. London: Methuen.

CLARK, J.G.D. 1970. *Aspects of Prehistory*. Berkeley: University of California Press.

CLARK, J.G.D. 1977 (third edn). *World Prehistory in New Perspective*. Cambridge: Cambridge University Press.

CLARK, J.G.D. 1982. *The Identity of Man*. London: Methuen.

HODDER, I. 1996. *On the Surface: Çatalhöyük 1993–95*. Cambridge and London: McDonald Archaeological Institute and British Institute of Archaeology at Ankara.

HODDER, I. 1997. *Çatalhöyük 1997: Archive Report*. Cambridge: Çatalhöyük Research Project.

HUMPHREY, C. & ONON, U. 1996. *Shamans and Elders*. Oxford: Clarendon Press.

KUNIHOLM, P. & NEWTON, M. 1996. Interim dendrochronological progress report 1995/6. In I. Hodder (ed.), *On the Surface: Çatalhöyük 1993–95*, 345–8. Cambridge and London: McDonald Archaeological Institute and British Institute of Archaeology at Ankara.

MATTHEWS, R. 1996. Surface scraping and planning. In I. Hodder (ed.), *On the Surface: Çatalhöyük 1993–95*, 79–100. Cambridge and London: McDonald Archaeological Institute and British Institute of Archaeology at Ankara.

MATTHEWS, W., FRENCH, C., LAWRENCE, T. & CUTLER, D. 1996. Multiple surfaces: the micromorphology. In I. Hodder (ed.), *On the Surface: Çatalhöyük 1993–95*, 301–42. Cambridge and London: McDonald Archaeological Institute and British Institute of Archaeology at Ankara.

MELLAART, J. 1967. *Çatalhöyük*. London: Thames and Hudson.

MOLLESON, T. & ANDREWS, P. 1997. The human remains. In I. Hodder (ed.), *Çatalhöyük 1997: Archive Report*, 96–111. Cambridge: Çatalhöyük Research Project.

SHELL, C. 1996. Magnetometric survey at Çatalhöyük East. In I. Hodder, (ed.), *On the Surface: Çatalhöyük 1993–95*, 101–14. Cambridge and London: McDonald Archaeological Institute and British Institute of Archaeology at Ankara.

Concluding Remarks and Recollections

JOHN MULVANEY

We have participated today in a remarkable tribute to Grahame Clark's significant pioneering role in economic, social, and intellectual archaeology. His own opinion on the British archaeology of his formative years during the 1930s was that though it 'was long on fact it was miserably short on thought and narrow in perspective' (Clark 1989, 52). His energetic efforts to transform the state of archaeology were recognized by many honours during his lifetime, including two Festschriften. Appropriately, the first of these was offered by the Prehistoric Society in 1971, while some 38 former pupils produced essays in his praise in 1976. The breadth of today's papers again recognizes his pioneering global achievements, and Grahame would have appreciated this occasion when his colleagues gathered to honour him.

Yet in his typically blunt manner, Grahame also may have queried the slate of chosen speakers. Readers of his 1989 account of *Prehistory at Cambridge and Beyond* could reasonably infer that in his opinion no real archaeology was practised beyond the imperium of the Cambridge Disneyland. So today's organizers may have had to do some explaining as to why six of today's chorus of 15 evidently have no direct Cambridge association! Upon reflection, however, he would have approved their selection, as demonstrating Cambridge intellectual influences on scholars in the regions of Beyond.

Clark's profound influence in so many areas has been illuminated—virtual father of the Mesolithic and of economic prehistory, innovator in methodology and data interpretation, synthesizer of world prehistory, a prophet of Unesco cultural ideas before that body existed, and in later years, champion of individual human artistic creativity in all ages and societies.

My brief was to offer some concluding observations upon the day's presentations. Unfamiliarity with this wealth of varied data and interpretation made me opt for a personal approach, for Grahame Clark has been a major influence upon my career across almost half a century. Indeed the Clark's, Grahame and Desmond, both advised me

Proceedings of the British Academy, **99**, 193–197

extensively on microlithic artefacts in 1959, after I excavated geometric microliths in South Australia.

My debt to Grahame Clark is profound, as it was also for the late Charles McBurney, who described himself in Clark's Festschrift as 'your oldest pupil' (though Desmond Clark might claim the same privilege). In this personal vein, three anecdotes involving Grahame reveal something of his forthright, self-centred, and essentially British imperial world view. Yet, as I go on to signify, he combined these often irritating features with traits which rendered his character more complex and easier to appreciate.

Upon my arrival as a Clare undergraduate, in 1951, I was instructed to report to Clark in Downing Street to discuss supervision arrangements. I proudly carried a copy of my 50,000 word First Class Honours Melbourne Master's History thesis, a library-based evaluation of the archaeological evidence for the economy of late Iron Age and Roman Britain. As 'The Belgae and British Economic History' criticized assumptions and explanations of current eminent persons, I looked forward to meeting my hero. For I had chosen Cambridge largely because of the deep intellectual stimulation provided from reading the spate of Clark's articles on economic prehistory. I was left in no doubt that it was pointless for him to look at such superficial work undertaken far overseas; and he never did.

Two years later I made my farewells to the, by then, Disney Professor. He mortified me by remarking that, although I was awarded only a II.1 degree, this was adequate enough because I was only returning to Australia. A decade on, Grahame accepted my report on excavations at Kenniff Cave, Queensland, for the *PPS*. Noting that my series of C14 dates showed stratigraphic disagreement between those produced by the National Physical Laboratory and the ANU Laboratory on the one hand, and Tokyo's Gakashuin Laboratory on the other, he proposed deleting the Japanese chronology as likely to be the result of inferior science. He eventually accepted my demand to publish, warts and all.

Despite such negative rebuffs, my relations with Grahame remained positive. Before I left Cambridge, he had already found me a position in New Zealand, unsolicited by myself. To his somewhat pained surprise I declined the offer, so Jack Golson was designated Cambridge begetter of Antipodean archaeology.

It was Grahame who invited me to attempt a synthesis of Australian prehistory, under the title 'The Stone Age of Australia'. Published in *PPS* 1961, that transfer of the European 'Age' mode to Australia would have been an unlikely title acceptable to either of us even a decade later. For by 1964, when Grahame first visited Australia, we both had experienced 'living archaeology'. Grahame's 1965 volume of *PPS* included my lengthy Kenniff report. Given the dearth of Australian publication sources in those times, this largesse was deeply appreciated. Today, when Australian and Pacific archaeology features frequently in *Antiquity*, such comment may seem unnecessary. It was different over three decades ago, and Grahame Clark was the first British archaeologist to recognize this overseas need. Near the end of his life, he cited Australian discoveries as the most dramatic global illustration of the role of radiocarbon and the physics of prehistory (Clark 1994, 124).

Clark discovered New Zealand and Australian prehistory during his 1964 tour, possibly the first of several journeys of discovery in which he encountered the past of other continents. His subsequent writing testifies to the influence of these worlds beyond Europe. It was evident to all involved in arranging an Australian itinerary for this austere scholar, always fascinated by and fixated upon the evidence in the latest fresh encounter, that Grahame was not a solitary visitor. It is appropriate here to pay tribute to his longtime intellectual partner, Mollie Clark, whose role sustained his scholarly career. Mollie combined throughout secretarial and public relations duties watchful of Grahame's needs as a loving and thoughtful minder. Grahame's dedication of his innovative and insightful book, *Archaeology and Society* (1939)—'to my wife'—was indeed a meaningful one; and Grahame was fully aware of his combined debt and good fortune.

Charles McBurney (Sieveking *et al.* 1976, xii) remarked of his 1935 experiences as a student in Downing Street, that from Clark, then commencing his lectureship, 'we began to hear . . . of new and exciting developments quite outside the scope of the classic textbooks of the day'. I felt a comparable sense of immediacy and excitement listening to both Clark and McBurney from 1951. Classes in Grahame's office were unusually cramped, because the Star Carr finds lay everywhere. Students had best be interested in that site, for Grahame thought and spoke of little else. But what a privilege to sit amongst the finds of one of the greatest prehistoric excavations of this century! When I returned briefly in 1961, Grahame's current fixation was with Neolithic bows. Significantly, in the 1970s his concerns lay with issues beyond Britain. Yet, at the mundane level of personal transport, hazards remained constant features in Grahame's changing intellectual world. Whereas in 1951 we students sped to a Roman site at Cardington at alarming speed in Grahame's Mercedes, a quarter of a century later, as Grahame's guests at Aldeburgh, Jean and I experienced perilous yachting adventures with him at the helm.

My compatriot, Gordon Childe, has been examined in numerous books and articles, chiefly appreciative, correctly crediting him with a significance in the front rank of twentieth-century archaeology; some rank his importance above all others. I venture the prediction that, as time perspectives lengthen, Clark's multipurpose role will be judged pivotal in prehistoric studies, ahead of Childe's cultural synthesis.

Childe was a hero of a left-wing intellectual generation which anticipated the triumph of the common people and universal justice. Contemporaneously, many students found Clark's freely expressed political opinions to be nationalistic, stridently and unfashionably right-wing. I suggest that such emotions influence judgements upon the relative merits of these outstanding scholars, so that changes in Clark's thinking over time have not been sufficiently credited. Even during Childe's lifetime two mutual relationships merit thought. First of all, it was Clark whom Childe chose to be his literary executor. Back in 1946, also, when Childe and Benjamin Farrington edited the Past and Present series for Cobbett Press, Clark wrote *From Savagery to Civilisation* for that leftist series. Even the title was borrowed from Lewis Henry Morgan, a luminary in the pantheon of Marxism.

Politics aside, Grahame Clark's intellectual journey merits the same detailed attention as Childe received. I note, for example, that when Lewis Binford and associates pioneered the American New Archaeology, they approvingly cited Clark and Childe for their emphasis upon process. In that challenging 1968 Binfordian text *New Perspectives in Archaeology*, authors cited *Star Carr* (Clark, 1954), *Prehistoric Europe: the Economic Basis* (Clark, 1952), and five of Clark's articles stretching back to 1948. Most other British archaeologists were listed only for their claimed logical or theoretical errors. At the same time, Grahame Clark made his case clearly, but without the jargon which was the badge of the New Archaeology. As I observed in 1975 (Mulvaney 1975, 13) his *Star Carr* makes sense today, even though he never referred in those terms to locational analysis, processual archaeology, systems analysis, or even models or paradigms!

Any future assessment of Clark's contribution should include his developing internationalist philosophy. Despite his political conservatism, he anticipated objectives of the future United Nations in his forthright assertion that, in 1943, 'to the peoples of the world generally, the peoples who willy nilly must in future cooperate and build or fall out and destroy, I venture to think that Palaeolithic man has more meaning than the Greeks' (Clark 1943, 118).

Such iconoclasm probably was dismissed at the time as outrageous by a Europocentric profession, yet his 1959 Presidential Address to the Prehistoric Society cannot be taken so lightly. He drew attention to the reality that almost one-fifth of the Society lived overseas, and he urged a more inclusive approach to publication policy. (By that date he had already solicited my Australian survey for *PPS*.) It is important to emphasize Clark's editorial role in encouraging young researchers and soliciting contributions. A full bibliography of his publications and editorial activities is overdue.

Clark continued with sentiments which have resonance in today's divided world. His Presidential Address (Clark 1959, 13) recognized that 'men nurtured in their own distinctive and parochial manners, beliefs, art conventions, and histories, and situated at the most diverse levels of economic and cultural development . . . cannot long survive without a common sentiment and allegiance more positive than the fear of mutual destruction'.

It was to those peoples without conventional written history that he turned his attention, urging the recovery of 'the common past of humanity'. Since that lecture, and partly through Clark's encouragement and publication space, the emerging nations of the Pacific region, including Papua New Guinea, the Solomon Islands, Fiji, and Vanuatu have found their insular cultural identities, chronologies, and cultural interconnections as a basis for their individual nationhood, largely through the research of prehistorians.

Grahame's latest writings voiced his concern with the reverse situation which has arisen following the uncovering and definition of the past of such unique cultures. Those individual components of humanity he feared, are today in danger of losing their cultural uniqueness and identity. He used the term 'homogenization'.

Grahame Clark's intellectual journey and priorities from flints, through economic prehistory and distribution maps to the human mind, merit detailed evaluation. Never one to concern himself with political correctness, he sturdily asserted his philosophy in 1979 (Clark 1979, 20): 'If our common aim is to enhance our lives our guiding light must surely be quality rather than quantity, hierarchy rather than equality, and diversity rather than homogeneity. By the same token, we should not be afraid to count archaeology as a human study.'

References

BINFORD, S.R. & BINFORD, L.R. (eds), 1968. *New Perspectives in Archaeology*. Chicago: Aldine.

CLARK, J.G.D. 1939. *Archaeology and Society*. London: Methuen.

CLARK, J.G.D. 1943. Education and the study of man. *Antiquity* 17, 113–21.

CLARK, J.G.D. 1952. *Prehistoric Europe: the Economic basis*. Cambridge: Cambridge University Press.

CLARK, J.G.D. 1954. *Excavations at Star Carr*. Cambridge: Cambridge University Press.

CLARK, J.G.D. 1959. Presidential Address. *Proceedings of the Prehistoric Society* 25, 1–14.

CLARK, J.G.D. 1979. Archaeology and human diversity. *Annual Review of Anthropology* 8, 1–20.

CLARK, J.G.D. 1989. *Prehistory at Cambridge and Beyond*. Cambridge: Cambridge University Press.

CLARK, J.G.D. 1994. *Space, Time and Man: A Prehistorian's View*. Cambridge: Cambridge University Press.

COLES, J. (ed.), 1971. Contributions to Prehistory offered to Grahame Clark. *Proceedings of the Prehistoric Society* 37(2).

MULVANEY, D.J. 1975. *The Prehistory of Australia*. Ringwood: Penguin Books.

SIEVEKING, G. DE G., LONGWORTH, I.H. & WILSON, K.E. (eds), 1976. *Problems in Economic and Social Archaeology*. London: Duckworth.

Abstracts

J. DESMOND CLARK

Grahame Clark and World Prehistory: A Personal Perspective

This paper traces the development of Grahame Clark's concepts of human cultural and biological evolution and identifies some of the factors that enhanced the depth and scope of his horizons from regional and national to international and global prehistory and interrelated behavioural traits of modern human populations of our present world.

BERNARD WOOD and MARK COLLARD

'Is *Homo* Defined by Culture?'

When the genus *Homo* was established by Linnaeus in 1758 it was described as consisting of two species components referred to as 'diurnal' and 'nocturnal'. We know now that 'nocturnal' Man referred to the orang-utan, which is now included in a separate genus, *Pongo*. The description of the second, 'diurnal', species, which Linnaeus called *Homo sapiens*, recognized six subgroups of which four were living, continental-based, geographic variants. It was more than a century later that the first fossil species, *Homo neanderthalensis* King, 1864, was added to *Homo* and since then other species referred to the genus have made it morphologically more inclusive.

Arguably the greatest single step in this process of relaxing the morphological criteria for including fossil species in *Homo* was made exactly a hundred years after the addition of *H. neanderthalensis*, when in 1964 Louis Leakey, Phillip Tobias, and John Napier proposed that gracile hominin remains from Olduvai Gorge, Tanzania, be included in the genus *Homo* as *Homo habilis*. Since then the hypodigm of *H. habilis* has accommodated specimens which have stretched the variability within that species to the point where many believe that the fossils attributed to it sample not one, but two species, *H. habilis sensu stricto* and *Homo rudolfensis*.

In this paper we trace the increasing inclusivity of the genus *Homo* and relate it to the apparently ever greater antiquity of stone tool manufacture. We also review the criteria for recognizing genera and examine whether our present understanding of the genus *Homo* conforms with the two main criteria, namely monophyly and adaptive homogeneity. We review the evidence for monophyly and refer to the results of an examination of a range of functionally-related variables to assess the adaptive levels of early hominin species.

Our conclusion is that the boundaries of *Homo* should be reset so that it includes early African *Homo erectus*, or *Homo ergaster*, and excludes *H. habilis sensu stricto* and *H. rudolfensis*. This would mean that the manufacture of stone tools would no longer be restricted to members of the genus *Homo*. However, we would contend that this has been an untenable association ever since the realization that synchronic taxa have existed in East Africa for much of the early phases of hominin evolution for which there is also evidence of stone artefact manufacture.

JOHN PARKINGTON

Western Cape Landscapes

The Atlantic coast of the western Cape is host to a vast quantity of archaeological sites of the past 100,000 years. Ecological studies of Middle and Late Stone Age sites provide opportunities to explore the development of behavioural patterns. The multitude of painted shelters and caves in the western Cape allow us to glimpse the systems of belief that structured early societies.

RHYS JONES

Dating the Human Colonization of Australia: Radiocarbon and Luminescence Revolutions

Dating the early colonization of Australia has for long been at the forefront of prehistoric archaeological enquiries. This paper reviews the historical progression from conjecture to fact, amplified by increasingly sophisticated methods of dating, and identifies those sites now acknowledged to be of paramount importance to a greater understanding of human colonization of the continent.

BRIAN FAGAN

Grahame Clark and American Archaeology

Grahame Clark exercised a seminal influence on American archaeology at a critical stage in its development. His ecological and subsistence researches in the Cambridgeshire Fenland and interest in settlement archaeology were known to but a few American scholars of the 1940s and 1950s. However, the publication of *Prehistoric Europe: The Economic Basis* (1952) and *Star Carr* (1954) came at a time when Americanists were turning from culture history to processual archaeology. Clark's analyses of environment and subsistence played a vital role in the formulation of some of the basic tenets of the so-called 'new archaeology' of the 1960s. His field researches provided a practical component to the influential theoretical models proposed by American anthropologist Julian Steward and others as the new cultural ecology. Clark was a pioneer in the teaching of world prehistory. He trained a whole generation of Cambridge graduates whom he encouraged to work in distant parts of the world. Some of them eventually moved to the United States, bringing his anthropological and ecological approach with them. Grahame Clark's most influential book was *World Prehistory* (1961), which provided the first synthesis that incorporated both New and Old World archaeology into a single global whole. This work, over three editions, provided the conceptual basis for the much more sophisticated world archaeology of today and the inspiration for important comparative studies of early civilizations.

C.F.W. HIGHAM

Recent Advances in the Prehistory of South-east Asia

Prehistoric archaeology in south-east Asia has often lagged behind that of other regions because of its terrain, languages, and politics. Yet the record of human diversity and achievement in colonization, subsistence, and metallurgy is now exceptionally well-documented through a series of multidisciplinary projects. The paper presents an overview of recent field studies and notes the encouragement given by Grahame Clark to south-east Asian archaeology.

LARS LARSSON

Settlement and Palaeoecology in the Scandinavian Mesolithic

Professor Grahame Clark devoted special interest to the Scandinavian Mesolithic, and his research in the area was to serve as a model for several generations of Mesolithic scholars in northern Europe and an encouragement to extend the forms of analysis. The aim of this paper is to follow up certain themes that Grahame Clark considered to be of particular interest, and also to add information from some current research efforts.

As regards the transition Late Palaeolithic–Mesolithic, important new investigations have given us a better knowledge of the deglaciation phase and have also shown that the Ahrensburg culture had a previously unrecognized spread along the west coast of Scandinavia, and it is in connection with this that we can trace the material change to a typical Mesolithic context.

Investigations in marine archaeology in recent years have given us some, albeit fragmentary, knowledge of submerged coastal settlement in southern Scandinavia in the Early Mesolithic. Work on the bottom of Öresund, the sound between present-day eastern Denmark and southern Sweden, shows how extensive this coastal settlement was. The results mean that we must reconsider earlier models of the relation between coastal and inland settlement.

The shell middens of south-western Scandinavia have been well known for a long time, not least as a result of Grahame Clark's publications. Renewed studies show, however, that there is still a great deal of new information to be derived from these features. The cemeteries of the Late Mesolithic in southern Scandinavia are a late observed phenomenon whose implications for research have been emphasized. There is a constant growth in factual material showing that an association between settlement sites and graves was common in the Late Mesolithic. A proposed function for the graves in an environmental perception of the Late Mesolithic conceptual world is presented. Greater consideration must be given in future analyses to the mental relationship between the people and the environment, in order to fully appreciate the Late Mesolithic coastal societies.

In recent years, knowledge of the Mesolithic in northernmost Scandinavia has increased significantly. In northern Sweden this is due to increased archaeological activity combined with extensive surveys. The art of ceramic fabrication appeared at roughly the same time in northern Sweden as in southern Scandinavia. In recent years graves, in a few cases in cemetery-like assemblages beside settlement sites belonging to the Late Mesolithic, have also been documented in northernmost Sweden.

In the study of the Mesolithic, our perspective on society and environment has been broadened by creative efforts in both theory and method. In some cases, new points of view can be obtained by choosing new ways to excavate a settlement site. A few examples of this are presented.

LEENDERT P. LOUWE KOOIJMANS

Shippea Hill and after: Wetlands in North European Prehistory and the Case of the *Donken*

Wetlands are like gold mines for our knowledge of the past and this is particularly so for north European prehistory. They have so many qualities: organic perishable materials are preserved and patterns are undisturbed in 'time capsules', while stratigraphy on all scales gives us a high time resolution. The contrast in all these aspects to upland sites invokes contrasts in our views of upland and wetland people. One can, however, question whether prehistoric people saw these same contrasts. We observe in this paper that most wetlands were used for 'cultic' deposition, and for traffic and settlement as well. The Dutch delta wetlands even seem to have been a preferred agricultural land in later prehistory. We should not transfer the historic or our own (negative) wetland appreciation to prehistoric communities and we realize that prehistoric people settled themselves there by free choice. So wetland data, if cautiously used, can be considered as representative of former subsistence and organization.

The second part of this paper is a case study. An overview is given of a research programme for which Grahame Clark was the inspiration in his Fenland work of the early 1930s. Outcropping dune tops in the Rhine delta deposits offer us a unique and rich dataset on the Late Mesolithic and Neolithic communities, 5500–2500 cal BC, and on the adoption of agriculture in the Dutch part of the North European Plain. We note that prospection and excavation down to 10 m below sea level require a special technology.

PETER ROWLEY-CONWY

Economic Prehistory in Southern Scandinavia

This contribution explores hunter-gatherer settlement and society, and the appearance of agriculture. It argues that zooarchaeology and radiocarbon dating have been the major sources of new information and have led to many theoretical changes.

Hunter-gatherer settlement and society: in the Danish early Mesolithic all the diagnosed sites were occupied in summer; the winter half of the year may have been spent in areas now below present sea level. The late Mesolithic is above or only just below sea level, and in Jutland is characterized by permanent central sites and small satellite camps; in southern Sweden the main base camps may have been seasonal, while in the Øresund it is unknown. The extent to which the Ertebølle was based on fishing has become clear in recent years, due to the finding of large static fish traps and the recovery of many large samples of fish bones. Various aspects of the archaeological record enhance the impression that the Ertebølle was what is commonly described as 'complex'; this is an adaptation to prevailing conditions rather than the result of internal social development, because the middle Mesolithic shows such features as soon as sea level nears the modern level and becomes accessible to study.

Appearance of agriculture: claimed chronological overlap between hunter gatherers and farmers in Denmark was the result of relative dating methods subsequently shown to be faulty by radiocarbon; the result was the development of a processual theory emphasizing a stable frontier between Danish hunter gatherers and German farmers that lasted at least a millennium. When agriculture finally appeared in Denmark, it apparently did so rapidly, in contrast to some current suggestions of gradual change. Less evidence is available from Norway because of poor organic preservation, but agriculture may not have reached south-western regions until the late Neolithic. In eastern Sweden there was a re-adoption of hunting and gathering in the middle Neolithic; recent work on Gotland has shown that after an early Neolithic based on agriculture, the middle Neolithic moved back to the sea shore and concentrated on marine resources.

JEAN CLOTTES

Twenty Thousand Years of Palaeolithic Cave Art in Southern France

Out of the 350 or so sites with rock art known in the Upper Palaeolithic about half are located in Southern France. A number of important discoveries have been made in the past few years. This overview will be mainly concerned with three points. The first deals with the results of direct radiocarbon dating for the art. The direct dates available range from 32,410±720 BP for a painted rhino in Chauvet to 11,600±150 BP for a painted horse in Portel. The realization that Aurignacians had mastered all the artistic techniques that were supposed to have developed gradually over the following millennia upsets the long-held theory of a gradual evolution of art from supposedly crude beginnings. The second point overturns the concept that particular themes, which were thought to be chronologically and/or spatially restricted (Placard signs, claviforms, hand stencils, composite creatures), are not. Finally, the third part examines some consistent types of behaviour all over the Upper Palaeolithic, relating to the deep caves. They testify to a common attitude in relation to the cave itself from the Aurignacian to the end of the Magdalenian, that is, to a common frame of beliefs that passed from generation to generation.

IAN HODDER

Symbolism at Çatalhöyük

This paper follows Grahame Clark's interest in the social character of art and in the diversity of cultural achievement. These themes are pursued in relation to the 9000 year old site of Çatalhöyük in central Turkey. Re-excavation of the site since 1993 has allowed questions to be asked about the environmental, economic, and social context of the art, although this paper deals only with social aspects. The detailed excavation of Building 1 in the north part of the Çatalhöyük East mound is described and the arrangement of activities in each phase of the building is shown. It is argued that two types of art relate to two different social rhythms. The relief sculpture is associated with the life cycles of buildings and whole extended family groups. It may be related to ancestral links between families and buildings. The painting, on the other hand, appears to be related to the burial of young people. It may have a specific and shorter-term role in dealing with the spiritual dangers of young death. These examples are presented as a first step in the understanding of the symbolism at Çatalhöyük.

JOHN MULVANEY

Concluding Remarks and Recollections

These personal reflections attempt to assess Clark's academic role and influence by adopting a 'warts and all' approach. The importance of visits to New Zealand and Australia in redirecting Clark's intellectual interests is emphasized.

Appendix

John Grahame Douglas Clark 1907–1995

'If anyone were to ask me why I have spent my life studying Prehistory, I would only say that I have remained under the spell of a subject which seeks to discover how we became human beings endowed with minds and souls before we had learned to write.' So begins Grahame Clark's own account of his career.[1]

He was born on 28 July 1907, the elder son of Charles Douglas Clark and Maude Ethel Grahame Clark (née Shaw). The family was based at Shortlands near Bromley in Kent. Grahame Clark last saw his father in 1914 as Lt Colonel Clark left for France, the Near East and then India. His father died of influenza in 1919 as his ship entered Plymouth Sound. Clark was brought up by his mother and his guardian uncle, Hugh Shaw, for whom he had real affection. As a small child, he was introduced to archaeology by an elderly neighbour, a Mr Bird, who had a collection of flints from Yorkshire. Clark's own collection began soon afterwards, and his overwhelming interest was signalled to his mother when his pony arrived home riderless; he had spied some flints while out exercising the animal and had dismounted, gathered the artefacts, and forgotten about the beast.

Clark was sent to Marlborough, a school at the heart of prehistoric Wessex, with Avebury, Silbury Hill, and even Windmill Hill lying within the reach of an ambitious young boy. By this time, the family had moved to Seaford on the Sussex Downs where again there were great opportunities for observing ancient monuments and for collecting stone tools. At school, Clark soon acquired the nickname of 'Stones and Bones', and he joined the Natural History Society. This brought him two advantages; he was excused games at least once a week in order to participate in Society activities, and he could engage in the pursuit of his two loves—the natural history of moths and butterflies, and flint collecting on the Downs. His first four publications, omitted from all the bibliographies usually consulted,[2] are reports on flint tools and weapons from the Marlborough and Seaford areas.[3] His first paper describes collections of flints with distribution maps, technological information and functional interpretations. As the 'weapons of war' (axes, arrowheads and

First published in *Proceedings of the British Academy*, **94**, 357–387 spear points) only made up three per cent of the assemblages, and domestic tools (scrapers, borers, knives, etc.) made up ninety-seven per cent, 'the community must have been essentially a peaceful one'. From 1923 to 1926, Clark was one of the Society's leading scholars, collecting, guiding and lecturing on archaeology, and still engaged in study of the natural history of the area. It would seem, from this distance, that even at this early age he had begun to develop that intense curiosity about the ancient world that would drive him for the rest of his life.

Partly due to the academic stimulus offered by his school teachers, Clark resolved to study prehistory at university. Cambridge was the only English university to offer instruction in prehistory to undergraduates, so he sat for a scholarship at Peterhouse. Unsuccessful in the examination, he was none the less offered a place as pensioner of the college and arrived in 1926. He first took the History Tripos then moved across to the newly-created Faculty of Archaeology and Anthropology; meantime, his uncle Hugh Shaw came across to enquire of the Disney Professor, Ellis Minns, about the prospects of future employment for an archaeologist. Receiving the same reply that one would expect today, Shaw none the less agreed to the new venture when he saw Clark's fierce determination to study prehistory. Clark was thus exposed to the excitement of the 'Arch and Anth' Tripos, studying social and physical anthropology along with archaeology, for two years. Prehistory was taught by Miles Burkitt, but equally valuable was the instruction indirectly provided by Cyril Fox's *Archaeology of the Cambridge Region*,[4] by J. Clapham's economic history and geographical research,[5] and by the Faculty's base in the University Museum of Archaeology and Ethnology. Clark was at once immersed in it all, walking daily by a huge totem pole from western Canada, past full-size casts of Mayan sculptures from central America, and proceeding underneath ethnographic hangings from the Torres Straits on his way to the lecture rooms. Across the court was the Botany School, and adjacent was the Sedgwick Museum of Geology. Among undergraduate books was Gordon Childe's *Dawn*,[6] and the new journal *Antiquity* was influential; visiting lecturers included Leonard Woolley, Grafton Elliot Smith, Gertrude Caton Thompson and Dorothy Garrod. Woolley was in the midst of his work at Ur (1922–34), Elliot Smith's *The Evolution of Man* was newly published (1924), Caton Thompson had just completed her survey of the North Fayum (1924–6) and was working on the sites as Field Director (1927–8), and Garrod had completed her excavations at the Devil's Tower, Gibraltar (1925–6), and was engaged in her survey of Southern Kurdistan (1928). Louis Leakey was also present, with news of his East African Archaeological Research Expeditions (1926–9). These scholars had an international awareness in contrast to the parochial west European view of Burkitt; here was the first inkling of a world prehistory.

Another omission from the standard teaching was any introduction to the ways by which prehistorians came into possession of the evidence. Burkitt was no excavator although he travelled widely to visit others' work. Clark was well aware of this gap and upon graduation he resolved to find instruction. An ideal teacher was soon to emerge, in Eliot Curwen who worked as an amateur archaeologist on the Sussex Downs.[7] In 1930 he and his son

Cecil invited Clark to help in the excavation of a causewayed enclosure. This was good instruction in field techniques for Clark, although he had to learn to avoid certain subjects dear to his own interests; Curwen was a Creationist and would not tolerate hearing opinions that the world had a longer prehistory than 4004 BC. It was not the last time that Clark had to put up with people who had, to his mind, divergent and non-scientific views of the world.

Following success in the Archaeological and Anthropological Tripos (a First), Clark began research for a higher degree, and held a Hugo de Balsham Studentship at Peterhouse (1930–2). He worked primarily on the Mesolithic industries of Britain, and when he published his first book, *The Mesolithic Age in Britain*, his supervisor M.C. Burkitt wrote the preface which included the phrases 'It is true that the cultures . . . were not so brilliant as those of Upper Palaeolithic date . . .. But at the same time though perhaps more miserable they are not at all despicable.'[8] Words such as these may or may not have encouraged Clark during his research.

At one of the Sussex enclosures, the Trundle, Clark met two people who were to become lifelong friends and advisers. Charles Phillips was teaching history at Cambridge, and Stuart Piggott was already engaged in his study of Neolithic pottery. Of the two, Phillips was the more influential; he had an uncanny eye for the landscape and soon involved Clark in a project to identify the traces of early communities in the hitherto unexplored rural landscape of Lincolnshire.[9] In Phillips's Austin car, the two men could drive into the prime areas, collect artefacts and map the sites, and return to Cambridge within the day. By evening, the finds were soaking in water, and Phillips's landlady was bringing macaroni cheese up the stairs to the team. Occasionally, Piggott would also be present, and Christopher Hawkes was there one day when extra supplies had to be summoned by a sharp tap on the floor. It was a good time for the men to debate how they hoped that British archaeology would develop. Clark was of the opinion that the archaeologists then controlling work were long on facts, miserably short on thought and narrow in perspective. No wonder Miles Burkitt put Clark up for election to the Society of Antiquaries of London in 1933, 'before too many enemies were made'.[10] Various Cambridge undergraduates were sometimes invited to sit in the back of Phillips's car on the Lincolnshire forays, T.G.E. Powell and C.T. Shaw among them, and doubtless they absorbed not only the experience of fieldwork but also the outspoken comments about their teachers.

Clark later joined Phillips in the excavation of a Lincolnshire long barrow, and one of the team was a young archaeologist Gwladys Maud (Mollie) White. Grahame Clark and Mollie White had already met, appropriately enough, in the University Museum of Archaeology and Ethnology. She came into the main gallery with a question for Miles Burkitt about some Mesolithic object. Burkitt at once said 'you should ask Grahame Clark about that', and there he was, leaning over the balustrade of the upper gallery. Grahame Clark and Mollie White were married in 1936. Mollie gave up her job with the Welsh Commission and became an indispensable part of Clark's academic life as well as a source of immense happiness to him. Their honeymoon was spent in Norway and Sweden, visiting hunter-gatherer rock carvings recently studied by Gjessing;[11] they went on to Oslo to attend the Congress of Pre- and Protohistoric Sciences. Clark wrote an account of the carvings for *Antiquity* in 1937,[12] which helped him establish a long and good relationship with O.G.S. Crawford, founder and editor of the journal.

This period was crucial for Clark's future direction in prehistory. He was in regular contact with C.W. Phillips and the botanist Harry Godwin, both men later acknowledging Clark's influence on them as well, and Piggott was involved in even more serious discussions about the future of British prehistoric studies. It was agreed that Piggott would take on the Neolithic, Clark staying with the Mesolithic, and each had his own priorities for research, which were advanced through lectures and publications. Piggott modelled his later book on *The Neolithic Cultures of the British Isles* on Clark's concepts, especially in efforts to set the communities in an appropriate environmental frame. But Phillips was the prime source of inspiration for landscape archaeology, strengthened from a distance by Crawford. O.G.S. Crawford had already published his *Air Survey and Archaeology* (1924) and *Wessex from the Air* had appeared in 1928; these were influential books but Crawford's work as Archaeological Officer for the Ordnance Survey (1920–46) was more crucial for Clark's understanding of the potential of landscape archaeology. The writings of Cyril Fox were dismissed as too theoretical and unyielding.

From this distance, it may be difficult to envisage the character of the archaeology of the period. Eager as Clark and Piggott were, to gain entry to the establishment they had to subscribe to the traditions of work and offer carefully-couched words of advice to their elders but not necessarily their betters. There were few significant excavations, and fewer still where methods were much beyond recovery of the most obvious structures and artefacts. At the stone circle of Avebury, all was well, as Piggott was employed as Assistant Director. The work was directed and funded by Alexander Keiller,[13] and Grahame and Mollie Clark were invited for a visit. The site was viewed with mutual satisfaction, but dinner at Keiller's residence required full evening dress which neither possessed. Clark's somewhat worn trousers were of course collected by a servant at bedtime for cleaning and pressing, with the contents of its pockets laid carefully and symmetrically on the elaborate dressing table—a piece of string and a broken penknife.

As a junior research student, Clark found the time and the encouragement to publish his thoughts on a group of flint tools that he had long ago identified from the chalklands of southern England. His first professional paper, on discoidal flint knives, appeared in the *Proceedings of the Prehistoric Society of East Anglia* for 1928.[14] The Society was by then exactly 20 years old, and rather fewer of its members were resident in East Anglia than had been at the beginning; in addition, the mania for flint collecting was in decline. Clark was an active member of the old Society, as were Stuart Piggott, Christopher Hawkes and Charles Phillips. By 1933, their opinions had hardened and an effort was made to widen the scope of the Society's interests by dropping the East Anglian designation. It was not until the Annual General Meeting of 1935 that the crucial vote was taken; the principal supporter of the status quo, Reid Moir, had intimated that he would be absent and a small party, led by Piggott, made the journey from Avebury to Norwich in a borrowed car. The result was an overwhelming endorsement of the proposed change of title.[15] Clark was voted into the Editorship, Phillips became Secretary and the worn-out debates about the antiquity of man in East Anglia were at an end. It was ironic that Reid Moir gave a paper on 'worked flints' from beneath the Red Crag of Suffolk immediately after the Society had dropped its East Anglian title and just when the new generation were empowered to publicly dismiss the eoliths from further debate.[16]

The first meeting of the new Prehistoric Society was on 2 May 1935 at Burlington House, when nine members were present, and Clark was one of six speakers on recent archaeological research. In 1935, the Society had 353 members; by 1938, the total was already 668. The precarious nature of the finances, as evidenced in the accounts for the early years, never deterred the Council from its aim of publishing an annual *Proceedings*. In Clark's first year as editor of the new journal, 1000 copies were printed even as the accounts showed an uneasy state, cash in hand £156. 4s. 7d., money owing £179. 2s. -. The confidence of Council in what it was doing must have been overwhelmingly strong.

Clark served as Editor of the *Proceedings* for 35 years, and worked to enhance its standing as a journal of international importance. Invited papers were secured from most of the rising stars of prehistoric studies (Piggott, W.F. Grimes, Glyn Daniel) as well as by the established leaders (Childe, Fox, Garrod, Curwen). Clark's aim was to promote prehistory as a subject and discipline in its own right, and to expose British readers to the European dimensions and, eventually, to the world. Although he had various Assistant Editors, among them Stuart Piggott and Kenneth Oakley, he never released his grip on the structure of the journal and rarely allowed a paper to pass to press without some alteration of style or content. Many papers went off barely legible, such was the rewriting between the typed lines.

In 1931, Clark was on the point of completing his book on the Mesolithic of Britain when he heard of a remarkable discovery made in the North Sea. From a depth of some 20 fathoms, a trawler had hauled up some moorlog containing a barbed antler point of Maglemosian type. This find, from the Leman and Ower bank, confirmed Clark's theory that the south-east of Britain had been colonized from lands across the present North Sea, at a time when there had existed a wide and welcoming plain between the higher lands of what were to become southern England and the north-west of continental Europe. Harry Godwin and his wife Margaret applied the new science of pollen analysis to the moorlog and dated it to the Boreal phase, just the period of the Maglemosian in Denmark.[17] Subsequent redating of the point to an earlier time is immaterial; the object stimulated great interest in and enthusiasm for Fenland research.

In the summer of 1932, Clark had seen enough Fenland landscapes, and had sufficient knowledge of the limitations of the existing archaeological evidence, to take the lead in an act that has had a profound influence on modern archaeology. He summoned a gathering of scientists, historians and archaeologists to a meeting in Peterhouse, and, with Charles Phillips and Harry Godwin, the Fenland Research Committee was formed.[18] The Committee brought the subjects of botany, geology, geography, biology, history and prehistory together—almost certainly for the first time—in a combined approach to a diminishing resource, that of the Fenland of East Anglia. The Committee met three times a year, at different Cambridge colleges, and under the influence of competitive dinners the members could debate the programme of work, and resolve to undertake the necessary tasks. One of the first sites to be selected for work was Shippea Hill, a prehistoric site not far east of Cambridge. Clark led the excavation, with Godwin in regular attendance; the work was designed to explore the context of Mesolithic and Bronze Age flints eroding out of a sand ridge mostly submerged by peat. An enormously deep trench was excavated by labourers accustomed to working through damp peat, and the hole was stepped back; even so, the photo of Clark at the bottom, with the peaty sides entirely lacking shoring planks, is unnerving.[19] At a depth of 15 feet, Neolithic material was found, and at 17 feet was the Mesolithic. The Bronze Age occupation lay near the top of the sequence and Godwin was able to examine both pollen and the sand-peat-clay sequences he had predicted. From here, the Research Committee moved on to other sites, publishing their results mostly in the *Antiquaries Journal*,[20] and in the short space of a decade managed to imprint the idea that an ecological approach to archaeological evidence was not only desirable at all times but essential wherever and whenever conditions allowed the full panoply of disciplines to be applied. In terms of British archaeology, the Fenland work did not make the permanent impression that Clark wanted; this was not due to an inadequacy of the approach, but was due in great measure to the general impression that the Fenland was a freak, unmatched elsewhere, both in its original and its current status, and thus ill-serving as a model. Time has shown how wrong that impression was, and how the opportunities were missed; Clark became well aware of this after the War.

The *Mesolithic Age in Britain* was published in 1932, and Clark obtained his Ph.D. the following year. His dissertation was not the same as his book, as in the former he covered the flint industries of the Mesolithic, Neolithic and early Metal Age. His collaboration with Piggott in publications began with a paper on the flint mines,[21] and continued soon after with a report on work on the Essex coastline.[22] Clark's interest in flint industries, so often ignored in considerations of his other, organic, archaeology, was always prominent in his many visits to museums and to sites throughout the world. His papers on microlithic industries in Britain and in western Europe served as landmarks for many years.[23]

By 1935 Clark had almost 30 papers in print. All were on British sites and subjects. He was elected to a Bye-Fellowship at Peterhouse in 1932 and one of his early tasks as a junior Fellow was to introduce the Abbé Breuil to High Table in College; this passed off well enough, perhaps in part because both Breuil, surprisingly enough, and Clark were of the same mind in asserting that in the Stone Age, Europe was no more than a small northern projection of the greater land masses of Africa and Asia. To this view not everyone agreed, especially most of the French prehistorians.

Clark set off in 1933, and again in 1934, on his first major study tours to northern Europe. His aim was to collect material relating to early human settlement and ecological change in the northern lands, and he visited Holland, Denmark and Germany, meeting three men in particular who influenced his work very significantly. Therkel Mathiassen was in mid-campaign on Mesolithic sites, J. Troels-Smith was engaged in refinements of pollen analysis, and Gudmun Hatt was studying primitive cultivation; most of their work was published three or four years later, but Clark was able to observe their individual environmental and ecological approaches in the field.[24]

But there were others at work too, and the sites visited included some from which inorganics were wholly absent. The fishing stations in particular, some in current use, and older examples then being investigated,[25] must have encouraged Clark in his quest to secure material for a major book. In 1936, *The Mesolithic Settlement of Northern Europe* appeared.[26] In this, he set out his aim—to put archaeology in the context of a totality of an ecosystem. He applied a battery of newly-developed and well-established techniques to the dating of the various industrial complexes so far identified over the vast territory of northern Europe, and he did not lose sight of the fact that environmental change in such a severe climate could have profound impacts on communities. Yet equally important to future work was his realization that while he was dabbling with the lithic industries of the British Mesolithic, in Denmark his contemporaries were studying not only flints but also the wood, fibre, bone and antler artefacts surviving in the bogs. His chance to make the case for wetland sites to a wider public was made in his 1939 book *Archaeology and Society*, a wide-ranging essay on modern archaeology, its strengths and its weaknesses.[27] By this time, of course, the wave of nationalistic exaggeration was about to break upon Europe and the world. The book touched upon the threat, but concentrated on ancient economies, technology, housing, exchange of goods, and intellectual life.

Clark was appointed as University Assistant Lecturer in Archaeology at Cambridge in 1935, at an annual salary of £150. He worked under the Departmental Head, Ellis Minns, who had encouraged him throughout his undergraduate and graduate days. Minns gave Clark an offprint of his paper on 'The Art of the Northern Nomads' in 1942, inscribing it 'To Grahame Clark my most surpassing pupil'. In the Department, Clark could indulge himself by teaching the Mesolithic, by forays into the fields of Cambridgeshire and beyond, by serious involvement with the *Proceedings of the Prehistoric Society* and by a close acquaintance with the ethnographic collections of the University Museum. Here it was that he began to plan for major field projects, into the Fens with his Research Committee, and elsewhere for sites that would yield the sort of evidence he needed for his aim—societies in their true ecological setting. In 1937–8 he made a bad decision to excavate a Mesolithic site in Surrey, which yielded thousands of flints but little or nothing in the way of structures, and organic survival was poor.[28] He admitted later that he should have gone farther afield to the Somerset Levels where Godwin was already achieving much, and well-preserved sites were appearing.[29]

Several of the most successful of the students he taught soon ventured into archaeologically-uncharted lands. Thurstan Shaw, who graduated in 1936, became Curator of the Anthropological Museum of the Gold Coast (1937–45), and Desmond Clark became

Director of the Rhodes-Livingstone Museum of Northern Rhodesia (1938–61). These men provided inspiration for Clark's eventual adoption of the world as his prehistoric theme. In 1939 he was able to anticipate the future with the unexpected (to readers) publication in the *Proceedings* of Donald Thompson's paper on the seasonal activities of the people of Cape York in Australia;[30] this paper had a profound effect on the editor and, had the war not intervened, he would have instigated a campaign in the Fens to try out his theory on the Mesolithic and Neolithic communities. By the time he could do this, the opportunity in the Fens had passed. He made a plea for the survival of the ancient heritage, in all its forms, in his 1939 book *Archaeology and Society*.

While waiting to be called up for military service, he took lessons in Russian from Ellis Minns and apparently found this much less formidable than expected; deflation set in when presented with the poems of Pushkin, but his limited knowledge was put to good use later in life. In the RAF Volunteer Reserves he was first sent to Medmenham to the aerial photograph interpretation unit, and here he met again Stuart Piggott, Glyn Daniel, Charles McBurney and Dorothy Garrod (the new Disney Professor of Archaeology). Most of them were sent overseas, but Clark remained in Britain because of a health problem. In 1944 he transferred to the Air Historical branch in London; this allowed him to re-establish a home in Cambridge from where he commuted to work each day, writing on the train and editing papers for the *Proceedings*. He also found time for visits to art galleries in London, arousing an interest in modern art in which he could indulge later on. In great part stimulated by his pre-war travels, he also began to assemble material and thoughts on a new approach, that of an economic prehistory, one not based on typologies, and inorganics, but one more securely founded on seasonalities and organic survivals. Papers on bees, water, seals, whales, forests, sheep, fishing, and fowling flowed from his pen in the years 1942–8;[31] these short papers were revelatory to almost all archaeologists except those then working in the water-saturated sites of Denmark and north Germany. From here, the different work and emphases of Johannes Iversen and Alfred Rust made Clark ever more determined in his ecological approach.[32] There had to be comparable opportunities in Britain, and all the necessary multi-disciplinary studies were ready to be mobilized.

At the war's end, Clark was made a full University Lecturer and helped Dorothy Garrod develop a new Part II in Archaeology for the Tripos. Soon he was able to make another extended tour of northern Europe, this time to the far north with a Leverhulme Scholarship. He travelled up the west coast of Norway in a small boat which called at fishing villages in every fjord to deliver mail and stores. Clark could go ashore for daily supplies of milk and other food, and could observe how much the communities depended on the sea, their only means of travel, on fishing, and on preserving the catches for the long winters. From Norway and Sweden he travelled to Finland where his Helsinki hotel sheets were made of paper, and his coffee was brewed from parched grain, such were the reparation demands. This tour of 1947, and a later Australian visit in 1964, were probably the most influential on Clark's own evolution as a prehistorian. The Scandinavian visit allowed him to experience in part the wide landscapes, the environmental harshness yet also its richness, and to observe the seemingly primitive yet highly developed economic practices of the people both inland and coastal. He could hardly avoid noticing the wide use of organic substances for tools, nor the richness of folk culture; on a northern train he was rudely disturbed by a bunch of drunken travellers, which presumably added something to his appreciation of folk behaviour. He wrote a short account of the more archaeologically satisfying aspects of folk culture and prehistory in 1951.[33]

In 1950 Clark was offered a Fellowship at Peterhouse, which he held for 45 years. Here in College he encountered a wide range of disciplines, among them the economic history of Michael Postan. Postan was Lecturer, then Professor, of Economic History at the University, and a Fellow of Peterhouse since 1935. His *Historical Methods in Social Sciences* had appeared in 1939, but it was his work towards *The Medieval Economy and Society* and *Essays on Medieval Agriculture and the Medieval Economy* (1973) that were the stimulus. Postan awakened Clark's interest in prehistoric agriculture that had remained dormant for some years, although Godwin had pursued the evidence from pollen analysis for some time for the Fenland Research Committee. The emerging Neolithic was important, but it did not alter Clark's own opinion of those who devoted themselves solely to the developed Neolithic, and especially those inclined to visit megaliths; these people were 'secondary archaeologists'. There may have been a deliberate attempt here to distance himself from certain of his colleagues, but he said the same of the research students who went the way of the big stones.

As a University Lecturer, Clark was not always appreciated by his students. His lectures were generally considered to be rather poorly constructed, and he often wandered from the subject in hand. More than once he gave a detailed Part II lecture by mistake to a bunch of first-year students who may have felt happy to be considered able to take it, but who mostly could not understand what was going on. For those legitimately taking his courses on the Mesolithic or the beginnings of agriculture, the *post mortem* of the lectures would take place in a nearby coffee house, either 'The Bun Shop' or 'Hawkins' (both alas no more); here the delivery of the information was criticized, but no one would think of missing the lectures, and sometimes there was excitement when Clark would launch into an off-the-cuff description of a recent discovery that might even be relevant to the course of instruction. He never much ventured, throughout his many years as a prominent archaeologist, to get absorbed into popular archaeology. Glyn Daniel was very successful both in television and in writing for the public, and Clark must have felt unable to compete at this level. He mostly kept quiet about the public face of archaeology, with the occasional swipe at 'what might charitably be termed post-T.V. books'.[34]

In 1948, Clark was told about the discovery of some microliths at Seamer Carr in Yorkshire. He was already aware of a number of antler barbed points from Holderness, and hastened to the site. Here he found pieces of antler and bone sticking out from the side of a ditch. Godwin was appraised of the potential and he and Clark mounted an ambitious campaign in 1949–51.[35] The site, Star Carr, was explored with great care, and the organic material, for so long sought after by Clark, emerged in great quantities. The British

Museum (Natural History) undertook the faunal analyses and introduced a vacuum chamber to ensure the continued preservation of the bone and antler. The story of Star Carr has been told so often, and the reinterpretations so frequent, that little needs to be said here. Inorganic flintwork could be seen in a proper subsidiary, yet still important, relationship to the bark, wood, bone and antler artefacts made and used by the occupants of a wooden platform built out into the pool. Godwin's environmental analyses were crucial to the interpretation of the site, and Clark could assert with some justification that here was a British site to rival, indeed surpass, almost all of the Danish sites. The inventor of the radiocarbon dating method, Willard Libby, undertook to process a sample of the wooden platform and produced a date of 9488±350 years before present; the site was on all counts the contemporary of Klosterlund in Denmark, where only flint and stone objects had survived. In the monograph of the site, published in 1954,[36] Clark produced a classic diagram showing how the Mesolithic group had exploited the animal, vegetable and mineral resources, for food, clothing, fire, tools and weapons, and adornment. He also made the point, again, that Quaternary Research was vital in any serious prehistoric research project, particularly those dealing with the Stone Age. Godwin had only recently assumed charge of the newly-formed Sub-Department of Quaternary Research in the Botany School and Star Carr was the best possible example of the great future that that institution was to have. For Clark, the successful use of the rich faunal remains in his interpretation, and the inspiring and entirely satisfactory radiocarbon date, were to remain with him as guides to future research projects.

Meanwhile, his more theoretical studies of subsistence practices and the exploitation of natural resources continued and an opportunity arose to bring his various papers together. Gordon Childe had retired as Abercromby Professor in Edinburgh and Clark was a candidate for the chair. Piggott was chosen and at once invited his friend and colleague to deliver the 1949 Munro Lectures in Scotland. Clark accepted, and the lectures appeared in printed form as *Prehistoric Europe: The Economic Basis*, in 1952.[37] To many, this is Clark's major triumph. The book went into various languages, including Russian; Minns would be pleased. In the same year, Dorothy Garrod made way and Clark was elected to the Disney Professorship in Cambridge. In the next year he took the Sc.D. degree at Cambridge on the basis of his published work. He was unsure about the degree, whether it should have been the Litt.D. or the Sc.D., but in part was persuaded towards science by the offer of a free scarlet gown of a deceased geologist; for a prehistorian, it was a fitting choice.

His 1953 Albert Reckitt Archaeological Lecture to the British Academy gave Clark an opportunity to express his economic prehistory in other ways, and foreshadowed the path he wanted to follow in his later writings. He used this lecture as one of the bases for his final manuscripts: '. . . economic progress, in the sense of a growing capacity to utilise natural resources such as we can trace in prehistory, marks stages in the liberation of the human spirit by making possible more varied responses and so accelerates the processes of change and diversification over the whole realm of culture'.[38]

In 1952 Clark broke out of Europe to attend the inaugural meeting of the Wenner-Gren Foundation for Anthropological Research in New York. This brought opportunities for archaeological fieldwork in many areas of the world, and Clark was soon to benefit his students and others by Wenner-Gren activities. However, he set himself the task first of carrying out more local excavations, partly to test his observations on sites where skilful work had revealed surprisingly detailed information about settlements in particular. In Norfolk, first, he tested an Iron Age site but conditions were very poor.[39] Then in 1957–8 he undertook a major piece of excavation at Hurst Fen near Cambridge where, according to expectations, he might have found Neolithic house plans and settlement organization along the lines of the sand-based Neolithic structures just across the North Sea. Although the site yielded vast amounts of flint implements and pottery, severe erosion of the Fen soils had removed all trace of structures. This was a great disappointment and the report on the site, as prompt as ever, was Clark's last excavation paper.[40]

Henceforth he was in analytical mode, and increasingly involved with committees both inside and outside the University. He served on the Ancient Monuments Board, on the Royal Commission on the Historical Monuments of England, on various management committees and councils, and continued to edit the *Proceedings*. He never took kindly to University politics or the machinations needed then, and now, to ensure progress both structural (plant) and academic (staff); his time as Disney Professor and as occasional Chairman of the Faculty was propitious for augmenting his staff but he never bothered to work the system and press for new developments. Yet he was assiduous in encouraging every member of his existing staff to conduct research of almost whatever kind, and wherever in the world, and to help in its publication. One aspect of his Headship was widely appreciated; he never felt it necessary to have a formal Departmental meeting. Decisions for Faculty were made 'on the hoof' and communicated as and when necessary, or not at all. He was Chairman of the Faculty for three years and would race through the Agenda, overriding other Departmental Heads whenever discussion and decision seemed to be developing into debate. His aims for his Department were always clear—make time for study and research, and for graduate students, and for undergraduate teaching, in that descending order.

He had a succession of research students for whom he acted as supervisor or in other capacities, and he was immensely proud of their achievements. Some reflect wryly on the lack of real supervision of their subjects; Clark would often launch into a discourse on a totally unrelated topic, interesting perhaps but not much practical use for a student aiming to complete a dissertation on a specific subject, generally one suggested by Clark in the first place. His own graduate students went on to create new concepts in archaeological research or to direct major institutions in various parts of the world. More than one he sent off to new jobs in Africa or Australia, the recruit sometimes never having heard of the particular region or the precise subject which was to be the focus of research. Most survived the encounters, and were anxious to reciprocate when Clark, later on, began to travel the world.[41] He suffered two terrible blows in his later years, with the deaths of

David Clarke and Glyn Isaac, both Peterhouse men and world leaders in their fields. He took comfort in their accomplishments and those of the others, and while still Disney Professor he was assiduous in monitoring and encouraging the progress of all the graduates of his Department who participated in the expansion of world archaeology in the late 1960s and 1970s. Clark's famous map of the world, with its many coloured pins showing where the graduates had landed to establish outposts of the Cambridge school, was never prominently displayed, but he kept a mental image of the world with its Cambridge diaspora, and he could identify every region with its current 'holder', the work underway, and the latest publications emanating from the colonies. Of course he knew it was an exaggeration of the prominence of his school, but that was no hindrance to encouragement. Although his book *Prehistory at Cambridge and Beyond* appeared only in 1989, it reflected upon the flow of talent that had passed into and through Cambridge, with only a few remaining at home. Much autobiographical material appears in this book, and it shows Clark in a rightfully expansionist mode, and the pride which he had for the accomplishments of his students.

As Head of a prestigious Department and therefore on the receiving end of a succession of visitors to Cambridge, Clark used his College Fellowship to the full, and many a foreign archaeologist recalls dining at High Table where the talk could veer wildly from the quality of the food to University politics and inevitably to archaeology, without any noticeable break in the flow either of words or of food. Another divertissement for newcomers was a tour with Clark to visit local sites, or to travel together by car to meetings outside Cambridge. His abilities as the operator of a motor vehicle are legendary, and some of the stories told by former passengers are certainly true. Colleagues, visiting scholars and students all had variously unnerving experiences with Clark at the wheel of his Mercedes or other powerful car. Sudden braking, as a monument was sighted in the distance, created as much alarm to passengers as it did to the drivers of following vehicles; it was one way of picking up local terms of abuse. Clark's sense of direction was not often wrong but in any event there was little opportunity for anyone, especially a student, to suggest a change of course as the flow of words continued without respite. Many visitors recall with delight their times in the Fens with Clark; a few still shudder. Clark was wholly unconcerned with such matters, as one specific example may indicate. In the early 1960s, en route from Cambridge to Birmingham on the hitherto untried M1 motorway, and in driving rain, Clark placed his Mercedes firmly in the outside lane and rushed northwards at over 100 mph, growling only as a very occasional Jaguar passed by on the inside lane. On approaching the Bull Ring, an innovative and terrifying ring road recently constructed, Clark handed over his only map to his newly-appointed Assistant Lecturer, suggesting that this would help us find our way into the city centre. The map was in an AA book of 1935 when, presumably, horse and cart were the order of the day. Cars, like bicycles and typewriters (but not his staff), were there to be used without respite until they were deemed unfit for the task; a new machine was then purchased.

Like most field archaeologists of the day, Clark was obliged to make most of his own maps, plans and drawings. He was surprisingly patient and talented at this, not so well able to create attractive artwork as Stuart Piggott could, but none the less entirely competent. His maps were invariably models of clarity. For the Star Carr report, he was able to take time to delineate over 100 barbed antler points and various pieces of bone and wood, in part because his literary activities were curtailed by a broken arm. The fact that Clark of all people was doing this kind of work amazed a small group of visiting Dutch archaeologists who were accustomed to assigning such tasks to draughtsmen; yet there was no better way to become acquainted with the artefacts. Photography was a craft never fully mastered and not often employed as a serious expression of the evidence. Site photography was a haphazard affair; at Hurst Fen he decided that a high elevation photograph was called for, but after trying to mount a contraption made of chairs and planks, he abandoned the attempt with the words, 'No, the loss to science would be too great'. Whether this referred to the potential damage to site or to archaeologist is unclear.

Clark was elected to the British Academy in 1951 and was Chairman of Section 10 (Archaeology) from 1974 to 1978. He was an active member of the Section but it was not until the late 1960s that he seized the opportunities to involve the Section and the Academy in major projects. Before that time, he embarked on a series of journeys to various parts of the world, rarely on holiday (apart from a Scandinavian visit in 1955) and often as a visiting lecturer or professor. He was the Grant MacCurdy Lecturer at Harvard in 1957, W. Evans Professor at Otago and Commonwealth Visiting Fellow in Australia in 1964, between which times he attended the Congress of Pre- and Protohistoric Sciences at Hamburg and Rome. A notable excursion to the Netherlands with the Prehistoric Society in 1960 allowed a group of recent graduates to observe the leading British prehistorians, Clark, Piggott *et al.*, in earnest and sometimes amicably heated discourse with W. van Giffen and his formidable graduates and associates P. Modderman, W. Glasbergen and H. Waterbolk. Clark was always held in very considerable respect by his contemporaries and it was not surprising to see even Piggott and his colleague R.J.C. Atkinson anxious to make a favourable impression on one of Clark's visits to their site at Wayland's Smithy. Lounging in their directorial hut one day, drinking gin with a visitor, they were roused to frantic action when told that Professor Clark was walking up to the excavation. Clark did nothing to cultivate this superior position, but probably did little to undermine it. He was by far the most respected British prehistorian on the continent of Europe where his reputation was regularly enhanced by his visits and the encouragement given to young research workers in particular.

In 1961 Clark published the first edition of *World Prehistory: An Outline*, basing his syntheses in part on his own travels and visits, on the work of his own students, and to a considerable extent on his contacts in various parts of the world.[42] One of the basic elements of the book, and indeed essential for comparative studies, was the ever-wider presentation of absolute dates from all parts of the world. This was the master key that unlocked the doors of the world for Clark. It gave him the framework for the patterns of behaviour that he could deduce from the material culture observed, and it allowed him to speculate on contacts, influences and indigenous development. He pursued this in more detailed ways soon after his *World Prehistory* appeared. The first edition was flawed by omissions and some errors, as he well knew. But he also knew that some senior archaeologists could not find it in themselves to accept a theory of world prehistory, arguing that it was only possible to comprehend more specific, solid, site or landscape-based archaeology. Clark ignored such criticism because he knew the time had come to move outwards to the widest concepts of space and time. Almost at once, he began to reassemble the evidence and to augment it by his own research. A pleasant interruption to this was his installation as Commander, Order of the Danebrog, in 1961; as someone who had always looked to Denmark for both evidence and inspiration, this award was particularly gratifying.

In 1968 he was in Japan, Taiwan, the Philippines and New Zealand. In Taipei en route to some meeting or other, his host stepped into a bookshop and brought out a pirated copy of Clark's *Archaeology and Society*. This was not the only such unauthorized version of his books. But in this case, redress, if not financial then emotional, was secured in the Philippines. Clark was able to see the fabulous Locsin collection of Chinese porcelain of the Sung, Yuan and early Ming periods, and was then invited to the Locsin estate where the excavation of a cemetery was in progress. The grave goods already found included Chinese porcelain of the Yuan dynasty (AD 1279–1368), and Clark was asked to continue the excavation of a grave where the labourers had dug down to the level of the burial. Lo and behold, he soon exposed some fine porcelain. Lunch was then taken under the palm trees, with white-coated waiters serving suckling pig on fine china. Upon departure, Clark was presented with a box containing 'his' excavated porcelain. A perfect day.

From 1964 to 1969 he travelled widely, not only to the east but also to Canada and America, and to parts of the Near East and central Europe. In Australia in 1964 on a Commonwealth Visiting Scholarship he had a particularly satisfying time, with a field trip into Central Australia with Norman Tindale. Here he could observe the aboriginal people's use of space in their hunting and gathering economies, and he could try to comprehend their complex cultural patterns; this visit was profoundly important for Clark's vision of prehistory. He generally made assiduous records of all his observations, but on this journey his notebook vanished into some crevice in the great outback; this loss may account for a slip of the pen in one of Clark's later publications where the Wombah midden appears as Wombat.[43] More importantly, Clark's observations of work at the stone quarries and long-distance distributions led him to an appraisal of traffic in stone axe and adze blades which appeared in 1965.[44] In New Zealand, as W. Evans Professor at Otago, Clark was intensely interested in the contrasting ways of life of the Maoris of the North Island and those of the South Island, due in good measure to the cultivation of introduced food plants in the North, and the implications therefrom for exchanges in materials and commodities. The impressions gained in Australia and New Zealand were to direct Clark in his future writings, not only in the *World Prehistory: A New Outline* of 1969,[45] but also in his later thoughts on symbols and interactions which appeared as lengthy essays in the 1980s.

In 1967 he received the Hodgkins Medal of the Smithsonian Institution, and in 1971 the Viking Fund Medal of the Wenner-Gren Foundation. These were followed by the Lucy Wharton Gold Medal from the University of Pennsylvania in 1974, the Gold Medal of the Society of Antiquaries of London in 1978 and the Chandra Medal of the Asiatic Society in 1979. He was a Corresponding or Foreign Member of a large number of European and American Academies.[46]

In 1969 he was Hitchcock Professor at Berkeley in California where his close friend J. Desmond Clark was based, and in his lectures he returned to the importance of basic archaeological evidence. Artefacts were the signposts of the course of prehistory, as everyone should know, but they were also the mechanism that distinguished humans from other animals. They signified the human capacity to identify and assign importance both to the everyday elements of prehistoric life and to the symbols of the thought processes that reflected forces beyond the grasp of humans. This statement served notice that Clark was not about to fall into the abyss of writing prehistory without evidence to back it up, but it was also a comment on those close at hand, both in America and in Europe, who were content to pick at the cherries and ignore the branches and trunk without which the fruit would not exist. The powerful theme pursued here, and in his Albert Reckitt Archaeological Lecture as long ago as 1953, was simple: economic progress empowered the human spirit. It was a theme that Clark continued to develop throughout his later years.

Clark did not devote as much research time to the Americas as he did to other parts of the world, but he made an impassioned plea to North American archaeologists when he made a tour across much of Canada in 1976. He commented upon the tendency of some current archaeologists to treat their subject as a science, and almost a pure science at that.[47] Clark stated that this view was misguided and 'it is also pathetic'. Natural science was a mere artefact of man, elaborate and expensive, and yet nothing more than a means by which man could comprehend and manipulate his environment; he might have included culture in his argument. In this, he signalled his intention to devote time and writing to the development of his thoughts on the uniqueness of the human condition, and on the particular elements in the archaeological record that could most easily identify that state.

In the late 1960s, while writing two slighter books on *Prehistoric Societies* (with Stuart Piggott) and *The Stone Age Hunters*,[48] Clark took up a theme that was to develop into a major research project. By using the newly-available radiocarbon dates for the earliest agriculturally based communities throughout Europe and the Near East, he could produce a map that conclusively showed the spread of farming from the Near East into south-eastern Europe and across to the north and west.[49] This map, however refined and with a multiplicity of new spots, has never been seriously disputed although Clark was doubtless happy to accept minor adjustments and local innovations. But having secured the academic background and demonstrated the dynamics of economic change, he took steps to implement active research into the subject of early European agriculture. With the encouragement of the Sub-Department of Quaternary Research, Robert Rodden was despatched to Greece to begin a major excavation on the early Neolithic site of Nea Nikomedeia.[50] Eric Higgs, already attached to the Department of Archaeology and with practical experience of animal husbandry, went the same way and began investigations into earlier sites in the Aegean region.[51] Clark visited Greece and was inspired by what he saw. He worked with others in the British Academy to establish a Major Research Project on the Early History of Agriculture. A small committee was assembled in 1966, meeting in the same parlour in Peterhouse as had been used over 30 years before, when the Fenland Research Committee was established. Indeed, a majority of the new committee had been there at the earlier meeting. This initiated a major project that took much of Clark's time and energy, although Higgs was made director. The work done in Greece and elsewhere by the team was designed to explore the economic aspects of prehistory set within an ever-increasingly detailed palaeoenvironmental frame. Clark pressed for rapid publication of results, in a monograph series,[52] and provided much-needed encouragement and control at times of stress when the original aims of the project were threatened by the sheer speed of the work being done.

At the same time as he was demonstrating the spread of farming across Europe, and initiating the project, Clark took some of his British colleagues to task in a classic paper on the invasion hypothesis in British archaeology.[53] He could not accept that every innovation that appeared in the record had to be the result of new arrivals from the continent. That was too easy and, as he reiterated in the first Gordon Childe Memorial Lecture, 'it has tended in the past to inhibit research into alternative causes'.[54] His 1966 paper was not universally welcomed but it had the desired effect on the bulk of British prehistorians, who now looked more carefully before they leaped across the channel seeking originators for developments in these islands.

The Early History of Agriculture project absorbed much of Clark's emotions in the active years of its work. He was more content to see from a distance the work of his colleague Charles McBurney. McBurney's great excavations in North Africa and on Jersey absorbed much space and energy within the confines of the Department, and Clark had the greatest respect for the work of post-excavation analyses and the painstaking way by which McBurney put together the monograph of the Haua Fteah.[55] It was a happier relationship between the two than existed between Clark and the other senior figure, Glyn Daniel, but a working pattern was established with all and there can be little doubt that the Department offered an exciting spectrum of approaches to graduate students in particular. Undergraduates had their turn too, but only those who went the way of one camp or another had much hope of success in the Tripos; the rest left somewhat bemused by it all, with Second Class degrees. Clark did better; he became Commander, Order of the British Empire, in 1971.

Although much absorbed with his travels and new experiences, and assembling vast quantities of new information in the late 1960s and early 1970s, Clark was always aware of his original base of research in Northern Europe, and of his environmental and economic approaches, and in his debt to the site of Star Carr. He was anxious that the evidence from Star Carr should be capable of reworking and although his excavation records were not stratigraphically detailed enough for intricate work patterns to be deduced, none the less the bulk of the material and its excellent condition permitted new appraisals over the years. Clark made an effort himself to expose new thoughts in a widely-quoted paper of 1972, subtitled *A Case Study in Bioarchaeology*.[56] This long paper, essentially a small book, was a very substantial reworking and rethinking of the data from Star Carr. The 1954 monograph had appeared soon after the field seasons ended, and Clark felt that he wanted to expose the evidence to new and more fully-considered thoughts. A major section of the paper, titled 'Bioarchaeological interpretation', allowed him to deal with environment, social context, seasonality, site territory and food supply. It remains a model of his own archaeological evolution up to the early 1970s.

In 1972, Clark was a Visiting Professor at the University of Uppsala, and he became once more absorbed into the study of the earliest traces of human occupation in northern Europe. He received a Filosofie Doktor (*honoris causa*) from Uppsala University in 1976, an award that gave him much pleasure in the recognition by a Scandinavian university of his contributions to prehistory. Equally satisfying was a Doctor of Letters awarded by the National University of Ireland in the same year.

In 1975, *The Earlier Stone Age Settlement of Scandinavia* appeared, in which Clark tried to bring together the evidence newly-acquired since his pioneering book of 1936.[57] Many new discoveries had been made, and new techniques applied to their elucidation, but the new book was not as warmly received as had been the first, and it was obvious to Clark that the task of identifying the significant developments in a land with which he was familiar, but in which he was not resident, was beyond him; the pace of discovery was too great, and more importantly the new approaches made by a generation of Scandinavian scholars included concepts that Clark could not fully accept and therefore did not recognize in his book. He had planned a second book, *The Later Stone Age Settlement*, but did not pursue this as he would have been on less familiar chronological territory.

The multiplicity of scientific interests brought to bear on the Early History of Agriculture Project led easily enough to thoughts about the expansion of science-based archaeology, and Clark was instrumental in calling a meeting in 1972 between representatives of the British Academy, the Natural Environment Research Council, and the Royal Society. Archaeology and the natural sciences were debated in terms of equality of opportunity, but it was clear that the former would be the greater beneficiary of any union of resources. By 1974, Science-based Archaeology was on the agenda of the Science Research Council and in 1975 the Academy pressed for a solution to the problem of funding archaeological science from a wholly inadequate and inappropriate resource. In 1976, Clark assumed the Chair at the first Science-based Archaeology Committee, which consisted of a formidable array of scientists sympathetic to archaeology in one way or another. In 1980 he relinquished the Chair but by then major advances had been made, including the establishment of the Radiocarbon Accelerator Unit at Oxford. In that year, Clark gave the J.C. Jacobsen Memorial Lecture to the Danish Academy of Science, and he could point with some satisfaction to the results of the dating programme, on a world basis, and to the advances in an understanding of global environmental change.[58] These tools were essential in the efforts by archaeologists to comprehend the character and the pace of change within and between prehistoric communities.

Another abiding interest was in collecting porcelain. Clark had always been intrigued by Jomon pottery, not least by its early dating, and from 1968 when he had attended a Congress in Tokyo he became an avid collector of Far Eastern porcelain, some of it rare and extremely fragile. He probably took some amusement from the terrified looks on the faces of his students when they, invited to tea, were handed a piece, told its age (but not its price) and asked to admire it.

At Peterhouse, where he was Master 1973–80, he and his wife entertained scholars from all parts of the world, and without exception the visitors speak of their joy at being received so warmly in such dignified surroundings. Clark felt passionate about the College, and firmly believed that anyone fortunate enough to become attached to a place of learning and Fellowship should accept an obligation to work towards the general good rather than holing up in a room for personal study alone. He has been described as 'an absolutely perfect Master of Peterhouse'. The College had such a hold on him that sometimes even prehistory had to wait; visitors who came during the Bumps were promptly bundled off with the Master to support Peterhouse. Clark would say: 'these things are important, we can't spend all of our time thinking about archaeology'. The College elected him to an Honorary Fellowship in 1980 and he continued to participate in College matters whenever possible. Welcome breaks from University and College politics were taken at Aldeburgh in Suffolk where he could sail his small boat in peace; rumour has it that he sailed as he drove. This time was a particularly happy one for him and Mollie. Gardening at his home in Cambridge was another interest and their Wilberforce Road garden had always been proudly displayed to a constant flow of visitors.

By the early 1970s, he was now wholly immersed in a world prehistory which he alone it seemed could grasp. His first two editions of the *World Prehistory* book had exposed the gaps in information, some real and some of his own, and he set to in 'the sanctuary of the Master's lodge at Peterhouse' to work up the material flowing into Cambridge through visiting scholars, and also the information he had accumulated on his world travels. He had a formidable card index system that allowed him to build up a body of evidence which he could search at will for the latest references, discoveries, personalities and above all concepts. Quotations were liberally sprinkled throughout the cards, and he was always generous in acknowledging help of any kind in the lengthy dedications and lists in his publications. Writing drafts of his papers and books was an ever-absorbing task and pleasure, and when one report went off to the press, another was promptly initiated at his desk in the Master's lodge or in the comfortable home he and Mollie acquired after 1980.

Clark was invited to India in 1978 by B.K. Thapar, Director-General of the Archaeological Survey. Thapar had spent some time in Cambridge and had provided Clark with material for his revision of *World Prehistory*. In India, Clark gave the first Wheeler Memorial Lectures, on the contribution of Sir Mortimer to Indian archaeology. The two lectures, published soon after,[59] allowed Clark to expound on Wheeler's disciplined approach to fieldwork and to ponder on his legacy to Indian archaeology. Clark was generous in his praise of the first subject, but less so of the second; he felt that Indian archaeologists should now break out of the shackles that a too-rigid approach to fieldwork *à la* Wheeler might create. The chronologies had now been established, and it was time to ask more searching questions of the evidence. Of course, it was phrased well, as it had to be in the circumstances.

In 1977 Clark published the third and final edition of his book, *World Prehistory in New Perspective*.[60] This was a total rewrite of his previous efforts, was far longer and better constructed. It bore all the signs of a greater awareness of the prehistoric world in all its variety, and of the need to refine the information by more, and more-refined, research. Radiocarbon dating was extensively used to correlate events, if not on a world-wide basis, then at least on a continental frame. This book, like the other two editions, went into translations in various languages, but only the 1969 version appeared in Serbo-Croat. World prehistory is now beyond the capabilities of any one person, and although it may be said that any synthesis that tries to cover the world will, like a British Rail timetable, inevitably have gaps and missed connections, it is the chronology of Clark's work that is important. He it was who tried, and succeeded in part, to present the prehistoric world in such a way that the themes of humanity, of invention and innovation, of contact and stress, of a community of necessities, and of demonstrable variations in behaviour, were always before us. Understated in places, exaggerated in others, the humanity of the race was always implicit in his text. The place of the natural sciences, the cornerstone of much of Clark's own work, was there, of course, but it was the human condition that interested him.

There followed, in a way as anticlimax, other books, of essay proportions and thematic approaches. *Mesolithic Prelude* (1980), *The Identity of Man* (1983), *Symbols of Excellence* (1986) and *Space, Time and Man* (1992) were books designed for more general readership and helped to advance the archaeological and prehistoric causes that Clark still wanted to pursue.[61] *Space, Time and Man* drew heavily upon Clark's own *World Prehistory* but extended the enquiry into relatively modern societies. His premise was that once humans and other animals had exploited the spatial dimensions of their environments, and had successfully occupied their territories over time, a parting of the ways occurred. Only humans could perceive the dimensionality of space and time, by consciously and at times illogically expanding their spatial horizons, and by deliberately setting out to document the passage of time.

The Identity of Man as Seen by an Archaeologist was another essay directing attention to the features that distinguished humans from other primates, namely culture and cultural behaviour. The awareness of other times, of times long ago, of ancestors, and the quest for immortality, each necessitating attempts to try to grasp some conception of the cosmos, could be traced in prehistory, and delineated in ethno-historical societies. This book had a logical but less well-argued successor in *Symbols of Excellence*, subtitled *Precious Materials as Expressions of Status*, in which Clark's admiration for the artistic expressions of the Stone Age could be followed through time into the realms of modern societies in which extraordinary combinations of precious substances came to signify position and power. In the conclusion, he deemed it a privilege to be able to study objects that oozed status, and to thereby acknowledge the power that they conveyed to mere citizens of the state. Here, as much as anywhere else, Clark exhibited his own political proclivities, and why not? His great and good friend Gordon Childe had done the same from the opposite end and that had not disturbed their close relationship and mutual admiration. Both men subscribed to the view that it was essential for all people of whatever political hue to co-operate, or else to perish, and Clark's writings through the years carried that stark message—facing up to our predicament as self-conscious human beings was how he expressed it.[62] In 1976 Clark had been able to publish his view of Gordon Childe in a wide assessment of developments in prehistoric studies since Childe's death.[63]

In 1990, the Praemium Erasmianum Foundation of The Netherlands awarded its Erasmus Prize to Grahame Clark, and the citation referred to his interdisciplinary work, his interest in prehistoric economics, his definitions and descriptions of ancient societies, and his contribution to the Cambridge school of archaeology. In accepting the award, Clark at once identified the uses to which it would be put. The Prehistoric Society would administer a Europa Fund to provide an annual award to a Europa Lecturer who was judged to have made significant contributions to European prehistoric studies. And the British Academy would administer an endowment for a medal which would recognize achievements in prehistoric research. The first recipient of the medal was Clark's former colleague and collaborator Stuart Piggott, whose delight at the award was a reminder to those present of the long friendship of the two men. There followed, in 1992, a knighthood for Grahame Clark on the grounds of his lifetime of research and his leadership in the study of the prehistory of the world. In 1994, the emergence of the Macdonald Institute for Archaeological Research at Cambridge was witnessed by Sir Grahame and Lady Clark, and the Grahame Clark Laboratory for Archaeology was dedicated. At the time of his death on 12 September 1995 he was planning another book, to be called *Man the Spiritual Primat*e, and sections exist for future research into arguably the greatest prehistorian of the twentieth century.

At the end of the day, how best to sum up the career and contributions of Grahame Clark? Much has been written, and more will appear, about his pioneering work in prehistoric economies, in the ecological approach, in the study of organic artefacts, in his initiation of science-based archaeology, in his Academy projects, and in his world view of prehistory. But perhaps above all else was the encouragement given to his own graduates and to all those he met in Cambridge or abroad, to pursue an archaeology that could bind the world together both in the prehistoric past and in the future, through the identification of a commonality of aspiration and endeavour.

On 10 July 1926, the young Grahame Clark delivered a paper to the Natural History Society of Marlborough College; the paper was called 'Progress in Prehistoric Times' and the Secretary of the Society reported: 'He knew his subject very well'.

JOHN COLES
Fellow of the Academy

Note. I am grateful to many people who have helped in the compilation of this Memoir. I am particularly grateful to Lady Clark who has provided many papers for me to read, and who has given me insights into Grahame Clark's life. Information and comments have been sent to me by many colleagues, and I am happy to acknowledge the assistance of the following: C.J. Becker FBA; J.D. Clark FBA; B.J. Coles; B.W. Cunliffe FBA; J.D. Evans FBA; P. Gathercole; B. Gräslund; N.D.C. Hammond FBA; C.F.C. Higham; M.S.F. Hood FBA; R.R. Inskeep; I.H. Longworth; M.P. Malmer FBA; A. McBurney; C. McVean; P.A. Mellars FBA; P.J.R. Modderman; D.J. Mulvaney FBA; the late S. Piggott FBA; Lord Renfrew FBA; D.A. Roe; P. Rowley-Conwy; C.T. Shaw FBA; G.R. Willey FBA; and Sir David Wilson FBA.

Endnotes

[1] 'A Path to Prehistory', unpublished manuscript, 1993.

[2] G. Clark, *Economic Prehistory. Papers on Archaeology by Grahame Clark* (Cambridge, 1989); the bibliography in this book is incomplete in other respects although the omissions are minor. To the books can now be added *Space, Time and Man. A Prehistorian's view* (Cambridge, 1992).

[3] *Report of the Marlborough College Natural History Society* (1923), pp. 85–9; (1924), pp. 75–9; (1925), p. 114; (1926), pp. 73–5.

[4] C. Fox, *The Archaeology of the Cambridge Region* (Cambridge, 1923).

[5] Clapham became Professor of Economic History at Cambridge in 1928 but had variously been a Fellow of King's College since 1898; his *Study of Economic History* appeared in 1929.

[6] V.G. Childe, *The Dawn of European Civilization* (London, 1925).

[7] E.C. Curwen, *The Archaeology of Sussex* (London, 1937).

[8] J.G.D. Clark, *The Mesolithic Age in Britain* (Cambridge, 1932).

[9] C.W. Phillips, *My Life in Archaeology* (Gloucester, 1987).

[10] Clark served on Council in 1938 and again in 1946–7; he was Vice-President in 1959–62.

[11] G. Gjessing, *Arktische Helleristninger: Nord-Norge* (Oslo, 1932).

[12] J.G.D. Clark, 'Scandinavian rock engravings', *Antiquity*, 11 (1937), 56–69.

[13] I.F. Smith, *Windmill Hill and Avebury. Excavations by Alexander Keiller 1925–39* (Oxford, 1965).

[14] J.G.D. Clark, 'Discoidal polished flint knives: their typology and distribution', *Proceedings of the Prehistoric Society of East Anglia*, 6 (1928), 40–54.

[15] G. Clark, 'The Prehistoric Society: from East Anglia to the world', *Proceedings of the Prehistoric Society*, 51 (1985), 1–13. The brief report of the AGM in *Proceedings*, 1 (1935), 162 can be amplified by the notice sent out to members beforehand, and a notice sent out after the event. These survive in the Society's archive.

[16] Burkitt was one of the few prehistorians who continued to give house room to eoliths, and in his *The Old Stone Age* (3rd edn, London, 1955) he was still arguing that 'the existence of Tertiary man seems incontestable'; in his University Museum collection he had labelled a flint flake from an impossibly ancient Crag 'this is a fine specimen', but of what we never were told.

[17] H. Godwin, *Fenland: Its Ancient Past and Uncertain Future* (Cambridge, 1978); original report, H. and M.E Godwin, 'British Maglemose harpoon sites', *Antiquity*, 7 (1933), 36–48.

[18] C.W. Phillips, 'The Fenland Research Committee, its past achievements and future prospects', in W.F. Grimes (ed.), *Aspects of Archaeology in Britain and Beyond* (London, 1957), pp. 258–73.

[19] J.G.D. Clark, H. and M.E. Godwin, and M.H. Clifford, 'Report on recent excavations at Peacock's Farm, Shippea Hill, Cambridgeshire', *Antiquaries Journal*, 15 (1935), 284–319.

[20] J.G.D. Clark, 'Report on an Early Bronze Age site in the south-eastern Fens', *Antiquaries Journal*, 13 (1933), 266–96; H. and M.E. Godwin, J.G.D. Clark, and M.H. Clifford, 'A Bronze Age spearhead found in Methwold Fen, Norfolk', *Proceedings of the Prehistoric Society of East Anglia*, 7 (1934), 395–8; J.G.D. Clark, H. and M.E. Godwin, and M.H. Clifford, 'Peacock's Farm', (1935) see above, n.19; J.G.D. Clark, 'Report on a Late Bronze Age site in

Mildenhall Fen, West Suffolk', *Antiquaries Journal*, 16 (1936), 29–50; J.G.D. Clark and H. Godwin, 'A Late Bronze Age find near Stuntney, Isle of Ely', *Antiquaries Journal*, 20 (1940), 52–71.

[21] J.G.D. Clark and S. Piggott, 'The Age of the British flint mines', *Antiquity*, 7 (1933), 166–83.

[22] S. Hazzledine Warren, S. Piggott, J.G.D. Clark, M.C. Burkitt and H. and M.E. Godwin, 'Archaeology of the submerged land surface of the Essex coast', *Proceedings of the Prehistoric Society*, 2 (1936), 178–210.

[23] J.G.D. Clark, 'The classification of a microlithic culture: the Tardenoisian of Horsham', *Archaeological Journal*, 90 (1933), 52–77; 'Derivative forms of the petit tranchet in Britain', *Archaeological Journal*, 91 (1934), 32–58; 'A microlithic industry from the Cambridgeshire Fenland and other industries of Sauveterrian affinities from Britain', *Proceedings of the Prehistoric Society*, 21 (1955), 3–20; 'Blade and trapeze industries of the European Stone Age', *Proceedings of the Prehistoric Society*, 24 (1958), 24–42.

[24] T. Mathiassen, 'Gudenaa-Kulturen. En Mesolitish Inlands bebyggelse i Jylland', *Aarbøger* (1937), 1–186; J. Troels-Smith, 'Stammebade fra Aamosen'. *Fra Nationalmuseets Arbejdsmark* (1946); G. Hatt 1937, *Landbrug i Danmarks Oldtid* (Copenhagen, 1937).

[25] e.g. I. Arwidsson, 'Några fasta fisken i Södra Bullaren från äldre tider', Göteborgs och Bohusläns Fornminnesförenings Tidsskrift, (1936), 92–122. Arwidsson's work here was only one of the family's contributions to Clark's development; Greta Arwidsson's later work at Valsgårde and Birka played a part in Clark's increasing interest in symbols of prestige—a far cry from the wooden stakes on the Bullaren Lake.

[26] J.G.D. Clark, *The Mesolithic Settlement of Northern Europe: A Study of the Food Gathering Peoples of Northern Europe During the Early Post-glacial Period* (Cambridge, 1936).

[27] Grahame Clark, *Archaeology and Society* (London, 1939).

[28] J.G.D. Clark and W.F. Rankine, 'Excavations at Farnham, Surrey (1937–38): the Horsham culture and the question of Mesolithic dwellings', *Proceedings of the Prehistoric Society*, 5 (1939), 61–118.

[29] H. Godwin, *The Archives of the Peat Bogs* (Cambridge, 1981).

[30] D. Thompson, 'The seasonal factor in human culture', *Proceedings of the Prehistoric Society*, 5 (1939), 209–21.

[31] 'Bees in antiquity', *Antiquity*, 16 (1942), 208–15; 'Water in antiquity', *Antiquity*, 18 (1944), 1–15; 'Seal-hunting in the Stone Age of north-western Europe: a study in economic prehistory', *Proceedings of the Prehistoric Society*, 12 (1946), 12–48; 'Forest clearance and prehistoric farming', *Economic History Review*, 17 (1947), 45–51; 'Sheep and swine in the husbandry of prehistoric Europe', *Antiquity*, 21 (1947), 122–36; 'Whales as an economic factor in prehistoric Europe', *Antiquity*, 21 (1947), 84–104; 'The development of fishing in prehistoric Europe', *Antiquaries Journal*, 28 (1948), 45–85; 'Fowling in prehistoric Europe', *Antiquity*, 22 (1948), 116–30.

These papers were reprinted in *Economic Prehistory* (1989).

[32] J. Iversen, 'Land occupation in Denmark's Stone Age. A pollen-analytical study of the influence of farming culture on the vegetational development', *Danmarks Geologiske Undersøgelse II R 66* (Copenhagen, 1941). A. Rust, *Die alt- und mittelsteinzeitlichen funde von Stellmoor* (Neumünster, 1943); *Das altsteinzeitliche rentierjägerlager Meiendorf* (Neumünster, 1937).

[33] J.G.D. Clark, 'Folk-culture and the study of European prehistory', in Grimes (ed.), *Aspects of Archaeology* (1951), pp. 49–65.

[34] J.G.D. Clark, 'Prehistory since Childe', *Bulletin of the Institute of Archaeology*, 13 (1976), 1–21.

[35] J.G.D. Clark, 'A preliminary report on excavations at Star Carr, Seamer, Scarborough, Yorkshire, 1949', *Proceedings of the Prehistoric Society*, 15 (1949), 52–65.

[36] J.G.D. Clark, *Excavations at Star Carr: An Early Mesolithic Site at Seamer, near Scarborough, Yorkshire* (Cambridge, 1954).

[37] J.G.D. Clark, *Prehistoric Europe: The Economic Basis* (London, 1952).

[38] J.G.D. Clark, 'The economic approach to prehistory: Albert Reckitt Archaeological Lecture, 1953', *Proceedings of the British Academy*, 39 (1953), 215–38. This quotation varies only in some slight degree from the published lecture, and is Clark's own annotated version which he aimed to present in his *A Path to Prehistory* (see above, n. 1), or in his *Man the Spiritual Primate* of which only one chapter, and various notes, exist in manuscript.

[39] J.G.D. Clark and C.I. Fell, 'The early Iron Age site at Micklemoor-Hill, West Harling, Norfolk, and its pottery', *Proceedings of the Prehistoric Society*, 19 (1953), 1–39.

[40] J.G.D. Clark, E.S. Higgs, and I.H. Longworth, 'Excavations at the Neolithic site Hurst Fen, Mildenhall, Suffolk (1954, 1957 and 1958)', *Proceedings of the Prehistoric Society*, 26 (1960), 202–45.

[41] Clark wrote, often movingly, about his many students and their achievements in his book *Prehistory at Cambridge and Beyond* (Cambridge, 1989).

[42] G. Clark, *World Prehistory: An Outline* (Cambridge, 1961). It was about this time that he began to publish consistently under the name Grahame Clark rather than J.G.D. Clark. This was in part because J.D. Clark (Desmond Clark) was also actively publishing and some confusion could, and did, arise. In 1990 the laudation of the Erasmus Foundation cited the book *The Prehistory of Africa* as one of Grahame's major publications; it was Desmond's.
[43] John Mulvaney has the last photograph of the book, and the reference is G. Clark, *World Prehistory: A New Outline* (Cambridge, 1969), p. 260.
[44] G. Clark, 'Traffic in stone axe and adze blades', *Economic History Review*, 2nd ser., 18 (1965), 1–28. He had already touched on this subject in his 1948 paper on South Scandinavian flint in the far north, *Proceedings of the Prehistoric Society*, 14 (1948), 221–32.
[45] G. Clark, *World Prehistory: A New Outline* (Cambridge, 1969).
[46] Royal Society of Northern Antiquaries (Copenhagen); Swiss Prehistoric Society; German Archaeological Institute; Archaeological Institute of America; Finnish Archaeological Society; American Academy of Arts and Sciences; Royal Danish Academy of Sciences and Letters; Royal Netherlands Academy of Sciences; Royal Society of Sciences, Uppsala; National Academy of Sciences, America; Royal Society of Humane Letters, Lund.
[47] G. Clark, 'New perspectives in Canadian archaeology: a summation', in A.G. McKay (ed.), *New Perspectives in Canadian Archaeology* (Ottawa, 1976), pp. 237–48.
[48] G. Clark, *The Stone Age Hunters* (London, 1967).
[49] G. Clark, 'Radiocarbon dating and the expansion of farming culture from the Near East over Europe', *Proceedings of the Prehistoric Society*, 31 (1965), 58–73.
[50] R.J. Rodden, 'Excavations at the Early Neolithic site at Nea Nikomedeia, Greek Macedonia (1961 Season)', *Proceedings of the Prehistoric Society*, 28 (1962), 267–88.
[51] S.I. Dakaris, E.S. Higgs, and R.W. Hey, 'The climate, environment and industries of Stone Age Greece: Part 1', *Proceedings of the Prehistoric Society*, 30 (1964), 194–214; E.S. Higgs and C. Vita-Finzi, 'The climate, environment and industries of Stone Age Greece: Part 2', *Proceedings of the Prehistoric Society*, 32 (1966), 1–29; E.S. Higgs, C. Vita-Finzi, D.R. Harris and A.E. Fagg, 'The climate, environment and industries of Stone Age Greece: Part 3', *Proceedings of the Prehistoric Society*, 33 (1967), 1–29.
[52] E.S. Higgs (ed.), *Papers in Economic Prehistory* (Cambridge, 1972); E.S. Higgs (ed.), *Palaeoeconomy* (Cambridge, 1975); E.S. Higgs, M.R. Jarman, G.N. Bailey, and H.N. Jarman, *Early European Agriculture* (Cambridge, 1982).
[53] J.G.D. Clark, 'The invasion hypothesis in British archaeology', *Antiquity*, 40 (1966), 172–89.
[54] J.G.D. Clark, 'Prehistory since Childe', see above, n. 34.
[55] C.B.M. McBurney, *The Haua Fteah (Cyrenaica)* (Cambridge, 1967). The Jersey excavations had to be published after McBurney's death: P. Callow and J.M. Cornford (eds.), *La Cotte de St Brelade 1961–1978* (Norwich, 1986).
[56] G. Clark, '*Star Carr: A Case Study in Bioarchaeology*' in *Addison-Wesley Modular Publication* (Reading, Mass., 1972).
[57] G. Clark, *The Earlier Stone Age Settlement of Scandinavia* (Cambridge, 1975).
[58] In 1980, Clark was able to publish some of his thoughts about the relationships in 'World prehistory and natural science', the J.C. Jacobsen Memorial Lecture, *Historisk-filosofiske Meddelelser*, 50 (1980), 1–40.
[59] G. Clark, *Sir Mortimer and Indian Archaeology* (New Delhi, 1979).
[60] G. Clark, *World Prehistory in New Perspective* (Cambridge, 1977). This book had 554 pages, in contrast to the earlier editions of about 300 pages.
[61] G. Clark, *Mesolithic Prelude: The Palaeolithic-Neolithic Transition in Old World Prehistory* (Edinburgh, 1980) should logically have been written decades before its appearance; *The Identity of Man as Seen by an Archaeologist* (London, 1983); *Symbols of Excellence: Precious Materials as Expressions of Status* (Cambridge, 1986); *Space, Time and Man: A Prehistorian's View* (Cambridge, 1992). Several of these appeared in translation and, in all, about a dozen of his books appeared in one or more of 13 languages.
[62] e.g., in his Inaugural Lecture, *The Study of Prehistory* (Cambridge, 1954).
[63] J.G.D. Clark, 'Prehistory since Childe', see above, n. 34. In this essay, Clark gave no real indication of his friendship with Childe; their surviving correspondence speaks of a familiarity and warmth that does not come through in his publications.

Index

Prepared by Barbara Hird

NOTE: References in italics denote illustrations. The abbreviation GC refers to Grahame Clark.